DATE DUE

HIGHSMITH #45115

The Maine Woods

The Maine Woods

HENRY D. THOREAU

A FULLY ANNOTATED EDITION

Edited by Jeffrey S. Cramer

Yale University Press   New Haven and London

Designed by Sonia Shannon.
Set in Adobe Garamond type by Tseng Information
Systems, Inc.
Printed in the United States of America.

Library of Congress Cataloging-in-Publication-Data
Thoreau, Henry David, 1817–1862.
The Maine woods : a fully annotated edition /
Henry D. Thoreau ; edited by Jeffrey S. Cramer.
    p.   cm.
Includes bibliographical references and index.
ISBN 978-0-300-12283-1 (cloth : alk. paper)
1. Piscataquis County (Me.)—Description and travel.
2. Maine—Description and travel. 3. Thoreau, Henry
David, 1817–1862—Travel—Maine. 4. Authors,
American—19th century—Biography. I. Cramer,
Jeffrey S., 1955–. II. Title.
F27.P5T43 2009
917.4′1043—dc22

                                        2009015161

A catalogue record for this book is available from the
British Library.

This paper meets the requirements of ANSI/NISO
Z39.48-1992 (Permanence of Paper).

10 9 8 7 6 5 4 3 2 1

To Greg Joly

Often on bare rocky carries the trail was so indistinct that I repeatedly lost it,

but when I walked behind him I observed that he could keep it almost like a hound,

and rarely hesitated, or, if he paused a moment on a bare rock, his eye immediately

detected some sign which would have escaped me.

—"The Allegash and East Branch"

Contents

Preface

My purpose in editing *The Maine Woods: A Fully Annotated Edition* has been twofold: to examine the text of *The Maine Woods* in light of the research and commentary that has appeared in the 135 years since it was first published, and to present a reliable text with a comprehensive series of annotations. While paying tribute to and honoring the work that has come before, I have tried to correct errors and omissions of previous editions without creating new ones.

Acknowledgments

The Maine Woods: A Fully Annotated Edition could not have been made without the help of literally hundreds of people, known and unknown. Many are acknowledged below, but there are some who, I regret, have become anonymous, and for these omissions of credit I apologize. There is generosity and enthusiasm in the world for which I am appreciative, and it is rewarding to know that such dedication and passion exists.

I am grateful to previous editors of *The Maine Woods,* particularly Joseph J. Moldenhauer, and to the work of William Howarth and J. Parker Huber. Their work has contributed greatly to this new edition of *The Maine Woods.*

No work such as this could be completed without the indispensable work and dedication of librarians who, with the advent of the Internet, have each become my local librarian wherever they may sit. In particular I would like to thank the State of Maine Law and Legislative Reference Library; the Old Town (Maine) Public Library; the Caribou (Maine) Public Library; Raymond H. Fogler Library, University of Maine; Maine Folklife Center; Geography and Map Division, Library of Congress; Moosehead Historical Society; Monson Historical Society; Bangor (Maine) Public Library; American Museum of Natural History; Kansas City Public Library; Geography and Map Division, Library of Congress; Boston Public Library; Houghton Library at Harvard University; the Berg Collection of the New York Public Library; Henry E. Huntington Library in San Marino, California; and the Pierpont Morgan Library.

In addition, the following have been indispensable in offering help in various ways: Everett Parker; John Neff; Tom Kelleher,

Old Sturbridge Village; Micah A. Pawling; Zip Kellogg; Cliff Bart on Marm Howard; David Gamage on the Whitehead Light; Stanley F. Lombardo on Homer; Mark Griffith and Michael Lloyd on Aeschylus; Melanie Mohney and Scott Michaud on Waite's Farm; Philippe Charland, Université du Quebec a Montreal, for his help with the Abenaki language; Debbie (Pelletier) Tajmajer on the Sawyers of Greenville; Glen Blouin on Native American medicinal uses of alder bark; Tony L. Nette, Arthur R. Rodgers, and Mike Schrage on moose horns; Ray Angelo on spruce trees; Rick Sisco on snakes; and Jan Hokes.

I am indebted to Don Henley, Founder and President of the Walden Woods Project, and to Kathi Anderson, its Executive Director, for their vision of a center for Thoreau studies, and to the many scholars who have donated their research to the collections of the Walden Woods Project, the Thoreau Society, and the Ralph Waldo Emerson Society. These collections, housed at the Thoreau Institute at Walden Woods, Lincoln, Massachusetts, and managed by the Walden Woods Project, constitute an invaluable and unparalleled resource, without which this book could not have been completed.

I would also like to express gratitude to Jennifer Banks, my editor at Yale University Press, for her support, and to Dan Heaton for his masterful editing of the manuscript.

Thanks to my daughters, Kazia and Zoë, for again sharing time with this dead nineteenth century Transcendentalist.

And finally, always and forever, Julia—as Thoreau wrote, "Till we have loved we have not imagined the heights of love."

Permissions

Grateful acknowledgment is made to the Thoreau Society and the Walden Woods Project's Thoreau Institute at Walden Woods for permission to quote from the unpublished correspondence of Fanny Eckstorm to Walter Harding, October 1840, in the Walter Harding Collection (Thoreau Society Collections), Thoreau Institute at Walden Woods.

Introduction

*Shall we not quit our companions, as if they were thieves and
pot-companions, and betake ourselves to some desert cliff of
mount Katahdin, some unvisited recess of Moosehead Lake,
to bewail our innocency and to recover it, and with it the power
to communicate again with these sharers of a more sacred idea?
—Ralph Waldo Emerson, "The Method of Nature" (1841)*

The Maine woods were present in Thoreau's consciousness for
more than half his life. He is known to have made six excursions
to Maine: in May 1838 to search for a teaching position; in 1846
to climb Mount Katahdin; in 1849 and 1851 to lecture on economy and Cape Cod, respectively; in 1853 to observe a moose hunt;
and in 1857 to travel the Allegash and Penobscot Rivers. In his
journal are numerous references to Maine, to Indians, and to the
life it represented. Thoreau's last recorded intelligible words were
"moose" and "Indian."

Thoreau made his Ktaadn excursion during his second year at
Walden Pond, despite his statement at the end of *Walden* that
his "second year was similar" to the first. Thoreau was invited to
accompany his cousin George Thatcher, who was in the lumber
business in Maine and would be traveling to look at some property. During this time Thoreau made one of the few early ascents
of Mount Katahdin by a non–Native American, finding a primordial landscape in which he felt like an intruder. "For what canst
thou pray here," he wrote in his journal, "but to be delivered from
here."

It was this feeling, expanded and manipulated in the published essay, which led to one of Thoreau's most powerful comments on man's place in nature: "Think of our life in nature,—daily to be shown matter, to come in contact with it,—rocks, trees, wind on our cheeks! the *solid* earth! the *actual* world! the *common sense! Contact! Contact! Who* are we? *where* are we?"

Thoreau lectured about his Ktaadn excursion in Concord in January 1848, and published his account, begun while at Walden, in five installments in Sartain's *Union Magazine of Literature and Art,* from July through November 1848.

"Chesuncook" describes a moose-hunting expedition Thoreau took in September 1853. It was his object to accompany Thatcher on a hunt. Thoreau distanced himself from the actual hunt by explaining that he "had not come a-hunting, and felt some compunctions about accompanying the hunters." He had gone to see a moose, confessing at the same time that he "was not sorry to learn how the Indian managed to kill one." Thoreau went as a "reporter" to the hunt, and his description of "that still warm and palpitating body pierced with a knife," of the "warm milk" that streamed "from the rent udder, and the ghastly naked red carcass appearing from within its seemly robe," rivals, in less epic proportion, scenes of whale hunting in *Moby-Dick.*

Almost equally well known as the essay itself, however, is the incident regarding its publication in the *Atlantic Monthly.* A sentence about the pine tree—"It is as immortal as I am, and perchance will go to as high a heaven, there to tower above me still"— had been expurgated. Thoreau was outraged at this liberty, writing to James Russell Lowell, then editor of the magazine, on 22 June 1858: "The editor has, in this case, no more right to omit a sentiment than to insert one, or put words into my mouth. . . . I am not willing to be associated in any way, unnecessarily, with parties who will confess themselves so bigoted & timid as this implies. I could excuse a man who was afraid of an uplifted fist, but if one manifests fear at the utterance of a sincere thought, I must think that his life is a kind of nightmare continued into broad daylight." He did not publish anything else in the *Atlantic Monthly* until after Lowell's resignation as editor in early 1861.

It was during Thoreau's final excursion to Maine, in 1857, that he met the Native American Joe Polis, who became his guide and earned his great respect. When originally asked for a piece for the *Atlantic Monthly,* Thoreau declined sending "The Allegash and East Branch"—instead submitting "Chesuncook"—because, as he wrote to Lowell: "The more fatal objection to printing my last Maine-wood experience, is that my Indian guide, whose words & deeds I report very faithfully,—and they are the most interesting part of the story,—knows how to read, and takes a newspaper, so that I could not face him again."

"The Allegash and East Branch" is the least formed of the pieces, never having been redacted from its journal-entry structure—a style Thoreau did not use in his published writings—to an essay that finally expressed what Thoreau summed up about this excursion on 18 August 1857 to visit his friend, H. G. O. Blake:

I have now returned, and think I have had a quite profitable journey, chiefly from associating with an intelligent Indian. . . . I have made a short excursion into the new world which the Indian dwells in, or is. He begins where we leave off. It is worth the while to detect new faculties in man, he is so much the more divine; and anything that fairly excites our admiration expands us. The Indian who can find his way so wonderfully in the woods possesses so much intelligence which the white man does not, and it increases my own capacity as well as faith to observe it. I rejoice to find that intelligence flows in other channels than I knew.

Despite Robert Louis Stevenson's dismissal that "Thoreau could not clothe his opinions in the garment of art, for that was not his talent," the essays in *The Maine Woods* are paradigms of the writer's art presented in the guise of unadorned travel narrative. The traveler, Thoreau wrote in his journal, "is to be reverenced as such. His profession is the best symbol of our life. Going from ————toward————; it is the history of every one of us." In the construction of his literary excursions, Thoreau clearly outlined a progression, not just in the physical distance from Massachusetts to Maine, but from the man who left Concord to the man who returned.

Always, and foremost, Thoreau was a writer, and each essay is more than a factual account of a single excursion to Maine. In a letter to Ralph Waldo Emerson of 12 January 1848, Thoreau wrote: "I read a part of the story of my excursion to Ktaadn to quite a large audience of men and boys, the other night, whom it interested. It contains many facts and some poetry."

Poetry, Thoreau wrote in his journal, "puts an interval between the impression and the expression,—waits till the seed germinates naturally." It is the poetry and deliberation of thought that makes a Thoreauvian excursion. The poet "must be something more than natural. . . . Nature will not speak through but along with him. His voice will not proceed from her midst, but, breathing on her, will make her the expression of his thought."

Thoreau knew, as he wrote in his journal, that there is "no such thing as pure objective observation." To be "interesting, i.e. to be significant" the writer's observations "must be subjective. The sum of what the writer of what ever class has to report is simply some human experience." The essays of *The Maine Woods* report the human experience as Thoreau understood it in relation to external conditions: the human experience in relation to the wild; the human experience in relation to the animal; the human experience of European descent in relation to the Native American.

As a writer Thoreau understood the importance of setting "down something besides facts," as he also wrote in his journal. Facts were to stand only as the "frame to my pictures; they should be the material to the mythology which I am writing." As he wrote in "Autumnal Tints": "The actual objects which one man will see from a particular hilltop are just as different from those which another will see as the beholders are different. . . . We cannot see anything until we are possessed with the idea of it, take it into our heads, and then we can hardly see anything else. . . . A man sees only what concerns him."

What concerned Thoreau was not the progress of the pilgrimage but what the mountains and the rivers and the woods said to him, and they spoke to him of man's place in nature, of that which is sacred and that which is profane. Contemplation of the natural world was as important a factor in the development of Thoreau's philosophy and ethic as was association with Emerson, John Brown, Joe Polis, Walt Whitman, and other representative men. Although it is common to distinguish between Thoreau's natural history essays and his reform essays, it is to make, to use a phrase Thoreau often used, a distinction without a difference.

In a journal entry of 6 May 1851 Thoreau wrote: "How important is a constant intercourse with nature and the contemplation of natural phenomena to the preservation of moral and intellectual health! . . . The philosopher contemplates human affairs as calmly and from as great a remoteness as he does natural phenomena. The ethical philosopher needs the discipline of the natural philosopher. He approaches the study of mankind with great advantages who is accustomed to the study of nature."

When he returned from a trip to Minnesota in July 1861, where he had gone to improve his health, it was clear that his time and strength were limited by the tuberculosis that would end his life in less than a year. Much of the time that remained was spent in preparing various works for posthumous publication, including his writings about Maine—two previously published essays, his journal entries about his 1857 excursion, and his notes that formed the appendix—which he redacted into *The Maine Woods*.

The Maine Woods was the second posthumous volume of Thoreau's writings. Like its predecessor, *Excursions,* it was compiled by Thoreau's sister, Sophia, with help from friends, in this case William Ellery Channing. Unlike *Excursions,* however, *The Maine Woods* did have some authorial approval. The first extant record by Thoreau of his possible intention to use his Maine essays in some way beyond their initial publication was in an 1858 letter to Lowell in relation to "Chesuncook": "I reserve the right to publish it in another form after it has appeared in your magazine."

Unlike another posthumous book, *Cape Cod,* which had been more carefully and cohesively planned and written during Thoreau's lifetime, *The Maine Woods* fails as a unified volume and is better considered as a collection of three thematically related but separate essays than as an organized whole. Had Thoreau lived, *The Maine Woods* might have been a completely different work. What that work might have been, no one can competently conjecture.

The following abbreviations for Thoreau's works are used in the notes:

C   *The Correspondence of Henry David Thoreau*. Edited by Walter Harding and Carl Bode. New York: New York University Press, 1958.

ITM   *I to Myself: An Annotated Selection from the Journal of Henry D. Thoreau*. Edited by Jeffrey S. Cramer. New Haven: Yale University Press, 2007.

J   *The Journal of Henry Thoreau*. Edited by Bradford Torrey and Francis H. Allen. Boston: Houghton Mifflin, 1906.

MJ   Manuscript journal, Pierpont Morgan Library.

PJ   *Journal*. Edited by John C. Broderick et al. Princeton: Princeton University Press, 1981–.

W   *The Writings of Henry D. Thoreau*. Walden edition. Boston: Houghton Mifflin, 1906.

Wa   *Walden: A Fully Annotated Edition*. Edited by Jeffrey S. Cramer. New Haven: Yale University Press, 2004.

All biblical quotations in the notes are from the King James Version. Native American words, plants, and other items identified in Thoreau's appendix are not separately annotated in the texts of the essays.

The Maine Woods

Ktaadn

On the 31st of August, 1846, I left Concord in Massachusetts for Bangor and the backwoods of Maine, by way of the railroad and steamboat,[1] intending to accompany a relative[2] of mine engaged in the lumber trade in Bangor, as far as a dam on the west branch of the Penobscot, in which property he was interested. From this place, which is about one hundred miles by the river above Bangor, thirty miles from the Houlton military road,[3] and five miles beyond the last log hut, I proposed to make excursions to mount Ktaadn, the second highest mountain in New England,[4] about thirty miles distant, and to some of the lakes of the Penobscot, either alone or with such company as I might pick up there. It is unusual to find a camp so far in the woods at that season, when lumbering operations have ceased, and I was glad to avail myself of the circumstance of a gang of men being employed there at that time in repairing the injuries caused by the great freshet in the spring.[5] The mountain may be approached more easily and directly on horseback and on foot from the north-east side, by the Aroostook road,[6] and the Wassataquoik river; but in that case you see much less of the wilderness, none of the glorious river and lake scenery, and have no experience of the batteau and the boatman's life. I was fortunate also in the season of the year, for in the summer myriads of black flies, mosquitoes, and midges, or, as the Indians call them, "no-see-ems," make travelling in the woods almost impossible; but now their reign was nearly over.

1 Thoreau took the railroad from Concord to Boston, and the steamer from Boston to Bangor.
2 George Augustus Thatcher (1806–1885), husband of Thoreau's paternal cousin Rebecca Jane Billings (1813–1883).
3 In 1828 Congress made provision for a military road from Bangor to Houlton to provide access for militia and supplies to northern Maine in case of border friction. John James Audubon (1785–1851) described it in 1833 as a "fine turnpike of great breadth, almost straight in its whole length, and perhaps the best now in the Union."
4 Ktaadn is the second highest if, as was common in Thoreau's day, the Presidential Range, which includes Mounts Washington, Adams, Jefferson, Monroe, and Madison, is considered as a whole with several peaks rather than as separate mountains.
5 The editor of the *Bangor Courier* wrote: "It will be difficult for people who did not witness it to realize that all the business part of the city was a pool in which large vessels might sail—that Exchange street, and Main street, and others lower down, were deep canals for half their length, and that Central street was a running river. But such things were, and hundreds of stores were under water!"
6 The Aroostook Road extends from the military road, seven miles above Mattawamkeag Point, to Ashland.

7 The ascent was made by Charles Turner, Jr. (1760–1839), and his party. Turner's "Description of Natardin or Catardin Mountain" was published in 1819.

8 Jacob Whitman Bailey (1811–1857) was professor of chemistry, mineralogy, and geology at West Point from 1834 until his death. His "Account of an Excursion to Mount Katahdin in Maine" was published in 1837.

9 Charles Thomas Jackson (1805–1880), brother of Lucy Jackson Brown (1798–1868), who boarded in the Thoreau family home, and of Lidian Emerson (1802–1892), the wife of Ralph Waldo Emerson (1803–1882). His climb is reported in the *Second Annual Report on the Geology of the Public Lands, Belonging to the Two States of Maine and Massachusetts.* He was assisted by James T. Hodge (1816–1871) from Massachusetts, whose report is included in Jackson's *Second Annual Report,* and William Clark Larrabee (1802–1859) from Maine, whose report appeared in the *Lincoln Telegraph* in January 1840. Jackson presented a lecture on geology at the Concord Lyceum on 1 February 1843, while Thoreau was curator. In a brief obituary in the 1862–1863 *Proceedings of the Boston Society of Natural History* he praised Thoreau's writings as "full of knowledge of the secrets of nature, . . . enlivened by much quaint humor, and warmed with kindness towards all living beings."

10 Edward Everett Hale (1822–1909), who published an account of the climb in the *Boston Daily Advertiser,* 15 August 1845, and William Francis Channing (1820–1901), cousin of Thoreau's friend William Ellery Channing (1817–1901).

11 Marcus R. Keep (1816–1894) published two accounts in the *Bangor Democrat*—"Katahdin" in December 1847 and "Mount Katahdin, Again" in October 1849—although Thoreau may have read Keep's account only as quoted by John S. Springer (1811–1852) in his *Forest Life and Forest Trees.* Aaron Young, Jr. (1819–1898), reported on his botanical survey of Ktaadn in "Report: Botanical Exploration of Mt. Katahdn" and in his 1848 *Flora of Maine.* George Thurber (1821–1890), a member of

Ktaadn, whose name is an Indian word signifying highest land, was first ascended by white men in 1804.[7] It was visited by Professor J. W. Bailey of West Point in 1836,[8] by Dr. Charles T. Jackson, the State Geologist, in 1837,[9] and by two young men from Boston in 1845.[10] All these have given accounts of their expeditions. Since I was there, two or three other parties have made the excursion and told their stories.[11] Besides these, very few, even among backwoodsmen and hunters, have ever climbed it,[12] and it will be a long time before the tide of fashionable travel sets that way. The mountainous region of the State of Maine stretches from near the White Mountains,[13] northeasterly one hundred and sixty miles, to the head of the Aroostook river, and is about sixty miles wide. The wild or unsettled portion is far more extensive. So that some hours only of travel in this direction will carry the curious to the verge of a primitive forest, more interesting, perhaps, on all accounts, than they would reach by going a thousand miles westward.

The next forenoon, Tuesday, Sept. 1st, I started with my companion in a buggy from Bangor for "up river," expecting to be overtaken the next day night, at Mattawamkeag Point,[14] some sixty miles off, by two more Bangoreans,[15] who had decided to join us in a trip to the mountain. We had each a knapsack or bag filled with such clothing and other articles as were indispensable, and my companion carried his gun.

Within a dozen miles of Bangor we passed through the villages of Stillwater and Oldtown,[16] built at the falls of the Penobscot, which furnish the principal power by which the Maine woods are converted into lumber. The mills are built directly over and across the river. Here is a close jam, a hard rub, at all seasons; and then the once green tree, long since white,[17] I need not say as the driven snow,[18] but as a driven log, becomes lumber merely. Here your inch, your two and your three inch stuff[19] begin to be, and Mr. Sawyer marks off those spaces which decide the destiny of so many prostrate forests. Through this steel riddle,[20] more or less coarse, is the arrowy[21] Maine forest, from Ktaadn and Chesuncook, and the head waters of the St. John,[22] relentlessly sifted, till it comes out boards, clapboards, laths, and shingles such as the wind can take, still perchance to be slit and slit again, till men get a size that will suit. Think how stood the white-pine tree on the shore of Chesuncook, its branches soughing with the four winds, and every individual needle trembling in the sunlight—think how it stands with it now—sold, perchance, to the New England Friction Match Company![23] There were in 1837, as I read, two hundred and fifty saw mills on the Penobscot and its tributaries above Bangor, the greater part of them in this immediate neighborhood, and they sawed two hundred millions of feet of boards annually.[24] To this is to be added, the lumber of the Kennebec, Androscoggin, Saco, Passamaquoddy, and other streams. No wonder that we hear so often of vessels which are becalmed off our coast, being surrounded a week at a time by floating lumber from the Maine woods. The mission of men there seems to be, like so many busy demons, to drive the forest all out of the country, from every solitary beaver swamp, and mountain side, as soon as possible.

At Oldtown we walked into a batteau manufactory. The making of batteaux is quite a business here for the supply of the Penobscot river. We examined some on the stocks. They are light and shapely vessels, calculated for rapid and rocky streams, and to be carried over long portages on men's shoulders, from twenty to thirty feet long, and only four or four and a half wide, sharp at both ends like a canoe, though broadest forward on the bottom, and reaching seven or eight feet over the water, in order that they may slip over rocks as gently as possible. They are made very slight, only two boards to a side, com-

Young's party, also published an account in the *Providence Journal*, 26 September 1847.

12 The first partial ascent by a nonnative actually occurred in 1764 by Joseph Chadwick. Other ascents were made by surveying parties: in October 1819 by a British expedition and in August 1820 by a joint expedition of British and American surveyors. Another early ascent, unknown to Thoreau, was made by Henry Boynton Smith (1815–1877) and two friends, in September 1836.

13 In New Hampshire.

14 A gravel bar formed by the junction of the Mattawamkeag and Penobscot Rivers, described by Ezekiel Holmes (1801–1865) in his *Report of an Exploration and Survey of the Territory on the Aroostook River* as "an elevated alluvial plain [that] commands three views of the two rivers,—viz: up and down the Penobscot and up the Mattawamkeag."

15 Charles Lowell (1803–1885), who was the husband of Thoreau's paternal cousin Mary Ann Billings (1819–1888), and Horatio ("Raish") P. Blood (1806–1883).

16 In 1806 the township of Orono, previously called Stillwater, was incorporated, including at that time the region of Oldtown. In 1840 Oldtown was incorporated as a separate town.

17 From the bark having rubbed off during the logjam.

18 Common phrase found in such works as John Lyly's (1554–1606) *Eupheus* and William Shakespeare's (1564–1616) *A Winter's Tale*.

19 Boards.

20 A coarse sieve with a perforated bottom used for cleaning grain, as in separating the grain from the chaff.

21 Descriptive also used by Thoreau to describe the "arrowy" pines around Walden [Wa 39].

22 River rising in Somerset County, Maine, and flowing northeastward through New Brunswick to empty into the Bay of Fundy.

23 One of the names by which the match company established by Ezekiel Byam (1795–1863), who began manufacturing matches commercially

in 1837 in Chelmsford, Massachusetts, and briefly in Boston, was known.

24 Thoreau read in John Hayward's (1781–1869) *New England Gazetteer:* "On the Penobscot river and its tributary streams, above Bangor, more than 250 saw-mills, capable of cutting at least two hundred million feet of boards a year; all of which, except what is used in building, must be shipped at the harbor of Bangor."

25 Arched or bowed.

26 Pierre-François-Xavier de Charlevoix (1682–1761), French Jesuit missionary to Canada from 1720 to 1722. His *Histoire et Description Générale de la Nouvelle France* was published in 1744.

27 A woodsman, boatman, or guide employed by a fur company to transport goods and supplies between remote stations in Canada or the U.S. Northwest, from the French, *voyager,* meaning to travel. In 1837 Thoreau wrote "Voyager's Song":

> Gentle river, gentle river
> Swift as glides thy stream along,
> Many a bold Canadian voyageur,
> Bravely swelled the gay chanson.
>
> . . . .
>
> Thus we lead a life of pleasure,
> While we while the hours away,
> Thus we revel beyond measure,
> Gaily live we while we may.

28 In 1819, before Maine became a separate state, the Commonwealth of Massachusetts entered into treaties with the remaining tribes establishing them as nations within that state. These treaties also gave each nation certain lands. In consideration for a quitclaim to certain lands, all the islands in the Penobscot River above and including Indian Island (Old Town) were to be enjoyed by the Penobscot in perpetuity.

29 From Hayward's *New England Gazetteer:* "The whole number of souls in the tribe was three hundred and sixty-two."

30 Inversion of the phrase *"aut militiae aut domi"*

monly secured to a few light maple or other hard-wood knees, but inward are of the clearest and widest white-pine stuff, of which there is a great waste on account of their form, for the bottom is left perfectly flat, not only from side to side, but from end to end. Sometimes they become "hogging"[25] even, after long use, and the boatmen then turn them over and straighten them by a weight at each end. They told us that one wore out in two years, or often in a single trip, on the rocks, and sold for from fourteen to sixteen dollars. There was something refreshing and wildly musical to my ears in the very name of the white man's canoe, reminding me of Charlevoix[26] and Canadian Voyageurs.[27] The batteau is a sort of mongrel between the canoe and the boat, a fur-trader's boat.

The ferry here took us past the Indian island.[28] As we left the shore, I observed a short shabby washerwoman-looking Indian; they commonly have the woe-begone look of the girl that cried for spilt milk—just from "up river,"—land on the Oldtown side near a grocery, and drawing up his canoe, take out a bundle of skins in one hand, and an empty keg or half-barrel in the other, and scramble up the bank with them. This picture will do to put before the Indian's history, that is, the history of his extinction. In 1837, there were three hundred and sixty-two souls left of this tribe.[29] The island seemed deserted to-day, yet I observed some new houses among the weather-stained ones, as if the tribe had still a design upon life; but generally they have a very shabby, forlorn, and cheerless look, being all back side and woodshed, not homesteads, even Indian homesteads, but instead of home or abroad-steads, for their life is *domi aut militiae,*[30] at home or at war, or now rather *venatus,* that is, a-hunting, and most of the latter. The church is the only trim-looking building, but that is not Abenaki,[31] that was Rome's doings.[32] Good Canadian it may be, but it is poor Indian. These were once a powerful tribe. Politics are all the rage with them now. I even thought that a row of wigwams, with a dance of pow-wows, and a prisoner tortured at the stake, would be more respectable than this.

We landed in Milford, and rode along on the east side of the Penobscot, having a more or less constant view of the river, and the Indian islands in it, for they retain all the islands as far up as Nickatow, at the mouth of the East Branch. They are generally well-timbered, and are said to be better soil than the neighboring shores. The river seemed shallow and rocky, and interrupted by rapids, rippling and gleaming in the sun. We paused a moment to see a fish-hawk dive for a fish down straight as an arrow, from a great height, but he missed his prey this time. It was the Houlton Road on which we were now travelling, over which some troops were marched once towards Mars' Hill, though not to Mars' *field,*[33] as it proved. It is the main, almost the only, road in these parts, as straight and well made, and kept in as good repair, as almost any you will find anywhere. Everywhere we saw signs of the great freshet—this house standing awry, and that where it was not founded, but where it was found, at any rate, the next day; and that other with a water-logged look, as if it were still airing and drying its basement, and logs with everybody's marks[34] upon them, and sometimes the marks of their having served as bridges, strewn along the road. We crossed the Sunkhaze, a summery Indian name, the Olemmon, Passadumkeag, and other streams, which make a greater show on the map than they now did on the road. At Passadumkeag, we found anything but what the name implies,[35] earnest politicians, to wit—white ones, I mean—on the alert, to know how the election was likely to go;[36] men who talked rapidly, with subdued voice, and a sort of factitious earnestness, you could not help believing, hardly waiting for an introduction, one on each side of your

(Latin: at war or at home), from Marcus Tullius Cicero's (106–43 B.C.E.) oration *In Pisonem.*

31 Native American people located in the Canadian Maritime Provinces and northeastern United States, most commonly found in Maine.

32 The Christianized Abenaki were Roman Catholic.

33 Allusion to the Aroostook War, a bloodless boundary dispute in 1839 between the United States (Maine) and Great Britain (New Brunswick). It was not Mars' field—so named for the Roman god of war—because no fighting actually occurred.

34 Logger's mark or brand that Springer compared to the way "one farmer distinguishes his sheep from those of his neighbor by the particular mark they bear, each differing in some particular from every other."

35 Passadumkeag in Abenaki means "where the water goes into the river above the falls."

36 The United States elections in 1846 for the House of Representatives, during which the Whigs took back control of the House. The biggest issues during this election were the Mexican-American War and the slavery question.

37 Land under federal jurisdiction but not part of a local municipality.

38 Allusion to Royall Tyler's (1757–1826) *The Contrast*, in which the character of Jonathan, in differentiating between a "servant" and a "waiter," is said to have made a "true Yankee distinction, egad, without a difference."

39 John Partridge Treat, Sr. (1783–1857), who settled in March 1823 in what would be incorporated as Enfield in 1835.

40 In "Wild Apples" Thoreau wrote: "I love better to go through the old orchards of ungrafted apple-trees, at whatever season of the year,—so irregularly planted: sometimes two trees standing close together; and the rows so devious that you would think that they not only had grown while the owner was sleeping, but had been set out by him in a somnambulic state. The rows of grafted fruit will never tempt me to wander amid them like these," and praised natural fruit of trees grown from seed as having "a certain volatile and ethereal quality which represents their highest value, and which cannot be vulgarized, or bought and sold" [W 5:299, 295].

41 Twigs or cut shoots with buds used in grafting.

42 A deepwater spring-fed lake located in Enfield.

43 Specifically, Mattanawacook Island.

buggy, endeavoring to say much in little, for they see you hold the whip impatiently, but always saying little in much. Caucuses they have had, it seems, and caucuses they are to have again—victory and defeat: somebody may be elected, somebody may not. One man, a total stranger, who stood by our carriage, in the dusk, actually frightened the horse with his asseverations, growing more solemnly positive as there was less in him to be positive about. So Passadumkeag did not look on the map. At sundown, leaving the river-road awhile for shortness, we went by way of Enfield, where we stopped for the night. This, like most of the localities bearing names on this road, was a place to name, which, in the midst of the unnamed and unincorporated[37] wilderness, was to make a distinction without a difference,[38] it seemed to me. Here, however, I noticed quite an orchard of healthy and well-grown apple trees, in a bearing state, it being the oldest settler's house in this region,[39] but all natural fruit, and comparatively worthless for want of a grafter.[40] And so it is generally lower down the river. It would be a good speculation, as well as a favor conferred on the settlers, for a Massachusetts boy to go down there with a trunk full of choice scions,[41] and his grafting apparatus, in the spring.

The next morning we drove along through a high and hilly country, in view of Cold-Stream Pond,[42] a beautiful lake, four or five miles long, and came into the Houlton road again, here called the Military road, at Lincoln, forty-five miles from Bangor, where there is quite a village, for this country—the principal one above Old-town. Learning that there were several wigwams here, on one of the Indian islands,[43] we left our horse and wagon, and walked through the forest half a mile, to the river, to procure a guide to the mountain. It was not till after considerable search that we discovered their habitations—small huts, in a retired place, where the scenery was unusually soft and beautiful, and the shore skirted with pleasant meadows and graceful elms. We paddled ourselves across to the island-side in a canoe, which we found on the shore. Near where we landed, sat an Indian girl, ten or twelve years old, on a rock in the water, in the sun, washing, and humming or moaning a song meanwhile. It was an aboriginal strain. A salmon-spear, made wholly of wood, lay on the shore, such as they might have used before white men came. It had an elastic piece of wood fastened to one side of its point, which slipped over and closed upon the fish, somewhat like the contrivance for holding a bucket at the end of a well-pole. As we walked up to the nearest house, we were met by a sally of a dozen wolfish-looking dogs, which may have been lineal descendants from the ancient Indian dogs, which the first voyageurs describe as "their wolves."[44] I suppose they were. The occupant soon appeared, with a long pole in his hand, with which he beat off the dogs, while he parleyed with us. A stalwart, but dull and greasy-looking fellow, who told us, in his sluggish way, in answer to our questions, as if it were the first serious business he had to do that day, that there *were* Indians going "up river,"—he and one other—to-day, before noon. And who was the other? Louis Neptune,[45] who lives in the next house. Well, let us go over and see Louis together. The same doggish reception, and Louis Neptune makes his appearance—a small, wiry man, with puckered and wrinkled face, yet he seemed the chiefer man of the two; the same, as I remembered, who had accompanied Jackson to the mountain in '37. The same questions were put to Louis, and the same information obtained, while the other Indian stood by. It appeared, that they were going to start by noon, with two canoes, to go up to Chesuncook, to hunt moose—to be gone a month. "Well, Louis, suppose you get to the Point,[46] [to the Five Islands, just below Mattawamkeag,][47] to camp, we walk on up the

44 Quoted from Thomas Hariot's (1560–1621) *A Brief and True Report of the New Found Land of Virginia:* "The inhabitants sometime kill the *Lion* & eat him: & we sometime as they came to our hands of their *Wolves* or *wolfish Dogs,* which I have not set down for good meat, least that some would understand my judgment therein to be more simple than needed, although I could allege the difference in taste of those kinds from ours, which by some of our company have been experimented in both."

45 Guide who replaced Peol Michael, Jackson's original guide, who had cut his leg with a hatchet while chopping wood. He may also be the same Neptune described by Emerson as an "able man" on his visit to Maine in July 1834.

46 Mattawamkeag Point.

47 Now Winn, it was originally named Snowville when first settled in 1820, and was also known as River Township No. 4 and Five Islands. Thoreau's brackets.

48 According to the Abenaki, Pomola, also known as Bmola and Bumole, a bird and night spirit, bringer of storms and cold weather, was said to live atop Katahdin. When Jackson's 1837 ascent was interrupted by a snowstorm, Neptune said that "Pomola was angry with us for presuming to measure the height of the mountain, and revenged himself upon us by this storm." Turner wrote that Pamola "flies off in the Spring with tremendous rumbling noises. They have a tradition that no person i.e. native, who has attempted to ascend it, has lived to return. They alledge, that many moons ago, seven Indians resolutely ascended the mountain, and that they were never heard of afterwards, having been undoubtedly killed by Pamola in the mountain. The two Indians, whom we hired to pilot and assist us . . . refused to proceed ahead—however, when they found that we were determined to proceed, even without them, they again went forward courageously, and seemed ambitious to be first on the summit."

49 Turner's party "deposited the Initials of our names . . . and the date, cut upon sheet lead, and a bottle of Rum corked and leaded, on the highest part." Another member of the party, Joseph Treat (1775–1853), wrote when he returned in 1820: "— we deposited a bottle of Rum, and a bottle containing the Constitution of Maine and a _____ by each of us on lead placed under a rock." (blank space Treat's). Louis Neptune was with Treat when he planted the Constitution and probably their initials, following Turner, under a rock.

West Branch to-morrow—four of us—and wait for you at the dam, or this side. You overtake us to-morrow or next day, and take us into your canoes. We stop for you, you stop for us. We pay you for your trouble." "Ye!" replied Louis, "may be you carry some provision for all—some pork—some bread—and so pay." He said, "Me sure get some moose;" and when I asked, if he thought Pomola[48] would let us go up, he answered that we must plant one bottle of rum on the top, he had planted good many; and when he looked again, the rum was all gone. He had been up two or three times: he had planted letter,—English, German, French, etc.[49] These men were slightly clad in shirt and pantaloons, like laborers with us in warm weather. They did not invite us into their houses, but met us outside. So we left the Indians, thinking ourselves lucky to have secured such guides and companions.

There were very few houses along the road, yet they did not altogether fail, as if the law by which men are dispersed over the globe were a very stringent one, and not to be resisted with impunity or for slight reasons. There were even the germs of one or two villages just beginning to expand. The beauty of the road itself was remarkable. The various evergreens, many of which are rare with us—delicate and beautiful specimens of the larch, arbor-vitae, ball spruce, and fir-balsam, from a few inches to many feet in height, lined its sides, in some places like a long front yard, springing up from the smooth grass-plots which uninterruptedly border it, and are made fertile by its wash; while it was but a step on either hand to the grim untrodden wilderness, whose tangled labyrinth of living, fallen, and decaying trees,—only the deer and moose, the bear and wolf, can easily penetrate. More perfect specimens than any front yard plot can show, grew there to grace the passage of the Houlton teams.

About noon we reached the Mattawamkeag, fifty-six

miles from Bangor by the way we had come, and put up at a frequented house,[50] still on the Houlton road, where the Houlton stage stops. Here was a substantial covered bridge over the Mattawamkeag, built, I think they said, some seventeen years before.[51] We had dinner—where, by the way, and even at breakfast, as well as supper[52]—at the public-houses on this road, the front rank is composed of various kinds of "sweet cakes,"[53] in a continuous line from one end of the table to the other. I think I may safely say that there was a row of ten or a dozen plates of this kind set before us two here. To account for which, they say, that when the lumberers come out of the woods, they have a craving for cakes and pies, and such sweet things, which there are almost unknown, and this is the *supply* to satisfy that *demand*[54]— the supply is always equal to the demand,—and these hungry men think a good deal of getting their money's worth. No doubt, the balance of victuals is restored by the time they reach Bangor: Mattawamkeag takes off the raw edge. Well, over this front rank, I say, you coming from the "sweet cake" side, with a cheap philosophic indifference though it may be, have to assault what there is behind, which I do not by any means mean to insinuate is insufficient in quantity or quality to supply that other demand of men not from the woods, but from the towns, for venison and strong country fare. After dinner, we strolled down to the "Point," formed by the junction of the two rivers, which is said to be the scene of an ancient battle between the Eastern Indians and the Mohawks,[55] and searched there carefully for relics,[56] though the men at the bar-room had never heard of such things; but we found only some flakes of arrow-head stone, some points of arrow-heads, one small leaden-bullet, and some colored beads, the last to be referred, perhaps, to early fur-trader days. The Mattawamkeag, though wide, was a mere river's bed, full of rocks and shallows at this time,

50 A hotel built in 1830 by James Penley and George Wallace of Old Town, on the site of the old Mattawamkeag Stagehouse, and bought in 1835 by Asa Smith (1786–1867).

51 The Mattawamkeag Bridge was begun in 1831 by Stephen H. Long (1784–1864) of the U.S. Army Corps of Topographical Engineers. Long's bridges were not covered but consisted of a rigid timber truss form that incorporated panels consisting of intersecting diagonals and counters.

52 Although used synonymously now, dinner was a mid-day meal while supper was the evening meal.

53 James Fenimore Cooper (1789–1851) described different cakes in *The Pioneers:* "The four corners were garnished with plates of cake. On one was piled certain curiously twisted and complicated figures, called 'nut-cakes.' On another were heaps of a black-looking substance, which, receiving its hue from molasses, was properly termed 'sweet-cake.'" Thoreau below differentiates these from "hot cakes not sweetened."

54 Classical economic theory developed as Say's Law, or Say's Law of Economics, from a principle attributed to French businessman and economist Jean-Baptiste Say (1767–1832) that supply creates demand.

55 Numerous battles took place in the seventeenth century between the Penobscot (Eastern Indians) and the Mohawks.

56 Thoreau collected approximately nine hundred Native American artifacts in his lifetime.

57 James Libby (1808–1874).
58 Phrase possibly coined by Washington Irving (1783–1859) in his *Knickerbocker's History of New York* to describe the log houses built by Yankee settlers and farmers.
59 A platform scale (ca. 1830) invented by Thaddeus Fairbanks (1796–1886), a Vermont farmer, to weigh a cartload of hay. The balance-box was the cart-size shallow chamber level with the ground, eliminating the need to hoist a cart for weighing.

so that you could cross it almost dry-shod in boots; and I could hardly believe my companion, when he told me that he had been fifty or sixty miles up it in a batteau, through distant and still uncut forests. A batteau could hardly find a harbor now at its mouth. Deer, and caribou, or reindeer, are taken here in the winter, in sight of the house.

Before our companions arrived, we rode on up the Houlton road seven miles, to Molunkus, where the Aroostook road comes into it, and where there is a spacious public house in the woods, called the "Molunkus House," kept by one Libbey,[57] which looked as if it had its hall for dancing and for military drills. There was no other evidence of man but this huge shingle palace[58] in this part of the world; but sometimes even this is filled with travellers. I looked off the piazza round the corner of the house up the Aroostook road, on which there was no clearing in sight. There was a man just adventuring upon it this evening, in a rude, original, what you may call Aroostook, wagon—a mere seat, with a wagon swung under it, a few bags on it, and a dog asleep to watch them. He offered to carry a message for us to anybody in that country, cheerfully. I suspect, that if you should go to the end of the world, you would find somebody there going further, as if just starting for home at sundown, and having a last word before he drove off. Here, too, *was* a small trader, whom I did not see at first, who kept a store—but no great store, certainly—in a small box over the way, behind the Molunkus sign-post. It looked like the balance-box of a patent hay-scales.[59] As for his house, we could only conjecture where that was; he may have been a boarder in the Molunkus House. I saw him standing in his shop-door—his shop was so small, that, if a traveller should make demonstrations of entering in, *he* would have to go out by the back way, and confer with his customer through a window, about his goods in the cellar, or, more probably, bespoken,[60] and yet on the way. I should have gone in, for I felt a real impulse to trade, if I had not stopped to consider what would become of him. The day before, we had walked into a shop, over against an inn where we stopped, the puny beginning of trade, which would grow at last into a firm copartnership, in the future town or city—indeed, it was already "Somebody & Co.," I forget who. The woman came forward from the penetralia[61] of the attached house, for "Somebody & Co." was in the burning,[62] and she sold us percussion-caps, canalés and smooth;[63] and knew their prices and qualities, and which the hunters preferred. Here was a little of everything in a small compass to satisfy the wants and the ambition of the woods, a stock selected with what pains and care, and brought home in the wagon box, or a corner of the Houlton team; but there seemed to me, as usual, a preponderance of children's toys, dogs to bark, and cats to mew, and trumpets to blow, where natives there hardly are yet. As if a child, born into the Maine woods, among the pine cones and cedar berries, could not do without such a sugar-man,[64] or skipping-jack,[65] as the young Rothschild[66] has.

I think that there was not more than one house on the road to Molunkus, or for seven miles. At that place we got over the fence into a new field, planted with potatoes, where the logs were still burning between the hills; and, pulling up the vines, found good-sized potatoes, nearly ripe, growing like weeds, and turnips mixed with them. The mode of clearing and planting, is, to fell the trees, and burn once what will burn, then cut them up into suitable lengths, roll into heaps, and burn again; then, with a hoe, plant potatoes where you can come at the ground between the stumps and charred logs, for a first crop, the ashes sufficing for manure, and no hoeing being necessary the first year. In the fall, cut, roll, and burn again, and so on, till the land is cleared; and soon

60 Goods ordered or arranged for.

61 The innermost part or most private recess.

62 Area of land being cleared by burning.

63 Percussion caps, respectively, for grooved and smooth bored rifles.

64 Sugar molded into the shape of a man.

65 Also known as a skipjack or jumping jack: the forked bone of a fowl's breast (merrythought or wishbone) made into a little toy by a twisted thread and a small stick. Sometimes made by twisting a piece of twine with a stick attached to it between the costal processes of the bone, one end of the stick being held by a small bit of shoemaker's wax. When the wax would give way from the tension of the twine, the toy skipped into the air or turned a somersault.

66 Prominent family of European bankers equated with great wealth.

67 Let grow to grass after the soil has been exhausted as a method to reclaim the soil's fertility.

68 A common epithet for the grave used by several poets, including William Wordsworth (1770–1850), Ossian (James MacPherson [1736–1796]), Robert Burns (1759–1796), and William Cullen Bryant (1794–1878). Thoreau used the epithet twice in *Walden*.

69 A person from the Canadian provinces, although Thoreau more regularly used the term *Canadian*.

70 A native of New England or northern United States. Of uncertain etymology, although in *A Week on the Concord and Merrimack Rivers* Thoreau, following Noah Webster's (1758–1843) 1828 *American Dictionary*, derived the epithet from the "New West Saxons, whom the red men call, not Angle-ish or English, but Yengeese, and so at last they are known for Yankees" [W 1:53].

71 Equal or nominal face value.

72 Provincial capital of New Brunswick.

73 Common nineteenth-century name for an American, similar to the use of John Bull for the English, but in "Life without Principle" Thoreau also used the name to mean someone "essentially provincial still, not metropolitan" [W 4:447].

74 The Yankee propensity for whittling was well known and sometimes caricatured. Michel Chevalier (1806–1879) in his 1839 *Society, Manners, and Politics in the United States*, wrote of the "pure Yankee" whose "fingers must be in action, he must be whittling a piece of wood."

75 Third edition (1844) of *Map of the State of Maine with the Province of New Brunswick* by cartographer Moses Greenleaf (1777–1834), first published to accompany his *Survey of the State of Maine*.

76 Coarse flax or hemp fibers that have been separated from the finer part.

77 To make the tablecloth waterproof.

78 "A Plan of the Public Lands in the State of Maine." The purpose of this map was to help settle land disputes between Massachusetts and Maine.

it is ready for grain, and to be laid down.[67] Let those talk of poverty and hard times who will, in the towns and cities; cannot the emigrant, who can pay his fare to New York or Boston, pay five dollars more to get here,—I paid three, all told, for my passage from Boston to Bangor, 250 miles,—and be as rich as he pleases, where land virtually costs nothing, and houses only the labor of building, and he may begin life as Adam did? If he will still remember the distinction of poor and rich, let him bespeak him a narrower house[68] forthwith.

When we returned to the Mattawamkeag, the Houlton stage had already put up there; and a Province man[69] was betraying his greenness to the Yankees[70] by his questions.—Why Province money won't pass here at par,[71] when States' money is good at Frederickton[72]—though this, perhaps, was sensible enough. From what I saw then, it appeared that the Province man was now the only real Jonathan,[73] or raw country bumpkin, left so far behind by his enterprising neighbors, that he didn't know enough to put a question to them. No people can long continue provincial in character, who have the propensity for politics and whittling,[74] and rapid travelling, which the Yankees have, and who are leaving the mother country behind in the variety of their notions and inventions. The possession and exercise of practical talent merely, are a sure and rapid means of intellectual culture and independence.

The last edition of Greenleaf's Map of Maine[75] hung on the wall here, and, as we had no pocket map, we resolved to trace a map of the lake country: so dipping a wad of tow[76] into the lamp, we oiled a sheet of paper on the oiled table-cloth,[77] and, in good faith, traced what we afterwards ascertained to be a labyrinth of errors, carefully following the outlines of the imaginary lakes which that map contains. The Map of the Public Lands of Maine and Massachusetts[78] is the only one I have seen that at all deserves the name. It was while we were engaged in this operation that our companions arrived. They had seen the Indians' fire on the Five Islands, and so we concluded that all was right.

Early the next morning we had mounted our packs, and prepared for a tramp up the West Branch, my companion having turned his horse out to pasture for a week or ten days, thinking that a bite of fresh grass, and a taste of running water, would do him as much good as backwoods fare, and new country influences his master. Leaping over a fence, we began to follow an obscure trail up the northern bank of the Penobscot. There was now no road further, the river being the only highway, and but half a dozen log huts confined to its banks, to be met with for thirty miles; on either hand, and beyond, was a wholly uninhabited wilderness, stretching to Canada. Neither horse, nor cow, nor vehicle of any kind, had ever passed over this ground. The cattle, and the few bulky articles which the loggers use, being got up in the winter on the ice, and down again before it breaks up. The evergreen woods had a decidedly sweet and bracing fragrance; the air was a sort of diet-drink,[79] and we walked on buoyantly in Indian file, stretching our legs. Occasionally there was a small opening on the bank, made for the purpose of log-rolling, where we got a sight of the river—always a rocky and rippling stream. The roar of the rapids, the note of a whistler-duck[80] on the river, of the jay and chicadee around us, and of the pigeon-woodpecker[81] in the openings, were the sounds that we heard. This was what you might call a bran new[82] country; the only roads were of Nature's making, and the few houses were camps. Here, then, one could no longer accuse institutions and society, but must front the true source of evil.[83]

There are three classes of inhabitants, who either frequent or inhabit the country which we had now entered;

[79] A medicinal decoction, often of guaiacum, sarsaparilla, or sassafras, taken either singly or in combination as normal drink throughout the day, usually for months, to change the habit of the body. Thoreau wrote in his journal: "Live in each season as it passes; breathe the air, drink the drink, taste the fruit, and resign yourself to the influences of each. Let these be your only diet drink and botanical medicines" [J 5:394].

[80] The common goldeneye (*Bucephala clangula*) colloquially called the "whistler" duck from the distinctive whistling sound its wings make during flight.

[81] Yellow-shafted flicker (*Colaptes auratus*).

[82] More properly "brand new," although commonly spelled "bran new" in the nineteenth century, from the sixteenth century usage meaning fresh or new from the fire.

[83] As Thoreau wrote in his journal of 3 January 1853:

> Man, man is the devil,
> The source of all evil. [ITM 172]

That man is the source of evil is found in many religious texts, such as Mark 7:21–23: "For from within, out of the heart of men, proceed evil thoughts, adulteries, fornications, murders, Thefts, covetousness, wickedness, deceit, lasciviousness, an evil eye, blasphemy, pride, foolishness: All these evil things come from within, and defile the man."

84 The Maine historian Fannie Hardy Eckstorm (1865–1946) described it as "a platform on wheels, carried down a short wooden track by gravity to the river."
85 Unidentified.
86 Also known as "penny books" or "one cent toy books."
87 Mary Doe Howard (1776–1869).

first, the loggers, who, for a part of the year, the winter and spring, are far the most numerous, but in the summer, except a few explorers for timber, completely desert it; second, the few settlers I have named, the only permanent inhabitants, who live on the verge of it, and help raise supplies for the former; third, the hunters, mostly Indians, who range over it in their season.

At the end of three miles we came to the Mattaseunk stream and mill, where there was even a rude wooden railroad running down to the Penobscot, the last railroad we were to see.[84] We crossed one tract, on the bank of the river, of more than a hundred acres of heavy timber, which had just been felled and burnt over, and was still smoking. Our trail lay through the midst of it, and was well nigh blotted out. The trees lay at full length, four or five feet deep, and crossing each other in all directions, all black as charcoal, but perfectly sound within, still good for fuel or for timber; soon they would be cut into lengths and burnt again. Here were thousands of cords, enough to keep the poor of Boston and New York amply warm for a winter, which only cumbered the ground, and were in the settler's way. And the whole of that solid and interminable forest is doomed to be gradually devoured thus by fire, like shavings, and no man be warmed by it. At Crocker's log hut,[85] at the mouth of Salmon River, seven miles from the Point, one of the party commenced distributing a store of small cent picture-books[86] among the children, to teach them to read; and also newspapers, more or less recent, among the parents, than which nothing can be more acceptable to a backwoods people. It was really an important item in our outfit, and, at times, the only currency that would circulate. I walked through Salmon River with my shoes on, it being low water, but not without wetting my feet. A few miles further we came to "Marm Howard's,"[87] at the end of an extensive clearing, where there were two or three log huts in sight at once, one on the opposite side of the river, and a few graves, even surrounded by a wooden paling, where already the rude forefathers of *a* hamlet lie;[88] and a thousand years hence, perchance, some poet will write his "Elegy in a Country Churchyard." The "Village Hampdens," the "mute, inglorious Miltons,"[89] and Cromwells,[90] "guiltless of" their "country's blood,"[91] were yet unborn.

> "Perchance in this *wild* spot *there will be* laid
>   Some heart once pregnant with celestial fire;
> Hands that the rod of empire might have swayed,
>   Or waked to ecstasy the living lyre."[92]

The next house was Fisk's,[93] ten miles from the Point, at the mouth of the East Branch, opposite to the island Nickatow, or the Forks,[94] the last of the Indian islands. I am particular to give the names of the settlers and the distances, since every log hut in these woods is a public house, and such information is of no little consequence to those who may have occasion to travel this way. Our course here crossed the Penobscot, and followed the southern bank. One of the party, who entered the house in search of some one to set us over, reported a very neat dwelling, with plenty of books, and a new wife, just imported from Boston,[95] wholly new to the woods. We found the East Branch a large and rapid stream at its mouth, and much deeper than it appeared. Having with some difficulty discovered the trail again, we kept up the south side of the West Branch, or main river, passing by some rapids called Rock-Ebeeme,[96] the roar of which we heard through the woods, and, shortly after, in the thickest of the wood, some empty loggers' camps, still new, which were occupied the previous winter. Though we saw a few more afterwards, I will make one account serve for all. These were such houses as the lumberers of

88 Allusion to Thomas Gray's (1716–1771) "Elegy Written in a Country Churchyard," line 16: "The rude forefathers of the hamlet sleep."

89 John Milton (1608–1674), British author known for such works as his poetic epic *Paradise Lost*, his elegy "Lycidas," and his treatise on censorship, *Areopagitica*.

90 Oliver Cromwell (1599–1658), who ruled England as lord protector from 1653 to 1658 following the English Civil War (1642–1651).

91 Quoted from Gray's "Elegy" 57–60:

> Some village Hampden that with dauntless breast
>   The little tyrant of his fields withstood,
> Some mute inglorious Milton here may rest,
>   Some Cromwell guiltless of his country's blood.

92 Quoted from Gray's "Elegy" 45–48, the first line of which Thoreau altered from: "Perhaps in that neglected spot is laid."

93 Benjamin Nutting Fiske (1815–1902).

94 The confluence of the east and west branches of the Penobscot.

95 Fiske married Eliza Pierce Warren (1811–1893) of Boston on 1 July 1846.

96 In his journal Thoreau interlined: "The water is comparatively smooth below Nickatow—though rough enough to daunt an inexperienced boatman, but above this the serious difficulties commence" [PJ 2:274].

97 *Pork barrel* became a standard unit of measurement equivalent to two hundred pounds.

Maine spend the winter in, in the wilderness. There were the camps and the hovel for the cattle, hardly distinguishable, except that the latter had no chimney. These camps were about twenty feet long by fifteen wide, built of logs—hemlock, cedar, spruce, or yellow birch—one kind alone, or all together, with the bark on; two or three large ones first, one directly above another, and notched together at the ends, to the height of three or four feet, then of smaller logs resting upon transverse ones at the ends, each of the last successively shorter than the other, to form the roof. The chimney was an oblong square hole in the middle, three or four feet in diameter, with a fence of logs as high as the ridge. The interstices were filled with moss, and the roof was shingled with long and handsome splints of cedar, or spruce, or pine, rifted with a sledge and cleaver. The fire-place, the most important place of all, was in shape and size like the chimney, and directly under it, defined by a log fence or fender on the ground, and a heap of ashes a foot or two deep within, with solid benches of split logs running round it. Here the fire usually melts the snow, and dries the rain before it can descend to quench it. The faded beds of arborvitae leaves extended under the eaves on either hand. There was the place for the water-pail, pork-barrel,[97] and wash-basin, and generally a dingy pack of cards left on a log. Usually a good deal of whittling was expended on the latch, which was made of wood, in the form of an iron one. These houses are made comfortable by the huge fires that can be afforded night and day. Usually the scenery about them is drear and savage enough; and the logger's camp is as completely in the woods as a fungus at the foot of a pine in a swamp; no outlook but to the sky overhead; no more clearing than is made by cutting down the trees of which it is built, and those which are necessary for fuel. If only it be well sheltered and convenient to his work, and near a spring, he wastes no thought on the prospect. They are very proper forest houses, the stems of the trees collected together and piled up around a man to keep out wind and rain: made of living green logs, hanging with moss and lichen, and with the curls and fringes of the yellow-birch bark, and dripping with resin, fresh and moist, and redolent of swampy odors, with that sort of vigor and perennialness even about them that toad-stools suggest.[98] The logger's fare consists of tea, molasses, flour, pork,—sometimes beef,—and beans. A great proportion of the beans raised in Massachusetts find their market here. On expeditions it is only hard bread[99] and pork, often raw, slice upon slice, with tea or water, as the case may be.

The primitive wood is always and everywhere damp and mossy, so that I travelled constantly with the impression that I was in a swamp; and only when it was remarked that this or that tract, judging from the quality of the timber on it, would make a profitable clearing, was I reminded, that if the sun were let in it would make a dry field, like the few I had seen, at once. The best shod for the most part travel with wet feet. If the ground was so wet and spongy at this, the driest part of a dry season, what must it be in the spring? The woods hereabouts abounded in beech and yellow-birch, of which last there were some very large specimens; also spruce, cedar, fir, and hemlock; but we saw only the stumps of the white pine[100] here, some of them of great size, these having been already culled out, being the only tree much sought after, even as low down as this. Only a little spruce and hemlock beside had been logged here. The eastern wood, which is sold for fuel in Massachusetts, all comes from below Bangor. It was the pine alone, chiefly the white pine, that had tempted any but the hunter to precede us on this route.

Waite's farm,[101] thirteen miles from the Point, is an extensive and elevated clearing, from which we got a

98 Thoreau's footnote, referring to Springer's *Forest Life and Forest Trees*, added in the 1864 edition of *The Maine Woods*: "Springer, in his 'Forest Life' (1851), says that they first remove the leaves and turf from the spot where they intend to build a camp, for fear of fire; also, that 'the spruce-tree is generally selected for camp-building, it being light, straight, and quite free from sap'; that 'the roof is finally covered with the boughs of the fir, spruce, and hemlock, so that when the snow falls upon the whole, the warmth of the camp is preserved in the coldest weather'; and that they make the log seat before the fire, called the 'Deacon's Seat,' of a spruce or fir split in halves, with three or four stout limbs left on one side for legs, which are not likely to get loose."

99 Also called hardtack: coarse, hard, unleavened, unsalted, kiln-dried biscuit used especially as rations for sailors or soldiers.

100 The largest tree in the old-growth forests of New England, used for lumber and ship masts.

101 Farm of George Washington Waite (1793–1870), although by this time the farm may have belonged to his son, William (1826–1915). Thoreau wrote in his journal: "We here met with a very hospitable reception from Mrs Waite who would not be paid for the luncheon she provided but seemed content with the sight of strangers" [PJ 2:297]. Mrs. Waite was George's wife, Mary Haskell Waite (1797–1864).

102 George McCauslin (1798–1884), the first white settler in the Burnt Land Rips area now known as East Millinocket.
103 Chiefly a New England term meaning a tract of low-lying land between hills.
104 Now, Schoodic Stream.
105 From the Kennebec River region in central Maine.

fine view of the river, rippling and gleaming far beneath us. My companions had formerly had a good view of Ktaadn and the other mountains here, but to-day it was so smoky that we could see nothing of them. We could overlook an immense country of uninterrupted forest, stretching away up the East Branch toward Canada, on the north and northwest, and toward the Aroostook valley on the northeast: and imagine what wild life was stirring in its midst. Here was quite a field of corn for this region, whose peculiar dry scent we perceived a third of a mile off before we saw it.

Eighteen miles from the Point brought us in sight of McCauslin's, or "Uncle George's,"[102] as he was familiarly called by my companions, to whom he was well known, where we intended to break our long fast. His house was in the midst of an extensive clearing of intervale,[103] at the mouth of the Little Schoodic River,[104] on the opposite or north bank of the Penobscot. So we collected on a point of the shore, that we might be seen, and fired our gun as a signal, which brought out his dogs forthwith, and thereafter their master, who in due time took us across in his batteau. This clearing was bounded abruptly on all sides but the river, by the naked stems of the forest, as if you were to cut only a few feet square in the midst of a thousand acres of mowing, and set down a thimble therein. He had a whole heaven and horizon to himself, and the sun seemed to be journeying over his clearing only, the live-long day. Here we concluded to spend the night, and wait for the Indians, as there was no stopping place so convenient above. He had seen no Indians pass, and this did not often happen without his knowledge. He thought that his dogs sometimes gave notice of the approach of Indians, half an hour before they arrived.

McCauslin was a Kennebec man,[105] of Scotch descent, who had been a waterman twenty-two years, and had driven on the lakes and head waters of the Penobscot five or six springs in succession, but was now settled here to raise supplies for the lumberers and for himself. He entertained us a day or two with true Scotch hospitality,[106] and would accept no recompense for it. A man of a dry wit and shrewdness, and a general intelligence which I had not looked for in the backwoods. In fact, the deeper you penetrate into the woods, the more intelligent, and, in one sense, less countrified do you find the inhabitants; for always the pioneer has been a traveller, and, to some extent, a man of the world; and, as the distances with which he is familiar are greater, so is his information more general and far reaching than the villager's. If I were to look for a narrow, uninformed, and countrified mind, as opposed to the intelligence and refinement which are thought to emanate from cities, it would be among the rusty inhabitants of an old-settled country, on farms all run out and gone to seed with life-everlasting,[107] in the towns about Boston, even on the high road[108] in Concord, and not in the backwoods of Maine.

Supper was got before our eyes, in the ample kitchen, by a fire which would have roasted an ox; many whole logs, four feet long, were consumed to boil our tea-kettle—birch, or beech, or maple, the same summer and winter; and the dishes were soon smoking on the table, late the arm-chair, against the wall, from which one of the party was expelled. The arms of the chair formed the frame on which the table rested; and, when the round top was turned up against the wall, it formed the back of the chair, and was no more in the way than the wall itself. This, we noticed, was the prevailing fashion in these log houses, in order to economize in room. There were piping hot wheaten-cakes, the flour having been brought up the river in batteaux,—no Indian bread,[109] for the upper part of Maine, it will be remembered, is a wheat country,—and ham, eggs, and potatoes, and milk

106 The legendary hospitality of the Scot has been mentioned by such authors as Charles Dickens (1812–1870), Samuel Johnson (1709–1784), and Sir Walter Scott (1771–1832). Nathaniel Parker Willis (1806–1867) in his *Famous Persons and Places* described it as aiming "to convince you that the house and all that is in it is your own."
107 Pearly everlasting (*Antennaria Margaritaceum*).
108 Now Lexington Road.
109 Plant with edible parts, such as the breadroot (*Psoralea esculenta*), eaten by some Native American peoples.

110 Also called the rock cranberry and cowberry, about which Thoreau wrote in his journal on 3 June 1851 following the initial publication of this essay in *Sartain's Union Magazine:* "Dr. Harris suggests that the mountain cranberry which I saw at Ktaadn was the *Vaccinium Vitis-Idaea,* cowberry, because it was edible and not the *Uva-Ursi,* or bear-berry, which we have in Concord" [J 2:224]. Thaddeus William Harris (1795–1856) was the librarian of Harvard from 1831 to 1856 and lectured on natural history there from 1837 to 1842. Thoreau often appealed to him for help with questions of natural history.

111 In *Walden* Thoreau wrote: "As if you could kill time without injuring eternity" [Wa 7].

112 Berries of the eastern red cedar (*Juniperus virginiana*).

113 Axe handles.

114 Famine swept Ireland in the 1840s, when the potato crop failed, causing the death of approximately one million people. At this time hundreds of thousands of Irish emigrated, many to the United States. The potato rot soon reached the United States, and in 1844 the Maine potato crop began to fail.

and cheese, the produce of the farm; and, also, shad and salmon, tea sweetened with molasses, and sweet cakes in contradistinction to the hot cakes not sweetened, the one white, the other yellow, to wind up with. Such, we found, was the prevailing fare, ordinary and extraordinary, along this river. Mountain cranberries (*Vaccinium Vitis-Idaea*),[110] stewed and sweetened, were the common dessert. Everything here was in profusion, and the best of its kind. Butter was in such plenty, that it was commonly used, before it was salted, to grease boots with.

In the night we were entertained by the sound of rain-drops on the cedar splints which covered the roof, and awaked the next morning with a drop or two in our eyes. It had set in for a storm, and we made up our minds not to forsake such comfortable quarters with this prospect, but wait for Indians and fair weather. It rained and drizzled, and gleamed by turns, the live-long day. What we did there, how we killed the time,[111] would, perhaps, be idler to tell; how many times we buttered our boots, and how often a drowsy one was seen to sidle off to the bedroom. When it held up, I strolled up and down the bank and gathered the harebell and cedar berries,[112] which grew there; or else we tried by turns the long-handled axe on the logs before the door. The axe-helves[113] here were made to chop standing on the log — a primitive log of course — and were, therefore, nearly a foot longer than with us. One while we walked over the farm, and visited his well-filled barns with McCauslin. There were one other man and two women only here. He kept horses, cows, oxen, and sheep. I think he said that he was the first to bring a plough and a cow so far; and, he might have added, the last, with only two exceptions. The potato rot had found him out here, too, the previous year,[114] and got half or two-thirds of his crop, though the seed was of his own raising. Oats, grass, and potatoes, were his staples; but he raised, also, a few carrots and turnips, and "a little corn for the hens," for this was all that he dared risk, for fear that it would not ripen. Melons, squashes, sweet-corn, beans, tomatoes, and many other vegetables, could not be ripened there.[115]

The very few settlers along this stream were obviously tempted by the cheapness of the land mainly. When I asked McCauslin why more settlers did not come in, he answered, that one reason was, they could not buy the land, it belonged to individuals or companies who were afraid that their wild lands would be settled, and so incorporated into towns, and they be taxed for them; but to settling on the State's land there was no such hinderance. For his own part, he wanted no neighbors— he didn't wish to see any road by his house. Neighbors, even the best, were a trouble and expense, especially on the score of cattle and fences. They might live across the river, perhaps, but not on the same side.

The chickens here were protected by the dogs. As McCauslin said, "The old one took it up first, and she taught the pup, and now they had got it into their heads that it wouldn't do to have anything of the bird kind on the premises." A hawk hovering over was not allowed to alight, but barked off by the dogs circling underneath; and a pigeon, or a "yellow-hammer," as they called the pigeon-woodpecker, on a dead limb or stump, was instantly expelled. It was the main business of their day, and kept them constantly coming and going. One would rush out of the house on the least alarm given by the other.

When it rained hardest, we returned to the house, and took down a tract from the shelf. There was the Wandering Jew,[116] cheap edition, and fine print, the Criminal Calendar,[117] and Parish's Geography,[118] and flash novels[119] two or three. Under the pressure of circumstances, we read a little in these. With such aid, the press is not so feeble an engine after all. This house,

115 Maine has a short growing season, from approximately 110 days in the north to 180 in the south. Thoreau's home state, in comparison, has a growing season of approximately 160 days in the eastern and central parts of the state, with a longer growing season on the coast, and just north of Boston, of about 200 days.
116 Translation of Eugène Sue's (1804–1857) *Le Juif errant*. Sue was a popular French writer whose sensational and melodramatic works were published serially in newspapers. The circulation of *Le Constitutionnel* quadrupled during the 1844–1845 serialization of *Le Juif errant*. *The Wandering Jew* was first published in the United States in 1844.
117 Reference to *The United States Criminal Calendar; or, An Awful Warning to the Youth of America; Being an Account of the Most Horrid Murders, Piracies, Highway Robberies*, compiled by Henry St. Clair (Boston: C. Gaylord, 1835).
118 Elijah Parish's (1762–1825) *Compendious System of Universal Geography* (1804) or his *New System of Modern Geography* (1810).
119 Cheap, paperbound popular fiction, quickly written and published. In his journal Thoreau mentioned one such work by name: Joseph Holt Ingraham's (1809–1860) *Belle of the Penobscots* [J 2:293]. Ingraham produced more than eighty such novels in a six-year period.

120 The chinks filled.
121 One who drives logs downstream, using a cant hook, or cant dog, a handspike with a swivel hook.
122 Allusion to the popular weather adage originating from Matthew 16.2: "When it is evening, ye say, It will be fair weather: for the sky is red."

which was a fair specimen of those on this river, was built of huge logs, which peeped out everywhere, and were chinked[120] with clay and moss. It contained four or five rooms. There were no sawed boards, or shingles, or clapboards, about it; and scarcely any tool but the axe had been used in its construction. The partitions were made of long clapboard-like splints, of spruce or cedar, turned to a delicate salmon color by the smoke. The roof and sides were covered with the same, instead of shingles and clapboards, and some of a much thicker and larger size were used for the floor. These were all so straight and smooth, that they answered the purpose admirably; and a careless observer would not have suspected that they were not sawed and planed. The chimney and hearth were of vast size, and made of stone. The broom was a few twigs of arbor-vitae tied to a stick; and a pole was suspended over the hearth, close to the ceiling, to dry stockings and clothes on. I noticed that the floor was full of small, dingy holes, as if made with a gimlet, but which were, in fact, made by the spikes, nearly an inch long, which the lumberers wear in their boots to prevent their slipping on wet logs. Just above McCauslin's, there is a rocky rapid, where logs jam in the spring; and many "drivers"[121] are there collected, who frequent his house for supplies: these were their tracks which I saw.

At sundown, McCauslin pointed away over the forest, across the river, to signs of fair weather amid the clouds—some evening redness there.[122] For even there the points of compass held; and there was a quarter of the heavens appropriated to sunrise and another to sunset.

The next morning, the weather proving fair enough for our purpose, we prepared to start; and, the Indians having failed us, persuaded McCauslin, who was not unwilling to re-visit the scenes of his driving, to accompany us in their stead, intending to engage one other boatman on the way. A strip of cotton-cloth for a tent, a couple of blankets, which would suffice for the whole party, fifteen pounds of hard bread, ten pounds of "clear" pork,[123] and a little tea, made up "Uncle George's" pack. The last three articles were calculated to be provision enough for six men for a week, with what we might pick up. A tea-kettle, a frying-pan and an axe, to be obtained at the last house, would complete our outfit.

We were soon out of McCauslin's clearing, and in the ever-green woods again. The obscure trail made by the two settlers above, which even the woodman is sometimes puzzled to discern, ere long crossed a narrow open strip in the woods overrun with weeds, called the Burnt Land, where a fire had raged formerly, stretching northward nine or ten miles, to Millinocket Lake. At the end of three miles we reached Shad Pond, or Noliseemack, an expansion of the river. Hodge, the Assistant State Geologist, who passed through this on the twenty-fifth of June, 1837, says, "We pushed our boat through an acre or more of buck-beans,[124] which had taken root at the bottom, and bloomed above the surface in the greatest profusion and beauty."[125] Thomas Fowler's[126] house is four miles from McCauslin's, on the shore of the pond, at the mouth of the Millinocket River, and eight miles from the lake of the same name, on the latter stream. This lake affords a more direct course to Ktaadn, but we preferred to follow the Penobscot and the Pamadumcook Lakes. Fowler was just completing a new log hut, and was sawing out a window through the logs nearly two feet thick when we arrived. He had begun to paper his house with spruce bark, turned inside out, which had a good effect, and was in keeping with the circumstances. Instead of water we got here a draught of beer,[127] which, it was allowed, would be better; clear and thin, but strong and stringent as the cedar sap. It was as if we sucked at the very teats of Nature's pine-clad bosom in these parts—

123 Best class of barreled pork, comprising the sides of large hogs free from bones and clear of lean.
124 *Menyanthes trifoliate*, also known as bog bean.
125 Quoted from "Mr. Hodge's Report on the Allegash section, from the Penobscot to the St. Lawrence River," in Jackson's *Second Annual Report*.
126 Thomas Fowler, Jr. (1822–1902).
127 Spruce beer that is described in William Durkee Williamson's (1779–1846) *History of the State of Maine* as "a most wholesome and palatable drink." On 13 July 1852 Thoreau wrote to his sister, Sophia 1819–1876): "I would exchange my immortality for a glass of small beer this hot weather" [C 6:194]. Thoreau made his own birch beer, as attested to by his friend Daniel Ricketson (1813–1898): "My friend Thoreau has a very pleasant acidulous drink, requiring only the addition of sugar. The sap of the birch, white, black and yellow. The former the most aromatic."

128 Allusion to Orpheus, in Greek mythology, whose music had supernatural powers and could charm animals and inanimate objects.
129 Thomas Fowler, Sr. (1792–1874), the first white settler in the area now known as Millinocket.
130 Muskrat.

the sap of all Millinocket botany commingled—the topmost most fantastic and spiciest sprays of the primitive wood, and whatever invigorating and stringent gum or essence it afforded, steeped and dissolved in it—a lumberer's drink, which would acclimate and naturalize a man at once—which would make him see green, and, if he slept, dream that he heard the wind sough among the pines. Here was a fife, praying to be played on, through which we breathed a few tuneful strains,—brought hither to tame wild beasts.[128] As we stood upon the pile of chips by the door, fish-hawks were sailing over head; and here, over Shad Pond, might daily be witnessed, the tyranny of the bald-eagle over that bird. Tom pointed away over the Lake to a bald-eagle's nest, which was plainly visible more than a mile off, on a pine, high above the surrounding forest, and was frequented from year to year by the same pair, and held sacred by him. There were these two houses only there, his low hut, and the eagles' airy cart-load of fagots. Thomas Fowler, too, was persuaded to join us, for two men were necessary to manage the batteau, which was soon to be our carriage, and these men needed to be cool and skilful for the navigation of the Penobscot. Tom's pack was soon made, for he had not far to look for his waterman's boots, and a red flannel shirt. This is the favorite color with lumbermen; and red flannel is reputed to possess some mysterious virtues, to be most healthful and convenient in respect to perspiration. In every gang there will be a large proportion of red birds. We took here a poor and leaky batteau, and began to pole up the Millinocket two miles, to the elder Fowler's,[129] in order to avoid the Grand Falls of the Penobscot, intending to exchange our batteau there for a better. The Millinocket is a small, shallow and sandy stream, full of what I took to be lamprey-eel's or sucker's nests, and lined with musquash[130] cabins, but free from rapids, according to Fowler, excepting at its outlet from the Lake. He was at this time engaged in cutting the native grass—rush grass[131] and meadow-clover,[132] as he called it—on the meadows and small, low islands, of this stream. We noticed flattened places in the grass on either side, where, he said, a moose had lain down the night before, adding, that there were thousands in these meadows.

Old Fowler's, on the Millinocket, six miles from Mc-Causlin's, and twenty-four from the Point, is the last house. Gibson's, on the Sowadnehunk,[133] is the only clearing above, but that had proved a failure, and was long since deserted.[134] Fowler is the oldest inhabitant of these woods. He formerly lived a few miles from here, on the south side of the West Branch, where he built his house sixteen years ago,[135] the first house built above the Five Islands. Here our new batteau was to be carried over the first portage of two miles, round the Grand Falls of the Penobscot, on a horse-sled made of saplings, to jump the numerous rocks in the way, but we had to wait a couple of hours for them to catch the horses, which were pastured at a distance, amid the stumps, and had wandered still further off. The last of the salmon for this season had just been caught, and were still fresh in pickle, from which enough was extracted to fill our empty kettle, and so graduate our introduction to simpler forest fare. The week before, they had lost nine sheep here out of their first flock, by the wolves. The surviving sheep came round the house, and seemed frightened, which induced them to go and look for the rest, when they found seven dead and lacerated, and two still alive. These last they carried to the house, and, as Mrs. Fowler[136] said, they were merely scratched in the throat, and had no more visible wound than would be produced by the prick of a pin. She sheared off the wool from their throats, and washed them and put on some salve, and turned them out, but in a few moments they were missing, and had not been

131 Sheathed rush-grass (*Sporobolus vaginiflorus*), a wiry grass with panicles more or less included in the leaf-sheaths, thus having a slightly rushlike appearance.
132 Red clover (*Trifolium pratense*).
133 Now Nesowadnehunk.
134 This clearing is described briefly in Jackson's *Second Annual Report:* "We then came to Gibson's clearing of 80 acres on the eastern side. The banks are from 10 to 15 feet high, and the soil, judging from the fine growth of grass which then covered the open intervale, is very good. The place is not inhabited."
135 Fowler first built at Grand Falls before moving to Millinocket Stream ca. 1829–1830.
136 Betsy (Martin) Fowler (1801–1890).

137 Aesopian fables such as "The Wolves and the Sheep," "The Wolf in Sheep's Clothing," and "The Shepherd-Boy and the Wolf."

138 Allusion to the "The Shepherd-Boy and the Wolf": "A shepherd-boy, who tended his flock not far from a village, used to amuse himself at times in crying out 'Wolf! Wolf!' Twice or thrice his trick succeeded. The whole village came running out to his assistance; when all the return they got was to be laughed at for their pains. At last one day the Wolf came indeed. The Boy cried out in earnest. But his neighbours, supposing him to be at his old sport, paid no heed to his cries, and the Wolf devoured the Sheep. So the Boy learned, when it was too late, that liars are not believed even when they tell the truth."

139 George W. Fowler (1824–1890).

140 In Hodge's report "Quakis" is described as "a narrow pond, 3 miles long, through which the current runs to its outlet. It is surrounded by low banks, which are covered with pine, birch, and oak."

found since. In fact, they were all poisoned, and those that were found swelled up at once, so that they saved neither skin nor wool. This realized the old fables of the wolves and the sheep,[137] and convinced me that that ancient hostility still existed. Verily, the shepherd boy did not need to sound a false alarm this time.[138] There were steel traps by the door of various sizes, for wolves, otter, and bears, with large claws instead of teeth, to catch in their sinews. Wolves are frequently killed with poisoned bait.

At length, after we had dined here on the usual backwoods fare, the horses arrived, and we hauled our batteau out of the water, and lashed it to its wicker carriage, and, throwing in our packs, walked on before, leaving the boatmen and driver, who was Tom's brother,[139] to manage the concern. The route, which led through the wild pasture where the sheep were killed, was in some places the roughest ever travelled by horses, over rocky hills, where the sled bounced and slid along, like a vessel pitching in a storm; and one man was as necessary to stand at the stern, to prevent the boat from being wrecked, as a helmsman in the roughest sea. The philosophy of our progress was something like this: when the runners struck a rock three or four feet high, the sled bounced back and upwards at the same time; but, as the horses never ceased pulling, it came down on the top of the rock, and so we got over. This portage probably followed the trail of an ancient Indian carry round these falls. By 2 o'clock we, who had walked on before, reached the river above the falls, not far from the outlet of Quakish Lake,[140] and waited for the batteau to come up. We had been here but a short time, when a thundershower was seen coming up from the west, over the still invisible lakes, and that pleasant wilderness which we were so eager to become acquainted with; and soon the heavy drops began to patter on the leaves around us. I had just selected the prostrate trunk of a huge pine, five or six feet in diameter, and was crawling under it, when, luckily, the boat arrived. It would have amused a sheltered man to witness the manner in which it was unlashed, and whirled over, while the first water-spout[141] burst upon us. It was no sooner in the hands of the eager company than it was abandoned to the first revolutionary impulse, and to gravity, to adjust it; and they might have been seen all stooping to its shelter, and wriggling under like so many eels, before it was fairly deposited on the ground. When all were under, we propped up the lee side, and busied ourselves there, whittling thole pins[142] for rowing, when we should reach the lakes; and made the woods ring, between the claps of thunder, with such boat-songs as we could remember.[143] The horses stood sleek and shining with the rain, all drooping and crestfallen, while deluge after deluge washed over us; but the bottom of a boat may be relied on for a tight roof. At length, after two hours' delay at this place, a streak of fair weather appeared in the northwest, whither our course now lay, promising a serene evening for our voyage; and the driver returned with his horses, while we made haste to launch our boat, and commence our voyage in good earnest.

There were six of us, including the two boatmen. With our packs heaped up near the bows, and ourselves disposed as baggage to trim[144] the boat, with instructions not to move in case we should strike a rock, more than so many barrels of pork, we pushed out into the first rapid, a slight specimen of the stream we had to navigate. With Uncle George in the stern, and Tom in the bows, each using a spruce pole about twelve feet long, pointed with iron,[145] and poling on the same side, we shot up the rapids like a salmon, the water rushing and roaring around, so that only a practised eye could distinguish a safe course, or tell what was deep water and what

141 A tornado passing over a body of water.

142 Wooden pegs set in part in the gunwales of a boat to serve as an oarlock.

143 Thoreau was familiar with the nautical songs of Charles Dibdin (1745–1814). He referred to Dibdin's "Blow High, Blow Low" in his 1849 journal [ITM 43], and Dibdin's "Poor Tom Bowling; or, The Sailor's Epitaph"—sometimes spelled "Tom Bowline"—was a favorite song. Edward Emerson, on recalling Thoreau singing it, wrote: "To this day that song, heard long years ago, rings clear and moving to me."

144 To balance a vessel by shifting its cargo.

145 Thoreau's footnote added in the 1864 edition of *The Maine Woods:* "The Canadians call it *picquer de fond.*"

146 The ship in Greek mythology on which Jason sailed in search of the Golden Fleece.

147 In Greek mythology, two floating cliffs guarding the entrance to the Euxine Sea that crashed together when ships attempted to pass through.

148 Thoreau often boated, and in 1839 he and his brother John built a boat named *Musketaquid*, after the Indian name for the Concord River, for their 1839 river excursion described in *A Week on the Concord and Merrimack Rivers*. In his notebook of 1 September 1842 Nathaniel Hawthorne (1804–1864) wrote: "Mr. Thoreau managed the boat so perfectly, either with two paddles or with one, that it seemed instinct with his own will, and to require no physical effort to guide it. He said that, when some Indians visited Concord a few years since, he found that he had acquired, without a teacher, their precise method of propelling and steering a canoe."

149 Quoted from Thomas Campbell's (1777–1844) *Gertrude of Wyoming*, III.v.4.

rocks, frequently grazing the latter on one or both sides, with a hundred as narrow escapes as ever the Argo[146] had in passing through the Symplegades.[147] I, who had had some experience in boating,[148] had never experienced any half so exhilarating before. We were lucky to have exchanged our Indians, whom we did not know, for these men, who, together with Tom's brother, were reputed the best boatmen on the river, and were at once indispensable pilots and pleasant companions. The canoe is smaller, more easily upset, and sooner worn out; and the Indian is said not to be so skilful in the management of the batteau. He is, for the most part, less to be relied on, and more disposed to sulks and whims. The utmost familiarity with dead streams, or with the ocean, would not prepare a man for this peculiar navigation; and the most skilful boatman anywhere else would here be obliged to take out his boat and carry round a hundred times, still with great risk, as well as delay, where the practised batteau man poles up with comparative ease and safety. The hardy "voyageur" pushes with incredible perseverance and success quite up to the foot of the falls, and then only carries round some perpendicular ledge, and launches again in "the torrent's smoothness, ere it dash below,"[149] to struggle with the boiling rapids above. The Indians say, that the river once ran both ways, one half up and the other down, but, that since the white man came, it all runs down, and now they must laboriously pole their canoes against the stream, and carry them over numerous portages. In the summer, all stores, the grindstone and the plough of the pioneer, flour, pork, and utensils for the explorer, must be conveyed up the river in batteaux; and many a cargo and many a boatman is lost in these waters. In the winter, however, which is very equable and long, the ice is the great highway, and the loggers' team penetrates to Chesuncook Lake, and still higher up, even two hundred miles above Bangor.

Imagine the solitary sled-track running far up into the snowy and evergreen wilderness, hemmed in closely for a hundred miles by the forest, and again stretching straight across the broad surfaces of concealed lakes!

We were soon in the smooth water of the Quakish Lake, and took our turns at rowing and paddling across it. It is a small, irregular, but handsome lake, shut in on all sides by the forest, and showing no traces of man but some low boom[150] in a distant cove, reserved for spring use. The spruce and cedar on its shores, hung with gray lichens,[151] looked at a distance like the ghosts of trees.[152] Ducks were sailing here and there on its surface, and a solitary loon, like a more living wave—a vital spot on the lake's surface—laughed and frolicked, and showed its straight leg, for our amusement. Joe Merry Mountain[153] appeared in the northwest, as if it were looking down on this lake especially; and we had our first, but a partial view of Ktaadn, its summit veiled in clouds, like a dark isthmus in that quarter, connecting the heavens with the earth. After two miles of smooth rowing across this lake, we found ourselves in the river again, which was a continuous rapid for one mile, to the dam,[154] requiring all the strength and skill of our boatmen to pole up it.

This dam is a quite important and expensive work for this country, whither cattle and horses cannot penetrate in the summer, raising the whole river ten feet, and flooding, as they said, some sixty square miles by means of the innumerable lakes with which the river connects. It is a lofty and solid structure, with sloping piers some distance above, made of frames of logs filled with stones, to break the ice.[155] Here every log pays toll as it passes through the sluices.

We filed into the rude loggers' camp at this place, such as I have described, without ceremony, and the cook, at that moment the sole occupant, at once set about preparing tea for his visitors. His fire-place, which the rain

150 Springer in his *Forest Life and Forest Trees* defined a boom as being "made by fastening the ends of the trunks of long trees, so as to prevent them from scattering over the lake on the breaking up of the ice." These were sometimes used as barriers or to mark a channel or a boundary.

151 Usnea lichens.

152 Phrase that Thoreau read in Samuel Laing's *Journal of a Residence in Norway*, in which Laing described trees "standing with all their branches dead, stripped of the bark to make bread, and blanched by the weather, resembling white marble,—mere ghosts of trees." Thoreau used the phrase in his journal on 12 February 1855: "All trees covered this morning with a hoar frost, very handsome looking toward the sun,—the ghosts of trees" [J 7:179]; and on 18 January 1859: "The trees were the ghosts of trees appearing in their winding-sheets, an intenser white against the comparatively dusky ground of the fog" [J 11:403].

153 Now Jo-Mary Mountain.

154 North Twin Dam.

155 Thoreau's footnote added in the 1864 edition of *The Maine Woods*: "Even the Jesuit missionaries, accustomed to the St. Lawrence and other rivers of Canada, in their first expeditions to the Abnaquinois, speak of rivers *ferrées de rochers*, shod with rocks. See also No. 10 Relations, for 1647, p. 185." The Abnaquinois were the Abenaki. Thoreau's note is a reference to the tenth relation in *Jesuit Relations*, in which on page 182 ("p. 185" may have been a misreading of Thoreau's handwriting) he found the following, which he would have read in the original French: "I say nothing of the difficulties which must be experienced in a journey of nine or ten months,—in which one encounters rivers iron-bound with rocks, and the vessels which carry you are only of bark; wherein the perils of life recur oftener than the days and the nights; wherein the cold of Winter changes a whole country into snow and ice; where it is necessary to carry one's house, one's living, and one's provisions; where you have no other company than that of the Barbarians, as far removed

from our usages as the earth is removed from the Heavens."

156 Emerson's *Address Delivered in the Court-House in Concord, Massachusetts, on 1st August, 1844: On the Anniversary of the Emancipation of the Negroes in the British West Indies* (Boston: James Munroe, 1844).

157 Antislavery party founded in 1840.

158 British periodical founded in 1824 by James Mill (1773–1836) and Jeremy Bentham (1748–1832) and published in London.

159 Published in Utica, N.Y.: H. H. Curtis, 1844. Myron Holly (1779–1841) was an abolitionist and one of the founders of the Liberty Party.

160 John Morrison (1818–1905), who would later purchase the Grant Farm.

161 As Thoreau noted in his journal, the main difference between hot cakes and sweet cakes "being that the former are white and the latter yellow" [PJ 2:306].

162 An inflated, swollen, light, fluffy, or porous thing, as in a light, spongy, or friable cake.

had converted into a mud-puddle, was soon blazing again, and we sat down on the log benches around it to dry us. On the well-flattened, and somewhat faded beds of arbor-vitae leaves, which stretched on either hand under the eaves behind us, lay an odd leaf of the Bible, some genealogical chapter out of the Old Testament; and, half buried by the leaves, we found Emerson's Address on West India Emancipation,[156] which had been left here formerly by one of our company; and *had made two converts to the Liberty party*[157] *here*, as I was told; also, an odd number of the Westminster Review,[158] for 1834, and a pamphlet entitled History of the Erection of the Monument on the grave of Myron Holly.[159] This was the readable, or reading matter, in a lumberer's camp in the Maine woods, thirty miles from a road, which would be given up to the bears in a fortnight. These things were well thumbed and soiled. This gang was headed by one John Morrison,[160] a good specimen of a Yankee; and was necessarily composed of men not bred to the business of dam-building, but who were Jacks-at-all-trades, handy with the axe, and other simple implements, and well skilled in wood and water craft. We had hot cakes for our supper even here, white as snow-balls, but without butter, and the never-failing sweet cakes,[161] with which we filled our pockets, foreseeing that we should not soon meet with the like again. Such delicate puffballs[162] seemed a singular diet for backwoodsmen. There was also tea without milk, sweetened with molasses. And so, exchanging a word with John Morrison and his gang when we had returned to the shore, and also exchanging our batteau for a better still, we made haste to improve the little daylight that remained. This camp, exactly twenty-nine miles from Mattawamkeag Point, by the way we had come, and about one hundred from Bangor by the river, was the last human habitation of any kind in this direction. Beyond, there was no trail; and the river and lakes, by batteaux and canoes, was considered the only practicable route. We were about thirty miles by the river from the summit of Ktaadn, which was in sight, though not more than twenty, perhaps, in a straight line.

It being about the full of the moon, and a warm and pleasant evening, we decided to row five miles by moonlight to the head of the North Twin Lake, lest the wind should rise on the morrow. After one mile of river, or what the boatmen call "thoroughfare,"—for the river becomes at length only the connecting link between the lakes,—and some slight rapid which had been mostly made smooth water by the dam, we entered the North Twin Lake just after sundown, and steered across for the river "thoroughfare," four miles distant. This is a noble sheet of water, where one may get the impression which a new country and a "lake of the woods"[163] are fitted to create. There was the smoke of no log-hut nor camp of any kind to greet us, still less was any lover of nature or musing traveller[164] watching our batteau from the distant hills; not even the Indian hunter was there, for he rarely climbs them, but hugs the river like ourselves. No face welcomed us but the fine fantastic sprays of free and happy evergreen trees, waving one above another in their ancient home. At first the red clouds hung over the western shore as gorgeously as if over a city, and the lake lay open to the light with even a civilized aspect, as if expecting trade and commerce, and towns and villas. We could distinguish the inlet to the South Twin, which is said to be the larger, where the shore was misty and blue, and it was worth the while to look thus through a narrow opening across the entire expanse of a concealed lake to its own yet more dim and distant shore. The shores rose gently to ranges of low hills covered with forests; and though in fact the most valuable white-pine timber, even about this lake, had been culled out, this would never have been suspected by the voyager. The impres-

163 Allusion to the Lac des Bois (French for Lake of the Woods), where Minnesota and the Canadian provinces of Ontario and Manitoba meet. It was first visited by a European, the French explorer Jacques de Noyon (1668–1745), in 1688 and became an important fur-trading route.

164 In *Walden* Thoreau noted the "sweet-scented flowers each spring, to be plucked by the musing traveller" [Wa 255]. He could tell when such a traveler visited his house in his absence by "their cards, either a bunch of flowers, or a wreath of evergreen. . . . They who come rarely to the woods take some little piece of the forest into their hands to play with by the way, which they leave, either intentionally or accidentally. One has peeled a willow wand, woven it into a ring, and dropped it on my table. I could always tell if visitors had called in my absence, either by the bended twigs or grass, or the print of their shoes, and generally of what sex or age or quality they were by some slight trace left, as a flower dropped, or a bunch of grass plucked and thrown way" [Wa 125–126].

165 Rivers in New Brunswick and Maine, and Quebec, respectively.

166 Reference to the Lake District in the northwest of England, associated with Wordsworth, Samuel Taylor Coleridge (1772–1834), and Robert Southey (1774–1843).

167 Telos Canal.

168 Maine was described as a "wilderness of lakes" in *The North American Tourist*, published by A. T. Goodrich in 1839.

sion, which indeed corresponded with the fact, was, as if we were upon a high table land between the States and Canada, the northern side of which is drained by the St. John and Chaudiere,[165] the southern by the Penobscot and Kennebec. There was no bold mountainous shore, as we might have expected, but only isolated hills and mountains rising here and there from the plateau. The country is an archipelago of lakes,—the lake-country[166] of New England. Their levels vary but a few feet, and the boatmen, by short portages, or by none at all, pass easily from one to another. They say that at very high water the Penobscot and the Kennebec flow into each other, or at any rate, that you may lie with your face in the one and your toes in the other. Even the Penobscot and St. John have been connected by a canal,[167] so that the lumber of the Allegash, instead of going down the St. John, comes down the Penobscot; and the Indian's tradition that the Penobscot once ran both ways for his convenience, is, in one sense, partially realized to-day.

None of our party but McCauslin had been above this lake, so we trusted to him to pilot us, and we could not but confess the importance of a pilot on these waters. While it is river, you will not easily forget which way is up stream; but when you enter a lake, the river is completely lost, and you scan the distant shores in vain to find where it comes in. A stranger is, for the time at least, lost, and must set about a voyage of discovery first of all to find the river. To follow the windings of the shore when the lake is ten miles or even more in length, and of an irregularity which will not soon be mapped, is a wearisome voyage, and will spend his time and his provisions. They tell a story of a gang of experienced woodmen sent to a location on this stream, who were thus lost in the wilderness of lakes.[168] They cut their way through thickets, and carried their baggage and their boats over from lake to lake, sometimes several miles. They carried into Millinocket lake, which is on another stream, and is ten miles square, and contains a hundred islands.[169] They explored its shores thoroughly, and then carried into another and another, and it was a week of toil and anxiety before they found the Penobscot river again, and then their provisions were exhausted, and they were obliged to return.

While Uncle George steered for a small island near the head of the lake, now just visible like a speck on the water, we rowed by turns swiftly over its surface, singing such boat-songs as we could remember. The shores seemed at an indefinite distance in the moonlight. Occasionally we paused in our singing and rested on our oars, while we listened to hear if the wolves howled, for this is a common serenade, and my companions affirmed that it was the most dismal and unearthly of sounds; but we heard none this time. — If we did not *hear*, however, we did *listen*, not without a reasonable expectation;[170] that at least I have to tell, — only some utterly uncivilized, big-throated owl hooted loud and dismally[171] in the drear and boughy wilderness, plainly not nervous about his solitary life, nor afraid to hear the echoes of his voice there. We remembered also that possibly moose were silently watching us from the distant coves, or some surly bear, or timid caribou had been startled by our singing. It was with new emphasis that we sang there the Canadian boat-song—

"Row, brothers, row, the stream runs fast,
The Rapids are near and the daylight's past!"[172]—

which described precisely our own adventure, and was inspired by the experience of a similar kind of life, — for the rapids were ever near, and the daylight long past; the woods on shore looked dim, and many an Utawas' tide[173] here emptied into the lake.

169 Jackson in his *Second Annual Report* described it as "a most beautiful sheet of water, containing a great number of small islands, from which circumstance it takes its name."
170 As Thoreau wrote in his journal of 2 September 1856: "I think we may detect that some sort of preparation and faint expectation preceded every discovery we have made" [ITM 284]. He expressed this concept many times, as in his 19 May 1859 letter to Mary Brown: "In the long run, we find what we expect" [C 551].
171 In *Walden* Thoreau wrote: "When other birds are still, the screech owls take up the strain, like mourning women their ancient u-lu-lu. Their dismal scream is truly Ben Jonsonian" [Wa 120–121].
172 Quoted with minor variants from Thomas Moore's (1779–1852) "Canadian Boat Song" (ll. 5–6), written on the St. Lawrence River in 1804. Thoreau also referred to this poem in "An Excursion to Canada."
173 The Ottawa River that empties into both the Lake of Two Mountains and the Saint Lawrence River.

"Why should we yet our sail unfurl?
There is not a breath the blue wave to curl!
But, when the wind blows off the shore,
O sweetly we'll rest our weary oar."

"Utawas' tide! this trembling moon,
Shall see us float o'er thy surges soon."[174]

At last we glided past the "green isle"[175] which had been our landmark, all joining in the chorus; as if by the watery links of rivers and of lakes we were about to float over unmeasured zones of earth, bound on unimaginable adventures.

"Saint of this green isle! hear our prayers,
O grant us cool days and favoring airs!"

About nine o'clock we reached the river, and ran our boat into a natural haven between some rocks, and drew her out on the sand. This camping ground McCauslin had been familiar with in his lumbering days, and he now struck it unerringly in the moonlight, and we heard the sound of the rill which would supply us with cool water emptying into the lake. The first business was to make a fire, an operation which was a little delayed by the wetness of the fuel and the ground, owing to the heavy showers of the afternoon. The fire is the main comfort of a camp, whether in summer or winter, and is about as ample at one season as at another. It is as well for cheerfulness, as for warmth and dryness. It forms one side of the camp; one bright side at any rate. Some were dispersed to fetch in dead trees and boughs, while Uncle George felled the birches and beeches which stood convenient, and soon we had a fire some ten feet long by three or four high, which rapidly dried the sand before it. This was calculated to burn all night. We next proceeded to pitch our tent; which operation was performed by sticking our two spike poles into the ground in a slanting direction, about ten feet apart, for rafters, and then drawing our cotton cloth over them, and tying it down at the ends, leaving it open in front, shed-fashion. But this evening the wind carried the sparks on to the tent and burned it. So we hastily drew up the batteau just within the edge of the woods before the fire, and propping up one side three or four feet high, spread the tent on the ground to lie on; and with the corner of a blanket, or what more or less we could get to put over us, lay down with our heads and bodies under the boat, and our feet and legs on the sand toward the fire. At first we lay awake, talking of our course, and finding ourselves in so convenient a posture for studying the heavens, with the moon and stars shining in our faces, our conversation naturally turned upon astronomy, and we recounted by turns the most interesting discoveries in that science. But at length we composed ourselves seriously to sleep. It was interesting, when awakened at midnight, to watch the grotesque and fiend-like forms and motions of some one of the party, who, not being able to sleep, had got up silently to arouse the fire, and add fresh fuel, for a change; now stealthily lugging a dead tree from out the dark, and heaving it on, now stirring up the embers with his fork,[176] or tiptoeing about to observe the stars, watched, perchance, by half the prostrate party in breathless silence; so much the more intense because they were awake, while each supposed his neighbor sound asleep. Thus aroused, I too brought fresh fuel to the fire, and then rambled along the sandy shore in the moonlight, hoping to meet a moose come down to drink, or else a wolf. The little rill tinkled the louder, and peopled all the wilderness for me; and the glassy smoothness of the sleeping lake, laving the shores of a new world, with the dark, fantastic rocks rising here and there from its surface, made a scene not easily de-

176 Wood forks "neatly whittled" as Thoreau describes them later in this essay.

177 On 30 April 1844 Thoreau, with his companion Edward Hoar, accidentally set the woods on fire. A spark from their fire caught on the extremely dry grass nearby. Over 300 acres were burned, causing over $2,000 in damage. The *Concord Freeman* reported on 3 May 1844: "The fire, we understand, was communicated to the woods through the thoughtlessness of two of our citizens, who kindled it in a *pine stump*, near the Pond, for the purpose of making a chowder. As every thing around them was as combustible almost as a fire-ship, the flames spread with rapidity, and hours elapsed before it could be subdued. It is to be hoped that this unfortunate result of sheer carelessness, will be borne in mind by those who may visit the woods in future for recreation."

For years Thoreau had to endure being called "woods-burner" in whispers behind his back. His prolonged feelings of guilt caused him to write a lengthy journal account of the incident in May 1850, six years later.

178 Now Jo-Mary Lakes: a chain of three lakes (Upper, Middle and Lower) in central Maine.

179 Quoted from Hayward's *New England Gazetteer*.

scribed. It has left such an impression of stern yet gentle wildness on my memory as will not soon be effaced. Not far from midnight, we were one after another awakened by rain falling on our extremities; and as each was made aware of the fact by cold or wet, he drew a long sigh and then drew up his legs, until gradually we had all sidled round from lying at right angles with the boat, till our bodies formed an acute angle with it, and were wholly protected. When next we awoke, the moon and stars were shining again, and there were signs of dawn in the east. I have been thus particular in order to convey some idea of a night in the woods.

We had soon launched and loaded our boat, and, leaving our fire blazing, were off again before breakfast. The lumberers rarely trouble themselves to put out their fires, such is the dampness of the primitive forest; and this is one cause, no doubt, of the frequent fires in Maine, of which we hear so much on smoky days in Massachusetts. The forests are held cheap after the white pine has been culled out; and the explorers and hunters pray for rain only to clear the atmosphere of smoke. The woods were so wet to-day, however, that there was no danger of our fire spreading.[177] After poling up half a mile of river, or thoroughfare, we rowed a mile across the foot of Pamadumcook Lake, which is the name given on the map to this whole chain of lakes, as if there was but one, though they are, in each instance, distinctly separated by a reach of the river, with its narrow and rocky channel and its rapids. This lake, which is one of the largest, stretched north-west ten miles, to hills and mountains in the distance. McCauslin pointed to some distant and, as yet, inaccessible forests of white pine, on the sides of a mountain in that direction. The Joe Merry Lakes,[178] which lay between us and Moosehead, on the west, were recently, if they are not still, "surrounded by some of the best timbered land in the state."[179] By another thoroughfare we passed into Deep Cove, a part of the same lake, which makes up two miles, toward the northeast, and rowing two miles across this, by another short thoroughfare, entered Ambejijis Lake.[180]

At the entrance to a lake we sometimes observed what is technically called "fencing stuff," or the unhewn timbers of which booms are formed, either secured together in the water, or laid up on the rocks and lashed to trees, for spring use. But it was always startling to discover so plain a trail of civilized man there. I remember that I was strangely affected when we were returning, by the sight of a ring-bolt well drilled into a rock, and fastened with lead, at the head of this solitary Ambejijis Lake.

It was easy to see, that driving logs must be an exciting as well as arduous and dangerous business. All winter long the logger goes on piling up the trees which he has trimmed and hauled in some dry ravine at the head of a stream, and then in the spring he stands on the bank, and whistles for Rain and Thaw,[181] ready to wring the perspiration out of his shirt to swell the tide, till suddenly, with a whoop and halloo from him, shutting his eyes, as if to bid farewell to the existing state of things, a fair proportion of his winter's work goes scrambling down the country, followed by his faithful dogs, Thaw, and Rain, and Freshet, and Wind, the whole pack in full cry, toward the Orono Mills.[182] Every log is marked with the owner's name, cut in the sapwood with an axe, or bored with an auger, so deep as not to be worn off in the driving, and yet not so as to injure the timber; and it requires considerable ingenuity to invent new and simple marks where there are so many owners. They have quite an alphabet of their own, which only the practised can read. One of my companions read off from his memorandum book some marks of his own logs, among which there were crosses, belts, crow's feet, girdles, etc., as Y-girdle-crowfoot, and various other devices. When the

180 Now spelled Ambejejus Lake.

181 Possible allusion to the seaman's superstition of "whistling for the wind" during a calm, referred to by Henry Wadsworth Longfellow (1807–1882) in *The Golden Legend:*

> I was whistling to Saint Antonio
> For a capful of wind to fill our sail,
> And instead of a breeze he has sent a gale.

182 In J. C. Myers's 1849 *Sketches on a Tour through the Northern and Eastern States, the Canadas, and Nova Scotia,* Orono is noted as being "famous for its numerous Saw-Mills."

183 Sometimes, run the gantlet: to be exposed to danger, criticism, or other adversity. Dating from the early seventeenth century, it referred to a form of military punishment where a man ran between two rows of soldiers or sailors who struck him with sticks or knotted ropes, but also to a Native American form of humiliation and torture that Thoreau would have been aware of from such sources as the story of Hannah Dustan (b. 1657) in John Warner Barber's *Historical Collections*.
184 Ferruled: capped, or wrapped with a metal ring.
185 Thoreau's footnote, quoted from Springer's *Forest Life and Forest Trees*, added in 1864 edition of *The Maine Woods:* "A steady current or pitch of water is preferable to one either rising or diminishing; as, when rising rapidly, the water at the middle of the river is considerably higher than at the shores—so much so as to be distinctly perceived by the eye of a spectator on the banks, presenting an appearance like a turnpike road. The lumber, therefore, is always sure to incline from the centre of the channel toward either shore."
186 François André Michaux (1770–1855), French botanist who studied the forests of North America under the auspices of the French government, and whose *North American Sylva* was published in 1819.

logs have run the gauntlet[183] of innumerable rapids and falls, each on its own account, with more or less jamming and bruising, those bearing various owners' marks being mixed up together, since all must take advantage of the same freshet, they are collected together at the heads of the lakes, and surrounded by a boom fence of floating logs, to prevent their being dispersed by the wind, and are thus towed altogether, like a flock of sheep, across the lake, where there is no current, by a windlass, or boom-head, such as we sometimes saw standing on an island or head-land, and, if circumstances permit, with the aid of sails and oars. Sometimes, notwithstanding, the logs are dispersed over many miles of lake surface in a few hours by winds and freshets, and thrown up on distant shores, where the driver can pick up only one or two at a time, and return with them to the thoroughfare; and, before he gets his flock well through Ambejijis or Pamadumcook, he makes many a wet and uncomfortable camp on the shore. He must be able to navigate a log as if it were a canoe, and be as indifferent to cold and wet as a muskrat. He uses a few efficient tools—a lever commonly of rock-maple, six or seven feet long, with a stout spike in it, strongly ferruled on,[184] and a long spike-pole, with a screw at the end of the spike to make it hold. The boys along shore learn to walk on floating logs as city boys on sidewalks. Sometimes the logs are thrown up on rocks in such positions as to be irrecoverable but by another freshet as high, or they jam together at rapids and falls, and accumulate in vast piles, which the driver must start at the risk of his life. Such is the lumber business, which depends on many accidents, as the early freezing of the rivers, that the teams may get up in season, a sufficient freshet in the spring, to fetch the logs down, and many others.[185] I quote Michaux on Lumbering on the Kennebec,[186] then the source of the best white-pine lumber carried to England. "The persons engaged in this branch of industry are generally emigrants from New Hampshire. . . . In the summer they unite in small companies, and traverse these vast solitudes in every direction, to ascertain the places in which the pines abound. After cutting the grass and converting it into hay for the nourishment of the cattle to be employed in their labor, they return home. In the beginning of the winter they enter the forests again, establish themselves in huts covered with the bark of the canoe-birch, or the arbor-vitae; and, though the cold is so intense that the mercury sometimes remains for several weeks from 40° to 50° [Fahr.] below the point of congelation, they persevere, with unabated courage, in their work."[187] According to Springer, the company consists of choppers, swampers—who make roads—barker and loader, teamster, and cook.[188] "When the trees are felled, they cut them into logs from fourteen to eighteen feet long, and, by means of their cattle, which they employ with great dexterity, drag them to the river, and after stamping on them a mark of property, roll them on its frozen bosom. At the breaking of the ice, in the spring, they float down with the current. . . . The logs that are not sawn the first year," adds Michaux, "are attacked by large worms, which form holes about two lines[189] in diameter, in every direction; but, if stripped of their bark, they will remain uninjured for thirty years."[190]

Ambejijis, this quiet Sunday morning, struck me as the most beautiful lake we had seen. It is said to be one of the deepest.[191] We had the fairest view of Joe Merry, Double Top,[192] and Ktaadn, from its surface. The summit of the latter had a singularly flat table-land appearance, like a short highway, where a demigod might be let down to take a turn or two in an afternoon, to settle his dinner. We rowed a mile and a half to near the head of the lake, and, pushing through a field of lily pads, landed, to cook our breakfast by the side of a large rock, known

187 The prefatory line before the ellipses is quoted from John Claudius Loudon's (1783–1843) *Arboretum et fruticetum Britanicum;* the excerpt from Michaux Thoreau follows, with minor variants in punctuation, the original text of Michaux's *North American Sylva.* The brackets are Thoreau's.

188 The choppers, as described by Springer in his *Forest Life and Forest Trees,* were "those who select, fell, and cut the logs. . . . Next the swampers, who cut and clear the roads through the forest to the fallen trees. . . . Then comes the barker and loader, the man who hews off the bark from that part of the log which is to drag on the snow, and assists the teamster in loading. . . . Then we have the captain of the goad, or teamster . . . and finally the cook, whose duty is too generally known to require any particular description."

189 Paris line: a French unit of measurement equal to .0888 of an inch.

190 Quoted from Michaux's *North American Sylva,* although the sentence following the ellipses, including the quotation, is quoted from Loudon's *Arboretum et Fruticetum Britanicum.*

191 It has a varying depth between fifty and one hundred feet.

192 More commonly, Doubletop Mountain.

193 Pounded brick was one of many substances used for tamping, the material with which the hole made for blasting is filled after the placement of the charge of powder or other explosive.
194 The first missionaries among the Abenaki were Jesuit priests.
195 One rod is equal to 16.5 feet.

to McCauslin. Our breakfast consisted of tea, with hard bread and pork, and fried salmon, which we ate with forks neatly whittled from alder-twigs, which grew there, off strips of birch-bark for plates. The tea was black tea, without milk to color or sugar to sweeten it, and two tin dippers were our tea cups. This beverage is as indispensable to the loggers as to any gossiping old women in the land, and they, no doubt, derive great comfort from it. Here was the site of an old loggers' camp, remembered by McCauslin, now overgrown with weeds and bushes. In the midst of a dense underwood, we noticed a whole brick, on a rock, in a small run, clean, and red, and square, as in a brick-yard, which had been brought thus far formerly for tamping.[193] Some of us afterward regretted that we had not carried this on with us to the top of the mountain, to be left there for our mark. It would certainly have been a simple evidence of civilized man. McCauslin said, that large wooden crosses made of oak, still sound, were sometimes found standing in this wilderness, which were set up by the first Catholic missionaries who came through to the Kennebec.[194]

In the next nine miles, which were the extent of our voyage, and which it took us the rest of the day to get over, we rowed across several small lakes, poled up numerous rapids and thoroughfares, and carried over four portages. I will give the names and distances, for the benefit of future tourists. First, after leaving Ambejijis Lake, we had a quarter of a mile of rapids to the portage, or carry of ninety rods[195] around Ambejijis Falls; then a mile and a half through Passamagamet Lake, which is narrow and river-like, to the falls of the same name—Ambejijis stream coming in on the right; then two miles through Katepskonegan Lake to the portage of ninety rods around Katepskonegan Falls, which name signifies "carrying-place"—Passamagamet stream coming in on the left; then three miles through Pockwockomus Lake, a slight expansion of the river, to the portage of forty rods around the falls of the same name—Katepskonegan stream coming in on the left; then three quarters of a mile through Aboljacarmegus Lake, similar to the last, to the portage of forty rods around the falls of the same name; then half a mile of rapid water to the Sowadnehunk dead-water,[196] and the Aboljacknagesic stream.

This is generally the order of names as you ascend the river:—First, the lake, or, if there is no expansion, the dead-water; then the falls; then the stream emptying into the lake or river above, all of the same name. First we came to Passamagamet Lake, then to Passamagamet Falls, then to Passamagamet stream, emptying in. This order and identity of names, it will be perceived, is quite philosophical, since the dead-water or lake is always at least partially produced by the stream emptying in above; and the first fall below, which is the inlet of that lake, and where that tributary water makes its first plunge, also naturally bears the same name.

At the portage around Ambejijis Falls I observed a pork-barrel on the shore, with a hole eight or nine inches square cut in one side, which was set against an upright rock; but the bears, without turning or upsetting the barrel, had gnawed a hole in the opposite side, which looked exactly like an enormous rat hole, big enough to put their heads in; and at the bottom of the barrel were still left a few mangled and slabbered slices of pork. It is usual for the lumberers to leave such supplies as they cannot conveniently carry along with them at carries or camps, to which the next comers do not scruple to help themselves, they being the property commonly not of an individual, but a company, who can afford to deal liberally.

I will describe particularly how we got over some of these portages and rapids, in order that the reader may get an idea of the boatman's life. At Ambejijis Falls, for

196 Georges Louis Leclerc, comte de Buffon (1707–1788), in his *Natural History, General and Particular* described dead water as being "produced by an inactive cause, a projection of the land, an island, &c. Though this kind of regorging does not give rise to any extraordinary counter current, it often sensibly retards the progress of small boats, and produces what is called *dead water*, which observes not the natural course of the river, but turns about in such a manner as greatly obstructs the passage of vessels."

197 A line attached to the bow of a canoe.
198 Tow with a warp or towing line.

instance, there was the roughest path imaginable cut through the woods; at first up hill at an angle of nearly forty-five degrees, over rocks and logs without end. This was the manner of the portage:—We first carried over our baggage, and deposited it on the shore at the other end; then returning to the batteau, we dragged it up the hill by the painter,[197] and onward, with frequent pauses, over half the portage. But this was a bungling way, and would soon have worn out the boat. Commonly, three men walk over with a batteau weighing from three to five or six hundred pounds on their heads and shoulders, the tallest standing under the middle of the boat, which is turned over, and one at each end, or else there are two at the bows. More cannot well take hold at once. But this requires some practice, as well as strength, and is in any case extremely laborious, and wearing to the constitution, to follow. We were, on the whole, rather an invalid party, and could render our boatmen but little assistance. Our two men at length took the batteau upon their shoulders, and, while two of us steadied it, to prevent it from rocking and wearing into their shoulders, on which they placed their hats folded, walked bravely over the remaining distance, with two or three pauses. In the same manner they accomplished the other portages. With this crushing weight they must climb and stumble along over fallen trees and slippery rocks of all sizes, where those who walked by the sides were continually brushed off, such was the narrowness of the path. But we were fortunate not to have to cut our path in the first place. Before we launched our boat, we scraped the bottom smooth again with our knives, where it had rubbed on the rocks, to save friction.

To avoid the difficulties of the portage, our men determined to "warp up"[198] the Passamagamet Falls: so while the rest walked over the portage with the baggage, I remained in the batteau, to assist in warping up. We were soon in the midst of the rapids, which were more swift and tumultuous than any we had poled up, and had turned to the side of the stream for the purpose of warping, when the boatmen, who felt some pride in their skill, and were ambitious to do something more than usual, for my benefit, as I surmised, took one more view of the rapids, or rather the falls; and in answer to one's question, whether we couldn't get up there, the other answered that he guessed he'd try it: so we pushed again into the midst of the stream, and began to struggle with the current. I sat in the middle of the boat, to trim it, moving slightly to the right or left as it grazed a rock. With an uncertain and wavering motion we wound and bolted our way up, until the bow was actually raised two feet above the stern at the steepest pitch; and then, when everything depended upon his exertions, the bowman's pole snapped in two; but before he had time to take the spare one, which I reached him, he had saved himself with the fragment upon a rock; and so we got up by a hair's breadth; and Uncle George exclaimed, that that was never done before; and he had not tried it, if he had not known whom he had got in the bow—nor he in the bow, if he had not known him in the stern. At this place there was a regular portage cut through the woods; and our boatmen had never known a batteau to ascend the falls. As near as I can remember, there was a perpendicular fall here, at the worst place of the whole Penobscot River, two or three feet at least. I could not sufficiently admire the skill and coolness with which they performed this feat, never speaking to each other. The bowman, not looking behind, but knowing exactly what the other is about, works as if he worked alone; now sounding in vain for a bottom in fifteen feet of water, while the boat falls back several rods, held straight only with the greatest skill and exertion; or, while the sternman obstinately holds his ground, like a turtle, the bowman springs from side to

199 Name given to the North American domin-
ions of Great Britain.
200 Oak Hall was a famous mid-nineteenth-
century men's clothing store in Boston. Handbills,
as well paste-ups and painted announcements
advertising the store, appeared all over New
England. Started by George W. Simmons (1814–
1882), whom Edward Emerson called "the enterprising pioneer of the ready-made clothing business, and of extensive advertising."

side with wonderful suppleness and dexterity, scanning the rapids and the rocks with a thousand eyes; and now, having got a bite at last, with a lusty shove which makes his pole bend and quiver, and the whole boat tremble, he gains a few feet upon the river. To add to the danger, the poles are liable at any time to be caught between the rocks, and wrenched out of their hands, leaving them at the mercy of the rapids—the rocks, as it were, lying in wait, like so many alligators, to catch them in their teeth, and jerk them from your hands, before you have stolen an effectual shove against their palates. The pole is set close to the boat, and the prow is made to overshoot, and just turn the corners of the rocks, in the very teeth of the rapids. Nothing but the length and lightness, and the slight draught of the batteau, enables them to make any headway. The bowman must quickly choose his course; there is no time to deliberate. Frequently the boat is shoved between rocks where both sides touch, and the waters on either hand are a perfect maelstrom.

Half a mile above this, two of us tried our hands at poling up a slight rapid; and we were just surmounting the last difficulty, when an unlucky rock confounded our calculations; and while the batteau was sweeping round irrecoverably amid the whirlpool, we were obliged to resign the poles to more skilful hands.

Katepskonegan is one of the shallowest and weediest of the lakes, and looked as if it might abound in pickerel. The falls of the same name, where we stopped to dine, are considerable and quite picturesque. Here Uncle George had seen trout caught by the barrel-full; but they would not rise to our bait at this hour. Half way over this carry, thus far in the Maine wilderness on its way to the Provinces,[199] we noticed a large flaming Oak Hall handbill,[200] about two feet long, wrapped round the trunk of a pine, from which the bark had been stript, and to which it was fast glued by the pitch. This should be recorded among the advantages of this mode of advertising, that so, possibly, even the bears and wolves, moose, deer, otter, and beaver, not to mention the Indian, may learn where they can fit themselves according to the latest fashion, or, at least, recover some of their own lost garments. We christened this the Oak Hall carry.

The forenoon was as serene and placid on this wild stream in the woods as we are wont to imagine that Sunday in summer usually is in Massachusetts. We were occasionally startled by the scream of a bald-eagle, sailing over the stream in front of our batteau; or of the fish-hawks, on whom he levies his contributions.[201] There were, at intervals, small meadows of a few acres on the sides of the stream, waving with uncut grass, which attracted the attention of our boatmen, who regretted that they were not nearer to their clearings, and calculated how many stacks they might cut. Two or three men sometimes spend the summer by themselves, cutting the grass in these meadows, to sell to the loggers in the winter, since it will fetch a higher price on the spot than in any market in the state. On a small isle, covered with this kind of rush, or cut grass, on which we landed, to consult about our further course, we noticed the recent track of a moose, a large, roundish hole, in the soft wet ground, evincing the great size and weight of the animal that made it. They are fond of the water, and visit all these island-meadows, swimming as easily from island to island as they make their way through the thickets on land. Now and then we passed what McCauslin called a pokelogan,[202] an Indian term for what the drivers might have reason to call a poke-logs-in, an inlet that leads nowhere; if you get in, you have got to get out again the same way. These, and the frequent "run-rounds," which come into the river again, would embarrass an inexperienced voyager not a little.

The carry around Pockwockomus Falls was exceed-

[201] Audubon wrote in *Birds of America* that when the fish hawk, or osprey, "rises from the water, with a fish in its grasp, forth rushes the Eagle in pursuit. He mounts above the Fish-Hawk, and threatens it by actions well understood, when the latter, fearing perhaps that its life is in danger, drops its prey. In an instant, the Eagle, accurately estimating the rapid descent of the fish, closes his wings, follows it with the swiftness of thought, and the next moment grasps it. The prize is carried off in silence to the woods, and assists in feeding the ever-hungry brood of the marauder."
[202] Indian word, used by hunters and lumbermen, for a marshy or stagnant cove or bay extending into the land from a stream or river, and often used to hold logs during a drive.

ingly rough and rocky, the batteau having to be lifted directly from the water up four or five feet on to a rock, and launched again down a similar bank. The rocks on this portage were covered with the dents made by the spikes in the lumberers' boots while staggering over under the weight of their batteaux; and you could see where the surface of some large rocks on which they had rested their batteaux was worn quite smooth with use. As it was, we had carried over but half the usual portage at this place for this stage of the water, and launched our boat in the smooth wave just curving to the fall, prepared to struggle with the most violent rapid we had to encounter. The rest of the party walked over the remainder of the portage, while I remained with the boatmen to assist in warping up. One had to hold the boat while the others got in to prevent it from going over the falls. When we had pushed up the rapids as far as possible, keeping close to the shore, Tom seized the painter and leaped out upon a rock just visible in the water, but he lost his footing notwithstanding his spiked boots, and was instantly amid the rapids; but recovering himself by good luck, and reaching another rock, he passed the painter to me, who had followed him, and took his place again in the bows. Leaping from rock to rock in the shoal[203] water close to the shore, and now and then getting a bite with the rope round an upright one, I held the boat while one reset his pole, and then all three forced it upward against any rapid. This was "warping up." When a part of us walked round at such a place, we generally took the precaution to take out the most valuable part of the baggage, for fear of being swamped.

As we poled up a swift rapid for half a mile above Aboljacarmegus Falls, some of the party read their own marks on the huge logs which lay piled up high and dry on the rocks on either hand, the relics probably of a jam which had taken place here in the Great Freshet in the spring. Many of these would have to wait for another great freshet, perchance, if they lasted so long, before they could be got off. It was singular enough to meet with property of theirs which they had never seen, and where they had never been before, thus detained by freshets and rocks when on its way to them. Methinks that must be where all my property lies, cast up on the rocks on some distant and unexplored stream, and waiting for an unheard-of freshet to fetch it down. O make haste, ye gods, with your winds and rains, and start the jam before it rots!

The last half mile carried us to the Sowadnehunk dead-water, so called from the stream of the same name, signifying "running between mountains,"[204] an important tributary which comes in a mile above. Here we decided to camp, about twenty miles from the Dam, at the mouth of Murch Brook[205] and the Aboljacknagesic, mountain streams, broad off from Ktaadn, and about a dozen miles from its summit; having made fifteen miles this day.

We had been told by McCauslin that we should here find trout enough: so while some prepared the camp, the rest fell to fishing. Seizing the birch poles which some party of Indians or white hunters had left on the shore, and baiting our hooks with pork, and with trout, as soon as they were caught, we cast our lines into the mouth of the Aboljacknagesic, a clear, swift, shallow stream, which came in from Ktaadn. Instantly a shoal[206] of white chivin[207] (*Leucisci pulchelli*), silvery roaches, cousin-trout, or what not, large and small, prowling thereabouts, fell upon our bait, and one after another were landed amidst the bushes. Anon their cousins, the true trout, took their turn, and alternately the speckled trout, and the silvery roaches, swallowed the bait as fast as we could throw in; and the finest specimens of both that I have ever seen, the largest one weighing

204 Quoted from Jackson's *Second Annual Report*.
205 Now Katahdin Stream.
206 School.
207 In *A Week on the Concord and Merrimack Rivers,* Thoreau wrote of "the chivin, dace, roach, cousin trout, or whatever else it is called (*Leuciscus pulchellus*), white and red, always an unexpected prize, which, however, any angler is glad to hook for its rarity" [W 1:27].

three pounds, were heaved upon the shore, though at first in vain, to wriggle down into the water again, for we stood in the boat; but soon we learned to remedy this evil: for one, who had lost his hook, stood on shore to catch them as they fell in a perfect shower around him—sometimes, wet and slippery, full in his face and bosom, as his arms were outstretched to receive them. While yet alive, before their tints had faded, they glistened like the fairest flowers, the product of primitive rivers; and he could hardly trust his senses, as he stood over them, that these jewels should have swum away in that Aboljacknagesic water for so long, so many dark ages;—these bright fluviatile[208] flowers, seen of Indians only, made beautiful, the Lord only knows why, to swim there! I could understand better, for this, the truth of mythology, the fables of Proteus,[209] and all those beautiful sea-monsters,—how all history, indeed, put to a terrestrial use, is mere history; but put to a celestial, is mythology always.

But there is the rough voice of Uncle George, who commands at the frying-pan, to send over what you've got, and then you may stay till morning. The pork sizzles, and cries for fish. Luckily for the foolish race, and this particularly foolish generation of trout, the night shut down at last, not a little deepened by the dark side of Ktaadn, which, like a permanent shadow, reared itself from the eastern bank. Lescarbot,[210] writing in 1609, tells us that the Sieur Champdorée,[211] who, with one of the people of the Sieur de Monts,[212] ascended some fifty leagues up the St. John in 1608, found the fish so plenty, "qu'en mettant la chaudière sur le feu ils en avoient pris suffisamment pour eux dîsner avant que l'eau fust chaude."[213] Their descendants here are no less numerous. So we accompanied Tom into the woods, to cut cedar-twigs for our bed. While he went ahead with the axe, and lopped off the smallest twigs of the flat-leaved cedar,

---

208 Fluvial.
209 In Greek mythology, a sea god who had the power of assuming different shapes.
210 Marc Lescarbot (1570–1642), French explorer.
211 Pierre Angibault, called Champdoré, late-sixteenth-to-early-seventeenth-century captain.
212 Pierre du Gua, Sieur de Monts (ca. 1558–1628), French explorer, colonizer, and merchant.
213 Quoted from Lescarbot's *Histoire de la Nouvelle-France:* "Putting the kettle over the fire, they had taken fish sufficient for their dinner before the water was hot."

the arbor-vitae of the gardens, we gathered them up, and returned with them to the boat, until it was loaded. Our bed was made with as much care and skill as a roof is shingled; beginning at the foot, and laying the twig end of the cedar upward, we advanced to the head, a course at a time, thus successively covering the stub-ends, and producing a soft and level bed. For us six it was about ten feet long by six in breadth. This time we lay under our tent, having pitched it more prudently with reference to the wind and the flame, and the usual huge fire blazed in front. Supper was eaten off a large log, which some freshet had thrown up. This night we had a dish of arbor-vitae, or cedar tea, which the lumberer sometimes uses when other herbs fail,—

> "A quart of *arbor*-vitae,
> To make him strong and mighty,"—[214]

but I had no wish to repeat the experiment. It had too medicinal a taste for my palate. There was the skeleton of a moose here, whose bones some Indian hunters had picked on this very spot.

In the night I dreamed of trout-fishing; and, when at length I awoke, it seemed a fable, that this painted fish swam there so near my couch, and rose to our hooks the last evening—and I doubted if I had not dreamed it all. So I arose before dawn to test its truth, while my companions were still sleeping. There stood Ktaadn with distinct and cloudless outline in the moonlight; and the rippling of the rapids was the only sound to break the stillness. Standing on the shore, I once more cast my line into the stream, and found the dream to be real, and the fable true. The speckled trout and silvery roach, like flying fish, sped swiftly through the moonlight air, describing bright arcs on the dark side of Ktaadn, until moonlight, now fading into daylight, brought satiety to

214 Quoted, with Thoreau's substitution of *arbor* for *aqua*-vitae, and with other substantive variants, from the English ballad "The Dragon of Wantley" in Thomas Percy's (1729–1811) *Reliques of Ancient English Poetry:*

> As soon as he rose,
> To make him strong and mighty,
> He drank, by the tale, six pots of ale
> And a quart of aqua-vitae.

215 Quoted from Jackson's *Second Annual Report*.

216 South Peak, in Thoreau's day, was thought to be the highest peak.

217 Abol Slide, formed ca. 1816, and which Henry Boynton Smith described in 1836 as having made "a favorable pathway, disemboweling the mountain, and showing its internal resources, here and there exposing to view the solid granite."

218 Jackson wrote in his *Second Annual Report:* "Travelling steadily up the slide, clambering over loose boulders of granite, trap and grau-wacke, which are heaped up in confusion along its course, and are capable of being set in motion by a careless step, we at length reached a place where it was dangerous longer to walk on the loose rocks, and crossing over to the right hand side, clambered up among the dwarfish bushes that cling to the side of the mountain. . . . The ascent now became exceedingly laborious, owing to large overhanging rocks, which were covered with moss, and, being wet, were very slippery, so that it was difficult to mount over them. . . . The remainder of our ascent was extremely difficult, and required no small perseverance."

219 Rum Mountain.

my mind, and the minds of my companions, who had joined me.

By six o'clock, having mounted our packs and a good blanket full of trout, ready dressed, and swung up such baggage and provision as we wished to leave behind upon the tops of saplings, to be out of the reach of bears, we started for the summit of the mountain, distant, as Uncle George said the boatmen called it, about four miles, but as I judged, and as it proved, nearer fourteen. He had never been any nearer the mountain than this, and there was not the slightest trace of man to guide us further in this direction. At first, pushing a few rods up the Aboljacknagesic, or "open-land stream,"[215] we fastened our batteau to a tree, and travelled up the north side, through burnt lands, now partially overgrown with young aspens, and other shrubbery; but soon, recrossing this stream, where it was about fifty or sixty feet wide, upon a jam of logs and rocks, and you could cross it by this means almost anywhere, we struck at once for the highest peak,[216] over a mile or more of comparatively open land still, very gradually ascending the while. Here it fell to my lot, as the oldest mountain-climber, to take the lead: so scanning the woody side of the mountain, which lay still at an indefinite distance, stretched out some seven or eight miles in length before us, we determined to steer directly for the base of the highest peak, leaving a large slide,[217] by which, as I have since learned, some of our predecessors ascended,[218] on our left. This course would lead us parallel to a dark seam in the forest, which marked the bed of a torrent, and over a slight spur,[219] which extended southward from the main mountain, from whose bare summit we could get an outlook over the country, and climb directly up the peak, which would then be close at hand. Seen from this point, a bare ridge at the extremity of the open land, Ktaadn presented a different aspect from any mountain

I have seen, there being a greater proportion of naked rock, rising abruptly from the forest; and we looked up at this blue barrier as if it were some fragment of a wall which anciently bounded the earth in that direction. Setting the compass for a north-east course, which was the bearing of the southern base of the highest peak, we were soon buried in the woods.

We soon began to meet with traces of bears and moose, and those of rabbits were everywhere visible. The tracks of moose, more or less recent, to speak literally, covered every square rod on the sides of the mountain; and these animals are probably more numerous there now than ever before, being driven into this wilderness from all sides by the settlements. The track of a full-grown moose is like that of a cow, or larger, and of the young, like that of a calf. Sometimes we found ourselves travelling in faint paths, which they had made, like cow-paths in the woods, only far more indistinct, being rather openings, affording imperfect vistas through the dense underwood, than trodden paths; and everywhere the twigs had been browsed by them, clipt as smoothly as if by a knife. The bark of trees was stript up by them to the height of eight or nine feet, in long, narrow strips, an inch wide, still showing the distinct marks of their teeth. We expected nothing less than to meet a herd of them every moment, and our Nimrod[220] held his shooting-iron in readiness; but we did not go out of our way to look for them, and, though numerous, they are so wary, that the unskilful hunter might range the forest a long time before he could get sight of one. They are sometimes dangerous to encounter, and will not turn out for the hunter, but furiously rush upon him, and trample him to death, unless he is lucky enough to avoid them by dodging round a tree. The largest are nearly as large as a horse, and weigh sometimes one thousand pounds; and it is said that they can step over a five-foot gate in their ordinary walk. They

220 Mighty hunter described in Genesis 10:9.

are described as exceedingly awkward-looking animals, with their long legs and short bodies, making a ludicrous figure when in full run, but making great headway nevertheless. It seemed a mystery to us how they could thread these woods, which it required all our suppleness to accomplish, climbing, stooping, and winding, alternately. They are said to drop their long and branching horns, which usually spread five or six feet, on their backs, and make their way easily by the weight of their bodies. Our boatmen said, but I know not with how much truth, that their horns are apt to be gnawed away by vermin while they sleep.[221] Their flesh, which is more like beef than venison, is common in Bangor market.

We had proceeded on thus seven or eight miles, till about noon, with frequent pauses to refresh the weary ones, crossing a considerable mountain stream, which we conjectured to be Murch Brook,[222] at whose mouth we had camped, all the time in woods, without having once seen the summit,[223] and rising very gradually, when the boatmen, beginning to despair a little, and fearing that we were leaving the mountain on one side of us, for they had not entire faith in the compass, McCauslin climbed a tree, from the top of which he could see the peak, when it appeared that we had not swerved from a right line, the compass down below still ranging with his arm, which pointed to the summit. By the side of a cool mountain rill, amid the woods, where the water began to partake of the purity and transparency of the air, we stopped to cook some of our fishes, which we had brought thus far in order to save our hard bread and pork, in the use of which we had put ourselves on short allowance. We soon had a fire blazing, and stood around it, under the damp and sombre forest of firs and birches, each with a sharpened stick, three or four feet in length, upon which he had spitted his trout, or roach, previously well gashed and salted, our sticks radiating like the spokes of a wheel

221 Antlers, having a concentrated network of blood vessels and nerves in its velvet, are very sensitive, and are in fact gnawed by mice and other rodents only after they are shed.

222 This was Abol Stream, not Murch Brook.

223 Katahdin has two primary summits, or peaks, Baxter (5,267 feet) and South (5,240 feet), as well as several lesser peaks: Pamola, Chimney, Hamlin, South Howe, and North Howe.

from one centre, and each crowding his particular fish into the most desirable exposure, not with the truest regard always to his neighbor's rights. Thus we regaled ourselves, drinking meanwhile at the spring, till one man's pack, at least, was considerably lightened, when we again took up our line of march.

At length we reached an elevation sufficiently bare to afford a view of the summit, still distant and blue, almost as if retreating from us. A torrent, which proved to be the same we had crossed, was seen tumbling down in front, literally from out of the clouds. But this glimpse at our whereabouts was soon lost, and we were buried in the woods again. The wood was chiefly yellow birch, spruce, fir, mountain-ash, or round-wood, as the Maine people call it, and moose-wood. It was the worst kind of travelling; sometimes like the densest scrub-oak patches with us.[224] The cornel, or bunch-berries, were very abundant, as well as Solomon's seal[225] and moose-berries.[226] Blueberries were distributed along our whole route; and in one place the bushes were drooping with the weight of the fruit, still as fresh as ever. It was the seventh of September. Such patches afforded a grateful[227] repast, and served to bait the tired party forward. When any lagged behind, the cry of "blueberries" was most effectual to bring them up. Even at this elevation we passed through a moose-yard, formed by a large flat rock, four or five rods square, where they tread down the snow in winter. At length, fearing that if we held the direct course to the summit, we should not find any water near our camping-ground, we gradually swerved to the west, till, at four o'clock, we struck again the torrent which I have mentioned, and here, in view of the summit, the weary party decided to camp that night.

While my companions were seeking a suitable spot for this purpose, I improved the little daylight that was left in climbing the mountain alone. We were in

224 On 1 December 1856 Thoreau wrote: "The shrub oak, lowly, loving the earth and spreading over it, tough, thick-leaved. . . . How many rents I owe to you! how many eyes put out! how many bleeding fingers! How many shrub oak patches I have been through, stooping, winding my way, bending the twigs aside, guiding myself by the sun, over hills and valleys and plains, resting in clear grassy spaces! I love to go through a patch of shrub oak in a bee-line, where you tear your clothes and put your eyes out" [J 9:147–148].
225 *Maianthemum canadense*, also known as the Canada mayflower, although possibly Thoreau may have seen the False Solomon's Seal.
226 Hobblebush (*Viburnum lantanoides* or *alnifolium*).
227 In the sense of agreeable, pleasing, gratifying.

228 In Book 2 of Milton's *Paradise Lost* Satan passes through the gates of Hell, past Sin and Death, and continues through the realm of Chaos in order to reach Eden.

229 Baxter Peak, which Thoreau did not recognize as being the highest peak.

230 Stunted from freezing temperatures.

a deep and narrow ravine, sloping up to the clouds, at an angle of nearly forty-five degrees, and hemmed in by walls of rock, which were at first covered with low trees, then with impenetrable thickets of scraggy birches and spruce-trees, and with moss, but at last bare of all vegetation but lichens, and almost continually draped in clouds. Following up the course of the torrent which occupied this—and I mean to lay some emphasis on this word *up*—pulling myself up by the side of perpendicular falls of twenty or thirty feet, by the roots of firs and birches, and then, perhaps, walking a level rod or two in the thin stream, for it took up the whole road, ascending by huge steps, as it were, a giant's stairway, down which a river flowed, I had soon cleared the trees, and paused on the successive shelves, to look back over the country. The torrent was from fifteen to thirty feet wide, without a tributary, and seemingly not diminishing in breadth as I advanced; but still it came rushing and roaring down, with a copious tide, over and amidst masses of bare rock, from the very clouds, as though a water-spout had just burst over the mountain. Leaving this at last, I began to work my way, scarcely less arduous than Satan's anciently through Chaos,[228] up the nearest, though not the highest peak.[229] At first scrambling on all fours over the tops of ancient black spruce-trees, (*Abies nigra*), old as the flood, from two to ten or twelve feet in height, their tops flat and spreading, and their foliage blue and nipt[230] with cold, as if for centuries they had ceased growing upward against the bleak sky, the solid cold. I walked some good rods erect upon the tops of these trees, which were overgrown with moss and mountain-cranberries. It seemed that in the course of time they had filled up the intervals between the huge rocks, and the cold wind had uniformly levelled all over. Here the principle of vegetation was hard put to it. There was apparently a belt of this kind running quite round the mountain, though, perhaps, nowhere so remarkable as here. Once, slumping through, I looked down ten feet, into a dark and cavernous region, and saw the stem of a spruce, on whose top I stood, as on a mass of coarse basket-work, fully nine inches in diameter at the ground. These holes were bears' dens, and the bears were even then at home. This was the sort of garden I made my way *over,* for an eighth of a mile, at the risk, it is true, of treading on some of the plants, not seeing any path *through* it—certainly the most treacherous and porous country I ever travelled.

> "——nigh founder'd, on he fares,
> Treading the crude consistence, half on foot,
> Half flying."[231]

But nothing could exceed the toughness of the twigs,—not one snapped under my weight, for they had slowly grown.[232] Having slumped, scrambled, rolled, bounced, and walked, by turns, over this scraggy country, I arrived upon a side-hill, or rather side-mountain, where rocks, gray, silent rocks, were the flocks and herds that pastured, chewing a rocky cud at sunset. They looked at me with hard gray eyes, without a bleat or a low. This brought me to the skirt of a cloud, and bounded my walk that night. But I had already seen that Maine country when I turned about, waving, flowing, rippling, down below.

When I returned to my companions, they had selected a camping-ground on the torrent's edge, and were resting on the ground; one was on the sick list, rolled in a blanket, on a damp shelf of rock. It was a savage and dreary scenery enough; so wildly rough, that they looked long to find a level and open space for the tent. We could not well camp higher, for want of fuel; and the trees here seemed so evergreen and sappy, that we almost doubted if they would acknowledge the influence of fire; but fire prevailed at last, and blazed here, too, like a good citi-

231 Quoted from Milton's *Paradise Lost* 2:940–942.
232 Thoreau would write in his journal of 5 November 1860: "I am struck by the fact that the more slowly trees grow at first, the sounder they are at the core, and I think that the same is true of human beings. We do not wish to see children precocious, making great strides in their early years like sprouts, producing a soft and perishable timber, but better if they expand slowly at first, as if contending with difficulties, and so are solidified and perfected. Such trees continue to expand with nearly equal rapidity to an extreme old age" [J 14:217].

233 Allusion to Oliver Goldsmith's (1728–1774) series of letters "The Citizen of the World," or to Diogenes Laertius (ca. third century C.E.), who, when asked where he came from replied, "I am a citizen of the world [*kosmopolitēs*]."

234 Edward Hitchcock (1793–1864) in his *Report on the Geology, Mineralogy, Botany, and Zoology of Massachusetts* wrote: "But from Boston to the extremity of Cape Ann . . . the amount of bowlders is prodigious . . . and yet so powerful was the diluvial current, that these must have been removed from their original position, and many of them now occupy the summits of the highest hills in that region: presenting often a most singular outline to the landscape. When one of these erratic blocks is so poised upon a rock in place, as to be easily moved it constitutes a rocking stone. Some of these, weighing from 10 to 100 tons, can be perceptibly moved by the strength of a single man, applied to a lever; though the combined efforts of a hundred cannot move them, but a few inches."

zen of the world.[233] Even at this height we met with frequent traces of moose, as well as of bears. As here was no cedar, we made our bed of coarser feathered spruce; but at any rate the feathers were plucked from the live tree. It was, perhaps, even a more grand and desolate place for a night's lodging than the summit would have been, being in the neighborhood of those wild trees, and of the torrent. Some more aerial and finer-spirited winds rushed and roared through the ravine all night, from time to time arousing our fire, and dispersing the embers about. It was as if we lay in the very nest of a young whirlwind. At midnight, one of my bedfellows, being startled in his dreams by the sudden blazing up to its top of a fir-tree, whose green boughs were dried by the heat, sprang up, with a cry, from his bed, thinking the world on fire, and drew the whole camp after him.

In the morning, after whetting our appetite on some raw pork, a wafer of hard bread, and a dipper of condensed cloud or water-spout, we all together began to make our way up the falls, which I have described; this time choosing the right hand, or highest peak, which was not the one I had approached before. But soon my companions were lost to my sight behind the mountain ridge in my rear, which still seemed ever retreating before me, and I climbed alone over huge rocks, loosely poised, a mile or more, still edging toward the clouds—for though the day was clear elsewhere, the summit was concealed by mist. The mountain seemed a vast aggregation of loose rocks, as if sometime it had rained rocks, and they lay as they fell on the mountain sides, nowhere fairly at rest, but leaning on each other, all rocking-stones,[234] with cavities between, but scarcely any soil or smoother shelf. They were the raw materials of a planet dropped from an unseen quarry, which the vast chemistry of nature would anon work up, or work down, into the smiling and verdant plains and valleys of earth. This was an undone extremity of the globe; as in lignite we see coal in the process of formation.[235]

At length I entered within the skirts of the cloud which seemed forever drifting over the summit, and yet would never be gone, but was generated out of that pure air as fast as it flowed away; and when, a quarter of a mile further, I reached the summit of the ridge, which those who have seen in clearer weather say is about five miles long, and contains a thousand acres of table-land, I was deep within the hostile ranks of clouds, and all objects were obscured by them. Now the wind would blow me out a yard of clear sunlight, wherein I stood; then a gray, dawning light was all it could accomplish, the cloud-line ever rising and falling with the wind's intensity. Sometimes it seemed as if the summit would be cleared in a few moments and smile in sunshine: but what was gained on one side was lost on another. It was like sitting in a chimney and waiting for the smoke to blow away. It was, in fact, a cloud-factory,—these were the cloud-works, and the wind turned them off done from the cool, bare rocks. Occasionally, when the windy columns broke in to me, I caught sight of a dark, damp crag to the right or left; the mist driving ceaselessly between it and me. It reminded me of the creations of the old epic and dramatic poets, of Atlas, Vulcan, the Cyclops, and Prometheus.[236] Such was Caucasus and the rock where Prometheus was bound. Aeschylus[237] had no doubt visited such scenery as this. It was vast, Titanic,[238] and such as man never inhabits. Some part of the beholder, even some vital part, seems to escape through the loose grating of his ribs as he ascends. He is more lone than you can imagine. There is less of substantial thought and fair understanding in him, than in the plains where men inhabit. His reason is dispersed and shadowy, more thin and subtile like the air. Vast, Titanic, inhuman Nature has got him at disadvantage, caught him alone, and pilfers him of some of

235 Lignite is the intermediate stage between peat and coal.
236 In Greek mythology, Atlas was a Titan who was condemned by Zeus to support the Earth and the sky on his shoulders for eternity. The cyclopes were one-eyed giants who forged iron for Hephaestus, although Thoreau may be referring specifically to the cyclops Polyphemus, in Homer's *Odyssey*, who imprisoned Odysseus and his men in his cave. Making him drunk with wine, they blinded him and were able to escape by hiding under the cyclops's sheep as they went out of the cave. Prometheus stole fire from the gods and gave it to mankind. As a punishment, Zeus ordered him chained to a rock on Mount Caucasus, where a great eagle gnawed at his liver. In Roman mythology, Vulcan was the god of fire and metalworking; his Greek equivalent was Hephaestus.
237 Greek tragic poet (525–456 B.C.E.) and author of more than seventy plays, only seven of which are extant. Thoreau made translations of Aeschylus's *Prometheus Bound* (published in the January 1843 issue of the *Dial*) and *The Seven Against Thebes* (posthumously published).
238 Related to the Titans, the primordial giant gods of Greek mythology who ruled the earth before Zeus and a symbol of great power and force.

his divine faculty. She does not smile on him as in the plains. She seems to say sternly, why came ye here before your time? This ground is not prepared for you. Is it not enough that I smile in the valleys? I have never made this soil for thy feet, this air for thy breathing, these rocks for thy neighbors. I cannot pity nor fondle thee here, but forever relentlessly drive thee hence to where I *am* kind. Why seek me where I have not called thee, and then complain because you find me but a stepmother? Shouldst thou freeze or starve, or shudder thy life away, here is no shrine, nor altar, nor any access to my ear.

> "Chaos and ancient Night, I come no spy
> With purpose to explore or to disturb
> The secrets of your realm, but * * *
> * * * * * * * as my way
> Lies through your spacious empire up to
>   light."[239]

The tops of mountains are among the unfinished parts of the globe, whither it is a slight insult to the gods to climb and pry into their secrets, and try their effect on our humanity. Only daring and insolent men, perchance, go there. Simple races, as savages, do not climb mountains—their tops are sacred and mysterious tracts never visited by them. Pomola is always angry with those who climb to the summit of Ktaadn.

According to Jackson, who in his capacity of geological surveyor of the state, has accurately measured it—the altitude of Ktaadn is 5,300 feet, or a little more than one mile above the level of the sea—and he adds, "It is then evidently the highest point in the State of Maine, and is the most abrupt granite mountain in New England."[240] The peculiarities of that spacious table-land on which I was standing, as well as the remarkable semicircular precipice or basin on the eastern side, were all concealed

---

239 Quoted from Milton's *Paradise Lost* 2:970–974.
240 Quoted from Jackson's *Second Annual Report*.

by the mist. I had brought my whole pack to the top, not knowing but I should have to make my descent to the river, and possibly to the settled portion of the state alone and by some other route, and wishing to have a complete outfit with me. But at length, fearing that my companions would be anxious to reach the river before night, and knowing that the clouds might rest on the mountain for days, I was compelled to descend. Occasionally, as I came down, the wind would blow me a vista open through which I could see the country eastward, boundless forests, and lakes, and streams, gleaming in the sun, some of them emptying into the East Branch. There were also new mountains in sight in that direction. Now and then some small bird of the sparrow family would flit away before me, unable to command its course, like a fragment of the gray rock blown off by the wind.

I found my companions where I had left them, on the side of the peak, gathering the mountain cranberries, which filled every crevice between the rocks, together with blueberries, which had a spicier flavor the higher up they grew, but were not the less agreeable to our palates. When the country is settled and roads are made, these cranberries will perhaps become an article of commerce. From this elevation, just on the skirts of the clouds, we could overlook the country west and south for a hundred miles. There it was, the State of Maine, which we had seen on the map, but not much like that,—immeasurable forest for the sun to shine on, that eastern *stuff*[241] we hear of in Massachusetts. No clearing, no house. It did not look as if a solitary traveller had cut so much as a walking-stick there. Countless lakes,—Moosehead in the southwest, forty miles long by ten wide, like a gleaming silver platter at the end of the table; Chesuncook, eighteen long by three wide, without an island; Millinocket, on the south, with its hundred islands; and a hundred others without a name; and mountains also,

241 In the sense of unwrought matter, raw material to be worked over or used in the making or producing of something.

242 Quoted from John Kimball de Laski's (1814–1874) third of five installments of "Dr. Young's Botanical Expedition," clipped from the *Bangor Daily Whig and Courier* (9 September 1847) and sent to Thoreau by his sister Sophia. Thoreau wrote: "I thank you for those letters about Ktaadn, and hope you will save and send me the rest, and anything else you may meet with relating to the Maine woods. That Dr. Young is both young and green too at travelling in the woods" [W 6:132]. The five installments were printed 7–11 September 1847. De Laski later published three papers in the *American Journal of Science,* one of which referred to his 1847 ascent of Katahdin.

243 Hayward's *New England Gazetteer.*

244 At the time Thoreau was writing, Katahdin was no longer considered part of Penobscot County. It became part of Piscataquis County, which was incorporated in 1838 from townships in neighboring Penobscot and Somerset counties.

245 Stripped of bark.

whose names, for the most part, are known only to the Indians. The forest looked like a firm grass sward, and the effect of these lakes in its midst has been well compared by one who has since visited this same spot, to that of a "mirror broken into a thousand fragments, and wildly scattered over the grass, reflecting the full blaze of the sun."[242] It was a large farm for somebody, when cleared. According to the Gazetteer,[243] which was printed before the boundary question was settled, this single Penobscot county[244] in which we were, was larger than the whole State of Vermont, with its fourteen counties; and this was only a part of the wild lands of Maine. We are concerned now, however, about natural, not political limits. We were about eighty miles as the bird flies from Bangor, or one hundred and fifteen as we had ridden, and walked, and paddled. We had to console ourselves with the reflection that this view was probably as good as that from the peak, as far as it went, and what were a mountain without its attendant clouds and mists? Like ourselves, neither Bailey nor Jackson had obtained a clear view from the summit.

Setting out on our return to the river, still at an early hour in the day, we decided to follow the course of the torrent, which we supposed to be Murch Brook, as long as it would not lead us too far out of our way. We thus travelled about four miles in the very torrent itself, continually crossing and recrossing it, leaping from rock to rock, and jumping with the stream down falls of seven or eight feet, or sometimes sliding down on our backs in a thin sheet of water. This ravine had been the scene of an extraordinary freshet in the spring, apparently accompanied by a slide from the mountain. It must have been filled with a stream of stones and water, at least twenty feet above the present level of the torrent. For a rod or two on either side of its channel, the trees were barked[245] and splintered up to their tops, the birches bent over, twisted, and sometimes finely split like a stable-broom;[246] some a foot in diameter snapped off, and whole clumps of trees bent over with the weight of rocks piled on them. In one place we noticed a rock two or three feet in diameter, lodged nearly twenty feet high in the crotch of a tree. For the whole four miles, we saw but one rill emptying in, and the volume of water did not seem to be increased from the first. We travelled thus very rapidly with a downward impetus, and grew remarkably expert at leaping from rock to rock, for leap we must, and leap we did, whether there was any rock at the right distance or not. It was a pleasant picture when the foremost turned about and looked up the winding ravine, walled in with rocks and the green forest, to see at intervals of a rod or two, a red-shirted or green-jacketed mountaineer against the white torrent, leaping down the channel with his pack on his back, or pausing upon a convenient rock in the midst of the torrent to mend a rent in his clothes, or unstrap the dipper at his belt to take a draught of the water. At one place we were startled by seeing, on a little sandy shelf by the side of the stream, the fresh print of a man's foot, and for a moment realized how Robinson Crusoe felt in a similar case;[247] but at last we remembered that we had struck this stream on our way up, though we could not have told where, and one had descended into the ravine for a drink. The cool air above, and the continual bathing of our bodies in mountain water, alternate foot, sitz, douche, and plunge baths,[248] made this walk exceedingly refreshing, and we had travelled only a mile or two after leaving the torrent, before every thread of our clothes was as dry as usual, owing perhaps to a peculiar quality in the atmosphere.

After leaving the torrent, being in doubt about our course, Tom threw down his pack at the foot of the loftiest spruce tree at hand, and shinned up the bare trunk some twenty feet, and then climbed through the green

246 A stable broom is characteristically made of stiff bristles that are set practically at right angles to the handle. Thoreau's description more aptly identifies a splinter broom, also known as a birch or Indian broom, which was made by splintering or peeling back thin strips of the wood to form the brush while the remaining portion of the wood formed the handle.

247 Allusion to Daniel Defoe's (1660–1731) *Robinson Crusoe* and the discovery, in chapter 11, of "the Print of a Man's naked Foot on the Shore": "I stood like one thunderstruck, or as if I had seen an apparition. I listened, I looked round me, but I could hear nothing, nor see anything. . . . I went on, but terrified to the last degree, looking behind me at every two or three steps, mistaking every bush and tree, and fancying every stump at a distance to be a man. Nor is it possible to describe how many various shapes my affrighted imagination represented things to me in, how many wild ideas were found every moment in my fancy, and what strange, unaccountable whimsies came into my thoughts by the way."

248 Baths in increasing degrees of immersion: sitz is a hip bath; douche, a jet or current of water applied to a specific part of the body; plunge, a bath large enough to allow for complete immersion.

249 Thoreau's footnote added in the 1864 edition of *The Maine Woods:* "'The spruce-tree,' says Springer in '51, 'is generally selected, principally for the superior facilities which its numerous limbs afford the climber. To gain the first limbs of this tree, which are from twenty to forty feet from the ground, a smaller tree is undercut and lodged against it, clambering up which the top of the spruce is reached. In some cases, when a very elevated position is desired, the spruce-tree is lodged against the trunk of some lofty pine, up which we ascend to a height twice that of the surrounding forest.'

"To indicate the direction of pines, he throws down a branch, and a man at the ground takes the bearing."

tower, lost to our sight, until he held the topmost spray in his hand.[249] McCauslin, in his younger days, had marched through the wilderness with a body of troops, under General Somebody, and with one other man did all the scouting and spying service. The General's word was: "Throw down the top of that tree," and there was no tree in the Maine woods so high that it did not lose its top in such a case. I have heard a story of two men being lost once in these woods, nearer to the settlements than this, who climbed the loftiest pine they could find, some six feet in diameter at the ground, from whose top they discovered a solitary clearing and its smoke. When at this height, some two hundred feet from the ground, one of them became dizzy, and fainted in his companion's arms, and the latter had to accomplish the descent with him, alternately fainting and reviving, as best he could. To Tom we cried, where away does the summit bear? where the burnt lands? The last he could only conjecture; he descried, however, a little meadow and pond, lying probably in our course, which we concluded to steer for. On reaching this secluded meadow, we found fresh tracks of moose on the shore of the pond, and the water was still unsettled as if they had fled before us. A little further, in a dense thicket, we seemed to be still on their trail. It was a small meadow, of a few acres, on the mountain side, concealed by the forest, and perhaps never seen by a white man before, where one would think that the moose might browse and bathe, and rest in peace. Pursuing this course, we soon reached the open land, which went sloping down some miles toward the Penobscot.

Perhaps I most fully realized that this was primeval, untamed, and forever untameable *Nature,* or whatever else men call it, while coming down this part of the mountain. We were passing over "Burnt Lands," burnt by lightning, perchance, though they showed no recent marks of fire, hardly so much as a charred stump, but looked rather like a natural pasture for the moose and deer, exceedingly wild and desolate, with occasional strips of timber crossing them, and low poplars springing up, and patches of blueberries here and there. I found myself traversing them familiarly, like some pasture run to waste, or partially reclaimed by man; but when I reflected what man, what brother or sister or kinsman of our race made it and claimed it, I expected the proprietor to rise up and dispute my passage. It is difficult to conceive of a region uninhabited by man. We habitually presume his presence and influence everywhere. And yet we have not seen pure Nature, unless we have seen her thus vast, and drear, and inhuman, though in the midst of cities. Nature was here something savage and awful, though beautiful. I looked with awe at the ground I trod on, to see what the Powers[250] had made there, the form and fashion and material of their work. This was that Earth of which we have heard, made out of Chaos and Old Night.[251] Here was no man's garden, but the unhandselled[252] globe. It was not lawn, nor pasture, nor mead, nor woodland, nor lea, nor arable, nor waste-land. It was the fresh and natural surface of the planet Earth, as it was made forever and ever,[253]—to be the dwelling of man, we say,[254]—so Nature made it, and man may use it if he can. Man was not to be associated with it. It was Matter, vast, terrific,—not his Mother Earth that we have heard of, not for him to tread on, or be buried in,—no, it were being too familiar even to let his bones lie there—the home this of Necessity and Fate.[255] There was there felt the presence of a force not bound to be kind to man. It was a place for heathenism and superstitious rites,—to be inhabited by men nearer of kin to the rocks and to wild animals than we.[256] We walked over it with a certain awe, stopping from time to time to pick the blueberries which grew there, and had a smart and spicy taste. Perchance where *our* wild pines stand,

250 Allusion to the order of angels in the hierarchy of Heaven, the powers being the sixth order, above angels, archangels, and principalities and below virtues, dominations, thrones, cherubim, and seraphim, with a possible allusion to "the Powers that erst in Heaven sat on thrones" from Milton's *Paradise Lost*, 1:360.

251 Allusion to the "reign of Chaos and old Night" from Milton's *Paradise Lost* 1:540.

252 Unused or untried, as in Emerson's "The American Scholar": "unhandselled savage nature."

253 Biblical phrase for eternity, as in Exodus 15:18: "The Lord shall reign for ever and ever."

254 Probable reference to John Pye-Smith's (1774–1851) statement in *On the Relation between the Holy Scriptures and Some Parts of Geological Science* that earth was "the part of our world which God was adapting for the dwelling of man and the animals connected with him," and which was referred to in several works of geology, such as Edward Hitchcock's *Elementary Geology*, published in 1840.

255 Allusion to the doctrines of fate, the established order of the universe, and necessity, the incontrovertible power that follows fate, as exemplified in Stoic philosophy.

256 In the Puritan ideology America was a "wilderness, full of wild beasts and wild men," as William Bradford (1590–1657) wrote, and Native Americans were, as Cotton Mather (1663–1728) put it, "miserable animals."

257 In the sense of planet, as found in nineteenth-century works of natural philosophy. In Benjamin Peirce's (1809–1880) *An Elementary Treatise of Plane and Spherical Trigonometry* stars are defined as either fixed or wandering, and "Of the wandering stars there are eleven, which are called planets. They are Mercury . . . Venus . . . the Earth"; John Gibson MacVicar (1800–1884) in his *Elements of the Economy of Nature* (1830) referred to the "surface of a star such as the earth."

258 The Transcendentalists made a distinction between actual and real, or ideal, existence. On this distinction Thoreau wrote in his journal: "On one side of man is the actual, and on the other the ideal" [ITM 33] and "Some incidents in my life have seemed far more allegorical than actual; they were so significant that they plainly served no other use" [ITM 188].

259 In addition to its meaning as practical sense or knowledge, *common sense* also carried with it the meaning that came out of the Scottish common sense school of philosophy, in particular, Thomas Reid's (1710–1796) *Inquiry into the Human Mind, on the Principles of Common Sense,* in which he emphasized common sense as natural judgment from a set of innate principles of conception and belief implanted in the human mind by God. This is the antecedent of the concept of inspiration, of which Emerson, in "Self-Reliance," called "the essence of genius, of virtue, and of life, which we call Spontaneity or Instinct. We denote this primary wisdom as Intuition. . . . In that deep force, the last fact behind which analysis cannot go, all things find their common origin." "The wildest dreams of wild men, even," Thoreau wrote in "Walking," "are not the less true, though they may not recommend themselves to the sense which is most common among Englishmen and Americans to-day. It is not every truth that recommends itself to the common sense" [W 5:233].

260 Thoreau's reaction to his ascent of Ktaadn is a later addition and not part of his original journal. As Thoreau wrote to H. G. O. Blake on 11

and leaves lie on their forest floor in Concord, there were once reapers, and husbandmen planted grain; but here not even the surface had been scarred by man, but it was a specimen of what God saw fit to make this world. What is it to be admitted to a museum, to see a myriad of particular things, compared with being shown some star's[257] surface, some hard matter in its home! I stand in awe of my body, this matter to which I am bound has become so strange to me. I fear not spirits, ghosts, of which I am one,—*that* my body might,—but I fear bodies, I tremble to meet them. What is this Titan that has possession of me? Talk of mysteries!—Think of our life in nature,—daily to be shown matter, to come in contact with it,—rocks, trees, wind on our cheeks! the *solid* earth! the *actual*[258] world! the *common sense!*[259] *Contact! Contact! Who* are we? *where* are we?[260]

Ere long we recognized some rocks and other features in the landscape which we had purposely impressed on our memories, and quickening our pace, by two o'clock we reached the batteau.[261] Here we had expected to dine on trout, but in this glaring sunlight they were slow to take the bait, so we were compelled to make the most of the crumbs of our hard bread and our pork, which were both nearly exhausted. Meanwhile we deliberated whether we should go up the river a mile farther to Gibson's clearing on the Sowadnehunk, where there was a deserted log hut, in order to get a half-inch auger, to mend one of our spike-poles with. There were young spruce trees enough around us, and we had a spare spike, but nothing to make a hole with. But as it was uncertain whether we should find any tools left there, we patched up the broken pole as well as we could for the downward voyage, in which there would be but little use for it. Moreover, we were unwilling to lose any time in this expedition, lest the wind should rise before we reached the larger lakes, and detain us, for a moderate wind produces quite a sea on these waters, in which a batteau will not live for a moment; and on one occasion McCauslin had been delayed a week at the head of the North Twin, which is only four miles across. We were nearly out of provisions, and ill prepared in this respect for what might possibly prove a week's journey round by the shore, fording innumerable streams, and threading a trackless forest, should any accident happen to our boat.

It was with regret that we turned our backs on Chesuncook, which McCauslin had formerly logged on, and the Allegash lakes. There were still longer rapids and portages above; among the last the Rippogenus Portage, which he described as the most difficult on the river, and three miles long. The whole length of the Penobscot is two hundred and seventy-five miles,[262] and we are still nearly one hundred miles from its source. Hodge, the assistant State Geologist, passed up this river in 1837, and by a portage of only one mile and three quarters,[263] crossed over into the Allegash, and so went down that into the St. John, and up the Madawaska to the Grand Portage across to the St. Lawrence.[264] His is the only account that I know, of an expedition through to Canada in this direction. He thus describes his first sight of the latter river, which, to compare small things with great, is like Balboa's first sight of the Pacific from the mountains of the Isthmus of Darien.[265] "When we first came in sight of the St. Lawrence," he says, "from the top of a high hill, the view was most striking, and much more interesting to me from having been shut up in the woods for the two previous months. Directly below us lays the broad river, extending across nine or ten miles, its surface broken by a few islands and reefs; and two ships riding at anchor near the shore. Beyond, extended ranges of uncultivated hills, parallel with the river. The sun was just going down behind them, and gilding the whole scene with its parting rays."[266]

November 1857: "Let me suggest a theme for you: to state to yourself precisely and completely what that walk over the mountains amounted to for you. . . . It is after we get home that we really go over the mountain, if ever. What did the mountain say? What did the mountain do?" [C 498]

261 Thoreau's footnote added in the 1864 edition of *The Maine Woods:* "The bears had not touched things on our possessions. They sometimes tear a batteau to pieces for the sake of the tar with which it is besmeared."

262 According to Hayward's *New England Gazetteer.*

263 Hodge wrote in his report: "We crossed the south-east corner of it to the portage, which passes over to Ponguongamook or Mud lake, the head waters of the Allagash river. These two lakes are only 1¾ miles apart."

264 North American river in southeastern Canada, flowing northeastward from Lake Ontario into the Gulf of St. Lawrence.

265 Vasco Núñez de Balboa (1475–1519), Spanish explorer who discovered the Pacific Ocean.

266 Quoted from Hodge in Jackson's *Second Annual Report.*

267 Thoreau's footnote added in the 1864 edition of *The Maine Woods*: "I cut this from a newspaper. 'On the 11th (instant?) [May, '49], on Rappogenes Falls, Mr. John Delantee, of Orono, Me., was drowned while running logs. He was a citizen of Orono, and was twenty-six years of age. His companions found his body, enclosed it in bark, and buried it in the solemn woods.'" Thoreau's brackets.

268 These falls are described in the *Sixth Annual report of the Secretary of the Maine Board of Agriculture*: "We soon came to the Aboljacarmegus portage, which is about one-eighth of a mile in length. Three-quarters of a mile below this, is the 'Pockwockamus carry,' which is one-eighth of a mile long. At both these portages, the river falls over ledges of fine granite, which presents no signs of disintegration, and is well situated and easy for working."

About four o'clock the same afternoon, we commenced our return voyage, which would require but little if any poling. In shooting rapids, the boatmen use large and broad paddles, instead of poles, to guide the boat with. Though we glided so swiftly and often smoothly down, where it had cost us no slight effort to get up, our present voyage was attended with far more danger: for if we once fairly struck one of the thousand rocks by which we were surrounded, the boat would be swamped in an instant. When a boat is swamped under these circumstances, the boatmen commonly find no difficulty in keeping afloat at first, for the current keeps both them and their cargo up for a long way down the stream; and if they can swim, they have only to work their way gradually to the shore. The greatest danger is of being caught in an eddy behind some larger rock, where the water rushes up stream faster than elsewhere it does down, and being carried round and round under the surface till they are drowned. McCauslin pointed out some rocks which had been the scene of a fatal accident of this kind. Sometimes the body is not thrown out for several hours. He himself had performed such a circuit once, only his legs being visible to his companions; but he was fortunately thrown out in season to recover his breath.[267] In shooting the rapids, the boatman has this problem to solve: to choose a circuitous and safe course amid a thousand sunken rocks, scattered over a quarter or half a mile, at the same time that he is moving steadily on at the rate of fifteen miles an hour. Stop he cannot; the only question is, where will he go? The bow-man chooses the course with all his eyes about him, striking broad off with his paddle, and drawing the boat by main force into her course. The stern-man faithfully follows the bow.

We were soon at the Aboljacarmegus Falls.[268] Anxious to avoid the delay as well as the labor of the portage here, our boatmen went forward first to reconnoitre, and concluded to let the batteau down the falls, carrying the baggage only over the portage. Jumping from rock to rock until nearly in the middle of the stream, we were ready to receive the boat and let her down over the first fall, some six or seven feet perpendicular. The boatmen stand upon the edge of a shelf of rock where the fall is perhaps nine or ten feet perpendicular, in from one to two feet of rapid water, one on each side of the boat, and let it slide gently over, till the bow is run out ten or twelve feet in the air; then letting it drop squarely, while one holds the painter, the other leaps in, and his companion following, they are whirled down the rapids to a new fall, or to smooth water. In a very few minutes they had accomplished a passage in safety, which would be as fool-hardy for the unskilful to attempt as the descent of Niagara itself.[269] It seemed as if it needed only a little familiarity, and a little more skill, to navigate down such falls as Niagara itself with safety. At any rate, I should not despair of such men in the rapids above Table-Rock, until I saw them actually go over the falls, so cool, so collected, so fertile in resources are they. One might have thought that these were falls, and that falls were not to be waded through with impunity like a mud-puddle. There was really danger of their losing their sublimity in losing their power to harm us. Familiarity breeds contempt.[270] The boatman pauses, perchance, on some shelf beneath a table-rock under the fall, standing in some cove of back-water two feet deep, and you hear his rough voice come up through the spray, coolly giving directions how to launch the boat this time.

Having carried round Pockwockomus Falls, our oars soon brought us to the Katepskonegan, or Oak Hall carry, where we decided to camp half way over, leaving our batteau to be carried over in the morning on fresh shoulders. One shoulder of each of the boatmen showed a red spot as large as one's hand, worn by the batteau

269 In 1829 Sam Patch (1807–1829) made the first successful leap of Niagara Falls on record.
270 Familiar axiom adapted from the Latin: *Nimia familiaritas contemptum parit.*

on this expedition; and this shoulder, as it did all the work, was perceptibly lower than its fellow, from long service. Such toil soon wears out the strongest constitution. The drivers are accustomed to work in the cold water in the spring, rarely ever dry; and if one falls in all over, he rarely changes his clothes till night, if then, even. One who takes this precaution is called by a particular nickname, or is turned off. None can lead this life who are not almost amphibious. McCauslin said soberly, what is at any rate a good story to tell, that he had seen where six men were wholly under water at once, at a jam, with their shoulders to handspikes. If the log did not start, then they had to put out their heads to breathe. The driver works as long as he can see, from dark to dark, and at night has not time to eat his supper and dry his clothes fairly, before he is asleep on his cedar bed. We lay that night on the very bed made by such a party, stretching our tent over the poles which were still standing, but reshingling the damp and faded bed with fresh leaves.

In the morning, we carried our boat over and launched it, making haste lest the wind should rise. The boatmen ran down Passamagamet, and, soon after, Ambejijis Falls, while we walked round with the baggage. We made a hasty breakfast at the head of Ambejijis Lake, on the remainder of our pork, and were soon rowing across its smooth surface again, under a pleasant sky, the mountain being now clear of clouds in the northeast. Taking turns at the oars, we shot rapidly across Deep Cove, the Foot of Pamadumcook, and the North Twin, at the rate of six miles an hour, the wind not being high enough to disturb us, and reached the Dam at noon. The boatmen went through one of the log sluices in the batteau, where the fall was ten feet at the bottom, and took us in below. Here was the longest rapid in our voyage, and perhaps the running this was as dangerous and arduous a task as any. Shooting down sometimes at the rate, as we judged, of fifteen miles an hour, if we struck a rock, we were split from end to end in an instant. Now like a bait bobbing for some river monster amid the eddies, now darting to this side of the stream, now to that, gliding swift and smooth near to our destruction, or striking broad off with the paddle and drawing the boat to right or left with all our might, in order to avoid a rock. I suppose that it was like running the rapids of the Sault de St. Marie, at the outlet of Lake Superior, and our boatmen probably displayed no less dexterity than the Indians there do. We soon ran through this mile, and floated in Quakish Lake.

After such a voyage, the troubled and angry waters, which once had seemed terrible and not to be trifled with, appeared tamed and subdued; they had been bearded[271] and worried in their channels, pricked and whipped into submission with the spike-pole and paddle, gone through and through with impunity, and all their spirit and their danger taken out of them, and the most swollen and impetuous rivers seemed but playthings henceforth. I began, at length, to understand the boatman's familiarity with and contempt for the rapids. "Those Fowler boys," said Mrs. McCauslin, "are perfect ducks for the water." They had run down to Lincoln, according to her, thirty or forty miles, in a batteau, in the night, for a doctor, when it was so dark that they could not see a rod before them, and the river was swollen so as to be almost a continuous rapid, so that the doctor *cried,* when they brought him up by daylight, "Why, Tom, how did you see to steer?" "We didn't steer much,—only kept her straight." And yet they met with no accident. It is true, the more difficult rapids are higher up than this.

When we reached the Millinocket opposite to Tom's house, and were waiting for his folks to set us over, for we had left our batteau above the Grand Falls, we discovered two canoes with two men in each, turning up this

271 Having had one's beard plucked or pulled as an act of defiance, contradiction, or contempt.

272 Latin for woodlands, but also an allusion to the name given to the area which became Pennsylvania. In 1677 William Penn (1644–1718) and a group of Quakers received the colonial province of West New Jersey. Penn called this land, granted to him in 1681, Sylvania.

stream from Shad Pond, one keeping the opposite side of a small island before us, while the other approached the side where we were standing, examining the banks carefully for muskrats as they came along. The last proved to be Louis Neptune and his companion, now at last on their way up to Chesuncook after moose; but they were so disguised that we hardly knew them. At a little distance, they might have been taken for Quakers, with their broad-brimmed hats, and overcoats with broad capes, the spoils of Bangor, seeking a settlement in this Sylvania,[272]—or, nearer at hand, for fashionable gentlemen, the morning after a spree. Met face to face, these Indians in their native woods looked like the sinister and slouching fellows whom you meet picking up strings and paper in the streets of a city. There is, in fact, a remarkable and unexpected resemblance between the degraded savage and the lowest classes in a great city. The one is no more a child of nature than the other. In the progress of degradation, the distinction of races is soon lost. Neptune at first was only anxious to know what we "kill," seeing some partridges in the hands of one of the party, but we had assumed too much anger to permit of a reply. We thought Indians had some honor before. But—"Me been sick. O, me unwell now. You make bargain, then me go." They had in fact been delayed so long by a drunken frolic at the Five Islands, and they had not yet recovered from its effects. They had some young muskrats in their canoes, which they dug out of the banks with a hoe for food, not for their skins, for muskrats are their principal food on these expeditions. So they went on up the Millinocket, and we kept down the bank of the Penobscot, after recruiting ourselves with a draught of Tom's beer, leaving Tom at his home.

Thus a man shall lead his life away here on the edge of the wilderness, on Indian Millinocket stream, in a new world, far in the dark of a continent, and have a flute to play at evening here,[273] while his strains echo to the stars, amid the howling of wolves; shall live, as it were, in the primitive age of the world, a primitive man. Yet he shall spend a sunny day, and in this century be my contemporary; perchance shall read some scattered leaves of literature, and sometimes talk with me. Why read history then if the ages and the generations are now? He lives three thousand years deep into time, an age not yet described by poets. Can you well go further back in history than this? Ay! ay!—for there turns up but now into the mouth of Millinocket stream a still more ancient and primitive man, whose history is not brought down even to the former. In a bark vessel sewn with the roots of the spruce, with horn-beam paddles he dips his way along. He is but dim and misty to me, obscured by the aeons that lie between the bark canoe and the batteau. He builds no house of logs, but a wigwam of skins. He eats no hot-bread and sweet-cake, but muskrat and moose-meat and the fat of bears. He glides up the Millinocket and is lost to my sight, as a more distant and misty cloud is seen flitting by behind a nearer, and is lost in space. So he goes about his destiny, the red face of man.

After having passed the night and buttered our boots for the last time at Uncle George's, whose dogs almost devoured him for joy at his return, we kept on down the river the next day about eight miles on foot, and then took a batteau with a man to pole it to Mattawamkeag, ten more. At the middle of that very night, to make a swift conclusion to a long story, we dropped our buggy over the half-finished bridge[274] at Oldtown, where we heard the confused din and clink of a hundred saws which never rest, and at six o'clock the next morning one of the party was steaming his way to Massachusetts.[275]

What is most striking in the Maine wilderness is, the continuousness of the forest, with fewer open intervals

273 Thoreau played the flute, as did his brother and father. Franklin Benjamin Sanborn (1831–1917) wrote, "Henry's favorite instrument was the flute, which his father had played before him; he was accompanied on the piano sometimes by one of his sisters; but the best place for hearing its pastoral note was on some hillside, or the edge of the wood or stream; and Emerson took pleasure in its strains upon those excursions to the Cliffs, or Walden, which were so frequent in the youth of the musician." Louisa May Alcott (1832–1888) wrote in her reminiscence "Thoreau's Flute," published in the September 1863 *Atlantic Monthly*:

> Then from the flute, untouched by hands,
> There came a low, harmonious breath:
> "For such as he there is no death;—
> His life the eternal life commands;
> Above man's aims his nature rose:
> The wisdom of a just content
> Made one small spot a continent,
> And tuned to poetry Life's prose."

274 Pushaw Bridge, which was completed in 1847, as a bridge over the Stillwater branch of the Penobscot River, near Pushaw Falls, to connect Marsh Island with the mainland in Orono.
275 Although Thoreau traveled to Maine by railroad on this excursion, he returned by steamer.

276 Of the highest quality. In the gem trade, the clarity of diamonds is assessed by their translucence. The more translucent, the higher the quality. Clear white diamonds are called diamonds of the first water. Thoreau used a similar phrase to describe Walden Pond in "The Ponds" chapter of *Walden:* "It is a gem of the first water which Concord wears in her coronet" [Wa 174].

277 In England, a system of law established by William the Conqueror (ca. 1028–1087) to protect game animals and their forest habitat from destruction.

278 Disafforested: in English law, to free from the restrictions of forest laws, that is, change to common land, but also to defoliate, or convert from forest to arable land.

279 Generic name for small freshwater fish, including, in Thoreau's day, the shiner, dace, roach, and minnow.

or glades than you had imagined. Except the few burnt lands, the narrow intervals on the rivers, the bare tops of the high mountains, and the lakes and streams, the forest is uninterrupted. It is even more grim and wild than you had anticipated, a damp and intricate wilderness, in the spring everywhere wet and miry. The aspect of the country indeed is universally stern and savage, excepting the distant views of the forest from hills, and the lake prospects, which are mild and civilizing in a degree. The lakes are something which you are unprepared for: they lie up so high exposed to the light, and the forest is diminished to a fine fringe on their edges, with here and there a blue mountain, like amethyst jewels set around some jewel of the first water,[276] — so anterior, so superior to all the changes that are to take place on their shores, even now civil and refined, and fair, as they can ever be. These are not the artificial forests of an English king — a royal preserve merely. Here prevail no forest laws,[277] but those of nature. The aborigines have never been dispossessed, nor nature disforested.[278]

It is a country full of evergreen trees, of mossy silver birches and watery maples, the ground dotted with insipid, small red berries, and strewn with damp and moss-grown rocks — a country diversified with innumerable lakes and rapid streams, peopled with trout and various species of *leucisci,*[279] with salmon, shad and pickerel, and other fishes; the forest resounding at rare intervals with the note of the chicadee, the blue-jay, and the woodpecker, the scream of the fish-hawk and the eagle, the laugh of the loon, and the whistle of ducks along the solitary streams; and at night, with the hooting of owls and howling of wolves; and in summer, swarming with myriads of black flies and mosquitoes, more formidable than wolves to the white man. Such is the home of the moose, the bear, the caribou, the wolf, the beaver, and the Indian. Who shall describe the inexpressible tenderness and immortal life of the grim forest, where Nature, though it be mid-winter, is ever in her spring, where the moss-grown and decaying trees are not old, but seem to enjoy a perpetual youth; and blissful, innocent Nature, like a serene infant, is too happy to make a noise, except by a few tinkling, lisping birds and trickling rills?

What a place to live, what a place to die and be buried in! There certainly men would live forever, and laugh at death and the grave. There they could have no such thoughts as are associated with the village graveyard — that make a grave out of one of those moist evergreen hummocks!

> Die and be buried who will,
> I mean to live here still;
> My nature grows ever more young
> The primitive pines among.

I am reminded by my journey how exceedingly new this country still is. You have only to travel for a few days into the interior and back parts even of many of the old states, to come to that very America which the Northmen, and Cabot, and Gosnold, and Smith and Raleigh[280] visited. If Columbus was the first to discover the islands, Americus Vespucius,[281] and Cabot, and the Puritans, and we their descendants, have discovered only the shores of America. While the republic has already acquired a history world-wide, America is still unsettled and unexplored. Like the English in New Holland,[282] we live only on the shores of a continent even yet, and hardly know where the rivers come from which float our navy. The very timber and boards, and shingles, of which our houses are made, grew but yesterday in a wilderness where the Indian still hunts and the moose runs wild. New York has her wilderness within her own borders; and though the sailors of Europe are familiar with the

280 John Cabot (ca. 1450–1498), Italian explorer who led a 1497 English expedition that discovered the North American mainland. Bartholomew Gosnold (ca. 1572–1607), English explorer and colonizer, who navigated the North American east coast from Maine to Narragansett Bay, and who named Cape Cod. John Smith (ca. 1580–1631), English explorer who helped found Jamestown, Virginia. Sir Walter Raleigh (1552 or 1554–1618), English explorer, courtier, and writer. Thoreau lectured on Raleigh on 8 February 1843, incorporating parts of the lecture into *A Week on the Concord and Merrimack Rivers.*
281 Latinized form of Amerigo Vespucci (1454–1512), Florentine navigator who explored the coast of South America.
282 Australia, which, from its discovery in the seventeenth century by the Dutch, had been called New Holland.

283 North American river flowing from the Adirondack Mountain range in the northeastern part of New York to Upper New York Bay, and a bay or inland sea of east-central Canada connected to the Atlantic Ocean by the Hudson Strait.

284 Robert Fulton (1765–1815), engineer and inventor of the first commercially successful steamship. Fulton worked on the ship on the East River but the first established route for the steamship was on the Hudson between New York and Albany.

285 River in eastern Texas that flows into the Gulf of Mexico.

286 Also known as Rio Grande, a North American river forming the boundary between the United States and Mexico.

287 The first railroad in Maine was chartered in 1832–1833, and the first tracks, from Bangor to Old Town, were completed in 1836; the first telegraph lines, from Portland to Bangor, were strung in 1848.

288 Allusion to the phrase found in Deuteronomy 32:10: "He found him in a desert land, and in the waste howling wilderness; he led him about, he instructed him, he kept him as the apple of his eye."

289 According to Hayward's *Gazetteer* (507): "A railroad, 12 miles in length, between Bangor and the villages of Stillwater and Oldtown, in Orono, was opened for travel in 1836."

soundings of her Hudson,[283] and Fulton long since invented the steamboat on its waters,[284] an Indian is still necessary to guide her scientific men to its head-waters in the Adirondac country.

Have we even so much as discovered and settled the shores? Let a man travel on foot along the coast, from the Passamaquoddy to the Sabine,[285] or to the Rio Bravo,[286] or to wherever the end is now, if he is swift enough to overtake it, faithfully following the windings of every inlet and of every cape, and stepping to the music of the surf—with a desolate fishing-town once a week, and a city's port once a month to cheer him, and putting up at the light-houses, when there are any, and tell me if it looks like a discovered and settled country, and not rather, for the most part, like a desolate island, and No-man's Land.

We have advanced by leaps to the Pacific, and left many a lesser Oregon and California unexplored behind us. Though the railroad and the telegraph have been established on the shores of Maine,[287] the Indian still looks out from her interior mountains over all these to the sea. There stands the city of Bangor, fifty miles up the Penobscot, at the head of navigation for vessels of the largest class, the principal lumber depot on this continent, with a population of twelve thousand, like a star on the edge of night, still hewing at the forests of which it is built, already overflowing with the luxuries and refinement of Europe, and sending its vessels to Spain, to England, and to the West Indies for its groceries,—and yet only a few axe-men have gone "up river" into the howling wilderness[288] which feeds it. The bear and deer are still found within its limits; and the moose, as he swims the Penobscot, is entangled amid its shipping and taken by foreign sailors in its harbor. Twelve miles in the rear, twelve miles of railroad,[289] are Orono and the

Indian Island, the home of the Penobscot tribe, and then commence the batteau and the canoe, and the military road; and, sixty miles above, the country is virtually unmapped and unexplored, and there still waves the virgin forest of the New World.[290]

290 The Americas: the term was first used by the Italian historian Peter Martyr (1457–1526) in his *De Rebus Oceanicis et Novo Orbe* (1516), a chronicle of the discovery of America.

1 The steamer *Penobscot* on Sandford's Independent Line traveled via Cape Ann to Monhegan Island. It was captained by William Flowers (1814–1895), who developed a system of piloting in 1845 using timed courses, calculating distance against time and speed with adjustments for tide and wind, to pinpoint his exact location at all times.
2 Inclined so much to one side that the deck approaches a nearly vertical position.
3 Quoted, with minor variants in spelling and tense, from George Chapman's (ca. 1539–1634) *Tragedy of Charles, Duke of Byron*, III.i.xx:

> Give me a spirit that on this life's rough seas
> Loves t' have his sails fill'd with a lusty wind,
> Even till his sail-yards tremble, his masts
> crack,
> And his rapt ship run on her side so low
> That she drinks water, and her keel plows air.

4 A peninsula in Essex County, northeast of Boston, and a popular beach area lined with summer cottages.
5 Also known as the Twin Lights, originally constructed in 1771 on Thatcher Island.
6 A town in northeastern Massachusetts, known as a shipbuilding center and fishing port.
7 On sailing across the equator for the first time, seamen are summoned to the "court of Neptune" for trial, followed by a ritual ducking in a tub of seawater sometimes including a lathering and rough shave. Richard Henry Dana, Jr. (1815–1882), wrote on 1 October 1834: "Crossed the equator. . . . I now, for the first time, felt at liberty, according to the old usage, to call myself a son of Neptune, and was very glad to be able to claim the title without the disagreeable initiation which so many have to go through. After once crossing the line, you can never be subjected to the process, but are considered as a son of Neptune, with full powers to play tricks upon others. This ancient custom is now seldom allowed, unless there are passengers on board, in which case there is always a good deal of sport."

Chesuncook

At 5 P.M., September 13th, 1853, I left Boston in the steamer for Bangor by the outside course.[1] It was a warm and still night,—warmer, probably, on the water than on the land,—and the sea was as smooth as a small lake in summer, merely rippled. The passengers went singing on the deck, as in a parlor, till ten o'clock. We passed a vessel on her beam-ends[2] on a rock just outside the islands, and some of us thought that she was the "rapt ship" which ran

> "on her side so low
> That she drank water, and her keel ploughed
> air,"[3]

not considering that there was no wind, and that she was under bare poles. Now we have left the islands behind and are off Nahant.[4] We behold those features which the discoverers saw, apparently unchanged. Now we see the Cape Ann lights,[5] and now pass near a small village-like fleet of mackerel fishers at anchor, probably off Gloucester.[6] They salute us with a shout from their low decks; but I understand their "Good evening" to mean, "Don't run against me, Sir." From the wonders of the deep we go below to yet deeper sleep. And then the absurdity of being waked up in the night by a man who wants the job of blacking your boots! It is more inevitable than sea-sickness, and may have something to do with it. It is like the ducking you get on crossing the line[7] the first time. I trusted that these old customs were abolished. They might with the same propriety insist on blacking your face. I heard of one man who complained that somebody had stolen his boots in the night; and when he found them, he wanted to know what they had done to them,—they had spoiled them,—he never put that stuff on them; and the blacker narrowly escaped paying damages.[8]

Anxious to get out of the whale's belly,[9] I rose early, and joined some old salts, who were smoking by a dim light on a sheltered part of the deck. We were just getting into the river. They knew all about it, of course. I was proud to find that I had stood the voyage so well, and was not in the least digested. We brushed up and watched the first signs of dawn through an open port; but the day seemed to hang fire.[10] We inquired the time; none of my companions had a chronometer. At length an African prince[11] rushed by, observing, "Twelve o'clock, gentlemen!" and blew out the light. It was moon-rise. So I slunk down into the monster's bowels again.

The first land we make is Monhegan Island,[12] before dawn, and next St. George's Islands,[13] seeing two or three lights. Whitehead, with its bare rocks and funeral bell,[14] is interesting. Next I remember that the Camden Hills attracted my eyes, and afterward the hills about Frankfort. We reached Bangor about noon.

When I arrived, my companion[15] that was to be had gone up river, and engaged an Indian, Joe Aitteon,[16] a son of the Governor,[17] to go with us to Chesuncook Lake. Joe had conducted two white men a-moose-hunting in the same direction the year before. He arrived by cars at Bangor that evening, with his canoe and a companion, Sabattis Solomon,[18] who was going to leave Bangor the following Monday with Joe's father, by way of the Penobscot, and join Joe in moose-hunting at Chesuncook, when we had done with him. They took supper

8 In "An Excursion to Canada" Thoreau wrote similarly: "I should no more think of it than of putting on a clean dicky and blacking my shoes to go a-fishing. As if you were going out to dine, when in fact the genuine traveller is going out to work hard and fare harder, to eat a crust by the way-side whenever he can get it. Honest travelling is about as dirty work as you can do. Why, a man needs a pair of overalls for it. As for blacking my shoes in such a case, I should as soon think of blacking my face. I carry a piece of tallow to preserve the leather, and keep out the water, that's all; and many an officious shoe-black, who carried off my shoes when I was slumbering, mistaking me for a gentleman, has had occasion to repent it before he produced a gloss on them" [W 5:31–32].
9 Allusion to Jonah 1:17: "Now the Lord had prepared a great fish to swallow up Jonah. And Jonah was in the belly of the fish three days and three nights."
10 Showing unexpected delay, from its use in relation to firearms: to be slow in the explosion of a charge after its primer has been ignited.
11 Reference to William Ansah (or Unsah) Sessarakoo (fl. 1736–1749), whose life was the inspiration for such accounts as "A Young African Prince, Sold for a Slave, Afterwards Brought to England" (*Gentleman's Magazine*, February 1749) and William Dodd's (1729–1777) poem "The African Prince."
12 Williamson in his *History of the State of Maine* wrote: "Monhegan Island was in ancient times, without exception, the most famous one on the seaboard of this State. It was the land aimed at and first mentioned by the original voyagers and fishermen about these waters; and was so noted a stage for the latter as to be sometimes called a *plantation*. . . . It is situated nine miles southerly of George's Islands; five leagues east-southeast of Townsend, and 3 leagues westwardly of Metinic. It contains upwards of a thousand acres of good land, has a bold shore on all its sides, a large projection of rocks at its northeastward part, and has one good harbour. On its south side is the *Menan-*

nah Island of two acres, distant a cable's length, and the harbour is between the two Islands; the entrance into it on the southwest of Monhegan being safe and easy."

13 Williamson wrote that "*St. George's Islands,* so often mentioned by early navigators, are a large cluster, situated about the mouth of St. George's river eastwardly; and on the east margin of Broad bay, being about twenty in number; twelve or fourteen of which deserve to be described or mentioned. . . . It is well known that Capt. Weymouth, with his ship's crew visited this river, A.D. 1605, called the harbour *Pentacost harbour,* and gave to George's Islands the name they have since borne. Here he planted a garden, the first probably in this State."

14 Whitehead Light was first established on Whitehead Island in 1807, with a new lighthouse being built in 1852. The first bell, installed in 1830, was replaced in 1837 or 1838 by a "perpetual fog bell" that was controlled by the tide. When this stopped working in 1842, the bell was rung manually by the keeper, until it was replaced with a new bell in 1853.

15 George Thatcher; see "Ktaadn," n. 2.

16 Joseph Attien (1829–1870), river driver, guide, and Penobscot tribal governor. He drowned on 4 July 1870 at Grand Falls, near Millinocket, trying to save his boat's crew.

17 John Attien (1778–1858) was the last Penobscot tribal governor with a hereditary life term of office. After his death the office was filled through annual elections, of which his son Joseph won seven.

18 Probably Sabattis Solomon Swassian, who was listed in the 1858 census of the Penobscot Indians by J. C. Knowlton, supervisor of schools, Old Town, Maine, as age twenty-three.

19 In 1835 plans began for a road, to be known as the Avenue Road, to extend from Bangor to Moosehead Lake, through central Penobscot and western Piscataquis Counties.

20 Anthony Finley's (ca. 1790–1840) *New General Atlas.*

at my friend's house and lodged in his barn, saying that they should fare worse than that in the woods. They only made Watch bark a little, when they came to the door in the night for water, for he does not like Indians.

The next morning Joe and his canoe were put on board the stage for Moosehead Lake, sixty and odd miles distant, an hour before we started in an open wagon. We carried hard bread, pork, smoked beef, tea, sugar, etc., seemingly enough for a regiment; the sight of which brought together reminded me by what ignoble means we had maintained our ground hitherto. We went by the Avenue Road,[19] which is quite straight and very good, north-westward toward Moosehead Lake, through more than a dozen flourishing towns, with almost every one its academy,—not one of which, however, is on my General Atlas, published, alas! in 1824;[20] so much are they before the age, or I behind it! The earth must have been considerably lighter to the shoulders of General Atlas[21] then.

It rained all this day and till the middle of the next forenoon, concealing the landscape almost entirely; but we had hardly got out of the streets of Bangor before I began to be exhilarated by the sight of the wild fir and spruce tops, and those of other primitive evergreens, peering through the mist in the horizon. It was like the sight and odor of cake to a schoolboy. He who rides and keeps the beaten track studies the fences chiefly. Near Bangor, the fence-posts, on account of the frost's heaving them in the clayey soil, were not planted in the ground, but were mortised into a transverse horizontal beam lying on the surface. Afterwards, the prevailing fences were log ones, with sometimes a Virginia fence,[22] or else rails slanted over crossed stakes,—and these zigzagged or played leap-frog all the way to the lake, keeping just ahead of us. After getting out of the Penobscot Valley, the country was unexpectedly level, or consisted of very even and equal swells, for twenty or thirty miles, never rising above the general level, but affording, it is said, a very good prospect in clear weather, with frequent views of Ktaadn,—straight roads and long hills. The houses were far apart, commonly small and of one story, but framed. There was very little land under cultivation, yet the forest did not often border the road. The stumps were frequently as high as one's head, showing the depth of the snows. The white hay-caps,[23] drawn over small stacks of beans or corn in the fields, on account of the rain, were a novel sight to me. We saw large flocks of pigeons, and several times came within a rod or two of partridges in the road. My companion said, that, in one journey out of Bangor, he and his son[24] had shot sixty partridges from his buggy. The mountain-ash was now very handsome, as also the wayfarer's-tree or hobble-bush, with its ripe purple berries mixed with red. The Canada thistle, an introduced plant,[25] was the prevailing weed all the way to the lake,—the road-side in many places, and fields not long cleared, being densely filled with it as with a crop, to the exclusion of everything else. There were also whole fields full of ferns, now rusty and withering, which in older countries are commonly confined to wet ground. There were very few flowers, even allowing for the lateness of the season. It chanced that I saw no asters in bloom along the road for fifty miles, though they were so abundant then in Massachusetts,—except in one place one or two of the *Aster acuminatus,*—and no golden-rods till within twenty miles of Monson, where I saw a three-ribbed one. There were many late buttercups, however, and the two fire-weeds, erechthites and epilobium, commonly where there had been a burning, and at last the pearly everlasting. I noticed occasionally very long troughs which supplied the road with water, and my companion said that three dollars annually were granted by the State to one man in each school-district,

21 Allusion to the Greek Titan Atlas; see "Ktaadn," n. 236.

22 A fence of crossed rails supporting one another and forming a zigzag pattern, also known as a snake or worm fence.

23 Canvas covering for a haycock.

24 Probably George Thatcher's eldest son, George Putnam Thatcher (1833–1919).

25 *Cirsium arvense,* also called Cursed Thistle, was identified in John Torrey (1796–1873) and Asa Gray's (1810–1888) *Flora of North America* (1838) as having been "introduced with grain from Europe, and in many places becoming an extremely troublesome weed."

26 In 1852 the Maine legislature approved an "act encouraging persons to furnish watering places" that stipulated: "Any person in any city, town or plantation in this state, who shall construct and maintain and keep in repair a good watering trough beside the highway, and well supplied with water, the surface of which shall be at least two feet and a half above the ground, and made easily accessible for horses and carriages, shall be allowed by the city, town or plantation, three dollars out of his highway tax for each year he shall furnish the same."

27 Possible reference to Thomas Babington Macaulay's (1800–1859) *Critical and Historical Essays*, in which he wrote: "It is a common error in politics to confound means with ends. Constitutions, charters, petitions of right, declarations of right, representative assemblies, electoral colleges, are not good government; nor do they, even when most elaborately constructed, necessarily produce good government. Laws exist in vain for those who have not the courage and the means to defend them. Electors meet in vain where want makes them the slaves of the landlord, or where superstition makes them the slaves of the priest. Representative assemblies sit in vain unless they have at their command, in the last resort the physical power which is necessary to make their deliberations free, and their votes effectual."

28 In the sense of superior quality, valuable, applied to gems as a mark of excellence, and as opposed to occidental, which was a mark of less value.

29 Maine, from the fact that when a ship sailed north from Boston to Maine—Boston is longitudinally east of the ports in Maine—it sailed downwind, or down east.

30 The Maine Liquor Law, prohibiting the sale of intoxicating beverages, came into effect on 2 June 1851. In 1853 a search and seizure act was passed for the confiscation of liquors.

31 In 1817, Joseph Ripley Bearce (1797–1818), the first settler of Monson, placed a set of moose horns on a guide post to mark where the trail

who provided and maintained a suitable water-trough by the road-side, for the use of travellers,[26]—a piece of intelligence as refreshing to me as the water itself. That legislature did not sit in vain.[27] It was an Oriental[28] act, which made me wish that I was still further down East,[29]—another Maine law, which I hope we may get in Massachusetts. That State is banishing bar-rooms from its highways,[30] and conducting the mountain-springs thither.

The country was first decidedly mountainous in Garland, Sangerville, and onwards, twenty-five or thirty miles from Bangor. At Sangerville, where we stopped at mid-afternoon to warm and dry ourselves, the landlord told us that he had found a wilderness where we found him. At a fork in the road between Abbot and Monson, about twenty miles from Moosehead Lake, I saw a guide-post surmounted by a pair of moose-horns, spreading four or five feet, with the word "Monson" painted on one blade, and the name of some other town on the other.[31] They are sometimes used for ornamental hat-trees, together with deers' horns, in front entries; but, after the experience which I shall relate, I trust that I shall have a better excuse for killing a moose than that I may hang my hat on his horns. We reached Monson, fifty miles from Bangor, and thirteen from the lake, after dark.

At four o'clock the next morning, in the dark, and still in the rain, we pursued our journey. Close to the academy[32] in this town they have erected a sort of gallows for the pupils to practice on.[33] I thought that they might as well hang at once all who need to go through such exercises in so new a country, where there is nothing to hinder their living an out-door life. Better omit Blair, and take the air.[34] The country about the south end of the lake is quite mountainous, and the road began to feel the effects of it. There is one hill which, it is calculated, it takes twenty-five minutes to ascend. In many places the road was in that condition called *repaired,* having just been whittled into the required semi-cylindrical form with the shovel and scraper, with all the softest inequalities in the middle, like a hog's back with the bristles up, and Jehu[35] was expected to keep astride of the spine. As you looked off each side of the bare sphere into the horizon, the ditches were awful to behold,—a vast hollowness, like that between Saturn and his ring. At a tavern[36] hereabouts the hostler greeted our horse as an old acquaintance, though he did not remember the driver. He said that he had taken care of that little mare for a short time, a year or two before, at the Mount Kineo House,[37] and thought she was not in as good condition as then. Every man to his trade.[38] I am not acquainted with a single horse in the world, not even the one that kicked me.[39]

Already we had thought that we saw Moosehead Lake from a hill-top, where an extensive fog filled the distant lowlands, but we were mistaken. It was not till we were within a mile or two of its south end that we got our first view of it,—a suitably wild-looking sheet of water, sprinkled with small low islands, which were covered with shaggy spruce and other wild wood,—seen over the infant port of Greenville,[40] with mountains on each side and far in the north, and a steamer's smoke-pipe rising above a roof. A pair of moose-horns ornamented a corner of the public-house[41] where we left our horse, and a few rods distant lay the small steamer Moosehead,[42] Captain King.[43] There was no village, and no summer road any further in this direction,—but a winter road, that is, one passable only when deep snow covers its inequalities, from Greenville up the east side of the lake to Lily Bay, about twelve miles.

I was here first introduced to Joe. He had ridden all the way on the outside of the stage the day before, in the

diverged from Blanchard, then known as Million Acres, to Monson.

32 Monson Academy, a primary and secondary school, was founded in 1847 and open in the fall of 1848.

33 In his journal of 21 September 1853 Thoreau wrote: "Most towns have an academy. Even away up toward the lake we saw a sort of gallows erected near one for the pupils to exercise upon. I had not dreamed of such degeneracy so hard upon the primitive wilderness" [J 5:427].

34 Hugh Blair (1718–1800), Scottish Presbyterian theologian and professor of rhetoric at the University of Edinburgh, and author of *Lectures on Rhetoric and Belles Lettres,* about whom Thoreau wrote in his journal of 5 February 1852: "I do not believe that any writer who considered the ornaments, and not the truth simply, ever succeeded. So are made the *belles lettres* and the *beaux arts* and their *professors,* which we can do without" [J 3:278–279]. Thoreau's rhyme may have been written in response to Samuel Hoole's (ca. 1757–1839) *Modern manners; or, The Country Cousins in a Series of Poetical Epistles:*

> When the silver urn is gone,
> Cloth remov'd, and breakfast done,
> Uncle walk'd to take the air,
> Aunt to pore on Dr. Blair.

35 A coachman, often one who drives quickly, from 2 Kings 9:20: "the driving is like the driving of Jehu the son of Nimshi; for he driveth furiously."

36 Possibly Rice's Tavern, at which Jackson stopped in 1838. It was run by Peabody H. Rice, who came to Monson in 1835 and who was engaged in trading, lumbering, and farming, as well as tavern keeping.

37 Built in 1848 by Joshua Fogg (1796–1884) to accommodate the increased number of travelers. It was described by the poet James Russell Lowell (1819–1891) on 13 August 1853 in "A Moosehead Journal": "By this time we had arrived at Kineo, a flourishing village of one house, the tavern kept by 'Squire Barrows. The 'Squire is a large, hearty man, with a voice as clear and strong as a northwest wind, and a great laugh suitable to it. His table is neat and well supplied, and he waits upon it himself in the good old landlordly fashion. One may be much better off here, to my thinking, than in one of those gigantic Columbaria which are foisted upon us patient Americans for hotels, and where one is packed away in a pigeon-hole so near the heavens that, if the comet should flirt its tail, (no unlikely thing in the month of flies,) one would be in danger of being brushed away. Here one does not pay his diurnal three dollars for an undivided five-hundredth part of the pleasure of looking at gilt gingerbread. Here one's relations are with the monarch himself."

38 Axiom dating from as early as the sixteenth century in English, also used by Thoreau in *Cape Cod:* "But every man to his trade. Though he had little woodcraft, he was not the less weatherwise, and gave us one piece of information; viz. he had observed that when a thunder-cloud came up with a flood-tide it did not rain" [W 4:197].

39 In his journal of 4 October 1857 Thoreau wrote: "Going home with what nails were left in a flour bucket on my arm, in a rain, I was about getting into a hay-rigging, when my umbrella frightened the horse, and he kicked at me over the fills, smashed the bucket on my arm, and stretched me on my back; but while I lay on my back, his leg being caught over the shaft, I got up, to see him sprawling on the other side. This accident, the sudden bending of my body backwards, sprained my stomach so that I did not get quite strong there for several years, but had to give up some fence-building and other work which I had undertaken from time to time" [ITM 329].

40 Centered on the lower end of Moosehead Lake, the township was incorporated in 1836.

41 In his journal Thoreau mentioned putting up their horse "at Sawyer's the—Public house—A suitably wild view with low islands covered with ragged wild wood— . . . A pair of Moose-horns

ornamented a corner of Sawyer's piazza—" [MJ 16 September 1853]. As no formal public house belonging to a Sawyer has been identified, this may have been the house of Joel Sawyer (1808–1895).

42 Built in 1848 expressly as a passenger-boat, with modern furnishings, a locomotive-boiler and engine that allowed a speed of fourteen miles per hour. In his journal Thoreau wrote: "This steamer runs to the head of the Lake at the N.E. carry Every Tuesday and Friday and returns the same day—On Wednesday it runs about half way—or to *mt* Kennia. On other days she is at the service of those who please to hire her—It is used chiefly by lumberers for the transportation of themselves—their boats and supplies toward the interior" [MJ 16 September 1853].

43 Unidentified further.

rain, giving way to ladies, and was well wetted. As it still rained, he asked if we were going to "put it through." He was a good-looking Indian, twenty-four years old, apparently of unmixed blood, short and stout, with a broad face and reddish complexion, and eyes, methinks, narrower and more turned-up at the outer corners than ours, answering to the description of his race. Beside his under-clothing, he wore a red flannel shirt, woollen pants, and a black Kossuth hat,[44] the ordinary dress of the lumberman, and, to a considerable extent, of the Penobscot Indian. When, afterward, he had occasion to take off his shoes and stockings, I was struck with the smallness of his feet. He had worked a good deal as a lumberman, and appeared to identify himself with that class. He was the only one of the party who possessed an India-rubber jacket. The top strip or edge of his canoe was worn nearly through by friction on the stage.

At eight o'clock the steamer, with her bell and whistle, scaring the moose, summoned us on board. She was a well-appointed little boat, commanded by a gentlemanly captain, with patent life-seats[45] and metallic life-boat,[46] and dinner on board, if you wish. She is chiefly used by lumberers for the transportation of themselves, their boats, and supplies, but also by hunters and tourists. There was another steamer, named Amphitrite,[47] laid up close by; but, apparently, her name was not more trite[48] than her hull. There were also two or three large sail-boats in port. These beginnings of commerce on a lake in the wilderness are very interesting,—these larger white birds that come to keep company with the gulls. There were but few passengers, and not one female among them: a St. Francis Indian,[49] with his canoe and moose-hides, two explorers[50] for lumber, three men who landed at Sandbar Island, and a gentleman[51] who lives on Deer Island, eleven miles up the lake, and owns also Sugar Island,[52] between which and the former the

44 Named for Lajos Kossuth (1802–1894), a Hungarian patriot who worked, unsuccessfully, to establish Hungarian independence from Austria in the 1840s. Kossuth visited Concord and spoke in Lexington on 11 May 1952, during his 1851–1852 lecture tour in the United States, where he was collecting funds toward independence. *Scientific American* reported on 27 December 1851: "Since Kossuth came to New York, the Kossuth hat has become quite fashionable. This is a low crowned hat with a small black ostrich feather stuck at one side. . . . These are made of felted wool, and allow gas to pass from the head to escape freely. . . . Oldish people of a sedate turn, although they would prefer the 'Kossuth hat,' do not like to adopt it just yet, from a prudential fear of being conspicuous." The hat was promoted by the New York merchant John Nicholas Genin (1819–1878), who distributed several of these hats to Kossuth's followers and Hungarian refugees as they disembarked from the ship at Sandy Hook, creating the new fashion fad.

45 Probably the seats patented by Nathan Thompson, Jr., in 1853 and described in *The Life-Boat; or, The Journal of the National Life-Boat Institution* (October 1854) as being in form "nearly that of a common four-legged stool, or a chair with the back cut off; the upper portion of it, or the seat itself, as distinguished from the legs, possesses the buoyant power which is contained in two metallic air-tight chambers incased in wood. . . . When closed or shut up, it is a seat; when open, it is a life-buoy; the two air-chambers being then extended horizontally, connected at the sides, and allowing sufficient space for a stout person to stow between them, in which position he may float very much at ease, having the free use of his arms, with which and his feet he can readily propel himself through the water, the one chamber floating in front, and the other behind him."

46 In 1845 Joseph Francis (1801–1893) patented the use of stamped corrugated metal to make lifeboats. By 1853 he opened a dedicated factory for his Metallic Life-Boat Company.

47 Launched in 1844, the *Amphitrite* was ninety feet long and could travel at six miles per hour. It was named for the queen of the sea in Greek mythology, wife of Poseidon and mother of Triton.
48 In the sense of worn out.
49 Western Abenaki, or the Sokoki, were known in New England as the St. Francis Indians.
50 In Thoreau's journal one was identified simply as Hayley, the other unidentified.
51 Aaron Capen (1796–1886) moved to Maine from Massachusetts in 1834, purchasing two islands of nearly eight thousand acres. He had been a general in the Massachusetts Militia.
52 Deer and Sugar Islands are, respectively, the second-largest and the largest of the islands in Moosehead Lake.
53 A large compartment, usually decorated, and used as a drawing or dining room.
54 In the traditional hierarchy of angels, cherubim and seraphim are, respectively, the second-highest and highest in the nine orders of angels. Thoreau punned on the seraphine, a musical instrument invented in the 1830s by John Green of London, similar to the harmonium, of which it was the precursor. The name was used later for any free-standing reed organ. On 7 August 1856 Thoreau wrote: "Heard this forenoon what I thought at first to be children playing on pumpkin stems in the next yard, but it turned out to be the new steam-whistle music, what they call the Calliope (!) in the next town. It sounded still more like the pumpkin stem near at hand, only a good deal louder. Again I mistook it for an instrument in the house or at the door, when it was a quarter of a mile off, from habit locating it by its loudness. At Acton, six miles off, it sounded like some new seraphim in the next house with the blinds closed" [ITM 269].
55 Also known as Heron Lake, which name Thoreau uses in "The Allegash and East Branch" and "Appendix."
56 Sometimes Kenio, described by Hodge in his report as having "the appearance of a huge artificial wall of stone, rising directly out of the water. We paddled under its cliffs, which jutted out over

steamer runs; these, I think, were all beside ourselves. In the saloon[53] was some kind of musical instrument, cherubim or seraphim,[54] to soothe the angry waves; and there, very properly, was tacked up the map of the public lands of Maine and Massachusetts, a copy of which I had in my pocket.

The heavy rain confining us to the saloon awhile, I discoursed with the proprietor of Sugar Island on the condition of the world in Old Testament times. But at length, leaving this subject as fresh as we found it, he told me that he had lived about this lake twenty or thirty years, and yet had not been to the head of it for twenty-one years. He faces the other way. The explorers had a fine new birch on board, larger than ours, in which they had come up the Piscataquis from Howland, and they had had several messes of trout already. They were going to the neighborhood of Eagle[55] and Chamberlain Lakes, or the head-waters of the St. John, and offered to keep us company as far as we went. The lake to-day was rougher than I found the ocean, either going or returning, and Joe remarked that it would swamp his birch. Off Lily Bay it is a dozen miles wide, but it is much broken by islands. The scenery is not merely wild, but varied and interesting; mountains were seen, further or nearer, on all sides but the northwest, their summits now lost in the clouds; but Mount Kineo[56] is the principal feature of the lake, and more exclusively belongs to it. After leaving Greenville, at the foot, which is the nucleus of a town some eight or ten years old,[57] you see but three or four houses for the whole length of the lake, or about forty miles, three of them the public houses at which the steamer is advertised to stop, and the shore is an unbroken wilderness. The prevailing wood seemed to be spruce, fir, birch, and rock-maple. You could easily distinguish the hard wood from the soft, or "black growth,"[58] as it is called, at a great distance,—the former being smooth, round-topped, and light green, with a bowery and cultivated look.

Mount Kineo, at which the boat touched, is a peninsula with a narrow neck, about midway the lake on the east side. The celebrated precipice is on the east or land side of this, and is so high and perpendicular that you can jump from the top many hundred feet into the water which makes up behind the point. A man on board told us that an anchor had been sunk ninety fathoms at its base before reaching bottom! Probably it will be discovered ere long that some Indian maiden jumped off it for love once,[59] for true love never could have found a path more to its mind. We passed quite close to the rock here, since it is a very bold shore, and I observed marks of a rise of four or five feet on it. The St. Francis Indian expected to take in his boy here, but he was not at the landing. The father's sharp eyes, however, detected a canoe with his boy in it far away under the mountain, though no one else could see it. "Where is the canoe?" asked the captain, "I don't see it"; but he held on nevertheless, and by and by it hove in sight.

We reached the head of the lake about noon. The weather had in the meanwhile cleared up, though the mountains were still capped with clouds. Seen from this point, Mount Kineo, and two other allied mountains[60] ranging with it north-easterly, presented a very strong family likeness, as if all cast in one mould. The steamer here approached a long pier projecting from the northern wilderness and built of some of its logs,—and whistled, where not a cabin nor a mortal was to be seen. The shore was quite low, with flat rocks on it, overhung with black ash, arbor-vitae, etc., which at first looked as if they did not care a whistle for us. There was not a single cabman to cry "Coach!" or inveigle us to the United States Hotel.[61] At length a Mr. Hinckley,[62] who has a camp at the other end of the "carry," appeared with a truck[63] drawn by

our heads at a height of five or six hundred feet. Below they descended perpendicularly ninety feet. . . . On looking down from the edge of the precipice, we see the water directly beneath; and so steep and overhanging is the rock, that by a single leap, one might throw himself from almost the highest point, and strike the water six hundred feet below, and many feet distant from the base of the mountain. Mt. Kenio receives its name from that of an old Indian, who formerly lived and hunted in its vicinity. It is a mountain composed entirely of a blueish hornstone, like flint, exceedingly hard and compact. After long exposure, the surface of the stone becomes white."

57 The township of Haskell's Plantation, organized in 1831, was incorporated as Greenville in 1836.

58 Ezekiel Holmes (1801–1865) in his *Report of an Exploration and Survey of the Territory on the Aroostook River* defined this as "pine, cedar, spruce, fir &c."

59 There were several stories about the leap of an Indian maiden, including Longfellow's "Lover's Rock" about Lake Sebago, Maine, and the legend of Winona, or Wenonah, who leapt from Maiden Rock in Lake Pepin, Wisconsin. Thoreau may have been familiar with the Winona legend through Mary Eastman's (1818–1880) *Dahcotah; or, Life and Legends of the Sioux Around Fort Snelling*, published in 1849. The lover's leap legend became so prolific that it caused Mark Twain (1835–1910) to comment there were "fifty Lover's Leaps along the Mississippi from whose summit disappointed Indian girls have jumped."

60 Shaw and Little Kineo Mountains.

61 There were several hotels of this name, but Thoreau may mean the United States Hotel in Boston, on Beech and Lincoln Streets, which, when it was designed in 1838, was the largest hotel in the country.

62 Unidentified.

63 A low, small-wheeled carriage used for carrying goods, stone, etc.

64 Granted by charter of the Maine Legislature to the recently incorporated Moosehead Lake Railway Company in 1847 to "construct and maintain a railway with material of wood or otherwise, with one or more tracks, from the head of Moosehead Lake to the West Branch of the Penobscot River."

an ox and a horse over a rude log-railway through the woods.[64] The next thing was to get our canoe and effects over the carry from this lake, one of the heads of the Kennebec, into the Penobscot River. This railway from the lake to the river occupied the middle of a clearing two or three rods wide and perfectly straight through the forest. We walked across while our baggage was drawn behind. My companion went ahead to be ready for partridges, while I followed, looking at the plants.

This was an interesting botanical locality for one coming from the South to commence with; for many plants which are rather rare, and one or two which are not found at all, in the eastern part of Massachusetts, grew abundantly between the rails,—as Labrador tea, *Kalmia glauca,* Canada blueberry, which was still in fruit and a second time in bloom, *Clintonia* and *Linnaea borealis,* which last a lumberer called *moxon,* creeping snowberry, painted trillium, large-flowered bell-wort, etc. I fancied that the *Aster radula, Diplopappus umbellatus, Solidago lanceolatus,* red trumpet-weed, and many others which were conspicuously in bloom on the shore of the lake and on the carry, had a peculiarly wild and primitive look there. The spruce and fir trees crowded to the track on each side to welcome us, the arbor-vitae with its changing leaves prompted us to make haste, and the sight of the canoe-birch gave us spirits to do so. Sometimes an evergreen just fallen lay across the track with its rich burden of cones, looking, still, fuller of life than our trees in the most favorable positions. You did not expect to find such *spruce* trees in the wild woods, but they evidently attend to their toilets each morning even there. Through such a front-yard did we enter that wilderness.

There was a very slight rise above the lake,—the country appearing like, and perhaps being, partly a swamp,—and at length a gradual descent to the Penobscot, which I was surprised to find here a large stream, from twelve to fifteen rods wide, flowing from west to east, or at right angles with the lake, and not more than two and a half miles from it. The distance is nearly twice too great on the Map of the Public Lands, and on Colton's Map of Maine,[65] and Russell Stream is placed too far down. Jackson makes Moosehead Lake to be nine hundred and sixty feet above high water in Portland harbor.[66] It is higher than Chesuncook, for the lumberers consider the Penobscot, where we struck it, twenty-five feet lower than Moosehead, — though eight miles above it is said to be the highest, so that the water can be made to flow either way, and the river falls a good deal between here and Chesuncook. The carry-man called this about one hundred and forty miles above Bangor by the river, or two hundred from the ocean, and fifty-five miles below Hilton's on the Canada road, the first clearing above, which is four and a half miles from the source of the Penobscot.

At the north end of the carry, in the midst of a clearing of sixty acres or more, there was a log camp of the usual construction, with something more like a house adjoining, for the accommodation of the carry-man's family and passing lumberers. The bed of withered fir-twigs smelled very sweet, though really very dirty. There was also a store-house on the bank of the river, containing pork, flour, iron, batteaux, and birches, locked up.

We now proceeded to get our dinner, which always turned out to be tea, and to pitch canoes, for which purpose a large iron pot lay permanently on the bank. This we did in company with the explorers. Both Indians and whites use a mixture of rosin and grease for this purpose, — that is, for the pitching, not the dinner. Joe took a small brand from the fire and blew the heat and flame against the pitch on his birch, and so melted and spread it. Sometimes he put his mouth over the place and sucked, to see if it admitted air; and at one place,

65 George Woolworth Colton's (1827–1901) "Railroad and Township Map of the State of Maine with Portions of New Hampshire, New Brunswick, and Canada" (1855) which, according to Thoreau in "The Allegash and East Branch," copied Coffin's map.

66 Jackson wrote in the *Second Annual Report:* "I took careful observations to determine the altitude of the Lake above sea level, and upon the mean of many exact measurements, made under the most favorable circumstances, I find it to be exactly 960 feet above the high water mark of Portland harbor."

67 Allusion to Thoreau's readings in *Jesuit Relations*, such as Isaac Jogues's (1607–1646) *Novum Belgium*: "The position one must take in the canoe is very strained and uncomfortable. You cannot stretch out your legs, for the place is narrow and crowded."

where we stopped, he placed his canoe high on crossed stakes, and poured water into it. I narrowly watched his motions, and listened attentively to his observations, for we had employed an Indian mainly that I might have an opportunity to study his ways. I heard him swear once mildly, during this operation, about his knife being as dull as a hoe,—an accomplishment which he owed to his intercourse with the whites; and he remarked, "We ought to have some tea before we start; we shall be hungry before we kill that moose."

At mid-afternoon we embarked on the Penobscot. Our birch was nineteen and a half feet long by two and a half at the widest part, and fourteen inches deep within, both ends alike, and painted green, which Joe thought affected the pitch and made it leak. This, I think, was a middling-sized one. That of the explorers was much larger, though probably not much longer. This carried us three with our baggage, weighing in all between five hundred and fifty and six hundred pounds. We had two heavy, though slender, rock-maple paddles, one of them of bird's-eye maple. Joe placed birch bark on the bottom for us to sit on, and slanted cedar splints against the cross-bars to protect our backs, while he himself sat upon a cross-bar in the stern. The baggage occupied the middle or widest part of the canoe. We also paddled by turns in the bows, now sitting with our legs extended, now sitting upon our legs, and now rising upon our knees; but I found none of these positions endurable, and was reminded of the complaints of the old Jesuit missionaries of the torture they endured from long confinement in constrained positions in canoes, in their long voyages from Quebec to the Huron country;[67] but afterwards I sat on the cross-bars, or stood up, and experienced no inconvenience.

It was dead water for a couple of miles. The river had been raised about two feet by the rain, and lumberers were hoping for a flood sufficient to bring down the logs that were left in the spring. Its banks were seven or eight feet high, and densely covered with white and black spruce,—which, I think, must be the commonest trees thereabouts,—fir, arbor-vitae, canoe, yellow, and black birch, rock, mountain, and a few red maples, beech, black and mountain ash, the common and rarely the large-toothed aspen, many civil-looking elms, now imbrowned, along the stream, and at first a few hemlocks also. We had not gone far before I was startled by seeing what I thought was an Indian encampment, covered with a red flag, on the bank, and exclaimed, "Camp!" to my comrades. I was slow to discover that it was a red maple changed by the frost. The immediate shores were also densely covered with the speckled alder, red osier, shrubby willows or sallows, and the like. There were a few yellow-lily-pads still left, half drowned, along the sides, and sometimes a white one. Many fresh tracks of moose were visible where the water was shallow, and on the shore, and the lily-stems were freshly bitten off by them.

After paddling about two miles, we parted company with the explorers, and turned up Lobster Stream, which comes in on the right, from the south-east. This was six or eight rods wide, and appeared to run nearly parallel with the Penobscot. Joe said that it was so called from small fresh-water lobsters[68] found in it. It is the Matahumkeag of the maps. My companion wished to look for moose signs, and intended, if it proved worth the while, to camp up that way, since the Indian advised it. On account of the rise of the Penobscot, the water ran up this stream quite to the pond of the same name, one or two miles. The Spencer Mountains, east of the north end of Moosehead Lake, were now in plain sight in front of us. The kingfisher flew before us, the pigeon woodpecker was seen and heard, and nuthatches and chicadees close

68 Crayfish, or crawfish: any of various freshwater crustaceans of the genera *Cambarus* and *Astacus* resembling a lobster but considerably smaller.

69 In the First Annual Report of the *American Society for Promoting the Civilization and General Improvement of the Indian Tribes within the United States* (1824), Moses Greenleaf wrote: "It is rather difficult to spell Indian words, from the want of English letters to convey accurately some of the Indian sounds, and from the differences in pronunciation among the Indians themselves."

70 Cougar (*Felis concolor*), also known as a catamount and puma.

71 Wood duck (*Aix sponsa*).

at hand. Joe said that they called the chicadee *kecunni-lessu* in his language. I will not vouch for the spelling of what possibly was never spelt before,[69] but I pronounced after him till he said it would do. We passed close to a woodcock, which stood perfectly still on the shore, with feathers puffed up, as if sick. This, Joe said, they called *nipsquecohossus.* The kingfisher was *skuscumonsuck;* bear was *wassus;* Indian Devil,[70] *lunxus;* the mountain-ash, *upahsis.* This was very abundant and beautiful. Moose-tracks were not so fresh along this stream, except in a small creek about a mile up it, where a large log had lodged in the spring, marked "W-cross-girdle-crowfoot." We saw a pair of moose-horns on the shore, and I asked Joe if a moose had shed them; but he said there was a head attached to them, and I knew that they did not shed their heads more than once in their lives.

After ascending about a mile and a half, to within a short distance of Lobster Lake, we returned to the Penobscot. Just below the mouth of the Lobster we found quick water, and the river expanded to twenty or thirty rods in width. The moose-tracks were quite numerous and fresh here. We noticed in a great many places narrow and well-trodden paths by which they had come down to the river, and where they had slid on the steep and clayey bank. Their tracks were either close to the edge of the stream, those of the calves distinguishable from the others, or in shallow water; the holes made by their feet in the soft bottom being visible for a long time. They were particularly numerous where there was a small bay, or *pokelogan,* as it is called, bordered by a strip of meadow, or separated from the river by a low peninsula covered with coarse grass, wool-grass, etc., wherein they had waded back and forth and eaten the pads. We detected the remains of one in such a place. At one place, where we landed to pick up a summer duck,[71] which my companion had shot, Joe peeled a canoe-birch for bark for his hunting-horn. He then asked if we were not going to get the other duck, for his sharp eyes had seen another fall in the bushes a little further along, and my companion obtained it. I now began to notice the bright red berries of the tree-cranberry, which grows eight or ten feet high, mingled with the alders and cornel along the shore. There was less hard wood than at first.

After proceeding a mile and three quarters below the mouth of the Lobster, we reached, about sundown, a small island at the head of what Joe called the Moosehorn Dead-water, (the Moosehorn, in which he was going to hunt that night, coming in about three miles below,) and on the upper end of this we decided to camp. On a point at the lower end lay the carcass of a moose killed a month or more before. We concluded merely to prepare our camp, and leave our baggage here, that all might be ready when we returned from moosehunting. Though I had not come a-hunting, and felt some compunctions about accompanying the hunters, I wished to see a moose near at hand, and was not sorry to learn how the Indian managed to kill one. I went as reporter or chaplain to the hunters,—and the chaplain has been known to carry a gun himself.[72] After clearing a small space amid the dense spruce and fir trees, we covered the damp ground with a shingling of fir-twigs, and, while Joe was preparing his birch-horn and pitching his canoe,—for this had to be done whenever we stopped long enough to build a fire, and was the principal labor which he took upon himself at such times,— we collected fuel for the night, large wet and rotting logs, which had lodged at the head of the island, for our hatchet was too small for effective chopping; but we did not kindle a fire, lest the moose should smell it. Joe set up a couple of forked stakes, and prepared half a dozen poles, ready to cast one of our blankets over in case it rained in the night, which precaution, however,

72 Thoreau, although often averse to killing, did sometimes carry a gun. Although he had sold his gun before moving to Walden, at the time of his river excursion with his brother John a few years earlier, as they glided out of Concord, they "let our guns speak for us, when at length we had swept out of sight, and thus left the woods to ring again with their echoes" [W 1:17]. Later, on 15 February 1857, he noted in his journal: "Never undertake to ascend a mountain or thread a wilderness where there is any danger of being lost, without taking . . . perhaps a gun" [J 9:259–260].

73 Full moon nearest the autumnal equinox.
74 Myrtle warbler (*Dendroica coronata*).

was omitted the next night. We also plucked the ducks which had been killed for breakfast.

While we were thus engaged in the twilight, we heard faintly, from far down the stream, what sounded like two strokes of a woodchopper's axe, echoing dully through the grim solitude. We are wont to liken many sounds, heard at a distance in the forest, to the stroke of an axe, because they resemble each other under those circumstances, and that is the one we commonly hear there. When we told Joe of this, he exclaimed, "By George, I'll bet that was moose! They make a noise like that." These sounds affected us strangely, and by their very resemblance to a familiar one, where they probably had so different an origin, enhanced the impression of solitude and wildness.

At starlight we dropped down the stream, which was a dead-water for three miles, or as far as the Moosehorn; Joe telling us that we must be very silent, and he himself making no noise with his paddle, while he urged the canoe along with effective impulses. It was a still night, and suitable for this purpose,—for if there is wind, the moose will smell you,—and Joe was very confident that he should get some. The harvest moon[73] had just risen, and its level rays began to light up the forest on our right, while we glided downward in the shade on the same side, against the little breeze that was stirring. The lofty spiring tops of the spruce and fir were very black against the sky, and more distinct than by day, close bordering this broad avenue on each side; and the beauty of the scene, as the moon rose above the forest, it would not be easy to describe. A bat flew over our heads, and we heard a few faint notes of birds from time to time, perhaps the myrtle-bird[74] for one, or the sudden plunge of a musquash, or saw one crossing the stream before us, or heard the sound of a rill emptying in, swollen by the recent rain. About a mile below the island, when the

solitude seemed to be growing more complete every moment, we suddenly saw the light and heard the crackling
of a fire on the bank, and discovered the camp of the two
explorers; they standing before it in their red shirts, and
talking aloud of the adventures and profits of the day.
They were just then speaking of a bargain, in which, as
I understood, somebody had cleared twenty-five dollars.
We glided by without speaking, close under the bank,
within a couple of rods of them; and Joe, taking his horn,
imitated the call of the moose, till we suggested that they
might fire on us. This was the last we saw of them, and
we never knew whether they detected or suspected us.

I have often wished since that I was with them. They
search for timber over a given section, climbing hills
and often high trees to look off,—explore the streams
by which it is to be driven, and the like,—spend five or
six weeks in the woods, they two alone, a hundred miles
or more from any town,—roaming about, and sleeping
on the ground where night overtakes them,—depending
chiefly on the provisions they carry with them, though
they do not decline what game they come across,—and
then in the fall they return and make report to their em-
ployers, determining the number of teams[75] that will
be required the following winter. Experienced men get
three or four dollars a day for this work. It is a solitary
and adventurous life, and comes nearest to that of the
trapper of the West, perhaps. Working ever with a gun as
well as an axe, letting their beards grow, without neighbors, not on an open plain, but far within a wilderness.

This discovery accounted for the sounds which we
had heard, and destroyed the prospect of seeing moose
yet awhile. At length, when we had left the explorers far
behind, Joe laid down his paddle, drew forth his birch
horn,—a straight one, about fifteen inches long and
three or four wide at the mouth, tied round with strips
of the same bark,—and standing up, imitated the call

75 Springer wrote in his *Forest Life:* "What is called a team is variously composed of from four to six, and even eight oxen."

76 In Johann Wolfgang von Goethe's (1749–1832) *Italiänische Reise*, Thoreau read in German: "I plainly saw the tower of St. Mark's at Venice, with other smaller towers." On 8 December 1837 Thoreau wrote about Goethe: "He is generally satisfied with giving an exact description of objects as they appear to him, and his genius is exhibited in the points he seizes upon and illustrates. His description of Venice and her environs as seen from the Marcusthurm is that of an unconcerned spectator, whose object is faithfully to describe what he sees, and that, too, for the most part, in the order in which he saw it" [J 1:15].

of the moose,—*ugh ugh ugh*, or *oo oo oo oo*, and then a prolonged *oo-o-o-o-o-o-o*, and listened attentively for several minutes. We asked him what kind of noise he expected to hear. He said, that, if a moose heard it, he guessed we should find out; we should hear him coming half a mile off; he would come close to, perhaps into, the water, and my companion must wait till he got fair sight, and then aim just behind the shoulder.

The moose venture out to the river-side to feed and drink at night. Earlier in the season the hunters do not use a horn to call them out, but steal upon them as they are feeding along the sides of the stream, and often the first notice they have of one is the sound of the water dropping from its muzzle. An Indian whom I heard imitate the voice of the moose, and also the caribou and deer, using a much longer horn than Joe's, told me that the first could be heard eight or ten miles, sometimes; it was a loud sort of bellowing sound, clearer and more sonorous than the lowing of cattle,—the caribou's a sort of snort,—and the small deer's like that of a lamb.

At length we turned up the Moosehorn, where the Indians at the carry had told us that they killed a moose the night before. This was a very meandering stream, only a rod or two in width, but comparatively deep, coming in on the right, fitly enough named Moosehorn, whether from its windings or its inhabitants. It was bordered here and there by narrow meadows between the stream and the endless forest, which afforded favorable places for the moose to feed, and to call them out on. We proceeded half a mile up this, as through a narrow winding canal, where the tall, dark spruce and firs and arborvitae towered on both sides in the moonlight, forming a perpendicular forest-edge of great height, like the spires of a Venice[76] in the forest. In two places stood a small stack of hay on the bank, ready for the lumberer's use in the winter, looking strange enough there. We thought of the day when this might be a brook winding through smooth-shaven meadows on some gentleman's grounds; and seen by moonlight then, excepting the forest that now hems it in, how little changed it would appear!

Again and again Joe called the moose, placing the canoe close by some favorable point of meadow for them to come out on, but listened in vain to hear one come rushing through the woods, and concluded that they had been hunted too much thereabouts. We saw many times what to our imaginations looked like a gigantic moose, with his horns peering from out the forest-edge; but we saw the forest only, and not its inhabitant, that night. So at last we turned about. There was now a little fog on the water, though it was a fine, clear night above. There were very few sounds to break the stillness of the forest. Several times we heard the hooting of a great horned-owl, as at home, and told Joe that he would call out the moose for him, for he made a sound considerably like the horn,—but Joe answered, that the moose had heard that sound a thousand times, and knew better; and oftener still we were startled by the plunge of a musquash. Once, when Joe had called again, and we were listening for moose, we heard come faintly echoing, or creeping from far, through the moss-clad aisles, a dull, dry, rushing sound, with a solid core to it, yet as if half smothered under the grasp of the luxuriant and fungus-like forest, like the shutting of a door in some distant entry of the damp and shaggy wilderness. If we had not been there, no mortal had heard it. When we asked Joe in a whisper what it was, he answered,—"Tree fall." There is something singularly grand and impressive in the sound of a tree falling in a perfectly calm night like this, as if the agencies which overthrow it did not need to be excited, but worked with a subtle, deliberate, and conscious force, like a boa-constrictor, and more effectively then than even in a windy day. If there is any such

77 Thoreau wrote in his journal on 26 April 1857 that "a sermon is needed on economy of fuel. What right has my neighbor to burn ten cords of wood, when I burn only one? Thus robbing our half-naked town of this precious covering. Is he so much colder than I? It is expensive to maintain him in our midst. If some earn the salt of their porridge, are we certain that they earn the fuel of their kitchen and parlor? One man makes a little of the driftwood of the river or of the dead and refuse (unmarketable!) wood of the forest suffice, and Nature rejoices in him. Another, Herod-like, requires ten cords of the best of young white oak or hickory, and he is commonly esteemed a virtuous man. He who burns the most wood on his hearth is the least warmed by the sight of it growing. Leave the trim wood-lots to widows and orphan girls. Let men tread gently through nature. Let us religiously burn stumps and worship in groves, while Christian vandals lay waste the forest temples to build miles of meetinghouses and horse-sheds and feed their box stoves" [ITM 313–314].

78 Allusion to Paul LeJeune (1594–1662), about whom Thoreau read in *Jesuit Relations*: "As the night was coming on rapidly, I retired into the woods, to . . . get a little rest. While I was saying my prayers near a tree, the woman who managed the household of my host came to see me; and, gathering together some leaves of fallen trees, said to me, 'Lie down there and make no noise,' then, having thrown me a piece of bark as a cover, she went away. So this was my first resting place at the sign of the Moon, which shone upon me from all sides. Behold me an accomplished Chevalier, after the first day of my entrance into this Academy. The rain coming on, a little before midnight, made me fear that I might get wet, but it did not last long. The next morning I found that my bed, although it had not been made up since the creation of the world, was not so hard as to keep me from sleeping."

difference, perhaps it is because trees with the dews of the night on them are heavier than by day.

Having reached the camp, about ten o'clock, we kindled our fire and went to bed. Each of us had a blanket, in which he lay on the fir-twigs, with his extremities toward the fire, but nothing over his head. It was worth the while to lie down in a country where you could afford such great fires; that was one whole side, and the bright side, of our world. We had first rolled up a large log some eighteen inches through and ten feet long, for a back-log, to last all night, and then piled on the trees to the height of three or four feet, no matter how green or damp. In fact, we burned as much wood that night as would, with economy and an air-tight stove, last a poor family in one of our cities all winter.[77] It was very agreeable, as well as independent, this lying in the open air, and the fire kept our uncovered extremities warm enough. The Jesuit missionaries used to say, that, in their journeys with the Indians in Canada, they lay on a bed which had never been shaken up since the creation,[78] unless by earthquakes. It is surprising with what impunity and comfort one who has always lain in a warm bed in a close apartment, and studiously avoided drafts of air, can lie down on the ground without a shelter, roll himself in a blanket, and sleep before a fire, in a frosty autumn night, just after a long rain-storm, and even come soon to enjoy and value the fresh air.

I lay awake awhile, watching the ascent of the sparks through the firs, and sometimes their descent in half-extinguished cinders on to my blanket. They were as interesting as fireworks, going up in endless successive crowds, each after an explosion, in an eager serpentine course, some to five or six rods above the tree-tops before they went out. We do not suspect how much our chimneys have concealed; and now air-tight stoves have come to conceal all the rest. In the course of the night, I got up once or twice and put fresh logs on the fire, making my companions curl up their legs.

When we awoke in the morning, (Saturday, September 17,) there was considerable frost whitening the leaves. We heard the sound of the chickaree,[79] and a few faintly lisping birds, and also of ducks in the water about the island. I took a botanical account of stock of our domains before the dew was off, and found that the ground-hemlock, or American yew, was the prevailing under-shrub. We breakfasted on tea, hard bread, and ducks.

Before the fog had fairly cleared away, we paddled down the stream again, and were soon past the mouth of the Moosehorn. These twenty miles of the Penobscot, between Moosehead and Chesuncook Lakes, are comparatively smooth, and a great part dead-water; but from time to time it is shallow and rapid, with rocks or gravel-beds, where you can wade across. There is no expanse of water, and no break in the forest, and the meadow is a mere edging here and there. There are no hills near the river nor within sight, except one or two distant mountains seen in a few places. The banks are from six to ten feet high, but once or twice rise gently to higher ground. In many places the forest on the bank was but a thin strip, letting the light through from some alder-swamp or meadow behind. The conspicuous berry-bearing bushes and trees along the shore were the red osier, with its whitish fruit, hobble-bush, mountain-ash, tree-cranberry, choke-cherry, now ripe, alternate cornel, and naked viburnum. Following Joe's example, I ate the fruit of the last, and also of the hobble-bush, but found them rather insipid and seedy. I looked very narrowly at the vegetation, as we glided along close to the shore, and frequently made Joe turn aside for me to pluck a plant, that I might see by comparison what was primitive about my native river. Horehound, horsemint, and the sensi-

79 Common nineteenth-century name for the red squirrel (*Tamiasciurus hudsonicus*) from the sound it makes. In his *Week on the Concord and Merrimack Rivers* Thoreau described the chickaree's "warning of our approach by that peculiar alarum of his, like the winding up of some strong clock, in the top of a pine-tree, and dodged behind its stem, or leaped from tree to tree with such caution and adroitness, as if much depended on the fidelity of his scout, running along the white-pine boughs sometimes twenty rods by our side, with such speed, and by such unerring routes, as if it were some well-worn familiar path to him; and presently, when we have passed, he returns to his work of cutting off the pine-cones, and letting them fall to the ground" [W 1:206].

80 The olfactory sense in most birds is minimal, although it is unclear whether Thoreau was aware of this. Although Audubon conducted experiments to prove that the vulture did not use smell to locate carrion, and Thomas Nuttall (1786–1859) wrote that "the olfactory organ in birds is obviously inferior to that of quadrupeds," many works of natural history published earlier in the nineteenth century referred to the acute sense of smell in birds.

tive fern grew close to the edge, under the willows and alders, and wool-grass on the islands, as along the Assabet River in Concord. It was too late for flowers, except a few asters, golden-rods, etc. In several places we noticed the slight frame of a camp, such as we had prepared to set up, amid the forest by the river-side, where some lumberers or hunters had passed a night,—and sometimes steps cut in the muddy or clayey bank in front of it.

We stopped to fish for trout at the mouth of a small stream called Ragmuff, which came in from the west, about two miles below the Moosehorn. Here were the ruins of an old lumbering-camp, and a small space, which had formerly been cleared and burned over, was now densely overgrown with the red cherry and raspberries. While we were trying for trout, Joe, Indian-like, wandered off up the Ragmuff on his own errands, and when we were ready to start was far beyond call. So we were compelled to make a fire and get our dinner here, not to lose time. Some dark reddish birds, with grayer females, (perhaps purple finches,) and myrtle-birds in their summer dress, hopped within six or eight feet of us and our smoke. Perhaps they smelled[80] the frying pork. The latter bird, or both, made the lisping notes which I had heard in the forest. They suggested that the few small birds found in the wilderness are on more familiar terms with the lumberman and hunter than those of the orchard and clearing with the farmer. I have since found the Canada jay, and partridges, both the black and the common, equally tame there, as if they had not yet learned to mistrust man entirely. The chicadee, which is at home alike in the primitive woods and in our wood-lots, still retains its confidence in the towns to a remarkable degree.

Joe at length returned, after an hour and a half, and said that he had been two miles up the stream exploring, and had seen a moose, but, not having the gun, he did not get him. We made no complaint, but concluded to look out for Joe the next time. However, this may have been a mere mistake, for we had no reason to complain of him afterwards. As we continued down the stream, I was surprised to hear him whistling "O Susanna,"[81] and several other such airs, while his paddle urged us along. Once he said, "Yes, Sir-ee."[82] His common word was "Sartain." He paddled, as usual, on one side only, giving the birch an impulse by using the side as a fulcrum. I asked him how the ribs were fastened to the side rails. He answered, "I don't know, I never noticed." Talking with him about subsisting wholly on what the woods yielded, game, fish, berries, etc., I suggested that his ancestors did so; but he answered, that he had been brought up in such a way that he could not do it. "Yes," said he, "that's the way they got a living, like wild fellows, wild as bears. By George![83] I shan't go into the woods without provision,—hard bread, pork, etc." He had brought on a barrel of hard bread and stored it at the carry for his hunting. However, though he was a Governor's son, he had not learned to read.

At one place below this, on the east side, where the bank was higher and drier than usual, rising gently from the shore to a slight elevation, some one had felled the trees over twenty or thirty acres, and left them drying in order to burn. This was the only preparation for a house between the Moosehead carry and Chesuncook, but there was no hut nor inhabitants there yet. The pioneer thus selects a site for his house, which will, perhaps, prove the germ of a town.

My eyes were all the while on the trees, distinguishing between the black and white spruce and the fir. You paddle along in a narrow canal through an endless forest, and the vision I have in my mind's eye, still, is of the small dark and sharp tops of tall fir and spruce trees, and pagoda-like arbor-vitaes, crowded together on each side,

81 Stephen Foster's (1826–1864) minstrel song, written in 1847 and first published the following year.
82 Considered in John Russell Bartlett's (1805–1886) *Dictionary of Americanisms* (1877) as "vulgar slang, which originated in New York, [and] is now heard throughout the Union."
83 Minced oath for "by God."

84 Etched in and printed from copper plates which, being soft, have a short life and create a less-defined image, as opposed to steel engravings which are more durable and sharper.

85 Literary productions published annually, often handsomely bound, illustrated with plates, and containing prose tales, poems, and other literary works, published from the mid-1820s through the 1850s. American literary annuals included the *Boston Book,* the *Liberty Bell,* and the *Gift.*

86 A detail from an engraving from Jackson's *Second Report:*

with various hard woods intermixed. Some of the arbor-vitaes were at least sixty feet high. The hard woods, occasionally occurring exclusively, were less wild to my eye. I fancied them ornamental grounds, with farm-houses in the rear. The canoe and yellow birch, beech, maple, and elm are Saxon and Norman; but the spruce and fir, and pines generally, are Indian. The soft engravings[84] which adorn the annuals[85] give no idea of a stream in such a wilderness as this. The rough sketches in Jackson's Reports on the Geology of Maine[86] answer much better. At one place we saw a small grove of slender sapling white-pines, the only collection of pines that I saw on this voyage. Here and there, however, was a full-grown, tall, and slender, but defective one, what lumbermen call a *konchus* tree, which they ascertain with their axes, or by the knots. I did not learn whether this word was Indian or English. It reminded me of the Greek κόγχη, a conch or shell, and I amused myself with fancying that it might signify the dead sound which the trees yield when struck. All the rest of the pines had been driven off.

How far men go for the material of their houses! The inhabitants of the most civilized cities, in all ages, send into far, primitive forests, beyond the bounds of their civilization, where the moose and bear and savage dwell, for their pine-boards for ordinary use. And, on the other hand, the savage soon receives from cities iron arrow-points, hatchets, and guns to point his savageness with.

The solid and well-defined fir-tops, like sharp and regular spear-heads, black against the sky, gave a peculiar, dark, and sombre look to the forest. The spruce-tops have a similar, but more ragged outline, — their shafts also merely feathered below. The firs were somewhat oftener regular and dense pyramids. I was struck by this universal spiring upward of the forest evergreens. The tendency is to slender, spiring tops, while they are narrower below. Not only the spruce and fir, but even the arbor-vitae and white-pine, unlike the soft, spreading second-growth, of which I saw none, all spire upwards, lifting a dense spear-head of cones to the light and air, at any rate, while their branches straggle after as they may; as Indians lift the ball over the heads of the crowd in their desperate game.[87] In this they resemble grasses, as also palms somewhat. The hemlock is commonly a tent-like pyramid from the ground to its summit.

After passing through some long rips[88] and by a large island, we reached an interesting part of the river called the Pine-Stream Dead-Water, about six miles below Rag-muff, where the river expanded to thirty rods in width and had many islands in it, with elms and canoe-birches, now yellowing, along the shore, and we got our first sight of Ktaadn.

Here, about two o'clock, we turned up a small branch three or four rods wide, which comes in on the right from the south, called Pine Stream, to look for moose signs. We had gone but a few rods before we saw very recent signs along the water's edge, the mud lifted up by their feet being quite fresh, and Joe declared that they had gone along there but a short time before. We soon reached a small meadow on the east side, at an angle in the stream, which was for the most part densely covered with alders. As we were advancing along the edge of this, rather more quietly than usual, perhaps, on account of the freshness of the signs, — the design being to camp up this stream, if it promised well, — I heard a slight crack-ling of twigs deep in the alders, and turned Joe's atten-tion to it; whereupon he began to push the canoe back rapidly; and we had receded thus half a dozen rods, when we suddenly spied two moose standing just on the edge of the open part of the meadow which we had passed, not more than six or seven rods distant, looking round the alders at us. They made me think of great frightened rabbits, with their long ears and half-inquisitive, half-

87 Version of lacrosse which Alexander Henry (1739–1824) described in his *Travels and Adventures in Canada and the Indian Territories Between the Years 1760 and 1776*: "*Baggatiway*, called, by the Canadians, *le jeu de la crosse*, is played with a bat and ball. The bat is about four feet in length, curved, and terminating in a sort of racket. Two posts are planted in the ground, at a considerable distance from each other, as a mile, or more. Each party has its post, and the game consists in throw-ing the ball up to the post of the adversary. The ball, at the beginning, is placed in the middle of the course, and each party endeavours as well to throw the ball out of the direction of its own post, as into that of the adversary's."
88 Stretches of turbulent water in a river caused by one current crossing or flowing into another current.

89 Coarse, undyed cloth made of homespun wool.

frightened looks; the true denizens of the forest, (I saw at once,) filling a vacuum which now first I discovered had not been filled for me,—*moose*-men, *wood-eaters,* the word is said to mean,—clad in a sort of Vermont gray, or homespun.[89] Our Nimrod, owing to the retrograde movement, was now the furthest from the game; but being warned of its neighborhood, he hastily stood up, and, while we ducked, fired over our heads one barrel at the foremost, which alone he saw, though he did not know what kind of creature it was; whereupon this one dashed across the meadow and up a high bank on the northeast, so rapidly as to leave but an indistinct impression of its outlines on my mind. At the same instant, the other, a young one, but as tall as a horse, leaped out into the stream, in full sight, and there stood cowering for a moment, or rather its disproportionate lowness behind gave it that appearance, and uttering two or three trumpeting squeaks. I have an indistinct recollection of seeing the old one pause an instant on the top of the bank in the woods, look toward its shivering young, and then dash away again. The second barrel was levelled at the calf, and when we expected to see it drop in the water, after a little hesitation, it, too, got out of the water, and dashed up the hill, though in a somewhat different direction. All this was the work of a few seconds, and our hunter, having never seen a moose before, did not know but they were deer, for they stood partly in the water, nor whether he had fired at the same one twice or not. From the style in which they went off, and the fact that he was not used to standing up and firing from a canoe, I judged that we should not see anything more of them. The Indian said that they were a cow and her calf,—a yearling, or perhaps two years old, for they accompany their dams so long; but, for my part, I had not noticed much difference in their size. It was but two or three rods across the meadow to the foot of the bank, which, like all the world thereabouts, was densely wooded; but I was surprised to notice, that, as soon as the moose had passed behind the veil of the woods, there was no sound of footsteps to be heard from the soft, damp moss which carpets that forest, and long before we landed, perfect silence reigned. Joe said, "If you wound 'em moose, me sure get 'em."

We all landed at once. My companion reloaded; the Indian fastened his birch, threw off his hat, adjusted his waistband, seized the hatchet, and set out. He told me afterward, casually, that before we landed he had seen a drop of blood on the bank, when it was two or three rods off. He proceeded rapidly up the bank and through the woods, with a peculiar, elastic, noiseless, and stealthy tread, looking to right and left on the ground, and stepping in the faint tracks of the wounded moose, now and then pointing in silence to a single drop of blood on the handsome, shining leaves of the *Clintonia borealis*, which, on every side, covered the ground, or to a dry fern-stem freshly broken, all the while chewing some leaf or else the spruce gum. I followed, watching his motions more than the trail of the moose. After following the trail about forty rods in a pretty direct course, stepping over fallen trees and winding between standing ones, he at length lost it, for there were many other moose-tracks there, and, returning once more to the last blood-stain, traced it a little way and lost it again, and, too soon, I thought, for a good hunter, gave it up entirely. He traced a few steps, also, the tracks of the calf; but, seeing no blood, soon relinquished the search.

I observed, while he was tracking the moose, a certain reticence or moderation in him. He did not communicate several observations of interest which he made, as a white man would have done, though they may have leaked out afterward. At another time, when we heard a slight crackling of twigs and he landed to reconnoitre, he stepped lightly and gracefully, stealing through the bushes with the least possible noise, in a way in which no white man does,—as it were, finding a place for his foot each time.

About half an hour after seeing the moose, we pursued our voyage up Pine Stream, and soon, coming to a part which was very shoal and also rapid, we took out the baggage, and proceeded to carry it round, while Joe got up with the canoe alone. We were just completing our portage and I was absorbed in the plants, admiring the leaves of the *Aster macrophyllus,* ten inches wide, and plucking the seeds of the great round-leaved orchis, when Joe exclaimed from the stream that he had killed a moose. He had found the cow-moose lying dead, but quite warm, in the middle of the stream, which was so shallow that it rested on the bottom, with hardly a third of its body above water. It was about an hour after it was shot, and it was swollen with water. It had run about a hundred rods and sought the stream again, cutting off a slight bend. No doubt, a better hunter would have tracked it to this spot at once. I was surprised at its great size, horse-like, but Joe said it was not a large cow-moose. My companion went in search of the calf again. I took hold of the ears of the moose, while Joe pushed his canoe down stream toward a favorable shore, and so we made out, though with some difficulty, its long nose frequently sticking in the bottom, to drag it into still shallower water. It was a brownish black, or perhaps a dark iron-gray, on the back and sides, but lighter beneath and in front. I took the cord which served for the canoe's painter, and with Joe's assistance measured it carefully, the greatest distances first, making a knot each time. The painter being wanted, I reduced these measures that night with equal care to lengths and fractions of my umbrella, beginning with the smallest measures, and untying the knots as I proceeded; and when we arrived at Chesuncook the next day, finding a two-foot rule there, I reduced the last to feet and inches; and, moreover, I made myself a two-foot rule of a thin and narrow strip of black ash which would fold up conveniently to six inches. All this pains I took because I did not wish to be obliged to say merely that the moose was very large. Of the various dimensions which I obtained I will mention only two. The distance from the tips of the hoofs of the fore-feet, stretched out, to the top of the back between the shoulders, was seven feet and five inches. I can hardly believe my own measure, for this is about two feet greater than the height of a tall horse. [Indeed, I am now satisfied that this measurement was incorrect, but the other measures given here I can warrant to be correct, having proved them in a more recent visit to those woods.] The extreme length was eight feet and two inches. Another cow-moose, which I have since measured in those woods with a tape, was just six feet from the tip of the hoof to the shoulders, and eight feet long as she lay.[90]

When afterward I asked an Indian at the carry how much taller the male was, he answered, "Eighteen inches," and made me observe the height of a cross-stake over the fire, more than four feet from the ground, to give me an idea of the depth of his chest. Another Indian, at Old-town, told me that they were nine feet high to the top of the back, and that one which he tried weighed eight hundred pounds. The length of the spinal projections between the shoulders is very great. A white hunter,[91] who was the best authority among hunters that I could have, told me that the male was *not* eighteen inches taller than the female; yet he agreed that he was sometimes nine feet high to the top of the back, and weighed a thousand pounds. Only the male has horns, and they rise two feet or more above the shoulders,—spreading three or four, and sometimes six feet,—which would make him in all, sometimes, eleven feet high! According to this calculation, the moose is as tall, though it may not be as

90 That killed in "The Allegash and East Branch."
91 Probably Hiram Lewis Leonard, whom Thoreau met in July 1857 and referred to as the "chief white hunter of Maine" in "The Allegash and East Branch."

92 Quoted from Gideon Algernon Mantell's (1790–1862) *Wonders of Geology.*

93 Giraffe, so called from a certain resemblance in form to a camel, and from its leopardlike spotted coloration. Thoreau would have seen a stuffed camelopard at the Boston Museum, which opened in 1841. It is unlikely that he saw a living one—he does not, in any case, mention one—in the traveling menagerie about which he wrote on 26 June 1851: "I am always surprised to see the same spots and stripes on wild beasts from Africa and Asia and also from South America,—on the Brazilian tiger and the African leopard,—and their general similarity. All these wild animals—lions, tigers, chetas, leopards, etc." [J 2:271]. The first living giraffe Thoreau is known to have viewed was not until his post-Chesuncook excursion to New York in November 1854.

94 Kind of marine plant, seaweed or rockweed, characterized by dichotomously branching fronds in which there is no distinction of stem and leaves.

large, as the great Irish elk, *Megaceros Hibernicus,* of a former period, of which Mantell says that it "very far exceeded in magnitude any living species, the skeleton" being "upwards of ten feet high from the ground to the highest point of the antlers."[92] Joe said, that, though the moose shed the whole horn annually, each new horn has an additional prong; but I have noticed that they sometimes have more prongs on one side than on the other. I was struck with the delicacy and tenderness of the hoofs, which divide very far up, and the one half could be pressed very much behind the other, thus probably making the animal surer-footed on the uneven ground and slippery moss-covered logs of the primitive forest. They were very unlike the stiff and battered feet of our horses and oxen. The bare, horny part of the fore-foot was just six inches long, and the two portions could be separated four inches at the extremities.

The moose is singularly grotesque and awkward to look at. Why should it stand so high at the shoulders? Why have so long a head? Why have no tail to speak of? for in my examination I overlooked it entirely. Naturalists say it is one inch and a half long. It reminded me at once of the camelopard,[93] high before and low behind,—and no wonder, for, like it, it is fitted to browse on trees. The upper lip projected two inches beyond the lower for this purpose. This was the kind of man that was at home there; for, as near as I can learn, that has never been the residence, but rather the hunting-ground of the Indian. The moose will perhaps one day become extinct; but how naturally then, when it exists only as a fossil relic, and unseen as that, may the poet or sculptor invent a fabulous animal with similar branching and leafy horns,—a sort of fucus[94] or lichen in bone,—to be the inhabitant of such a forest as this!

Here, just at the head of the murmuring rapids, Joe now proceeded to skin the moose with a pocket-knife, while I looked on; and a tragical business it was,—to see that still warm and palpitating body pierced with a knife, to see the warm milk stream from the rent udder, and the ghastly naked red carcass appearing from within its seemly robe, which was made to *hide* it. The ball had passed through the shoulder-blade diagonally and lodged under the skin on the opposite side, and was partially flattened. My companion keeps it to show to his grandchildren. He has the shanks of another moose which he has since shot, skinned and stuffed, ready to be made into boots by putting in a thick leather sole. Joe said, if a moose stood fronting you, you must not fire, but advance toward him, for he will turn slowly and give you a fair shot. In the bed of this narrow, wild, and rocky stream, between two lofty walls of spruce and firs, a mere cleft in the forest which the stream had made, this work went on. At length Joe had stripped off the hide and dragged it trailing to the shore, declaring that it weighed a hundred pounds, though probably fifty would have been nearer the truth. He cut off a large mass of the meat to carry along, and another, together with the tongue and nose, he put with the hide on the shore to lie there all night, or till we returned. I was surprised that he thought of leaving this meat thus exposed by the side of the carcass, as the simplest course, not fearing that any creature would touch it; but nothing did. This could hardly have happened on the bank of one of our rivers in the eastern part of Massachusetts; but I suspect that fewer small wild animals are prowling there than with us. Twice, however, in this excursion I had a glimpse of a species of large mouse.

This stream was so withdrawn, and the moose-tracks were so fresh, that my companions, still bent on hunting, concluded to go further up it and camp, and then hunt up or down at night. Half a mile above this, at a place where I saw the *Aster puniceus* and the beaked hazel, as we paddled along, Joe, hearing a slight rustling amid the alders, and seeing something black about two rods off, jumped up and whispered, "Bear!" but before the hunter had discharged his piece, he corrected himself to "Beaver!"—"Hedgehog!" The bullet killed a large hedgehog, more than two feet and eight inches long. The quills were rayed out and flattened on the hinder part of its back, even as if it had lain on that part, but were erect and long between this and the tail. Their points, closely examined, were seen to be finely bearded or barbed, and shaped like an awl, that is, a little concave, to give the barbs effect. After about a mile of still water, we prepared our camp on the right side, just at the foot of a considerable fall. Little chopping was done that night, for fear of scaring the moose. We had moose-meat fried for supper. It tasted like tender beef, with perhaps more flavor,—sometimes like veal.

After supper, the moon having risen, we proceeded to hunt a mile up this stream, first "carrying" about the falls. We made a picturesque sight, wending single-file along the shore, climbing over rocks and logs,—Joe, who brought up the rear, twirling his canoe in his hands as if it were a feather, in places where it was difficult to get along without a burden. We launched the canoe again from the ledge over which the stream fell, but after half a mile of still water, suitable for hunting, it became rapid again, and we were compelled to make our way along the shore, while Joe endeavored to get up in the birch alone, though it was still very difficult for him to pick his way amid the rocks in the night. We on the shore found the worst of walking, a perfect chaos of fallen and drifted trees, and of bushes projecting far over the water, and now and then we made our way across the mouth of a small tributary on a kind of net-work of alders. So we went tumbling on in the dark, being on the shady side, effectually scaring all the moose and bears that might be thereabouts. At length we came to a standstill, and Joe went forward to reconnoitre; but he reported that it was still a continuous rapid as far as he went, or half a mile, with no prospect of improvement, as if it were coming down from a mountain. So we turned about, hunting back to the camp through the still water. It was a splendid moonlight night, and I, getting sleepy as it grew late,—for I had nothing to do,—found it difficult to realize where I was. This was much more unfrequented than the main stream, lumbering operations being no longer carried on in this quarter. It was only three or four rods wide, but the firs and spruce through which it trickled seemed yet taller by contrast. Being in this dreamy state, which the moonlight enhanced, I did not clearly discern the shore, but seemed, most of the time, to be floating through ornamental grounds,—for I associated the fir-tops with such scenes;—very high up some Broadway, and beneath or between their tops, I thought I saw an endless succession of porticos and columns, cornices and façades, verandas and churches.[95] I did not merely fancy this, but in my drowsy state such was the illusion. I fairly lost myself in sleep several times, still dreaming of that architecture and the nobility that dwelt behind and might issue from it; but all at once I would be aroused and brought back to a sense of my actual position by the sound of Joe's birch horn in the midst of all this silence calling the moose, *ugh, ugh, oo-oo-oo-oo-oo-oo,* and I prepared to hear a furious moose come rushing and crashing through the forest, and see him burst out on to the little strip of meadow by our side.

But, on more accounts than one, I had had enough of moose-hunting. I had not come to the woods for this purpose, nor had I foreseen it, though I had been willing to learn how the Indian manoeuvred; but one moose killed was as good, if not as bad, as a dozen. The afternoon's tragedy, and my share in it, as it affected the inno-

95 Sites familiar to Thoreau from the period, May through December 1843, when he served as a private tutor to the children of William Emerson (1801–1868) on Staten Island.

cence, destroyed the pleasure of my adventure. It is true, I came as near being a hunter and miss it, as possible myself; and as it is, I think that I could spend a year in the woods, fishing and hunting, just enough to sustain myself, with satisfaction. This would be next to living like a philosopher on the fruits of the earth which you had raised, which also attracts me. But this hunting of the moose merely for the satisfaction of killing him, — not even for the sake of his hide, — without making any extraordinary exertion or running any risk yourself, is too much like going out by night to some wood-side pasture and shooting your neighbor's horses. These are God's own horses, poor, timid creatures, that will run fast enough as soon as they smell you, though they *are* nine feet high. Joe told us of some hunters who a year or two before had shot down several oxen by night, somewhere in the Maine woods, mistaking them for moose. And so might any of the hunters; and what is the difference in the sport, but the name? In the former case, having killed one of God's and *your own* oxen, you strip off its hide, — because that is the common trophy, and, moreover, you have heard that it may be sold for moccasins, — cut a steak from its haunches, and leave the huge carcass to smell to heaven for you. It is no better, at least, than to assist at a slaughter-house.

This afternoon's experience suggested to me how base or coarse are the motives which commonly carry men into the wilderness. The explorers and lumberers generally are all hirelings, paid so much a day for their labor, and as such they have no more love for wild nature than wood-sawyers have for forests. Other white men and Indians who come here are for the most part hunters, whose object is to slay as many moose and other wild animals as possible. But, pray, could not one spend some weeks or years in the solitude of this vast wilderness with other employments than these, — employments perfectly sweet and innocent and ennobling? For one that comes with a pencil to sketch or sing, a thousand come with an axe or rifle. What a coarse and imperfect use Indians and hunters make of Nature! No wonder that their race is so soon exterminated. I already, and for weeks afterward, felt my nature the coarser for this part of my woodland experience, and was reminded that our life should be lived as tenderly and daintily as one would pluck a flower.

With these thoughts, when we reached our camping-ground, I decided to leave my companions to continue moose-hunting down the stream, while I prepared the camp, though they requested me not to chop much nor make a large fire, for fear I should scare their game. In the midst of the damp fir-wood, high on the mossy bank, about nine o'clock of this bright moonlight night, I kindled a fire, when they were gone, and, sitting on the fir-twigs, within sound of the falls, examined by its light the botanical specimens which I had collected that afternoon, and wrote down some of the reflections which I have here expanded;⁹⁶ or I walked along the shore and gazed up the stream, where the whole space above the falls was filled with mellow light. As I sat before the fire on my fir-twig seat, without walls above or around me, I remembered how far on every hand that wilderness stretched, before you came to cleared or cultivated fields, and wondered if any bear or moose was watching the light of my fire; for Nature looked sternly upon me on account of the murder of the moose.⁹⁷

Strange that so few ever come to the woods to see how the pine lives and grows and spires, lifting its evergreen arms to the light,—to see its perfect success; but most are content to behold it in the shape of many broad boards brought to market, and deem *that* its true success! But the pine is no more lumber than man is, and to be made into boards and houses is no more its true and

96 Thoreau's practice was to write minutes in a field notebook and afterward, usually the same evening when he got home, or in this case back to camp, he transcribed those entries into his journal. Later, they may be still further expanded, or combined with other journal entries, to form part of a lecture or essay.

97 Thoreau made several references to the taking of animal life as murder. In a letter of 16 February 1847 Thoreau wrote regarding birds: "I confess to a little squeamishness on the score of robbing their nests, though I could easily go to the length of abstracting an egg or two gently, now and then, and if the advancement of science obviously demanded it might be carried to the extreme of deliberate murder" [C 175]. Although in "The Ponds" chapter of *Walden* he somewhat lightly referred to fishing as "piscine murder" [Wa 181], in the "Higher Laws" chapter he explained: "We cannot but pity the boy who has never fired a gun; he is no more humane, while his education has been sadly neglected. This was my answer with respect to those youths who were bent on this pursuit, trusting that they would soon outgrow it. No humane being, past the thoughtless age of boyhood, will wantonly murder any creature, which holds its life by the same tenure that he does" [Wa 204].

98 Moral principles or laws of conscience that take precedence over the constitutions or statutes of society. The concept of higher law can be found in the Judeo-Christian belief in moral law, as well as in the idea of a natural law formulated by Plato and Cicero. In "On the Republic" Cicero wrote: "There is in fact a true law—namely, right reason—which is in accordance with nature, applies to all men, and is unchangeable and eternal. By its commands it summons men to the performance of their duties; by its prohibitions it restrains them from doing wrong. To invalidate this law by human legislation is never morally right, nor is it permissible ever to restrict its operation; and to annul it wholly is impossible."

99 Americanism from the mid-nineteenth century, meaning to have faced and overcome adversities, often used by those who had traveled west during the gold rush. It is a variation of the sixteenth century British expression, to see the lions, meaning to see something of celebrity or note.

100 Stripping trees of bark, a source of tannic acid, for use in the tanning of leather.

101 To make a hole or cut in a tree, to procure the sap.

102 In Greek mythology, the nymph Pitys was transformed into a pine to escape the advances of Pan.

103 Thoreau wrote in his journal 3 March 1839 that the poet "must be something more than natural,—even supernatural. Nature will not speak through but along with him. His voice will not proceed from her midst, but, breathing on her, will make her the expression of his thought. He then poetizes when he takes a fact out of nature into spirit. He speaks without reference to time or place. His thought is one world, hers another. He is another Nature,—Nature's brother. Kindly offices do they perform for one another. Each publishes the other's truth" [ITM 11]. Emerson explained in his essay "The Poet": "The poet is the sayer, the namer, and represents beauty. . . . The poet does not wait for the hero or the sage, but, as they act and think primarily, so he writes

highest use than the truest use of a man is to be cut down and made into manure. There is a higher law[98] affecting our relation to pines as well as to men. A pine cut down, a dead pine, is no more a pine than a dead human carcass is a man. Can he who has discovered only some of the values of whalebone and whale oil be said to have discovered the true use of the whale? Can he who slays the elephant for his ivory be said to have "seen the elephant"?[99] These are petty and accidental uses; just as if a stronger race were to kill us in order to make buttons and flageolets of our bones; for everything may serve a lower as well as a higher use. Every creature is better alive than dead, men and moose and pine-trees, and he who understands it aright will rather preserve its life than destroy it.

Is it the lumberman, then, who is the friend and lover of the pine, stands nearest to it, and understands its nature best? Is it the tanner who has barked it,[100] or he who has boxed[101] it for turpentine, whom posterity will fable was changed into a pine at last?[102] No! no! it is the poet;[103] he it is who makes the truest use of the pine,— who does not fondle it with an axe, nor tickle it with a saw, nor stroke it with a plane,—who knows whether its heart is false without cutting into it,—who has not bought the stumpage[104] of the township on which it stands. All the pines shudder and heave a sigh when *that* man steps on the forest floor. No, it is the poet, who loves them as his own shadow in the air, and lets them stand. I have been into the lumber-yard, and the carpenter's shop, and the tannery, and the lampblack-factory,[105] and the turpentine clearing;[106] but when at length I saw the tops of the pines waving and reflecting the light at a distance high over all the rest of the forest, I realized that the former were not the highest use of the pine. It is not their bones or hide or tallow that I love most. It is the living spirit of the tree, not its spirit of turpentine, with which I sympathize, and which heals my cuts.[107] It is as immortal as I am, and perchance will go to as high a heaven, there to tower above me still.

Ere long, the hunters returned, not having seen a moose, but, in consequence of my suggestions, bringing a quarter of the dead one, which, with ourselves, made quite a load for the canoe.

After breakfasting on moose-meat, we returned down Pine Stream on our way to Chesuncook Lake, which was about five miles distant. We could see the red carcass of the moose lying in Pine Stream when nearly half a mile off. Just below the mouth of this stream were the most considerable rapids between the two lakes, called Pine-Stream Falls, where were large flat rocks washed smooth, and at this time you could easily wade across above them. Joe ran down alone while we walked over the portage, my companion collecting spruce gum for his friends at home, and I looking for flowers. Near the lake, which we were approaching with as much expectation as if it had been a university,—for it is not often that the stream of our life opens into such expansions,—were islands, and a low and meadowy shore with scattered trees, birches, white and yellow, slanted over the water, and maples,— many of the white birches killed, apparently by inundations. There was considerable native grass; and even a few cattle—whose movements we heard, though we did not see them, mistaking them at first for moose—were pastured there.

On entering the lake, where the stream runs southeasterly, and for some time before, we had a view of the mountains about Ktaadn, (*Katahdinauguoh* one[108] says they are called,) like a cluster of blue fungi of rank growth, apparently twenty-five or thirty miles distant, in a southeast direction, their summits concealed by clouds. Joe called some of them the *Souadneunk* mountains. This is the name of a stream there, which another Indian told us meant "Running between mountains."

primarily what will and must be spoken. . . . For it is not metres, but a metre-making argument, that makes a poem."

104 Timber in standing trees, often sold without the land at a fixed price per tree or per stump.

105 Lampblack, also known as blacking: a fine soot formed by the condensation of the smoke of burning pitch or other resinous substances, used as a pigment in shoe polish.

106 Cleared area in a pine wood where pine resin is gathered, possibly distilled, and barreled.

107 Oil of turpentine: used externally as, among other properties, an antiseptic.

108 Moses Greenleaf on his 1829 *A Survey of the State of Maine.*

109 Probably a mistranscription from Jackson: "Chesuncook Lake is a fine sheet of water, extending N.E. and S.W. 18 miles, and about 2 in width. There are no islands in it."

110 Ansel Smith (1815–1879), who settled here in 1849, was not at home at the time of Thoreau's visit.

111 A large flat-bottomed boat.

112 Also known as head-works, a large raft mounted with a windlass or capstan, a broad revolving cylinder used for winding rope or cable.

113 In Greek mythology, the Argo launched from the ancient Thessalean city of Iolkus. See "Ktaadn," n. 146.

114 Ansel Smith's brother, unidentified further.

Though some lower summits were afterward uncovered, we got no more complete view of Ktaadn while we were in the woods. The clearing to which we were bound was on the right of the mouth of the river, and was reached by going round a low point, where the water was shallow to a great distance from the shore. Chesuncook Lake extends northwest and southeast, and is called eighteen miles long and three wide, without an island.[109] We had entered the northwest corner of it, and when near the shore could see only part way down it. The principal mountains visible from the land here were those already mentioned, between southeast and east, and a few summits a little west of north, but generally the north and northwest horizon about the St. John and the British boundary was comparatively level.

Ansel Smith's,[110] the oldest and principal clearing about this lake, appeared to be quite a harbor for batteaux and canoes; seven or eight of the former were lying about, and there was a small scow[111] for hay, and a capstan on a platform, now high and dry, ready to be floated and anchored to tow rafts with.[112] It was a very primitive kind of harbor, where boats were drawn up amid the stumps,—such a one, methought, as the Argo[113] might have been launched in. There were five other huts with small clearings on the opposite side of the lake, all at this end and visible from this point. One of the Smiths[114] told me that it was so far cleared that they came here to live and built the present house four years before, though the family had been here but a few months.

I was interested to see how a pioneer lived on this side of the country. His life is in some respects more adventurous than that of his brother in the West; for he contends with winter as well as the wilderness, and there is a greater interval of time at least between him and the army which is to follow. Here immigration is a tide which may ebb when it has swept away the pines; there it is not a tide, but an inundation, and roads and other improvements come steadily rushing after.

As we approached the log-house, a dozen rods from the lake, and considerably elevated above it, the projecting ends of the logs lapping over each other irregularly several feet at the corners gave it a very rich and picturesque look, far removed from the meanness of weatherboards.[115] It was a very spacious, low building, about eighty feet long, with many large apartments. The walls were well clayed between the logs, which were large and round, except on the upper and under sides, and as visible inside as out, successive bulging cheeks gradually lessening upwards and tuned to each other with the axe, like Pandean pipes.[116] Probably the musical forest-gods had not yet cast them aside; they never do till they are split or the bark is gone. It was a style of architecture not described by Vitruvius,[117] I suspect, though possibly hinted at in the biography of Orpheus;[118] none of your frilled or fluted columns, which have cut such a false swell, and support nothing but a gable end and their builder's pretensions,—that is, with the multitude; and as for "ornamentation," one of those words with a dead tail[119] which architects very properly use to describe their flourishes,[120] there were the lichens and mosses and fringes of bark, which nobody troubled himself about. We certainly leave the handsomest paint and clapboards behind in the woods, when we strip off the bark and poison ourselves with white-lead[121] in the towns. We get but half the spoils of the forest. For beauty, give me trees with the fur on. This house was designed and constructed with the freedom of stroke of a forester's axe, without other compass and square than Nature uses. Wherever the logs were cut off by a window or door, that is, were not kept in place by alternate overlapping, they were held one upon another by very large pins driven in diagonally on each side, where branches might have been, and then cut

115 A facing of thin boards, having usually a feather edge, and nailed lapping one over another, used as siding; similar to, although larger and wider than, clapboards.

116 Panpipes: musical wind instrument consisting of graduated tubes fastened together and closed at one end, named for the Greek god Pan.

117 Marcus Vitruvius Pollio (first century B.C.E.), Roman architect and author of *De Architectura*.

118 In Greek mythology, Orpheus raised the walls of Thebes with his music. Carlyle wrote in *Sartor Resartus*: "Were it not wonderful, for instance, had Orpheus, or Amphion, built the walls of Thebes by the mere sound of his Lyre? . . . Not only was Thebes built by the music of an Orpheus; but without the music of some inspired Orpheus was no city ever built, no work that man glories in ever done." Thoreau wrote in his journal of 11 January 1852: "Grow your own house, I say. Build it after an Orphean fashion. When R. W. E. and Greenough have got a few blocks finished and advertised, I will look at them. When they have got my ornaments ready I will wear them" [J 9:182].

119 On 26 January 1858 Thoreau wrote: "Some men have a peculiar taste for bad words, mouthing and licking them into lumpish shapes like the bear her cubs,—words like 'tribal' and 'ornamentation,' which drag a dead tail after them. They will pick you out of a thousand the still-born words, the falsettos, the wing-clipped and lame words, as if only the false notes caught their ears. They cry encore to all the discords" [J 10:261–262].

120 Allusion to Horatio Greenough (1805–1852), sculptor, who was an early proponent of the idea of functional architectural decoration and about whom Thoreau wrote in *Walden:* "I have heard of one at least possessed with the idea of making architectural ornaments have a core of truth, a necessity, and hence a beauty, as if it were a revelation to him. All very well perhaps from his point of view, but only a little better than the common dilettantism. A sentimental reformer in architecture, he began at the cornice, not at the foundation. . . . A great proportion of architectural ornaments are

literally hollow, and a September gale would strip them off, like borrowed plumes, without injury to the substantials" [Wa 45–46].

121 A carbonate of lead, primarily used in painting.

122 Pioneers would sometimes sleep in a hollow tree until a more permanent shelter could be built. Thoreau referred to the hollow tree as a residence several times in *Walden* and wrote in a journal entry of 15 May 1858: "Measured two apple trees by the road from the middle of Bedford and Fitch's mill. One, which divided at the ground, was thirteen and a half feet in circumference there, around the double trunk; but another, in a field on the opposite side of the road, was the most remarkable tree for size. This tree was exceedingly low for the size of its trunk, and the top rather small. At three feet from the ground it measured ten and a quarter feet in circumference, and immediately above this sent off a branch as big as a large apple tree. It was hollow, and on one side part of the trunk had fallen out. These trees mark the residence of an old settler evidently" [J 10:422].

123 In Thoreau's day, a place for keeping food or other articles cool, usually by means of ice.

124 Narrow two-hand saw for cutting timber lengthwise.

125 In the laying and overlapping of shingles, that part that remains exposed to the weather.

126 On the farm of Thomas J. Grant.

off so close up and down as not to project beyond the bulge of the log, as if the logs clasped each other in their arms. These logs were posts, studs, boards, clapboards, laths, plaster, and nails, all in one. Where the citizen uses a mere sliver or board, the pioneer uses the whole trunk of a tree. The house had large stone chimneys, and was roofed with spruce-bark. The windows were imported, all but the casings. One end was a regular logger's camp, for the boarders, with the usual fir floor and log benches. Thus this house was but a slight departure from the hollow tree,[122] which the bear still inhabits,—being a hollow made with trees piled up, with a coating of bark like its original.

The cellar was a separate building, like an ice-house, and it answered for a refrigerator[123] at this season, our moose-meat being kept there. It was a potato-hole with a permanent roof. Each structure and institution here was so primitive that you could at once refer it to its source; but our buildings commonly suggest neither their origin nor their purpose. There was a large, and what farmers would call handsome, barn, part of whose boards had been sawed by a whip-saw;[124] and the saw-pit, with its great pile of dust, remained before the house. The long split shingles on a portion of the barn were laid a foot to the weather,[125] suggesting what kind of weather they have there. Grant's barn at Caribou Lake[126] was said to be still larger, the biggest ox-nest in the woods, fifty feet by a hundred. Think of a monster barn in that primitive forest lifting its gray back above the tree-tops! Man makes very much such a nest for his domestic animals, of withered grass and fodder, as the squirrels and many other wild creatures do for themselves.

There was also a blacksmith's shop, where plainly a good deal of work was done. The oxen and horses used in lumbering operations were shod, and all the iron-work of sleds, etc., was repaired or made here. I saw them load a batteau at the Moosehead carry, the next Tuesday, with about thirteen hundred weight[127] of bar iron for this shop. This reminded me how primitive and honorable a trade was Vulcan's. I do not hear that there was any carpenter or tailor among the gods. The smith seems to have preceded these and every other mechanic at Chesuncook as well as on Olympus, and his family is the most widely dispersed, whether he be christened John or Ansel.

Smith owned two miles down the lake by half a mile in width. There were about one hundred acres cleared here. He cut seventy tons of English hay[128] this year on this ground, and twenty more on another clearing, and he uses it all himself in lumbering operations. The barn was crowded with pressed hay and a machine to press it.[129] There was a large garden full of roots, turnips, beets, carrots, potatoes, etc., all of great size. They said that they were worth as much here as in New York. I suggested some currants for sauce, especially as they had no apple-trees set out, and showed how easily they could be obtained.

There was the usual long-handled axe of the primitive woods by the door, three and a half feet long, — for my new black-ash rule was in constant use, — and a large, shaggy dog, whose nose, report said, was full of porcupine quills. I can testify that he looked very sober. This is the usual fortune of pioneer dogs, for they have to face the brunt of the battle for their race, and act the part of Arnold Winkelried[130] without intending it. If he should invite one of his town friends up this way, suggesting moose-meat and unlimited freedom,[131] the latter might pertinently inquire, "What is that sticking in your nose?" When a generation or two have used up all the enemies' darts, their successors lead a comparatively easy life. We owe to our fathers analogous blessings. Many old people receive pensions for no other reason, it seems to me, but as a compensation for having lived a long time ago. No

127 A hundredweight is equivalent to one hundred pounds.

128 Various imported crops, as timothy, redtop, and clover, cultivated in America as feed, called English hay to distinguish it from the less valuable meadow hay harvested for bedding.

129 Forerunner of the modern hay baler. Daniel Pereira Gardner (d. 1853) in his 1854 *Farmer's Dictionary: A Vocabulary of the Technical Terms Recently Introduced into Agriculture* described a hay press: "It consists of four upright posts strongly framed together, within which is a chamber of stout plank of the size of the intended bundle of hay. The press is firmly fixed between the lofts of a barn, the hay being thrown in above, and the horse power applied to the sweep and screw below. The sides of the chamber are opened to remove the pressed hay by doors hung upon rollers, and the upward pressure of the screw is resisted by a strong cap, which is pushed backward or forward at pleasure."

130 Arnold Winkelried (d. 1386), legendary Swiss hero who allegedly saved the victory of the Swiss Confederacy during the Battle of Sempach against an invading Austrian army. According to the legend, when the Swiss were unable to break the close ranks of the enemy soldiers, Winkelried rushed forward, gathering a number of Austrian spears together against his breast, thus breaching the enemy line.

131 In the fable of "The Country Mouse and the Town Mouse," the country mouse is invited to dine with the town mouse only to find the excitement of the town poor compensation for its dangers compared with the comforts of the country.

132 Allusion to Thomas Paine's (1737–1809) opening line to his pamphlet, *The Crisis* no. 1, published December 1776: "These are the times that try men's souls."

133 In his journal Thoreau wrote only: "I heard them call to Aleck" [MJ 18 September 1853].

134 Any of the wars between the Abenaki and the British, but probably the Fourth Abenaki War, part of Dummer's War (1721–1726), which included Lovewell's Fight and the death of Father Sebastian Rasles.

135 The period of which Homer wrote, ca. 1400–1000 B.C.E., not the period in which he wrote, ca. 850 B.C.E.

136 Probable allusion to Ithacus's speech in Homer's *Iliad* 19:167–178:

> Strength is derived from spirits and from
>   blood,
> And those augment by generous wine and
>   food:
> What boastful son of war, without that stay,
> Can last a hero through a single day?
> Courage may prompt; but, ebbing out his
>   strength,
> Mere unsupported man must yield at length;
> Shrunk with dry famine, and with toils
>   declined,
> The drooping body will desert the mind:
> But built anew with strength-conferring fare,
> With limbs and soul untamed, he tires a war.
> Dismiss the people, then, and give command.
> With strong repast to hearten every band.

137 Unidentified allusion. In "Ktaadn" Thoreau similarly wrote: "He eats no hot-bread and sweet-cake."

138 Reference to the simile found in Homer's *Iliad* XIII.739 as translated by Alexander Pope (1688–1744): "As on some ample barn's well-harden'd floor." Achilles is the Greek hero of the Trojan War in the epic.

doubt our town dogs still talk, in a snuffling way, about the days that tried dogs' noses.[132] How they got a cat up there I do not know, for they are as shy as my aunt about entering a canoe. I wondered that she did not run up a tree on the way; but perhaps she was bewildered by the very crowd of opportunities.

Twenty or thirty lumberers, Yankee and Canadian, were coming and going,—Aleck among the rest,[133]—and from time to time an Indian touched here. In the winter there are sometimes a hundred men lodged here at once. The most interesting piece of news that circulated among them appeared to be, that four horses belonging to Smith, worth seven hundred dollars, had passed by further into the woods a week before.

The white-pine-tree was at the bottom or further end of all this. It is a war against the pines, the only real Aroostook or Penobscot war.[134] I have no doubt that they lived pretty much the same sort of life in the Homeric age,[135] for men have always thought more of eating than of fighting;[136] then, as now, their minds ran chiefly on the "hot bread and sweet cakes";[137] and the fur and lumber trade is an old story to Asia and Europe. I doubt if men ever made a trade of heroism. In the days of Achilles, even, they delighted in big barns,[138] and perchance in pressed hay, and he who possessed the most valuable team was the best fellow.

We had designed to go on at evening up the Caucomgomoc, whose mouth was a mile or two distant, to the lake of the same name, about ten miles off; but some Indians of Joe's acquaintance, who were making canoes on the Caucomgomoc, came over from that side, and gave so poor an account of the moose-hunting, so many had been killed there lately, that my companions concluded not to go there. Joe spent this Sunday and the night with his acquaintances. The lumberers told me that there were many moose hereabouts, but no caribou or deer. A man from Oldtown had killed ten or twelve moose, within a year, so near the house that they heard all his guns. His name may have been Hercules, for aught I know, though I should rather have expected to hear the rattling of his club;[139] but, no doubt, he keeps pace with the improvements of the age, and uses a Sharps' rifle[140] now; probably he gets all his armor made and repaired at Smith's shop. One moose had been killed and another shot at within sight of the house within two years. I do not know whether Smith has yet got a poet to look after the cattle,[141] which, on account of the early breaking up of the ice, are compelled to summer in the woods, but I would suggest this office to such of my acquaintances as love to write verses and go a-gunning.

After a dinner, at which apple-sauce was the greatest luxury to me, but our moose-meat was oftenest called for by the lumberers, I walked across the clearing into the forest, southward, returning along the shore. For my dessert, I helped myself to a large slice of the Chesuncook woods, and took a hearty draught of its waters with all my senses. The woods were as fresh and full of vegetable life as a lichen in wet weather, and contained many interesting plants; but unless they are of white pine, they are treated with as little respect here as a mildew, and in the other case they are only the more quickly cut down. The shore was of coarse, flat, slate rocks, often in slabs, with the surf beating on it. The rocks and bleached drift-logs, extending some way into the shaggy woods, showed a rise and fall of six or eight feet, caused partly by the dam at the outlet. They said that in winter the snow was three feet deep on a level here, and sometimes four or five,—that the ice on the lake was two feet thick, clear, and four feet, including the snow-ice. Ice had already formed in vessels.

We lodged here this Sunday night in a comfortable bedroom, apparently the best one; and all that I noticed

139 In Greek mythology, Hercules was the son of Zeus, known for his great strength. In order to be released from servitude to Eurystheus, king of Tiryns, he had to complete twelve seemingly impossible labors. The first labor was to slay the Nemean lion, whose hide was so tough that it could not be pierced. Hercules stunned the beast with his olive-wood club and then strangled it with his bare hands.

140 A long-range cartridge rifle designed by Christian Sharps (1811–1874).

141 In Greek mythology, Apollo, god of music and poetry, during his nine-year banishment from heaven, was forced to tend the herds of the Pheraean king Admetus.

142 Fort Ticonderoga was surrendered without a fight by the British on 10 May 1775, Crown Point two days later.

143 Heavy overcoat.

144 When Ethan Allen (1738–1789), an American patriot and commander of the Green Mountain Boys, demanded the surrender of Fort Ticonderoga, the British commander asked, "By what authority?" Allen is reported to have replied, "I demand it in the name of the Great Jehovah, and the Continental Congress."

145 One of a body of regular or irregular troops, or other armed men, employed in ranging over a region, either for its protection or as marauders.

146 On 31 December 1775, after an expedition to Canada through the Maine woods, Benedict Arnold (1741–1801) made an unsuccessful attempt to capture Quebec.

147 War between the United States and Mexico (1846–1848) over the annexation of Texas, to which northern abolitionists objected on the grounds that it was an attempt to expand U.S. slavery. Referring to this war, Thoreau wrote in *Walden:* "I am less affected by their heroism who stood up for half an hour in the front line at Buena Vista, than by the steady and cheerful valor of the men who inhabit the snow-plough for their winter quarters" [Wa 114].

unusual in the night—for I still kept taking notes, like a spy in the camp—was the creaking of the thin split boards, when any of our neighbors stirred.

Such were the first rude beginnings of a town. They spoke of the practicability of a winter-road to the Moosehead carry, which would not cost much, and would connect them with steam and staging and all the busy world. I almost doubted if the lake would be then the self-same lake,—preserve its form and identity, when the shores should be cleared and settled; as if these lakes and streams which explorers report never awaited the advent of the citizen.

The sight of one of these frontier-houses, built of these great logs, whose inhabitants have unflinchingly maintained their ground many summers and winters in the wilderness, reminds me of famous forts, like Ticonderoga, or Crown Point, which have sustained memorable sieges.[142] They are especially winter-quarters, and at this season this one had a partially deserted look, as if the siege were raised a little, the snow-banks being melted from before it, and its garrison accordingly reduced. I think of their daily food as rations,—it is called "supplies"; a Bible and a great coat[143] are munitions of war, and a single man seen about the premises is a sentinel on duty. You expect that he will require the countersign, and will perchance take you for Ethan Allen, come to demand the surrender of his fort in the name of the Continental Congress.[144] It is a sort of ranger[145] service. Arnold's expedition[146] is a daily experience with these settlers. They can prove that they were out at almost any time; and I think that all the first generation of them deserve a pension more than any that went to the Mexican war.[147]

Early the next morning we started on our return up the Penobscot, my companion wishing to go about twenty-five miles above the Moosehead carry to a camp near the junction of the two forks,[148] and look for moose there. Our host allowed us something for the quarter of the moose which we had brought, and which he was glad to get. Two explorers from Chamberlain Lake started at the same time that we did.[149] Red flannel shirts should be worn in the woods, if only for the fine contrast which this color makes with the evergreens and the water. Thus I thought when I saw the forms of the explorers in their birch, poling up the rapids before us, far off against the forest. It is the surveyor's color also, most distinctly seen under all circumstances. We stopped to dine at Ragmuff, as before. My companion it was who wandered up the stream to look for moose this time, while Joe went to sleep on the bank, so that we felt sure of him; and I improved the opportunity to botanize and bathe. Soon after starting again, while Joe was gone back in the canoe for the frying-pan, which had been left, we picked a couple of quarts of tree-cranberries for a sauce.

I was surprised by Joe's asking me how far it was to the Moosehorn. He was pretty well acquainted with this stream, but he had noticed that I was curious about distances, and had several maps. He, and Indians generally, with whom I have talked, are not able to describe dimensions or distances in our measures with any accuracy. He could tell, perhaps, at what time we should arrive, but not how far it was. We saw a few wood-ducks, sheldrakes, and black ducks, but they were not so numerous there at that season as on our river at home. We scared the same family of wood-ducks before us, going and returning. We also heard the note of one fish-hawk, somewhat like that of a pigeon-woodpecker, and soon after saw him perched near the top of a dead white-pine against the island where we had first camped, while a company of peetweets were twittering and teetering about over the carcass of a moose on a low sandy spit just beneath. We drove the fish-hawk from perch to perch,

148 The Forks.
149 One was named Ross, according to Thoreau's journal, the other unidentified.

150 Sabatis (sometimes Sabattis or Sebattis)
Dana listed in the 1858 census of the Penobscot
Indians by J. C. Knowlton, supervisor of schools,
Old Town, Maine, as age thirty-seven and described by the Maine historian Fannie Eckstorm as
a "Maliseet from Quoddy, with a slightly negroid
look, though probably no negro blood."

151 Reference to "Arnold's Letters on his Expedition to Canada in 1775": "Here, on a small island
of a quarter of an acre, the party discovered a de-
licious cranberry, growing on a bush ten feet high,
and the fruit as large as a cherry."

each time eliciting a scream or whistle, for many miles
before us. Our course being up-stream, we were obliged
to work much harder than before, and had frequent use
for a pole. Sometimes all three of us paddled together,
standing up, small and heavily laden as the canoe was.
About six miles from Moosehead, we began to see the
mountains east of the north end of the lake, and at four
o'clock we reached the carry.

The Indians were still encamped here. There were
three, including the St. Francis Indian who had come
in the steamer with us. One of the others was called
Sabattis.[150] Joe and the St. Francis Indian were plainly
clear Indian, the other two apparently mixed Indian
and white; but the difference was confined to their features and complexions, for all that I could see. We here
cooked the tongue of the moose for supper,—having
left the nose, which is esteemed the choicest part, at
Chesuncook, boiling, it being a good deal of trouble to
prepare it. We also stewed our tree-cranberries, (*Viburnum opulus,*) sweetening them with sugar. The lumberers sometimes cook them with molasses. They were used
in Arnold's expedition.[151] This sauce was very grateful
to us who had been confined to hard bread, pork, and
moose-meat, and, notwithstanding their seeds, we all
three pronounced them equal to the common cranberry;
but perhaps some allowance is to be made for our forest
appetites. It would be worth the while to cultivate them,
both for beauty and for food. I afterward saw them
in a garden in Bangor. Joe said that they were called
ebeemenar.

While we were getting supper, Joe commenced curing
the moose-hide, on which I had sat a good part of the
voyage, he having already cut most of the hair off with
his knife at the Caucomgomoc. He set up two stout
forked poles on the bank, seven or eight feet high, and
as much asunder east and west, and having cut slits eight

or ten inches long, and the same distance apart, close to the edge, on the sides of the hide, he threaded poles through them, and then, placing one of the poles on the forked stakes, tied the other down tightly at the bottom. The two ends also were tied with cedar bark, their usual string, to the upright poles, through small holes at short intervals. The hide, thus stretched, and slanted a little to the north, to expose its flesh side to the sun, measured, in the extreme, eight feet long by six high. Where any flesh still adhered, Joe boldly scored it with his knife to lay it open to the sun. It now appeared somewhat spotted and injured by the duck shot. You may see the old frames on which hides have been stretched at many camping-places in these woods.

For some reason or other, the going to the forks of the Penobscot was given up, and we decided to stop here, my companion intending to hunt down the stream at night. The Indians invited us to lodge with them, but my companion inclined to go to the log-camp on the carry.[152] This camp was close and dirty, and had an ill smell, and I preferred to accept the Indians' offer, if we did not make a camp for ourselves; for, though they were dirty, too, they were more in the open air, and were much more agreeable, and even refined company, than the lumberers. The most interesting question entertained at the lumberers' camp was, which man could "handle" any other on the carry; and, for the most part, they possessed no qualities which you could not lay hands on. So we went to the Indians' camp or wigwam.

It was rather windy, and therefore Joe concluded to hunt after midnight, if the wind went down, which the other Indians thought it would not do, because it was from the south. The two mixed bloods, however, went off up the river for moose at dark, before we arrived at their camp. This Indian camp was a slight, patched-up affair, which had stood there several weeks, built

[152] Hinckley's camp.

153 Allusion to John White, sometimes With or Wyth, (ca. 1540–ca. 1593), whose watercolors formed the basis for the engravings in Theodore de Bry's (1528–1598) *Collectiones Peregrinationum in Indiam Orientalem et Indiam Occidentalem, XXV partibus comprehensae, a Theodoro, Joan: Theodoro de Bry, et a Matheo Merian pulicatae* (1590–1634).

154 Cannonball.

shed-fashion, open to the fire on the west. If the wind changed, they could turn it round. It was formed by two forked stakes and a cross-bar, with rafters slanted from this to the ground. The covering was partly an old sail, partly birch-bark, quite imperfect, but securely tied on, and coming down to the ground on the sides. A large log was rolled up at the back side for a headboard, and two or three moose-hides were spread on the ground with the hair up. Various articles of their wardrobe were tucked around the sides and corners, or under the roof. They were smoking moose-meat on just such a crate as is represented by With in De Bry's "Collectio Peregrinationum," published in 1592, and which the natives of Brazil called *boucan,* (whence buccaneer,) on which were frequently shown pieces of human flesh drying along with the rest.[153] It was erected in front of the camp over the usual large fire, in the form of an oblong square. Two stout forked stakes, four or five feet apart and five feet high, were driven into the ground at each end, and then two poles ten feet long were stretched across over the fire, and smaller ones laid transversely on these a foot apart. On the last hung large, thin slices of moose-meat smoking and drying, a space being left open over the centre of the fire. There was the whole heart, black as a thirty-two pound ball,[154] hanging at one corner. They said, that it took three or four days to cure this meat, and it would keep a year or more. Refuse pieces lay about on the ground in different stages of decay, and some pieces also in the fire, half buried and sizzling in the ashes, as black and dirty as an old shoe. These last I at first thought were thrown away, but afterwards found that they were being cooked. Also a tremendous rib-piece was roasting before the fire, being impaled on an upright stake forced in and out between the ribs. There was a moose-hide stretched and curing on poles like ours, and quite a pile of cured skins close by. They had killed twenty-two moose within two months, but, as they could use but very little of the meat, they left the carcasses on the ground. Altogether it was about as savage a sight as was ever witnessed, and I was carried back at once three hundred years. There were many torches of birch-bark, shaped like straight tin horns, lying ready for use on a stump outside.

For fear of dirt, we spread our blankets over their hides, so as not to touch them anywhere. The St. Francis Indian and Joe alone were there at first, and we lay on our backs talking with them till midnight. They were very sociable, and, when they did not talk with us, kept up a steady chatting in their own language. We heard a small bird just after dark, which, Joe said, sang at a certain hour in the night, — at ten o'clock, he believed. We also heard the hylodes[155] and tree-toads, and the lumberers singing in their camp a quarter of a mile off. I told them that I had seen pictured in old books pieces of human flesh drying on these crates; whereupon they repeated some tradition about the Mohawks eating human flesh, what parts they preferred, etc., and also of a battle with the Mohawks near Moosehead, in which many of the latter were killed; but I found that they knew but little of the history of their race, and could be entertained by stories about their ancestors as readily as any way. At first I was nearly roasted out, for I lay against one side of the camp, and felt the heat reflected not only from the birch-bark above, but from the side; and again I remembered the sufferings of the Jesuit missionaries, and what extremes of heat and cold the Indians were said to endure.[156] I struggled long between my desire to remain and talk with them, and my impulse to rush out and stretch myself on the cool grass; and when I was about to take the last step, Joe, hearing my murmurs, or else being uncomfortable himself, got up and partially dispersed the fire. I suppose that that is Indian manners, — to defend yourself.

155 The piping frog (*Hyla Pickeringii*).
156 Mentioned in many accounts in the *Jesuit Relations,* such as that of Francesco Giuseppe Bressani (1612–1672): "They endure cold, heat, pains, or diseases, without complaining."

157 War-chief of the Pequawkets, killed in King Philip's War, mentioned also in "A Walk to Wachusett."

158 John Eliot's (1604–1690) *Holy Bible, Containing the Old Testament and the New, Translated into the Indian Language*, which was written in the Algonquin language and published in 1633.

159 Christopher Columbus (Spanish: Cristóbal Colón) (1451–1506), Genoan explorer who, sailing under the Spanish flag, "discovered" the New World in 1492.

160 Untanned hide, also known as rawhide.

While lying there listening to the Indians, I amused myself with trying to guess at their subject by their gestures, or some proper name introduced. There can be no more startling evidence of their being a distinct and comparatively aboriginal race, than to hear this unaltered Indian language, which the white man cannot speak nor understand. We may suspect change and deterioration in almost every other particular, but the language which is so wholly unintelligible to us. It took me by surprise, though I had found so many arrow-heads, and convinced me that the Indian was not the invention of historians and poets. It was a purely wild and primitive American sound, as much as the barking of a *chickaree,* and I could not understand a syllable of it; but Paugus,[157] had he been there, would have understood it. These Abenakis gossiped, laughed, and jested, in the language in which Eliot's Indian Bible is written,[158] the language which has been spoken in New England who shall say how long? These were the sounds that issued from the wigwams of this country before Columbus was born;[159] they have not yet died away; and, with remarkably few exceptions, the language of their forefathers is still copious enough for them. I felt that I stood, or rather lay, as near to the primitive man of America, that night, as any of its discoverers ever did.

In the midst of their conversation, Joe suddenly appealed to me to know how long Moosehead Lake was.

Meanwhile, as we lay there, Joe was making and trying his horn, to be ready for hunting after midnight. The St. Francis Indian also amused himself with sounding it, or rather calling through it; for the sound is made with the voice, and not by blowing through the horn. The latter appeared to be a speculator in moose-hides. He bought my companion's for two dollars and a quarter, green.[160] Joe said that it was worth two and a half at Oldtown. Its chief use is for moccasins. One or two of these

Indians wore them. I was told, that, by a recent law of Maine, foreigners are not allowed to kill moose there at any season; white Americans can kill them only at a particular season, but the Indians of Maine at all seasons.[161] The St. Francis Indian accordingly asked my companion for a *wighiggin,* or bill, to show, since he was a foreigner. He lived near Sorel.[162] I found that he could write his name very well, *Tahmunt Swasen.*[163] One Ellis,[164] an old white man of Guilford, a town through which we passed, not far from the south end of Moosehead, was the most celebrated moose-hunter of those parts. Indians and whites spoke with equal respect of him. Tahmunt said, that there were more moose here than in the Adirondack country in New York, where he had hunted; that three years before there were a great many about, and there were a great many now in the woods, but they did not come out to the water. It was of no use to hunt them at midnight,—they would not come out then. I asked Sabattis, after he came home, if the moose never attacked him. He answered, that you must not fire many times so as to mad him. "I fire once and hit him in the right place, and in the morning I find him. He won't go far. But if you keep firing, you mad him. I fired once five bullets, every one through the heart, and he did not mind 'em at all; it only made him more mad." I asked him if they did not hunt them with dogs. He said, that they did so in winter, but never in the summer, for then it was of no use; they would run right off straight and swiftly a hundred miles.

Another Indian said, that the moose, once scared, would run all day. A dog will hang to their lips, and be carried along till he is swung against a tree and drops off. They cannot run on a "glaze," though they can run in snow four feet deep; but the caribou can run on ice. They commonly find two or three moose together. They cover themselves with water, all but their noses, to es-

161 In 1852 the Maine legislature approved the creation of moose wardens, appointed by the governor, one in each of the seven counties, each of which could appoint up to two deputies, for the purpose of upholding the 1841 ordinance defining the hunting season on deer and moose. The 1852 legislation specifically prohibited any "foreign citizens and Indians belonging in the British provinces . . . from killing any moose or deer within the limits of this state." In 1853 each town was allowed to appoint its own warden. Neither law extended unlimited hunting rights to the Indians.
162 Town and port in Quebec, at the confluence of the St. Lawrence and Richelieu Rivers.
163 Rowland Evans Robinson (1833–1900) wrote in his "On a Glass Roof": "I learned somewhat of my old acquaintances. One of them was Swasin Tahmont, who I doubt not was the Tahmunt Swasen of Thoreau's 'Maine Woods,' and of whom I was surprised to hear that he had gone to the happy hunting-grounds by the fire-water way, for when I knew him he would not touch whiskey and was very pious. He used to sing hymns to me in Waubanakee, and always said grace before his musquash-meat."
164 John Ellis (1784–1867) who settled in Guilford in 1844.

165 Although moose antlers are shed annually, the moose cannot move them independently of the head. The distinction between horns, which are permanent, and antlers, which are deciduous, was not in common usage in Thoreau's day.

166 In his journal Thoreau identified him only as "one intelligent Ind." (MJ 22 September 1853).

167 Father Sébastian Rasles, sometimes Rasle, Rale, or Ralle (1652–1724), compiled his *Dictionary of the Abnaki Language* while a missionary to the Abenaki at Norridgewock, Maine, from 1694 to 1724. He was killed and his dictionary stolen during a raid on the village by the British. The book was published in 1833 in the *Memoirs of the American Academy of Arts and Sciences.*

168 ꝏskanitéhaṅn, which Rasles defined as "os qui est au cœur de l'original." This is the *os cordis,* an ossification of the septum between the ventricles of the heart. The Greek character ꝏ was used by Rasles to denote a guttural *ou* sound for which the lips are not used.

169 ꝏkass, which Rasles defined as "le pié gauche de derr. [derrière]." The double ss was used by Rasles to denote the s sound as opposed to the z sound.

170 At Hemenway and Hersey, on Main Street, manufacturers of, according to an 1851 advertisement, "hats, caps, boots & shoes, fur goods, trunks, valises, gent's cravats, collars, bosoms, &c., &c."

171 Springer wrote: "There is an animal in the deep recesses of the forests of Maine, evidently belonging to the feline race, which, on account of its ferocity, is significantly called 'Indian Devil' — in the Indian language, 'the Lunk Soos'; a terror to the Indians, and the only animal in New England of which they stand in dread. You may speak of the moose, the bear, and the wolf even, and the red man is ready for the chase and the encounter. But name the object of his dread, and he will significantly shake his head, while he exclaims, 'He all one debil!'"

172 Wolverine.

cape flies. He had the horns of what he called "the black moose that goes in low lands." These spread three or four feet. The "red moose" was another kind, "running on mountains," and had horns which spread six feet. Such were his distinctions. Both can move their horns.[165] The broad flat blades are covered with hair, and are so soft, when the animal is alive, that you can run a knife through them. They regard it as a good or bad sign, if the horns turn this way or that. His caribou horns had been gnawed by mice in his wigwam, but he thought that the horns neither of the moose nor of the caribou were ever gnawed while the creature was alive, as some have asserted. An Indian, whom I met after this at Oldtown, who had carried about a bear and other animals of Maine to exhibit,[166] told me that thirty years ago there were not so many moose in Maine as now; also, that the moose were very easily tamed, and would come back when once fed, and so would deer, but not caribou. The Indians of this neighborhood are about as familiar with the moose as we are with the ox, having associated with them for so many generations. Father Rasles, in his Dictionary of the Abenaki Language,[167] gives not only a word for the male moose, (*aïaṅbé,*) and another for the female, (*hè'rar,*) but for the bone which is in the middle of the heart of the moose (!),[168] and for his left hind-leg.[169]

There were none of the small deer up there; they are more common about the settlements. One ran into the city of Bangor two years before, and jumped through a window of costly plate glass,[170] and then into a mirror, where it thought it recognized one of its kind, and out again, and so on, leaping over the heads of the crowd, until it was captured. This the inhabitants speak of as the deer that went a-shopping. The last-mentioned Indian spoke of the *lunxus* or Indian devil,[171] (which I take to be the cougar, and not the *Gulo luscus,*)[172] as the only animal in Maine which man need fear; it would follow a man, and did not mind a fire. He also said, that beavers were getting to be pretty numerous again, where we went, but their skins brought so little now that it was not profitable to hunt them.

I had put the ears of our moose, which were ten inches long, to dry along with the moose-meat over the fire, wishing to preserve them; but Sabattis told me that I must skin and cure them, else the hair would all come off. He observed, that they made tobacco-pouches of the skins of their ears, putting the two together inside to inside. I asked him how he got fire; and he produced a little cylindrical box of friction-matches. He also had flints and steel, and some punk,[173] which was not dry; I think it was from the yellow birch. "But suppose you upset, and all these and your powder get wet." "Then," said he, "we wait till we get to where there is some fire." I produced from my pocket a little vial, containing matches, stoppled water-tight, and told him, that, though we were upset, we should still have some dry matches; at which he stared without saying a word.

We lay awake thus a long while talking, and they gave us the meaning of many Indian names of lakes and streams in the vicinity,—especially Tahmunt. I asked the Indian name of Moosehead Lake. Joe answered, *Sebamook;* Tahmunt pronounced it *Sebemook.* When I asked what it meant, they answered, Moosehead Lake. At length, getting my meaning, they alternately repeated the word over to themselves, as a philologist might,— *Sebamook,—Sebamook,*—now and then comparing notes in Indian; for there was a slight difference in their dialects; and finally Tahmunt said, "Ugh! I know,"—and he rose up partly on the moose-hide,—"like as here is a place, and there is a place," pointing to different parts of the hide, "and you take water from there and fill this, and it stays here; that is *Sebamook.*" I understood him to mean that it was a reservoir of water which did not run

173 Also called spunk or sponk: wood decayed through the influence of a fungus or otherwise and used like tinder; touchwood.

away, the river coming in on one side and passing out again near the same place, leaving a permanent bay. Another Indian said, that it meant Large-Bay Lake, and that *Sebago* and *Sebec,* the names of other lakes, were kindred words, meaning large open water. Joe said that *Seboois* meant Little River. I observed their inability, often described, to convey an abstract idea.[174] Having got the idea, though indistinctly, they groped about in vain for words with which to express it. Tahmunt thought that the whites called it Moosehead Lake, because Mount Kineo, which commands it, is shaped like a moose's head, and that Moose River was so called "because the mountain points right across the lake to its mouth." John Josselyn, writing about 1673, says, "Twelve miles from Casco Bay, and passable for men and horses, is a lake, called by the Indians Sebug. On the brink thereof, at one end, is the famous rock, shaped like a moose deer or helk,[175] diaphanous, and called the Moose Rock."[176] He appears to have confounded Sebamook with Sebago, which is nearer, but has no "diaphanous" rock on its shore.

I give more of their definitions, for what they are worth,—partly *because* they differ sometimes from the commonly received ones. They never analyzed these words before. After long deliberation and repeating of the word, for it gave much trouble, Tahmunt said that *Chesuncook* meant a place where many streams emptied in (?), and he enumerated them,—Penobscot, Umbazookskus, Cusabexsex, Red Brook, etc.—"*Caucomgomoc,*—what does that mean?" "What are those large white birds?" he asked. "Gulls," said I. "Ugh! Gull Lake."—*Pammadumcook,* Joe thought, meant the Lake with Gravelly Bottom or Bed.—*Kenduskeag,* Tahmunt concluded at last, after asking if birches went up it, for he said that he was not much acquainted with it, meant something like this: "You go up Penobscot till you come to *Kenduskeag,* and you go by, you don't turn up there.

174 George Warburton (1816–1857) wrote in *The Conquest of Canada* that the Indian "has no abstract or universal ideas," and William Robertson (1721–1793) wrote in *The History of America* that the Indian is "unacquainted with all the ideas which have been denominated *universal,* or *abstract,* or *of reflection. . . . Time, space, substance,* and a thousand other terms which represent abstract and universal ideas, are altogether unknown to them."

175 Elk.

176 Quoted from John Josselyn's (ca. 1630–1675) *Account of Two Voyages to New-England.*

That is *Kenduskeag*." (?) Another Indian,[177] however, who knew the river better, told us afterward that it meant Little Eel River.—*Mattawamkeag* was a place where two rivers meet. (?)—*Penobscot* was Rocky River. One writer says, that this was "originally the name of only a section of the main channel, from the head of the tide-water to a short distance above Oldtown."[178]

A very intelligent Indian, whom we afterward met, son-in-law of Neptune, gave us also these other definitions:—*Umbazookskus*, Meadow Stream; *Millinoket*, Place of Islands; *Aboljacarmegus*, Smooth-Ledge Falls (and Dead-Water); *Aboljacarmeguscook*, the stream emptying in; (the last was the word he gave when I asked about *Aboljacknagesic*, which he did not recognize;) *Mattahumkeag*, Sand-Creek Pond; *Piscataquis*, Branch of a River.

I asked our hosts what *Musketaquid*, the Indian name of Concord, Mass., meant; but they changed it to *Musketicook,* and repeated that, and Tahmunt said that it meant Dead Stream, which is probably true.[179] *Cook* appears to mean stream, and perhaps *quid* signifies the place or ground. When I asked the meaning of the names of two of our hills, they answered that they were another language. As Tahmunt said that he traded at Quebec, my companion inquired the meaning of the word *Quebec,* about which there has been so much question.[180] He did not know, but began to conjecture. He asked what those great ships were called that carried soldiers. "Men-of-war," we answered. "Well," he said, "when the English ships came up the river, they could not go any further, it was so narrow there; they must go back,—go-back,— that's Que-bec." I mention this to show the value of his authority in the other cases.

Late at night the other two Indians came home from moose-hunting, not having been successful, aroused the fire again, lighted their pipes, smoked awhile, took some-

177 Mentioned again in the next paragraph and identified as Nicholai in "Appendix."
178 Quoted from Springer's *Forest Life and Forest Trees*.
179 In *A Week on the Concord and Merrimack River* Thoreau wrote of the name: "Compared with the other tributaries of the Merrimack, it appears to have been properly named Musketaquid, or Meadow River, by the Indians. For the most part, it creeps through broad meadows, adorned with scattered oaks, where the cranberry is found in abundance, covering the ground like a moss-bed" [W 1:8]. In "Natural History of Massachusetts" he wrote: "Among the rivers which empty into the Merrimack, the Concord is known to the boatmen as a dead stream. The Indians are said to have called it Musketaquid, or Prairie river" [W 5:115].
180 Thoreau would have read in many of his sources about the debate regarding the origin of the name. Alfred Hawkins (ca. 1802–1854) in *Hawkins's Picture of Quebec with Historical Recollections* wrote: "In the earlier period of the history of this country . . . the singular error was fallen into of supposing that Quebec was the Indian word which signified the place of the straight. Charlevoix is the writer on whose authority this error, as we conceive it to be, has been transmitted." Hawkins went on to say "there are strong grounds for believing that the name Quebec, *per se,* is in fact a Norman word. That some Indian name which resembled it in sound was heard by Champlain . . . and that from this word, it gradually acquired its present appellation." John Mactaggart (1791–1830) in his *Three Years in Canada* wrote: "'*Quel Bec!*' 'what a beak or promontory!' is considered by the learned, as we have said, to be the origin of *Quebec;* the same words being exclaimed by one of *Cartier's sailors* on first beholding the headland. Others again will argue that it is named from a small town in France . . . the name of which is Caudibec. On ancient boundary marks and brass plates lately discovered, it stands K———becque." The exclamation "Quel bec!" is attributed to Cartier's pilot. Henry Rowe School-

craft (1793–1864) in *The Red Race of America* related the name to the Algonquin language, "having its origin in Kebic, a fearful rock or cliff."

181 Mocotaugan, or crooked knife, a one-handed knife usually pulled toward the user. Rasles referred to it as *couteau croche* (hooked knife).

182 To cut down gradually by taking off thin shavings or parings, as in to shave shingles, strips, or hoops.

183 A cast-iron frying pan with three legs to hold it over the fire.

184 A feast, found among many Native American peoples, in which it is required to eat all that is put before you. If you are unable to eat all, it is required to offer a gift to someone to enlist their help. Thoreau read about this in Thaddeus Culbertson's *Journal of an Expedition to the Mauvaise Terres and the Upper Missouri in 1850* (published by the Smithsonian Institution in 1851): "I noticed quite a number passing their pans, well filled with mush, to their squaws who were standing about the door, which indicated generous and kind feeling. This was not an act of impoliteness, but just the reverse according to Indian etiquette, for with them it is very impolite not to eat all that is given at a feast—you must eat or *carry away*."

thing strong to drink, and ate some moose-meat, and, finding what room they could, lay down on the moose-hides; and thus we passed the night, two white men and four Indians, side by side.

When I awoke in the morning the weather was drizzling. One of the Indians was lying outside, rolled in his blanket, on the opposite side of the fire, for want of room. Joe had neglected to awake my companion, and he had done no hunting that night. Tahmunt was making a cross-bar for his canoe with a singularly shaped knife,[181] such as I have since seen other Indians using. The blade was thin, about three quarters of an inch wide, and eight or nine inches long, but curved out of its plane into a hook, which he said made it more convenient to shave with.[182] As the Indians very far north and northwest use the same kind of knife, I suspect that it was made according to an aboriginal pattern, though some white artisans may use a similar one. The Indians baked a loaf of flour bread in a spider[183] on its edge before the fire for their breakfast; and while my companion was making tea, I caught a dozen sizable fishes in the Penobscot, two kinds of sucker and one trout. After we had breakfasted by ourselves, one of our bedfellows, who had also breakfasted, came along, and, being invited, took a cup of tea, and finally, taking up the common platter, licked it clean. But he was nothing to a white fellow, a lumberer, who was continually stuffing himself with the Indians' moose-meat, and was the butt of his companions accordingly. He seems to have thought that it was a feast "to eat all."[184] It is commonly said that the white man finally surpasses the Indian on his own ground, and it was proved true in this case. I cannot swear to his employment during the hours of darkness, but I saw him at it again as soon as it was light, though he came a quarter of a mile to his work.

The rain prevented our continuing any longer in the

woods; so giving some of our provisions and utensils to the Indians, we took leave of them. This being the steamer's day, I set out for the lake at once.

I walked over the carry alone and waited at the head of the lake. An eagle, or some other large bird, flew screaming away from its perch by the shore at my approach. For an hour after I reached the shore there was not a human being to be seen, and I had all that wide prospect to myself. I thought that I heard the sound of the steamer before she came in sight on the open lake. I noticed at the landing, when the steamer came in, one of our bedfellows, who had been a-moose-hunting the night before, now very sprucely dressed in a clean white shirt and fine black pants, a true Indian dandy,[185] who had evidently come over the carry to show himself to any arrivers on the north shore of Moosehead Lake, just as New York dandies take a turn up Broadway and stand on the steps of a hotel.

Midway the lake we took on board two manly-looking middle-aged men, with their batteau, who had been exploring for six weeks as far as the Canada line, and had let their beards grow. They had the skin of a beaver, which they had recently caught, stretched on an oval hoop, though the fur was not good at that season. I talked with one of them, telling him that I had come all this distance partly to see where the white-pine, the Eastern stuff of which our houses are built, grew, but that on this and a previous excursion into another part of Maine I had found it a scarce tree; and I asked him where I must look for it. With a smile, he answered, that he could hardly tell me. However, he said that he had found enough to employ two teams the next winter in a place where there was thought to be none left. What was considered a "tip-top" tree now was not looked at twenty years ago, when he first went into the business; but they succeeded very well now with what was considered quite

185 Often used as a derisive term for a man who attracts attention by the unusual finery of his dress and a corresponding fastidious manner, after the 1820s it gradually came to be applied simply to those who were trim, neat, and careful in dressing according to the fashion of the day. As Thomas Carlyle (1795–1881) wrote in *Sartor Resartus:* "A Dandy is a clothes-wearing Man, a Man whose trade, office and existence consists in the wearing of Clothes. Every faculty of his soul, spirit, purse, and person is heroically consecrated to this one object, the wearing of Clothes wisely and well."

186 Full of shakes: a crack or fissure in timber, produced during growth by strain of wind or sudden changes of temperature, or formed during seasoning.

187 Charles Lowell, with whom Thoreau dined on 25 September 1853.

188 Measured or estimated.

189 Board feet.

190 Not cut into lumber.

191 The largest boom on the river was the Bangor Boom at Oldtown, chartered in 1825 and operated by the Bangor Boom Company, later the Bangor Boom Corporation, which had a six-mile jurisdiction on the river.

192 Also known as Webster Brook.

inferior timber then. The explorer used to cut into a tree higher and higher up, to see if it was false-hearted, and if there was a rotten heart as big as his arm, he let it alone; but now they cut such a tree, and sawed it all around the rot, and it made the very best of boards, for in such a case they were never shaky.[186]

One connected with lumbering operations at Bangor[187] told me that the largest pine belonging to his firm, cut the previous winter, "scaled"[188] in the woods four thousand five hundred feet,[189] and was worth ninety dollars in the log[190] at the Bangor boom[191] in Oldtown. They cut a road three and a half miles long for this tree alone. He thought that the principal locality for the white-pine that came down the Penobscot now was at the head of the East Branch and the Allegash, about Webster Stream[192] and Eagle and Chamberlain Lakes. Much timber has been stolen from the public lands. (Pray, what kind of forest-warden is the Public itself?) I heard of one man who, having discovered some particularly fine trees just within the boundaries of the public lands, and not daring to employ an accomplice, cut them down, and by means of block and tackle, without cattle, tumbled them into a stream, and so succeeded in getting off with them without the least assistance. Surely, stealing pine-trees in this way is not so mean as robbing hen-roosts.

We reached Monson that night, and the next day rode to Bangor, all the way in the rain again, varying our route a little. Some of the taverns on this road, which were particularly dirty, were plainly in a transition state from the camp to the house.

The next forenoon we went to Oldtown. One slender old Indian on the Oldtown shore, who recognized my companion, was full of mirth and gestures, like a Frenchman. A Catholic priest crossed to the island in the same batteau with us. The Indian houses are framed, mostly of one story, and in rows one behind another, at the south end of the island, with a few scattered ones. I counted about forty, not including the church and what my companion called the council-house. The last, which I suppose is their town-house, was regularly framed and shingled like the rest. There were several of two stories, quite neat, with front-yards inclosed, and one at least had green blinds. Here and there were moose-hides stretched and drying about them. There were no cart-paths, nor tracks of horses, but foot-paths; very little land cultivated, but an abundance of weeds, indigenous and naturalized; more introduced weeds than useful vegetables, as the Indian is said to cultivate the vices rather than the virtues of the white man.[193] Yet this village was cleaner than I expected, far cleaner than such Irish villages as I have seen.[194] The children were not particularly ragged nor dirty. The little boys met us with bow in hand and arrow on string, and cried, "Put up a cent." Verily, the Indian has but a feeble hold on his bow now; but the curiosity of the white man is insatiable, and from the first he has been eager to witness this forest accomplishment. That elastic piece of wood with its feathered dart,[195] so sure to be unstrung by contact with civilization, will serve for the type, the coat-of-arms of the savage. Alas for the Hunter Race![196] the white man has driven off their game, and substituted a cent in its place. I saw an Indian woman washing at the water's edge. She stood on a rock, and, after dipping the clothes in the stream, laid them on the rock, and beat them with a short club. In the graveyard, which was crowded with graves, and overrun with weeds, I noticed an inscription in Indian, painted on a wooden grave-board. There was a large wooden cross on the island.[197]

Since my companion knew him, we called on Governor Neptune,[198] who lived in a little "ten-footer,"[199] one of the humblest of them all. Personalities are allow-

193 The Committee on Indian Affairs of the House of Representatives in *American State Papers, Indian Affairs* reported in 1834: "The Indians are not now what they once were. They have partaken of our vices more than our virtues. Such is their condition, at present, that they must be civilized or exterminated; no other alternative exists." Calvin Colton (1789–1857) in his *Tour of the American Lakes* wrote that they were "more susceptible of the contagion of vice, than of improvement in virtue. The Indian, thrown into temptation, easily takes the vices of the white man."

194 Thoreau described the living conditions of the Irish immigrants around Concord in his journal, in one instance comparing hogs, which are "comparatively clean about their lodgings, and their shed, with its litter bed, was on the whole cleaner than an Irishman's shanty" [J 5:241]. In *Walden* he wrote: "It is a mistake to suppose that, in a country where the usual evidences of civilization exist, the condition of a very large body of the inhabitants may not be as degraded as that of savages. I refer to the degraded poor, not now to the degraded rich. To know this I should not need to look farther than to the shanties which every where border our railroads. . . . I see in my daily walks human beings living in sties. . . . Contrast the physical condition of the Irish with that of the North American Indian, or the South Sea Islander, or any other savage race before it was degraded by contact with the civilized man. . . . Their condition only proves what squalidness may consist with civilization" [Wa 34].

195 Common epithet for the arrow found in the works of many writers, including James MacPherson's purported translations from Ossian: "But, with the feathered dart, I have learned to pierce a distant foe."

196 Common epithet for Indians found in the works of many writers, including Henry Rowe Schoolcraft (1793–1864) in his many works on Indians.

197 A large wooden cross stood before the Indian Catholic Church with the inscription: "*Rogo—ut* omnes unum sint, Joan XVII" (I request—That they all may be one, John 17).

198 John Neptune (1767–1865) was lieutenant governor of the Penobscot Nation, and described by Gideon T. Ridlon (1841–1928), who met him in the 1850s, as "one of the most intelligent and distinguished of the Maine Indians. . . . His black hair was long and fell heavily upon his shoulders." He was a "good storyteller" who "reveled in his dramatic descriptions" and whose face, in the telling of a story, "became animated, his black eyes shot fire and his whole form became visibly agitated."

199 Ten-foot-square structures primarily used as shoe shops.

200 Political organization founded in 1841 by a state convention in Louisiana. Its principles were based on the opposition of those who professed the Roman Catholic faith, and the exclusion of foreign-born citizens from all offices of trust and emolument in the government, whether federal, state, or municipal. It was later known as the American, or Know-Nothing, Party.

201 Although according to his birth date on his tombstone Neptune would have been eighty-six, some newspaper accounts and notices indicate that he may have been born in 1764, thus making Neptune's age here correct.

202 The weather of New England was often maligned, as in Samuel Griswold Goodrich's (1793–1860) *Pictorial Geography of the World:* "New England is subject to great extremes of temperature. The winters are much colder, and the summers hotter than under the same parallels in Europe. Greece and Italy cannot boast of more exquisite days than the summer and autumn here exhibit; and the most foggy, ice-bound region of the north, does not endure a more disagreeable visitation than the cold mists of a New England spring. . . . If the spring is the finest season in Europe, it is the most unpleasant in New England. No weather can be more capricious." The 1853 *Buffalo Medical Journal* stated that the "New England climate has little in it that is sedative at any long season of the

able in speaking of public men, therefore I will give the particulars of our visit. He was a-bed. When we entered the room, which was one half of the house, he was sitting on the side of the bed. There was a clock hanging in one corner. He had on a black frock-coat, and black pants, much worn, white cotton shirt, socks, a red silk handkerchief about his neck, and a straw hat. His black hair was only slightly grayed. He had very broad cheeks, and his features were decidedly and refreshingly different from those of any of the upstart Native American party[200] whom I have seen. He was no darker than many old white men. He told me that he was eighty-nine;[201] but he was going a-moose-hunting that fall, as he had been the previous one. Probably his companions did the hunting. We saw various squaws dodging about. One sat on the bed by his side and helped him out with his stories. They were remarkably corpulent, with smooth, round faces, apparently full of good-humor. Certainly our much-abused climate[202] had not dried up their adipose substance. While we were there,—for we stayed a good while,—one went over to Oldtown, returned and cut out a dress, which she had bought, on another bed in the room. The Governor said, that "he could remember when the moose were much larger; that they did not use to be in the woods, but came out of the water, as all deer did. Moose was whale once. Away down Merrimack way, a whale came ashore in a shallow bay. Sea went out and left him, and he came up on land a moose. What made them know he was a whale was, that at first, before he began to run in bushes, he had no bowels inside, but"— and then the squaw who sat on the bed by his side, as the Governor's aid, and had been putting in a word now and then and confirming the story, asked me what we called that soft thing we find along the sea-shore. "Jelly-fish," I suggested. "Yes," said he, "no bowels, but jelly-fish."

There may be some truth in what he said about the

moose growing larger formerly; for the quaint John Josselyn, a physician who spent many years in this very district of Maine in the seventeenth century, says, that the tips of their horns "are sometimes found to be two fathoms asunder,"—and he is particular to tell us that a fathom is six feet,—"and [they are] in height, from the toe of the fore-foot to the pitch of the shoulder, twelve foot, both which hath been taken by some of my sceptique readers to be monstrous lies"; and he adds, "There are certain transcendentia[203] in every creature, which are the indelible characters of God, and which discover God."[204] This is a greater dilemma to be caught in than is presented by the cranium of the young Bechuana[205] ox, apparently another of the *transcendentia,* in the collection of Thomas Steel, Upper Brook Street, London, whose "entire length of horn, from tip to tip, along the curve, is 13 ft. 5 in.; distance (straight) between the tips of the horns, 8 ft. 8½ in."[206] However, the size both of the moose and the cougar, as I have found, is generally rather underrated than overrated, and I should be inclined to add to the popular estimate a part of what I subtracted from Josselyn's.

But we talked mostly with the Governor's son-in-law, a very sensible Indian; and the Governor, being so old and deaf, permitted himself to be ignored, while we asked questions about him. The former said, that there were two political parties among them,—one in favor of schools, and the other opposed to them, or rather they did not wish to resist the priest, who was opposed to them.[207] The first had just prevailed at the election and sent their man to the legislature.[208] Neptune and Aitteon and he himself were in favor of schools. He said, "If Indians got learning, they would keep their money." When we asked where Joe's father, Aitteon, was, he knew that he must be at Lincoln, though he was about going a-moose-hunting, for a messenger had just gone

year. The winters are broken and unsteady. . . . The character of New England spring weather is too well known to need comment. Nothing could be more uncertain and less reliable."

203 In medieval scholasticism, attributes that cannot be subsumed under categories defined by Aristotle (384–322 b.c.e.), thus: being (*ens*), one (*unum*), good (*bonum*), truth (*verum*), thing (*res*), and something (*aliquid*).

204 Quoted from Josselyn's *Account of Two Voyages to New-England.*

205 Common nineteenth-century spelling and pronunciation of Botswana, a member of a Bantu people inhabiting Bechuanaland (now Botswana and western South Africa).

206 Quoted, with minor variants, from Charles John (Karl Johann) Andersson's (1827–1867) *Lake Ngami,* 308. Sir Thomas Montague Steele (1820–1890) lived at 17 Upper Brook Street from 1824 to 1843 and had accompanied David Livingstone (1813–1873) to Africa.

207 The Penobscot split into two parties around 1826. The Old Party was headed by John Attean, and the New Party by John Neptune. The New Party adhered to policies as delineated by the Catholic missionaries. At this time the missionaries did not approve of the formal education system as exemplified in the public schools.

208 As tribal representative to the Maine legislature.

209 Probably John Pennowit, who was eighty-seven when he was interviewed in 1881 about Indian nomenclature by Lucius Lee Hubbard (1849–1933) for his *Woods and Lakes of Maine*. A pennyweight is a unit of weight equal to twenty-four grains or one-twentieth of an ounce.

210 Name used in New England for the small Spanish coin, the half-real, the value of which was four and one half pence in old New England currency.

211 Thoreau wrote a lengthy description of canoe building in his journal but did not incorporate it in *The Maine Woods*. See Appendix.

212 At this time not yet a term in common usage, as indicated in Springer, where it was similarly placed in quotation marks: "the 'boss,' or the principal in charge."

213 According to Williamson's *History of the State of Maine*, the Indian town, long-since destroyed, situated "on '*Fort-Hill*,' as the English have always called it, is supposed to have been the ancient *Negas*. It was never repaired; the Indians afterwards returning and reseating themselves at Old-town."

to him there to get his signature to some papers. I asked Neptune if they had any of the old breed of dogs yet. He answered, "Yes." "But that," said I, pointing to one that had just come in, "is a Yankee dog." He assented. I said that he did not look like a good one. "O yes!" he said, and he told, with much gusto, how, the year before, he had caught and held by the throat a wolf. A very small black puppy rushed into the room and made at the Governor's feet, as he sat in his stockings with his legs dangling from the bedside. The Governor rubbed his hands and dared him to come on, entering into the sport with spirit. Nothing more that was significant transpired, to my knowledge, during this interview. This was the first time that I ever called on a governor, but, as I did not ask for an office, I can speak of it with the more freedom.

An Indian who was making canoes behind a house, looking up pleasantly from his work,—for he knew my companion,—said that his name was Old John Penny-weight.[209] I had heard of him long before, and I inquired after one of his contemporaries, Joe Four-pence-ha'penny;[210] but, alas! he no longer circulates. I made a faithful study of canoe-building,[211] and I thought that I should like to serve an apprenticeship at that trade for one season, going into the woods for bark with my "boss,"[212] making the canoe there, and returning in it at last.

While the batteau was coming over to take us off, I picked up some fragments of arrow-heads on the shore, and one broken stone chisel, which were greater novelties to the Indians than to me. After this, on Old Fort Hill, at the bend of the Penobscot, three miles above Bangor, looking for the site of an Indian town which some think stood thereabouts,[213] I found more arrow-heads, and two little dark and crumbling fragments of Indian earthenware, in the ashes of their fires. The Indians on the Island appeared to live quite happily and to be well treated by the inhabitants of Oldtown.

We visited Veazie's mills,[214] just below the Island, where were sixteen sets of saws,—some gang saws,[215] sixteen in a gang, not to mention circular saws. On one side, they were hauling the logs up an inclined plane by water-power; on the other, passing out the boards, planks, and sawed timber, and forming them into rafts. The trees were literally drawn and quartered there. In forming the rafts, they use the lower three feet of hardwood saplings, which have a crooked and knobbed but-end, for bolts, passing them up through holes bored in the corners and sides of the rafts, and keying them.[216] In another apartment they were making fence-slats, such as stand all over New England, out of odds and ends,— and it may be that I saw where the picket-fence behind which I dwell at home came from. I was surprised to find a boy collecting the long edgings of boards as fast as cut off, and thrusting them down a hopper, where they were *ground up* beneath the mill, that they might be out of the way; otherwise they accumulate in vast piles by the side of the building, increasing the danger from fire,[217] or, floating off, they obstruct the river. This was not only a saw-mill, but a grist-mill, then. The inhabitants of Old-town, Stillwater, and Bangor cannot suffer for want of kindling-stuff, surely. Some get their living exclusively by picking up the drift-wood and selling it by the cord in the winter. In one place I saw where an Irishman, who keeps a team and a man for the purpose, had covered the shore for a long distance with regular piles, and I was told that he had sold twelve hundred dollars' worth in a year. Another, who lived by the shore, told me that he got all the material of his out-buildings and fences from the river; and in that neighborhood I perceived that this refuse wood was frequently used instead of sand to fill hollows with, being apparently cheaper than dirt.

214 Mill of General Samuel Veazie (1787–1868) who, at the time of his death, owned more than fifty mills.

215 A body of saws set in one frame for making simultaneous parallel cuts.

216 To fasten with a key, or with a wedge-shaped piece of wood or metal.

217 From the carbureted hydrogen, a flammable and explosive gaseous compound of carbon and hydrogen which occurs in stagnant pools such as the sawdust shoal around a mill.

I got my first clear view of Ktaadn, on this excursion, from a hill about two miles northwest of Bangor, whither I went for this purpose.[218] After this I was ready to return to Massachusetts.

Humboldt has written an interesting chapter on the primitive forest,[219] but no one has yet described for me the difference between that wild forest which once occupied our oldest townships, and the tame one which I find there to-day. It is a difference which would be worth attending to. The civilized man not only clears the land permanently to a great extent, and cultivates open fields, but he tames and cultivates to a certain extent the forest itself. By his mere presence, almost, he changes the nature of the trees as no other creature does. The sun and air, and perhaps fire, have been introduced, and grain raised where it stands. It has lost its wild, damp, and shaggy look, the countless fallen and decaying trees are gone, and consequently that thick coat of moss which lived on them is gone too. The earth is comparatively bare and smooth and dry. The most primitive places left with us are the swamps, where the spruce still grows shaggy with usnea.[220] The surface of the ground in the Maine woods is everywhere spongy and saturated with moisture. I noticed that the plants which cover the forest floor there are such as are commonly confined to swamps with us, — the *Clintonia borealis,* orchises, creeping snowberry, and others; and the prevailing aster there is the *Aster acuminatus,* which with us grows in damp and shady woods. The asters *cordifolius* and *macrophyllus* also are common, asters of little or no color, and sometimes without petals. I saw no soft, spreading, second-growth white-pines, with smooth bark, acknowledging the presence of the wood-chopper, but even the young white-pines were all tall and slender rough-barked trees.

Those Maine woods differ essentially from ours. There

218 Thoreau had already seen Ktaadn on this excursion on 17 September, although he may have been unable to get a clear view of the summit. In his journal he wrote: "Saw Ktaadn from a hill about 2 miles NW of Bangor on the road to Pushaw[.] It is about 80 mis from B. This was the nearest point from which we made out to see it" [MJ 17 September 1853].

219 Reference to "Nocturnal Life of Animals in the Primordial Forest" in Alexander von Humboldt's (1769–1859) *Views of Nature.*

220 *Usnea barbata:* a greenish gray pendulous lichen growing on trees, and sometimes referred to as beard moss, or old man's beard.

you are never reminded that the wilderness which you are threading is, after all, some villager's familiar wood-lot, some widow's thirds,[221] from which her ancestors have sledded fuel for generations, minutely described in some old deed which is recorded, of which the owner has got a plan too, and old bound-marks may be found every forty rods, if you will search. 'Tis true, the map may inform you that you stand on land granted by the State to some academy, or on Bingham's purchase;[222] but these names do not impose on you, for you see nothing to remind you of the academy or of Bingham. What were the "forests" of England to these? One writer relates of the Isle of Wight, that in Charles the Second's time "there were woods in the island so complete and extensive, that it is said a squirrel might have travelled in several parts many leagues together on the tops of the trees."[223] If it were not for the rivers, (and he might go round their heads,) a squirrel could here travel thus the whole breadth of the country.

We have as yet had no adequate account of a primitive pine-forest. I have noticed that in a physical atlas lately published in Massachusetts,[224] and used in our schools, the "wood land" of North America is limited almost solely to the valleys of the Ohio and some of the Great Lakes, and the great pine-forests of the globe are not represented. In our vicinity, for instance, New Brunswick and Maine are exhibited as bare as Greenland. It may be that the children of Greenville, at the foot of Moosehead Lake, who surely are not likely to be scared by an owl, are referred to the valley of the Ohio to get an idea of a forest; but they would not know what to do with their moose, bear, caribou, beaver, etc., there. Shall we leave it to an Englishman to inform us, that "in North America, both in the United States and Canada, are the most extensive pine-forests in the world"?[225] The greater part of New Brunswick, the northern half of

221 A widow's legal share of an inheritance, in English and American law: the third part of the husband's personal property, which goes to the widow absolutely in the case of his dying intestate and leaving a child or descendant, given (with various qualifications) by both common law and modern statute.

222 In 1786 Massachusetts disposed of large tracts of unsettled lands in Maine, which was at this time part of Massachusetts, approximately one million acres of which were purchased by the Philadelphian banker William Bingham (1752–1804). A second purchase added another million acres.

223 Quoted from William Gilpin's (1724–1804) *Observations on the Western Parts of England.*

224 Cornelius Sowle Cartée's (1806–1885) *School Atlas of Physical Geography . . . Designed to Accompany Cartée's "Elements of Physical Geography,"* published in Boston in 1856.

225 Quoted from Loudon's *Arboretum et Fruticetum Britanicum.*

226 Quoted from John Smith's (1580–1631) *Description of New England.* as found in Alonzo Lewis's (1794–1861) *History of Lynn, Including Nahant.*

227 William Wood (fl. 1629–1635?) wrote in his *New England's Prospects, Being a True, Lively, and Experimental Description of that Part of America Commonly Called New-England* that Nahant is "well wooded with Oakes, Pines, and Cedars," although Thoreau's source may have been Lewis's *History of Lynn:* "An early writer says it was 'well wooded with oaks, pines and cedars;' and it has a 'sandy beach within the promontory.'"

228 Frederick Tudor (1783–1864), founder of the Tudor Ice Company and known as the Ice King, who is referred to as a "Gentleman farmer" in *Walden.* After inheriting his family's grounds in Nahant, Tudor began a lifelong campaign to plant trees on the otherwise treeless rocky peninsula. An article in the *American Agriculturist* (1846) described Tudor's "series of fences. The outside line is 16 feet high, made of large cedar posts, deeply sunk and braced in the ground, connecting with joists 3 by 5 inches, to which slats or pickets, 3 inches wide and one inch thick, of the same length as the posts, are nailed in an upright position 2 inches apart. . . . A second fence of the same fashion and materials, but not quite so high, is run round the garden a short distance from the first. Then comes a third fence, with others to the number of nearly one hundred, short and long, running off at different angles from the first line, making a complete labyrinth of the garden. . . . In another part of the garden is a peachery by itself, of 300 trees, grown by the sides of short slatted fences, a few feet apart, protected in front by a thick hedge of dwarf willow."

229 County in Massachusetts of which Concord was part.

230 A tall flagpole to the top of which a liberty cap or the flag of a new republic is attached. Liberty poles were erected in town squares, including that of Concord, in the years before and during the American Revolutionary War.

Maine, and adjacent parts of Canada, not to mention the northeastern part of New York and other tracts further off, are still covered with an almost unbroken pine-forest.

But Maine, perhaps, will soon be where Massachusetts is. A good part of her territory is already as bare and commonplace as much of our neighborhood, and her villages generally are not so well shaded as ours. We seem to think that the earth must go through the ordeal of sheep-pasturage before it is habitable by man. Consider Nahant, the resort of all the fashion of Boston,—which peninsula I saw but indistinctly in the twilight, when I steamed by it, and thought that it was unchanged since the discovery. John Smith described it in 1614 as "the Mattahunts, two pleasant isles of groves, gardens, and cornfields";[226] and others tell us that it was once well wooded,[227] and even furnished timber to build the wharves of Boston. Now it is difficult to make a tree grow there, and the visitor comes away with a vision of Mr. Tudor's ugly fences a rod high, designed to protect a few pear-shrubs.[228] And what are we coming to in our Middlesex[229] towns?—a bald, staring town-house, or meeting-house, and a bare liberty-pole,[230] as leafless as it is fruitless, for all I can see. We shall be obliged to import the timber for the last, hereafter, or splice such sticks as we have;—and our ideas of liberty are equally mean with these. The very willow-rows lopped every three years for fuel or powder,[231]—and every sizable pine and oak, or other forest tree, cut down within the memory of man! As if individual speculators were to be allowed to export the clouds out of the sky, or the stars out of the firmament, one by one. We shall be reduced to gnaw the very crust of the earth for nutriment.

They have even descended to smaller game. They have lately, as I hear, invented a machine for chopping up huckleberry-bushes fine, and so converting them into fuel!—bushes which, for fruit alone, are worth all the pear-trees in the country many times over.[232] (I can give you a list of the three best kinds, if you want it.) At this rate, we shall all be obliged to let our beards grow at least, if only to hide the nakedness of the land and make a sylvan appearance. The farmer sometimes talks of "brushing up," simply as if bare ground looked better than clothed ground, than that which wears its natural vesture,—as if the wild hedges, which, perhaps, are more to his children than his whole farm beside, were *dirt*. I know of one who deserves to be called the Tree-hater,[233] and, perhaps, to leave this for a new patronymic to his children. You would think that he had been warned by an oracle that he would be killed by the fall of a tree, and so was resolved to anticipate them. The journalists think that they cannot say too much in favor of such "improvements" in husbandry; it is a safe theme, like piety; but as for the beauty of one of these "model farms,"[234] I would as lief[235] see a patent churn[236] and a man turning it. They are, commonly, places merely where somebody is making money, it may be counterfeiting. The virtue of making two blades of grass grow where only one grew before[237] does not begin to be superhuman.

Nevertheless, it was a relief to get back to our smooth, but still varied landscape. For a permanent residence, it seemed to me that there could be no comparison between this and the wilderness, necessary as the latter is for a resource and a background, the raw material of all our civilization. The wilderness is simple, almost to barrenness. The partially cultivated country it is which chiefly has inspired, and will continue to inspire, the strains of poets, such as compose the mass of any literature. Our woods are sylvan, and their inhabitants woodmen and rustics,—that is, *selvaggia*,[238] and the inhabitants are *salvages*.[239] A civilized man, using the word in the ordinary sense, with his ideas and associations, must at length pine

231 Willow-bark powder from willow-bark charcoal, used in the making of gunpowder. In his journal of 20 August 1851 Thoreau noted: "The willow reach by Lee's Bridge has been stripped for powder. None escapes. This morning, hearing a cart, I looked out and saw George Dugan going by with a horse-load of his willow toward Acton powder-mills, which I had seen in piles by the turnpike" [J 2:410].

232 In his journal of 19 September 1856 Thoreau asked "what is the pear crop to the huckleberry crop? They make a great ado about their pears, those who get any, but how many families raise or buy a barrel of pears all told? The pear crop is insignificant compared with the huckleberry crop" [J 9:86].

233 Possible reference to Charles Davis and the felling of the "Great Davis elm" in 1857. Thoreau noted: "Davis and the neighbors were much alarmed by the creaking in the late storms, for fear it would fall on their roofs. It stands two or three feet into Davis's yard" [J 8:117].

234 Defined by the *Cultivator* (April 1857) as being "in reality a model for the farmer who desires to make a good living and become wealthy," and by the *American Agriculturist* (1848) as "one upon which only the best practices are pursued; in other words, the *beau ideal* of a farm; and in order to become a model, it must necessarily show a greater annual return, in proportion to the outlay, than most of the neighboring farms."

235 Gladly, willingly.

236 Various redesigns of the common churn, such as "Kendall's Patent Churn," which had a removable dasher, or "Gault's Patent Churn," which utilized a special crank system.

237 Jonathan Swift (1667–1745) wrote in *Gulliver's Travels*: "And, he gave it for his Opinion, that whoever could make two Ears of Corn, or two blades of Grass to grow upon a spot of Ground where only one grew before, would deserve better of Mankind, and do more essential Service to his Country than the whole Race of Politicians put together."

238 Italian: savage, wild, belonging to a wood.
239 Early modern English, and old French and Provençal, variant of the modern English *savage*.
240 Thoreau similarly wrote in his journal of 30 December 1853: "The artic voyagers are obliged to invent and willfully engage in active amusements to keep themselves awake and alive" [J 6:38].
241 Allusion to Matthew 3:4 (and similarly in Mark 1:4): "Now John himself had his raiment of camel's hair, and a leathern girdle about his loins; and his food was locusts and wild honey." John the Baptist was a Jewish prophet who preceded Jesus.
242 Allusion to the Castilian Fountain on Mount Parnassus in Greek mythology, sacred to the Muses and a source of inspiration.
243 Definition of forest as found in Thomas Blount's (1618–1679) *Glossographia Anglicana Nova: "Forest,* is a large Wood priviledged to hold the King's game of all kind."

there, like a cultivated plant, which clasps its fibres about a crude and undissolved mass of peat. At the extreme North, the voyagers are obliged to dance and act plays for employment.[240] Perhaps our own woods and fields, — in the best wooded towns, where we need not quarrel about the huckleberries, — with the primitive swamps scattered here and there in their midst, but not prevailing over them, are the perfection of parks and groves, gardens, arbors, paths, vistas, and landscapes. They are the natural consequence of what art and refinement we as a people have, — the common which each village possesses, its true paradise, in comparison with which all elaborately and wilfully wealth-constructed parks and gardens are paltry imitations. Or, I would rather say, such *were* our groves twenty years ago. The poet's, commonly, is not a logger's path, but a woodman's. The logger and pioneer have preceded him, like John the Baptist; eaten the wild honey, it may be, but the locusts also;[241] banished decaying wood and the spongy mosses which feed on it, and built hearths and humanized Nature for him.

But there are spirits of a yet more liberal culture, to whom no simplicity is barren. There are not only stately pines, but fragile flowers, like the orchises, commonly described as too delicate for cultivation, which derive their nutriment from the crudest mass of peat. These remind us, that, not only for strength, but for beauty, the poet must, from time to time, travel the logger's path and the Indian's trail, to drink at some new and more bracing fountain of the Muses,[242] far in the recesses of the wilderness.

The kings of England formerly had their forests "to hold the king's game,"[243] for sport or food, sometimes destroying villages to create or extend them; and I think that they were impelled by a true instinct. Why should not we, who have renounced the king's authority, have our national preserves, where no villages need be destroyed,[244] in which the bear and panther,[245] and some even of the hunter race, may still exist, and not be "civilized off the face of the earth,"[246]—our forests, not to hold the king's game merely, but to hold and preserve the king himself also, the lord of creation,[247]—not for idle sport or food, but for inspiration and our own true recreation? or shall we, like villains, grub them all up, poaching on our own national domains?

244 For the purpose of establishing New Forest, William the Conqueror depopulated a district by destroying villages and driving out the inhabitants.
245 Cougar.
246 Allusion to Charles Dickens's "Noble Savage": "I call him a savage, and I call a savage something highly desirable to be civilized off the face of the earth" (*Household Words* [11 June 1853]).
247 Epithet used for both God, as the creator, and man, who, in Genesis 1:28–29, was given "dominion over the fish of the sea, and over the fowl of the air, and over every living thing that moveth upon the earth."

The Allegash and East Branch

I started on my third excursion to the Maine woods Monday, July 20th, 1857, with one companion,[1] arriving at Bangor the next day at noon.[2] We had hardly left the steamer, when we passed Molly Molasses[3] in the street. As long as she lives the Penobscots may be considered extant as a tribe. The succeeding morning, a relative of mine,[4] who is well acquainted with the Penobscot Indians, and who had been my companion in my two previous excursions into the Maine woods, took me in his wagon to Oldtown, to assist me in obtaining an Indian for this expedition.

We were ferried across to the Indian Island in a batteau. The ferryman's boy had got the key to it, but the father, who was a blacksmith, after a little hesitation, cut the chain with a cold-chisel[5] on a rock. He told us that the Indians were nearly all gone to the seaboard and to Massachusetts, partly on account of the small-pox, of which they are very much afraid,[6] having broken out in Oldtown, and it was doubtful whether we should find a suitable one at home. The old chief Neptune, however, was there still. The first man we saw on the island was an Indian named Joseph Polis,[7] whom my relative had known from a boy, and now addressed familiarly as "Joe." He was dressing a deer-skin in his yard. The skin was spread over a slanting log, and he was scraping it with a stick, held by both hands. He was stoutly built, perhaps a little above the middle height, with a broad face, and, as others said, perfect Indian features and

1 Edward Sherman Hoar (1823–1893), Thoreau's Concord friend and sometimes traveling companion, was the son of Samuel Hoar (1778–1856), judge and statesman. Hoar was with Thoreau when they accidentally set the woods on fire in April 1844, and he would accompany Thoreau to the White Mountains in July 1858.

2 Thoreau took the Fitchburg Railroad to Boston, then at 5 P.M. took the Boston and Maine Railroad to Portland. In his journal Thoreau described the railroad cars as "very hot and dusty" and in need of a veil "to exclude cinders as in the woods to keep off mosquitoes. Riding in the cars this weather like sitting in the flue of a chimney" [J 9:485]. From Portland he took the steamer, which was delayed by a night fog, to Bangor.

3 Molly Molasses (ca. 1775–1867), whose real name may have been Molly, or Mary, Balassee Nicola, was an Abenaki and considered to have *m'teoulin*, magic, including the ability to foretell the future. She was described as wearing "long calico jumpers, and men's tall silk hats" in Joseph Williamson's (1828–1902) *History of the City of Belfast*.

4 George Thatcher.

5 Tool made of tempered steel used for cutting cold metals, those not softened by heating in a forge or with a heating torch.

6 Smallpox, when introduced in North America by Europeans, had devastated Native American tribes across the continent. Williamson wrote in his *History of the State of Maine* that "the small pox and other diseases . . . carried off great numbers of the natives," and George Catlan (1796–1872) in his *Letters and Notes on the Manners, Customs, and Conditions of the North American Indians* called it "the great destroyer of the Indian race."

7 Joseph Polis, sometimes Poris or Porus (ca. 1808–1884), was described by Manly Hardy (1832–1910) as "a very mysterious man, full of quiet drollery. He would come up, and, extending his hand at full arm's length, look one gravely in the face and perhaps give some exclamation in Indian, asking its meaning, although he knew you complexion. His house was a two-story white one with blinds, the best looking that I noticed there, and as good as an average one on a New England village street. It was surrounded by a garden and fruit-trees, single cornstalks standing thinly amid the beans. We asked him if he knew any good Indian who would like to go into the woods with us, that is, to the Allegash Lakes, by way of Moosehead,[8] and return by the East Branch of the Penobscot, or vary from this as we pleased. To which he answered, out of that strange remoteness in which the Indian ever dwells to the white man, "Me like to go myself; me want to get some moose"; and kept on scraping the skin.[9] His brother[10] had been into the woods with my relative only a year or two before, and the Indian now inquired what the latter had done to him, that he did not come back, for he had not seen nor heard from him since.

At length we got round to the more interesting topic again. The ferryman had told us that all the best Indians were gone except Polis, who was one of the aristocracy.[11] He to be sure would be the best man we could have, but if he went at all would want a great price; so we did not expect to get him.

Polis asked at first two dollars a day, but agreed to go for a dollar and a half, and fifty cents a week for his canoe.[12] He would come to Bangor with his canoe by the seven o'clock train that evening,—we might depend on him. We thought ourselves lucky to secure the services of this man, who was known to be particularly steady and reliable.

I spent the afternoon with my companion, who had remained in Bangor, in preparing for our expedition, purchasing provisions, hard bread, pork, coffee, sugar, etc., and some India-rubber clothing.

We had at first thought of exploring the St. John from its source to its mouth, or else to go up the Penobscot by its East Branch to the lakes of the St. John, and re-

did not know." Thoreau wrote on 17 August 1857: "I have been associating for about a month with one Joseph Polis, the chief man of the Penobscot tribe of Indians, and have learned a great deal from him" [C 488].

8 The largest lake in Maine.

9 Thoreau wrote in his journal the following account that had taken place before Polis showed interest in accompanying them: "While we were talking with Polis, a young, very dark-complexioned Indian, named something like Nicholai Orson, came up, and Polis said, 'He go with you.' We found that the latter wanted to go very much, said he knew the country and all about it. But I said, 'We don't know you.' He was too dark-colored, as if with African blood,—P. said they did not mix with them,—and too young for me. While I was talking with him, Thatcher took Polis aside and inquired the other's character, when P. frankly told him that he wouldn't do for us at all, that he was a very good fellow except that he would get drunk whenever he had a chance" [J 9:486–487].

10 Peal Polis, who was listed in the 1858 census of the Penobscot Indians as age thirty-seven. In 1841 he petitioned the Maine legislature to learn to read and write English.

11 Possibly considered such through his association as a Penobscot representative to the Maine legislature during the 1830s and 1840s.

12 In a 28 January 1858 letter to Thomas Wentworth Higginson (1823–1911) Thoreau wrote: "We paid the Indian, who was a very good one, $1.50 per day & 50 cents a week for his canoe. This is enough in ordinary seasons. I had formerly paid $2 for an Indian & for white batteau-men" [W 6:325].

13 Thoreau's friend and first biographer, William Ellery Channing, wrote: "Once he made for himself a knapsack, with partitions for his books and papers,—india-rubber cloth, strong and large and spaced (the common knapsacks being unspaced). The partitions were made of stout book-paper."

14 Modeled after the Tremont House in Boston, the Bangor House opened in 1834. It was the largest hotel in Maine, having seventy-five rooms (sixty for guests and fifteen for the staff) on three and a half stories, with a spacious reception hall, dining room, bar, gentlemen's parlor, ladies' drawing room, ladies' dining room, smoking room, reading room, and a ballroom on the second floor that could seat two hundred for dining.

15 The leader of this hunting party was Hiram Lewis Leonard (1831–1907), who was, at this time, a well-known hunter and gunsmith in Bangor. According to the Maine historian Fannie Eckstorm, "The other three man were William H. Staples, of Patten . . . a man named Lane and one named Lunt, of Orono. Staples was going only to Moosehead Lake, the others through to Tobique River in Canada on a hunting trip."

turn by way of Chesuncook and Moosehead. We had finally inclined to the last route, only reversing the order of it, going by way of Moosehead, and returning by the Penobscot, otherwise it would have been all the way up stream and taken twice as long.

At evening Polis arrived in the cars, and I led the way while he followed me three quarters of a mile to my friend's house, with the canoe on his head. I did not know the exact route myself, but steered by the lay of the land, as I do in Boston, and I tried to enter into conversation with him, but as he was puffing under the weight of his canoe, not having the usual apparatus for carrying it, but, above all, was an Indian, I might as well have been thumping on the bottom of his birch the while. In answer to the various observations which I made by way of breaking the ice, he only grunted vaguely from beneath his canoe once or twice, so that I knew he was there.

Early the next morning (July 23d) the stage called for us, the Indian having breakfasted with us, and already placed the baggage in the canoe to see how it would go. My companion and I had each a large knapsack as full as it would hold, and we had two large India-rubber bags which held our provision and utensils.[13] As for the Indian, all the baggage he had, beside his axe and gun, was a blanket, which he brought loose in his hand. However, he had laid in a store of tobacco and a new pipe for the excursion. The canoe was securely lashed diagonally across the top of the stage, with bits of carpet tucked under the edge to prevent its chafing. The very accommodating driver appeared as much accustomed to carrying canoes in this way as bandboxes.

At the Bangor House[14] we took in four men bound on a hunting excursion,[15] one of the men going as cook. They had a dog, a middling-sized brindled cur, which ran by the side of the stage, his master showing his head and whistling from time to time; but after we had gone about three miles the dog was suddenly missing, and two of the party went back for him, while the stage, which was full of passengers, waited. I suggested that he had taken the back track for the Bangor House. At length one man came back, while the other kept on. This whole party of hunters declared their intention to stop till the dog was found; but the very obliging driver was ready to wait a spell longer. He was evidently unwilling to lose so many passengers, who would have taken a private conveyance, or perhaps the other line of stages, the next day. Such progress did we make with a journey of over sixty miles, to be accomplished that day, and a rain-storm just setting in. We discussed the subject of dogs and their instincts till it was threadbare, while we waited there, and the scenery of the suburbs of Bangor is still distinctly impressed on my memory. After full half an hour the man returned, leading the dog by a rope. He had overtaken him just as he was entering the Bangor House. He was then tied on the top of the stage, but being wet and cold, several times in the course of the journey he jumped off, and I saw him dangling by his neck. This dog was depended on to stop bears with. He had already stopped one somewhere in New Hampshire, and I can testify that he stopped a stage in Maine. This party of four probably paid nothing for the dog's ride, nor for his run, while our party of three paid nine dollars, and were charged four for the light canoe which lay still on the top.

It soon began to rain, and grew more and more stormy as the day advanced. This was the third time that I had passed over this route, and it rained steadily each time all day. We accordingly saw but little of the country. The stage was crowded all the way, and I attended the more to my fellow-travellers. If you had looked inside this coach you would have thought that we were prepared to run the gauntlet of a band of robbers, for there were

16 Twelve bullets per pound, although according to Eckstorm, this gun "carried nine bullets to the pound, not twelve."
17 River rising in northwest New Brunswick and flowing northeast 130 miles to Chaleur Bay.
18 Inlet of the Gulf of St. Lawrence, between north New Brunswick and the Gaspé Peninsula, discovered and named by Jacques Cartier in 1534.
19 In the sense of acting with politeness and civil manners as opposed to the sense of being a person of noble birth or superior social position.

four or five guns on the front seat, the Indian's included, and one or two on the back one, each man holding his darling in his arms. One had a gun which carried twelve to a pound.[16] It appeared that this party of hunters was going our way, but much further down the Allegash and St. John, and thence up some other stream, and across to the Ristigouche[17] and the Bay of Chaleur,[18] to be gone six weeks. They had canoes, axes, and supplies deposited some distance along the route. They carried flour, and were to have new bread made every day. Their leader was a handsome man about thirty years old, of good height, but not apparently robust, of gentlemanly dress and faultless toilet; such a one as you might expect to meet on Broadway. In fact, in the popular sense of the word, he was the most "gentlemanly"[19] appearing man in the stage, or that we saw on the road. He had a fair white complexion, as if he had always lived in the shade, and an intellectual face, and with his quiet manners might have passed for a divinity student who had seen something of the world. I was surprised to find, on talking with him in the course of the day's journey, that he was a hunter at all,—for his gun was not much exposed,—and yet more to find that he was probably the chief white hunter of Maine, and was known all along the road. He had also hunted in some of the States further south and west. I afterwards heard him spoken of as one who could endure a great deal of exposure and fatigue without showing the effect of it; and he could not only use guns, but make them, being himself a gunsmith. In the spring, he had saved a stage-driver and two passengers from drowning in the backwater of the Piscataquis in Foxcroft on this road, having swum ashore in the freezing water and made a raft and got them off,—though the horses were drowned,—at great risk to himself, while the only other man who could swim withdrew to the nearest house to prevent freezing. He could now ride over this road for nothing. He knew our man, and remarked that we had a good Indian there, a good hunter; adding that he was said to be worth $6,000. The Indian also knew him, and said to me, "the great hunter."

The former told me that he practised a kind of still hunting,[20] new or uncommon in those parts, that the caribou, for instance, fed round and round the same meadow, returning on the same path, and he lay in wait for them.

The Indian sat on the front seat, saying nothing to anybody, with a stolid expression of face, as if barely awake to what was going on. Again I was struck by the peculiar vagueness of his replies when addressed in the stage, or at the taverns. He really never said anything on such occasions. He was merely stirred up, like a wild beast, and passively muttered some insignificant response. His answer, in such cases, was never the consequence of a positive mental energy, but vague as a puff of smoke, suggesting no *responsibility,* and if you considered it, you would find that you had got nothing out of him. This was instead of the conventional palaver and smartness of the white man, and equally profitable. Most get no more than this out of the Indian, and pronounce him stolid accordingly.[21] I was surprised to see what a foolish and impertinent style a Maine man, a passenger, used in addressing him, as if he were a child, which only made his eyes glisten a little. A tipsy Canadian asked him at a tavern, in a drawling tone, if he smoked, to which he answered with an indefinite "yes." "Won't you lend me your pipe a little while?" asked the other. He replied, looking straight by the man's head, with a face singularly vacant to all neighboring interests, "Me got no pipe"; yet I had seen him put a new one, with a supply of tobacco, into his pocket that morning.

Our little canoe, so neat and strong, drew a favorable criticism from all the wiseacres among the tavern

20 Hunting by stalking stealthily or from under cover. As Thoreau wrote in his journal: "His mode of hunting seemed to be to go patiently in search of the game—& lie in wait for it in a quiet & stealthy manner—" [MJ 23 July 1857]

21 Native Americans were called stolid by many nineteenth-century writers, including Schoolcraft, Thomas de Quincy (1785–1859), and John Greenleaf Whittier (1807–1892).

22 In his journal Thoreau wrote: "There were two public houses near together, and they wanted to detain us at the first, even took off some of our baggage in spite of us; but, on our protesting, shouted, 'Let them go! let them go,' as if it was any of their business. Whereupon we, thanking them for the privilege, rode on. . . . Here we found a spacious house, quite empty, close to the lake, with an attentive landlord, which was what we wanted. A bright wood fire soon burned very comfortable in that fresh atmosphere in the ample barroom, very comfortable in that fresh and cool atmosphere, and we congratulated ourselves on having escaped the crowd at the other house" [J 9:489]. The first public house to which Thoreau went was the Eveleth House, constructed in 1846. The second was the inn built by Joshua Fogg in 1850 to replace the Seboomook House, later called the Lake House, that was built in 1835 and burned down on 15 March 1849.

loungers along the road. By the roadside, close to the wheels, I noticed a splendid great purple-fringed orchis with a spike as big as an epilobium, which I would fain have stopped the stage to pluck, but as this had never been known to stop a bear, like the cur on the stage, the driver would probably have thought it a waste of time.

When we reached the lake, about half past eight in the evening, it was still steadily raining, and harder than before; and, in that fresh, cool atmosphere, the hylodes were peeping and the toads ringing about the lake universally, as in the spring with us. It was as if the seasons had revolved backward two or three months, or I had arrived at the abode of perpetual spring.

We had expected to go upon the lake at once, and after paddling up two or three miles, to camp on one of its islands; but on account of the steady and increasing rain, we decided to go to one of the taverns[22] for the night, though, for my own part, I should have preferred to camp out.

About four o'clock the next morning, (July 24th,) though it was quite cloudy, accompanied by the landlord to the water's edge, in the twilight, we launched our canoe from a rock on the Moosehead Lake. When I was there four years before we had a rather small canoe for three persons, and I had thought that this time I would get a larger one, but the present one was even smaller than that. It was 18¼ feet long by 2 feet 6½ inches wide in the middle, and one foot deep within, as I found by measurement, and I judged that it would weigh not far from eighty pounds. The Indian had recently made it himself, and its smallness was partly compensated for by its newness, as well as stanchness and solidity, it being made of very thick bark and ribs. Our baggage weighed about 166 pounds, so that the canoe carried about 600 pounds in all, or the weight of four men. The principal part of the baggage was, as usual, placed in the middle of the broadest part, while we stowed ourselves in the chinks and crannies that were left before and behind it, where there was no room to extend our legs, the loose articles being tucked into the ends. The canoe was thus as closely packed as a market-basket, and might possibly have been upset without spilling any of its contents. The Indian sat on a cross-bar in the stern, but we flat on the bottom, with a splint or chip behind our backs, to protect them from the cross-bar, and one of us commonly paddled with the Indian. He foresaw that we should not want a pole till we reached the Umbazookskus River, it being either dead water or down stream so far, and he was prepared to make a sail of his blanket in the bows, if the wind should be fair; but we never used it.

It had rained more or less the four previous days, so that we thought we might count on some fair weather. The wind was at first southwesterly.

Paddling along the eastern side of the lake in the still of the morning, we soon saw a few sheldrakes, which the Indian called *Shecorways,* and some peetweets *Naramekechus,* on the rocky shore; we also saw and heard loons, *medawisla,* which he said was a sign of wind. It was inspiriting to hear the regular dip of the paddles, as if they were our fins or flippers, and to realize that we were at length fairly embarked. We who had felt strangely as stage-passengers and tavern-lodgers were suddenly naturalized there and presented with the freedom of the lakes and the woods. Having passed the small rocky isles within two or three miles of the foot of the lake, we had a short consultation respecting our course, and inclined to the western shore for the sake of its lee; for otherwise, if the wind should rise, it would be impossible for us to reach Mount Kineo, which is about midway up the lake on the east side, but at its narrowest part, where probably we could recross if we took the western side. The wind is the chief obstacle to crossing the lakes, especially in so

23 Formerly Big Squaw Mountain, now Big Moose Mountain.

24 Now Big Spencer Mountain.

25 Monkey flower.

26 Thoreau referred to several ducks as dippers in his journal, making specific attempts to identify this bird after returning from Maine. On 29 October 1857 Thoreau noted that the Concord trapper George Melvin (b. 1813) called a coot "a little black dipper! It has some clear white under its tail. Is this, then, the name of that dipper? and are the young dippers of Moosehead different? The latter were in flocks and had some white in front" [J 10:140]. On 27 November he noted that another person told him "that the little dipper is not a coot" [J 10:208–209], and again on 26 December a third person "saw the bird which Melvin shot last summer (a coot), but he never saw one of them before. The little dipper must, therefore, be different from a coot. Is it not a grebe?" [J 10:225] In his appendix Thoreau lists under *Fuligula albeola* the "spirit duck or dipper."

27 Following this sentence, Thoreau's manuscript journal has: "P. said the mother had perhaps been killed" [MJ 24 July 1857].

small a canoe. The Indian remarked several times that he did not like to cross the lakes "in littlum canoe," but nevertheless, "just as we say, it made no odds to him." He sometimes took a straight course up the middle of the lake between Sugar and Deer Islands, when there was no wind.

Measured on the map, Moosehead Lake is twelve miles wide at the widest place, and thirty miles long in a direct line, but longer as it lies. The captain of the steamer called it thirty-eight miles as he steered. We should probably go about forty. The Indian said that it was called "*Mspame,* because large water." Squaw Mountain[23] rose darkly on our left, near the outlet of the Kennebec, and what the Indian called Spencer Bay Mountain,[24] on the east, and already we saw Mount Kineo before us in the north.

Paddling near the shore, we frequently heard the *pe-pe* of the olive-sided fly-catcher, also the wood-pewee, and the kingfisher, thus early in the morning. The Indian reminding us that he could not work without eating, we stopped to breakfast on the main shore, southwest of Deer Island, at a spot where the *Mimulus ringens*[25] grew abundantly. We took out our bags, and the Indian made a fire under a very large bleached log, using white-pine bark from a stump, though he said that hemlock was better, and kindling with canoe-birch bark. Our table was a large piece of freshly peeled birch-bark, laid wrong-side-up, and our breakfast consisted of hard bread, fried pork, and strong coffee, well sweetened, in which we did not miss the milk.

While we were getting breakfast a brood of twelve black dippers,[26] half grown, came paddling by within three or four rods, not at all alarmed; and they loitered about as long as we stayed, now huddled close together, within a circle of eighteen inches in diameter, now moving off in a long line, very cunningly.[27] Yet they bore a certain proportion to the great Moosehead Lake on whose bosom they floated, and I felt as if they were under its protection.

Looking northward from this place it appeared as if we were entering a large bay, and we did not know whether we should be obliged to diverge from our course and keep outside a point which we saw, or should find a passage between this and the mainland. I consulted my map and used my glass, and the Indian did the same, but we could not find our place exactly on the map, nor could we detect any break in the shore. When I asked the Indian the way, he answered "I don't know," which I thought remarkable, since he had said that he was familiar with the lake; but it appeared that he had never been up this side. It was misty dog-day weather,[28] and we had already penetrated a smaller bay of the same kind, and knocked the bottom out of it, though we had been obliged to pass over a small bar, between an island and the shore, where there was but just breadth and depth enough to float the canoe, and the Indian had observed, "Very easy makum bridge here," but now it seemed that, if we held on, we should be fairly embayed. Presently, however, though we had not stirred, the mist lifted somewhat, and revealed a break in the shore northward, showing that the point was a portion of Deer Island, and that our course lay westward of it. Where it had seemed a continuous shore even through a glass, one portion was now seen by the naked eye to be much more distant than the other which overlapped it, merely by the greater thickness of the mist which still rested on it, while the nearer or island portion was comparatively bare and green. The line of separation was very distinct, and the Indian immediately remarked, "I guess you and I go there,—I guess there's room for my canoe there." This was his common expression instead of saying we. He never addressed us by our names, though curious to know how they were spelled and what

28 Hottest days of summer, from first week of July to second week of August, so named for Sirius, the Dog Star, that rises with the sun at that time of year.

they meant, while we called him Polis. He had already guessed very accurately at our ages, and said that he was forty-eight.

After breakfast I emptied the melted pork that was left into the lake, making what sailors call a "slick,"[29] and watching to see how much it spread over and smoothed the agitated surface. The Indian looked at it a moment and said, "That make hard paddlum thro'; hold 'em canoe. So say old times."

We hastily reloaded, putting the dishes loose in the bows, that they might be at hand when wanted, and set out again. The western shore, near which we paddled along, rose gently to a considerable height, and was everywhere densely covered with the forest, in which was a large proportion of hard wood to enliven and relieve the fir and spruce.

The Indian said that the usnea lichen which we saw hanging from the trees was called *chorchorque.* We asked him the names of several small birds which we heard this morning. The wood-thrush, which was quite common, and whose note he imitated, he said was called *Adelung-quamooktum;* but sometimes he could not tell the name of some small bird which I heard and knew, but he said, "I tell all the birds about here,—this country; can't tell littlum noise, but I see 'em, then I can tell."

I observed that I should like to go to school to him to learn his language, living on the Indian island the while; could not that be done? "O, yer," he replied, "good many do so." I asked how long he thought it would take. He said one week. I told him that in this voyage I would tell him all I knew, and he should tell me all he knew, to which he readily agreed.

The birds sang quite as in our woods,—the red-eye, red-start, veery, wood-pewee, etc., but we saw no blue-birds in all our journey, and several told me in Bangor that they had not the bluebird there. Mount Kineo, which was generally visible, though occasionally concealed by islands or the mainland in front, had a level bar of cloud concealing its summit, and all the mountain-tops about the lake were cut off at the same height. Ducks of various kinds—sheldrake, summer ducks, etc.—were quite common, and ran over the water before us as fast as a horse trots. Thus they were soon out of sight.

The Indian asked the meaning of *reality,* as near as I could make out the word, which he said one of us had used; also of "*interrent,*" that is, intelligent. I observed that he could rarely sound the letter r, but used l, as also r for l sometimes; as *load* for road, *pickelel* for pickerel, *Soogle* Island for Sugar Island, *lock* for rock, etc. Yet he trilled the r pretty well after me.[30]

He generally added the syllable *um* to his words when he could,—as padl*um,* etc. I have once heard a Chippewa lecture, who made his audience laugh unintentionally by putting *m* after the word *too,* which word he brought in continually and unnecessarily, accenting and prolonging this sound into *m-ah* sonorously as if it were necessary to bring in so much of his vernacular as a relief to his organs, a compensation for twisting his jaws about, and putting his tongue into every corner of his mouth, as he complained that he was obliged to do when he spoke English. There was so much of the Indian accent resounding through his English, so much of the "bow-arrow tang" as my neighbor calls it,[31] and I have no doubt that word seemed to him the best pronounced.[32] It was a wild and refreshing sound, like that of the wind among the pines, or the booming of the surf on the shore.

I asked him the meaning of the word *Musketicook,* the Indian name of Concord River. He pronounced it *Muskéeticook,* emphasizing the second syllable with a peculiar guttural sound, and said that it meant "Deadwater," which it is, and in this definition he agreed exactly with the St. Francis Indian with whom I talked in 1853.

30 Channing wrote: "Henry retained a peculiar pronunciation of the letter *r,* with a decided French accent. He says, 'September is the first month with a *burr* in it'; and his speech always had an emphasis, a *burr* in it."

31 Probably George Minott, sometimes Minot (1783–1861), of whom Thoreau wrote in "Wild Apples": "An old farmer in my neighborhood, who always selects the right word, says that 'they have a kind of bow-arrow tang.'" Thoreau called him a "most poetical farmer" who used "good old English words . . . though I never heard them before in my life" [J 3:41].

32 In his journal of 5 March 1858 Thoreau wrote: "Went to hear a Chippeway Indian. . . . He made the audience laugh unintentionally by putting an m after the word too, which he brought in continually and unnecessarily, and almost after this word alone, emphasizing and prolonging that sound, as, 'They carried them home toom-ah,' as if it were a necessity for bringing in so much of the Indian language for a relief to his organs or a compensation for 'twisting his jaws about,' as he said, in his attempt to speak English. So Polis and the Penobscots continually put the um or em to our words. . . . I have no doubt it was a great relief to him and seemed the word best pronounced" [J 10:291].

33 Squaw Point.
34 Thoreau had reached the mouth of the West Outlet of the Kennebec River, not the Moose River, as he believed from Coffin's 1835 map.
35 According to the 1861 *Annual Report upon the Natural History and Geology of Maine,* the steamer "goes from Greenville to the head of the lake once a week."

On a point on the mainland[33] some miles southwest of Sand-bar Island, where we landed to stretch our legs and look at the vegetation, going inland a few steps, I discovered a fire still glowing beneath its ashes, where somebody had breakfasted, and a bed of twigs prepared for the following night. So I knew not only that they had just left, but that they designed to return, and by the breadth of the bed that there was more than one in the party. You might have gone within six feet of these signs without seeing them. There grew the beaked hazel, the only hazel which I saw on this journey, the *Diervilla,* rue seven feet high, which was very abundant on all the lake and river shores, and *Cornus stolonifera,* or red osier, whose bark, the Indian said, was good to smoke, and was called *maquoxigill,* "tobacco before white people came to this country, Indian tobacco."

The Indian was always very careful in approaching the shore, lest he should injure his canoe on the rocks, letting it swing round slowly sidewise, and was still more particular that we should not step into it on shore, nor till it floated free, and then should step gently lest we should open its seams, or make a hole in the bottom. He said that he would tell us when to jump.

Soon after leaving this point we passed the mouth of the Kennebec,[34] and heard and saw the falls at the dam there, for even Moosehead Lake is dammed. After passing Deer Island, we saw the little steamer from Greenville,[35] far east in the middle of the lake, and she appeared nearly stationary. Sometimes we could hardly tell her from an island which had a few trees on it. Here we were exposed to the wind from over the whole breadth of the lake, and ran a little risk of being swamped. While I had my eye fixed on the spot where a large fish had leaped, we took in a gallon or two of water, which filled my lap; but we soon reached the shore and took the canoe over the bar, at Sand-bar Island, a few feet wide only, and so saved a considerable distance. One landed first at a more sheltered place, and walking round caught the canoe by the prow, to prevent it being injured against the shore.

Again we crossed a broad bay opposite the mouth of Moose River, before reaching the narrow strait at Mount Kineo, made what the voyageurs call a *traverse,*[36] and found the water quite rough. A very little wind on these broad lakes raises a sea which will swamp a canoe. Looking off from a lee shore, the surface may appear to be very little agitated, almost smooth, a mile distant, or if you see a few white crests they appear nearly level with the rest of the lake; but when you get out so far, you may find quite a sea running, and erelong, before you think of it, a wave will gently creep up the side of the canoe and fill your lap, like a monster deliberately covering you with its slime before it swallows you,[37] or it will strike the canoe violently and break into it. The same thing may happen when the wind rises suddenly, though it were perfectly calm and smooth there a few minutes before; so that nothing can save you, unless you can swim ashore, for it is impossible to get into a canoe again when it is upset. Since you sit flat on the bottom, though the danger should not be imminent, a little water is a great inconvenience, not to mention the wetting of your provisions. We rarely crossed even a bay directly, from point to point, when there was wind, but made a slight curve corresponding somewhat to the shore, that we might the sooner reach it if the wind increased.

When the wind is aft, and not too strong, the Indian makes a spritsail[38] of his blanket. He thus easily skims over the whole length of this lake in a day.

The Indian paddled on one side, and one of us on the other, to keep the canoe steady, and when he wanted to change hands he would say "t'other side." He asserted, in answer to our questions, that he had never upset a canoe himself, though he may have been upset by others.

36 Term used for the crossing of a wide, open stretch of water from point to point.
37 The boa constrictor, sometimes called a serpent or monster in early books of natural history, is described as covering its victims with slime to ease the process of ingesting.
38 Sail extended by a small sprit or spar. As Thoreau wrote earlier, Polis "was prepared to make a sail of his blanket in the bows, if the wind should be fair; but we never used it."

39 Troll or trawl: to drag or trail a fishing-line and hook behind a boat, at or near the surface of the water.

40 Burbot (*Lota maculosa*), also known as fresh-water cod and eel-pout.

41 The simultaneous firing of all the armament on one side of a ship.

Think of our little egg-shell of a canoe tossing across that great lake, a mere black speck to the eagle soaring above it!

My companion trailed[39] for trout as we paddled along, but the Indian warning him that a big fish might upset us, for there are some very large ones there, he agreed to pass the line quickly to him in the stern if he had a bite. Beside trout, I heard of cusk,[40] white-fish, etc., as found in this lake.

While we were crossing this bay, where Mount Kineo rose dark before us, within two or three miles, the Indian repeated the tradition respecting this mountain's having anciently been a cow moose,—how a mighty Indian hunter, whose name I forget, succeeded in killing this queen of the moose tribe with great difficulty, while her calf was killed somewhere among the islands in Penobscot Bay, and, to his eyes, this mountain had still the form of the moose in a reclining posture, its precipitous side presenting the outline of her head. He told this at some length, though it did not amount to much, and with apparent good faith, and asked us how we supposed the hunter could have killed such a mighty moose as that,—how we could do it. Whereupon a man-of-war to fire broadsides[41] into her was suggested, etc. An Indian tells such a story as if he thought it deserved to have a good deal said about it, only he has not got it to say, and so he makes up for the deficiency by a drawling tone, long-windedness, and a dumb wonder which he hopes will be contagious.

We approached the land again through pretty rough water, and then steered directly across the lake, at its narrowest part, to the eastern side, and were soon partly under the lee of the mountain, about a mile north of the Kineo House, having paddled about twenty miles. It was now about noon.

We designed to stop there that afternoon and night,

and spent half an hour looking along the shore northward for a suitable place to camp. We took out all our
baggage at one place in vain, it being too rocky and uneven, and while engaged in this search we made our first
acquaintance with the moose-fly. At length, half a mile
further north, by going half a dozen rods into the dense
spruce and fir wood on the side of the mountain, almost
as dark as a cellar, we found a place sufficiently clear and
level to lie down on, after cutting away a few bushes. We
required a space only seven feet by six for our bed, the
fire being four or five feet in front, though it made no
odds how rough the hearth was; but it was not always
easy to find this in those woods. The Indian first cleared
a path to it from the shore with his axe, and we then
carried up all our baggage, pitched our tent, and made
our bed, in order to be ready for foul weather, which
then threatened us, and for the night. He gathered a
large armful of fir twigs, breaking them off, which he said
were the best for our bed, partly, I thought, because they
were the largest and could be most rapidly collected. It
had been raining more or less for four or five days, and
the wood was even damper than usual, but he got dry
bark for the fire from the under-side of a dead leaning
hemlock, which, he said, he could always do.

This noon his mind was occupied with a law question, and I referred him to my companion, who was a
lawyer.[42] It appeared that he had been buying land lately,
(I think it was a hundred acres,) but there was probably
an incumbrance to it, somebody else claiming to have
bought some grass on it for this year. He wished to know
to whom the grass belonged, and was told that if the
other man could prove that he bought the grass before
he, Polis, bought the land, the former could take it,
whether the latter knew it or not. To which he only answered, "Strange!" He went over this several times, fairly
sat down to it, with his back to a tree, as if he meant to

[42] Hoar practiced law in New York following his graduation from Harvard in 1844.

43 Now Boundary Bald Mountain.

confine us to this topic henceforth; but as he made no headway, only reached the jumping-off place of his wonder at white men's institutions after each explanation, we let the subject die.

He said that he had fifty acres of grass, potatoes, etc., somewhere above Oldtown, beside some about his house; that he hired a good deal of his work, hoeing, etc., and preferred white men to Indians, because "they keep steady, and know how."

After dinner we returned southward along the shore, in the canoe, on account of the difficulty of climbing over the rocks and fallen trees, and began to ascend the mountain along the edge of the precipice. But a smart shower coming up just then, the Indian crept under his canoe, while we, being protected by our rubber coats, proceeded to botanize. So we sent him back to the camp for shelter, agreeing that he should come there for us with his canoe toward night. It had rained a little in the forenoon, and we trusted that this would be the clearing-up shower, which it proved; but our feet and legs were thoroughly wet by the bushes. The clouds breaking away a little, we had a glorious wild view, as we ascended, of the broad lake with its fluctuating surface and numerous forest-clad islands, extending beyond our sight both north and south, and the boundless forest undulating away from its shores on every side, as densely packed as a rye-field, and enveloping nameless mountains in succession; but above all, looking westward over a large island was visible a very distant part of the lake, though we did not then suspect it to be Moosehead,—at first a mere broken white line seen through the tops of the island trees, like hay-caps, but spreading to a lake when we got higher. Beyond this we saw what appears to be called Bald Mountain on the map,[43] some twenty-five miles distant, near the sources of the Penobscot. It was a perfect lake of the woods. But this was only a transient gleam, for the rain was not quite over.

Looking southward, the heavens were completely overcast, the mountains capped with clouds, and the lake generally wore a dark and stormy appearance, but from its surface just north of Sugar Island, six or eight miles distant, there was reflected upward to us through the misty air a bright blue tinge from the distant unseen sky of another latitude beyond. They probably had a clear sky then at Greenville, the south end of the lake. Standing on a mountain in the midst of a lake, where would you look for the first sign of approaching fair weather? Not into the heavens, it seems, but into the lake.

Again we mistook a little rocky islet seen through the "drisk,"[44] with some taller bare trunks or stumps on it, for the steamer with its smoke-pipes, but as it had not changed its position after half an hour, we were undeceived. So much do the works of man resemble the works of nature. A moose might mistake a steamer for a floating isle, and not be scared till he heard its puffing or its whistle.

If I wished to see a mountain or other scenery under the most favorable auspices, I would go to it in foul weather, so as to be there when it cleared up; we are then in the most suitable mood, and nature is most fresh and inspiring. There is no serenity so fair as that which is just established in a tearful eye.

Jackson, in his Report on the Geology of Maine, in 1838, says of this mountain: "Hornstone,[45] which will answer for flints, occurs in various parts of the State, where trap-rocks have acted upon silicious slate. The largest mass of this stone known in the world is Mount Kineo, upon Moosehead Lake, which appears to be entirely composed of it, and rises seven hundred feet above the lake level. This variety of hornstone I have seen in every part of New England in the form of Indian arrow-

44 On 29 July 1851 Thoreau noted in his journal: "In the afternoon I sailed to Plymouth 3 miles notwithstanding the drizzling rain or 'drisk' as Uncle Ned called it" [J 2:356].
45 Hornfels: subspecies of quartz, similar to flint but more brittle.

46 Quoted from Jackson's *Second Annual Report*.

47 On 28 March 1859 Thoreau wrote in his journal: "I have not decided whether I had better publish my experience in searching for arrowheads in three volumes, with plates and an index, or try to compress it into one" [ITM 389]. Whether he may have been seriously intending to compile a work specifically on arrowheads is unclear. Although Thoreau began compiling notebooks of his readings on Native Americans in 1850, his final intentions for this material are unspecified and indeterminate.

48 Having convex elevations and concave depressions, applied principally to such a surface produced by fracture, as exemplified in obsidian.

49 Quoted from "Mr. Hodge's Report" in Jackson's *Second Annual Report*.

heads, hatchets, chisels, etc., which were probably obtained from this mountain by the aboriginal inhabitants of the country."[46] I have myself found hundreds of arrow-heads made of the same material.[47] It is generally slate-colored, with white specks, becoming a uniform white where exposed to the light and air, and it breaks with a conchoidal[48] fracture, producing a ragged cutting edge. I noticed some conchoidal hollows more than a foot in diameter. I picked up a small thin piece which had so sharp an edge that I used it as a dull knife, and to see what I could do, fairly cut off an aspen one inch thick with it, by bending it and making many cuts; though I cut my fingers badly with the back of it in the meanwhile.

From the summit of the precipice which forms the southern and eastern sides of this mountain peninsula, and is its most remarkable feature, being described as five or six hundred feet high, we looked, and probably might have jumped down to the water, or to the seemingly dwarfish trees on the narrow neck of land which connects it with the main. It is a dangerous place to try the steadiness of your nerves. Hodge says that these cliffs descend "perpendicularly ninety feet"[49] below the surface of the water.

The plants which chiefly attracted our attention on this mountain were the mountain cinquefoil (*Potentilla tridentata*), abundant and in bloom still at the very base, by the water-side, though it is usually confined to the summits of mountains in our latitude; very beautiful harebells overhanging the precipice; bear-berry; the Canada blueberry (*Vaccinium Canadense*), similar to the *V. Pennsylvanicum,* our earliest one, but entire leaved and with a downy stem and leaf; I have not seen it in Massachusetts; *Diervilla trifida; Microstylis ophioglossoides,* an orchidaceous plant new to us; wild holly (*Nemopanthes Canadensis*); the great round-leaved orchis (*Platanthera orbiculata*), not long in bloom; *Spiranthes cernua,* at the top; bunch-berry, reddening as we ascended, green at the base of the mountain, red at the top; and the small fern, *Woodsia ilvensis,* growing in tufts, now in fruit. I have also received *Liparis liliifolia,* or twayblade, from this spot. Having explored the wonders of the mountain, and the weather being now entirely cleared up, we commenced the descent. We met the Indian, puffing and panting, about one third of the way up, but thinking that he must be near the top, and saying that it took his breath away. I thought that superstition had something to do with his fatigue. Perhaps he believed that he was climbing over the back of a tremendous moose. He said that he had never ascended Kineo. On reaching the canoe we found that he had caught a lake trout weighing about three pounds, at the depth of twenty-five or thirty feet, while we were on the mountain.

When we got to the camp, the canoe was taken out and turned over, and a log laid across it to prevent its being blown away. The Indian cut some large logs of damp and rotten hard wood to smoulder and keep fire through the night. The trout was fried for supper. Our tent was of thin cotton cloth and quite small, forming with the ground a triangular prism closed at the rear end, six feet long, seven wide, and four high, so that we could barely sit up in the middle. It required two forked stakes, a smooth ridge-pole, and a dozen or more pins to pitch it. It kept off dew and wind, and an ordinary rain, and answered our purpose well enough. We reclined within it till bedtime, each with his baggage at his head, or else sat about the fire, having hung our wet clothes on a pole before the fire for the night.

As we sat there, just before night, looking out through the dusky wood, the Indian heard a noise which he said was made by a snake. He imitated it at my request, making a low whistling note,—*pheet—pheet,*—two or

50 The first missionary work among the Abenaki began in 1611 with the Jesuits Pierre Biard (1576–1622) and Enemond Massé (1574–1646). Between 1852 and 1857 Thoreau read many volumes of *Jesuit Relations*.

51 San Salvador was the first land sighted by Christopher Columbus (1451–1506) on 12 October 1492. Francisco Pizarro (1475–1541) reached the territory of the Incas in 1526.

three times repeated, somewhat like the peep of the hylodes, but not so loud. In answer to my inquiries, he said that he had never seen them while making it, but going to the spot he finds the snake. This, he said on another occasion, was a sign of rain. When I had selected this place for our camp, he had remarked that there were snakes there,—he saw them. But they won't do any hurt, I said. "O no," he answered, "just as you say, it makes no difference to me."

He lay on the right side of the tent, because, as he said, he was partly deaf in one ear, and he wanted to lie with his good ear up. As we lay there, he inquired if I ever heard "Indian sing." I replied that I had not often, and asked him if he would not favor us with a song. He readily assented, and lying on his back, with his blanket wrapped around him, he commenced a slow, somewhat nasal, yet musical chant, in his own language, which probably was taught his tribe long ago by the Catholic missionaries.[50] He translated it to us, sentence by sentence, afterward, wishing to see if we could remember it. It proved to be a very simple religious exercise or hymn, the burden of which was, that there was only one God who ruled all the world. This was hammered (or sung) out very thin, so that some stanzas wellnigh meant nothing at all, merely keeping up the idea. He then said that he would sing us a Latin song; but we did not detect any Latin, only one or two Greek words in it,—the rest may have been Latin with the Indian pronunciation.

His singing carried me back to the period of the discovery of America, to San Salvador and the Incas, when Europeans first encountered the simple faith of the Indian.[51] There was, indeed, a beautiful simplicity about it; nothing of the dark and savage, only the mild and infantile. The sentiments of humility and reverence chiefly were expressed.

It was a dense and damp spruce and fir wood in which

we lay, and, except for our fire, perfectly dark; and when I awoke in the night, I either heard an owl from deeper in the forest behind us, or a loon from a distance over the lake. Getting up some time after midnight to collect the scattered brands together, while my companions were sound asleep, I observed, partly in the fire, which had ceased to blaze, a perfectly regular elliptical ring of light, about five inches in its shortest diameter, six or seven in its longer, and from one eighth to one quarter of an inch wide. It was fully as bright as the fire, but not reddish or scarlet like a coal, but a white and slumbering light, like the glowworm's. I could tell it from the fire only by its whiteness. I saw at once that it must be phosphorescent wood, which I had so often heard of, but never chanced to see.[52] Putting my finger on it, with a little hesitation, I found that it was a piece of dead moose-wood (*Acer striatum*) which the Indian had cut off in a slanting direction the evening before. Using my knife, I discovered that the light proceeded from that portion of the sapwood immediately under the bark, and thus presented a regular ring at the end, which, indeed, appeared raised above the level of the wood, and when I pared off the bark and cut into the sap, it was all aglow along the log. I was surprised to find the wood quite hard and apparently sound, though probably decay had commenced in the sap, and I cut out some little triangular chips, and placing them in the hollow of my hand, carried them into the camp, waked my companion, and showed them to him. They lit up the inside of my hand, revealing the lines and wrinkles, and appearing exactly like coals of fire raised to a white heat, and I saw at once how, probably, the Indian jugglers[53] had imposed on their people and on travellers, pretending to hold coals of fire in their mouths.

I also noticed that part of a decayed stump within four or five feet of the fire, an inch wide and six inches

52 Luminosity or phosphorescence of decaying wood, sometimes called fox fire. Thoreau may have recalled, among other sources, Hawthorne's "The Custom House" in *The Scarlet Letter:* "the phosphorescent glow of decaying wood." He would see phosphorescent wood in Concord in the following year: "4 October 1858: I saw on the sidewalk something bright like fire, as if molten lead were scattered along, and then I wondered if a drunkard's spittle were luminous, and proceeded to poke it on to a leaf with a stick. It was rotten wood. I found that it came from the bottom of some old fence-posts which had just been dug up near by and there glowed for a foot or two, being quite rotten and soft, and it suggested that a lamp-post might be more luminous at bottom than at top. I cut out a handful and carried it about. It was quite soft and spongy and a very pale brown—some almost white—in the light, quite soft and flaky; and as I withdrew it gradually from the light, it began to glow with a distinctly blue fire in its recesses, becoming more universal and whiter as the darkness increased. Carried toward a candle, it is quite a blue light. One man whom I met in the street was able to tell the time by his watch, holding it over what was in my hand. The posts were oak, probably white. Mr. Melvin, the mason, told me that he heard his dog barking the other night, and, going out, found that it was at the bottom of an old post he had dug up during the day, which was all aglow" [J 11:195–196].
53 Cheats or deceivers.

54 Allusion to John 1:5—"And the light shineth in darkness"—and to Exodus 13, in which the Lord went before the Hebrews as a pillar of fire to lead them from the wilderness, as further explained in Nehemiah 9:19: "Yet thou in thy manifold mercies forsookest them not in the wilderness: the pillar of the cloud departed not from them by day, to lead them in the way; neither the pillar of fire by night, to shew them light, and the way wherein they should go."

55 *Ignis fatuus:* a phosphorescent light that hovers or flits over marshy ground at night, possibly caused by the spontaneous combustion of gases produced by rotting organic matter.

56 Quoted from Wordsworth's sonnet, "The World Is Too Much with Us":

> Great God! I'd rather be
> A Pagan suckled in a creed outworn;
> So might I, standing on this pleasant lea,
> Have glimpses that would make me less
>   forlorn.

57 In the sense of costing little effort to obtain.

long, soft and shaking wood, shone with equal brightness.

I neglected to ascertain whether our fire had anything to do with this, but the previous day's rain and long-continued wet weather undoubtedly had.

I was exceedingly interested by this phenomenon, and already felt paid for my journey. It could hardly have thrilled me more if it had taken the form of letters, or of the human face. If I had met with this ring of light while groping in this forest alone, away from any fire, I should have been still more surprised. I little thought that there was such a light shining in the darkness of the wilderness for me.[54]

The next day the Indian told me their name for this light,—*Artoosoqu',*—and on my inquiring concerning the will-o'-the-wisp,[55] and the like phenomena, he said that his "folks" sometimes saw fires passing along at various heights, even as high as the trees, and making a noise. I was prepared after this to hear of the most startling and unimagined phenomena witnessed by "his folks," they are abroad at all hours and seasons in scenes so unfrequented by white men. Nature must have made a thousand revelations to them which are still secrets to us.

I did not regret my not having seen this before, since I now saw it under circumstances so favorable. I was in just the frame of mind to see something wonderful, and this was a phenomenon adequate to my circumstances and expectation, and it put me on the alert to see more like it. I exulted like "a pagan suckled in a creed"[56] that had never been worn at all, but was bran new, and adequate to the occasion. I let science slide, and rejoiced in that light as if it had been a fellow-creature. I saw that it was excellent, and was very glad to know that it was so cheap.[57] A scientific *explanation,* as it is called, would have been altogether out of place there. That is for pale daylight. Science with its *retorts* would have put me to sleep; it was the opportunity to be ignorant that I improved. It suggested to me that there was something to be seen if one had eyes. It made a believer of me more than before. I believed that the woods were not tenantless, but choke-full of honest spirits as good as myself any day,—not an empty chamber, in which chemistry was left to work alone, but an inhabited house,—and for a few moments I enjoyed fellowship with them. Your so-called wise man goes trying to persuade himself that there is no entity there but himself and his traps, but it is a great deal easier to believe the truth. It suggested, too, that the same experience always gives birth to the same sort of belief or religion. One revelation has been made to the Indian, another to the white man. I have much to learn of the Indian, nothing of the missionary.[58] I am not sure but all that would tempt me to teach the Indian my religion would be his promise to teach me *his*. Long enough I had heard of irrelevant things; now at length I was glad to make acquaintance with the light that dwells in rotten wood. Where is all your knowledge gone to? It evaporates completely, for it has no depth.

I kept those little chips and wet them again the next night, but they emitted no light.

SATURDAY, July 25.

At breakfast this Saturday morning, the Indian, evidently curious to know what would be expected of him the next day, whether we should go along or not, asked me how I spent the Sunday when at home. I told him that I commonly sat in my chamber reading, etc., in the forenoon, and went to walk in the afternoon.[59] At which he shook his head and said, "Er, that is ver bad." "How do you spend it?" I asked. He said that he did no work, that he went to church at Oldtown when he was at home; in short, he did as he had been taught by the whites. This led to a discussion in which I found myself

58 Thoreau wrote about missionaries on 31 December 1853: "The strains of the aeolian harp and of the wood thrush are the truest and loftiest preachers that I know now left on this earth. I know of no missionaries to us heathen comparable to them" [ITM 218].

59 In "Walking" Thoreau wrote: "In my afternoon walk I would fain forget all my morning occupations, and my obligations to society" [W 5:211].

60 Thoreau was anti-Sabbatarian. In the "Sunday" chapter of *A Week on the Concord and Merrimack Rivers,* on being observed traveling on Sunday, he calls himself and his brother "the true observers of this sunny day" [W 1:64]. Emerson wrote in his "Divinity School Address": "It is already beginning to indicate character and religion to withdraw from the religious meetings. I have heard a devout person, who prized the Sabbath, say in bitterness of heart, 'on Sundays, it seems wicked to go to church.'"

61 Emerson wrote in his eulogy of Thoreau, "It required a rare decision to refuse all the accustomed paths and keep his solitary freedom at the cost of disappointing the natural expectations of his family and friends: all the more difficult that he had a perfect probity, was exact in securing his own independence, and in holding every man to the like duty. But Thoreau never faltered. He was a born protestant."

62 Two-mile portage between Moosehead Lake and the West Branch of the Penobscot.

63 An ox railroad built in 1842 to carry supplies for the lumbermen.

64 The Tomhegan and Socatean are tributary streams flowing into Moosehead Lake.

in the minority.[60] He stated that he was a Protestant, and asked me if I was. I did not at first know what to say, but I thought that I could answer with truth that I was.[61]

When we were washing the dishes in the lake, many fishes, apparently chivin, came close up to us to get the particles of grease.

The weather seemed to be more settled this morning, and we set out early in order to finish our voyage up the lake before the wind arose. Soon after starting the Indian directed our attention to the Northeast Carry,[62] which we could plainly see, about thirteen miles distant in that direction as measured on the map, though it is called much further. This carry is a rude wooden railroad,[63] running north and south about two miles, perfectly straight, from the lake to the Penobscot, through a low tract, with a clearing three or four rods wide; but low as it is, it passes over the height of land there. This opening appeared as a clear bright, or light point in the horizon, resting on the edge of the lake, whose breadth a hair could have covered at a considerable distance from the eye, and of no appreciable height. We should not have suspected it to be visible if the Indian had not drawn our attention to it. It was a remarkable kind of light to steer for,—daylight seen through a vista in the forest,—but visible as far as an ordinary beacon by night.

We crossed a deep and wide bay which makes eastward north of Kineo, leaving an island on our left, and keeping up the eastern side of the lake. This way or that led to some Tomhegan or *Socatarian* stream,[64] up which the Indian had hunted, and whither I longed to go. The last name, however, had a bogus sound, too much like sectarian for me, as if a missionary had tampered with it; but I know that the Indians were very liberal. I think I should have inclined to the Tomhegan first.

We then crossed another broad bay, which, as we could no longer observe the shore particularly, afforded ample time for conversation. The Indian said that he had got his money by hunting, mostly high up the west branch of the Penobscot, and toward the head of the St. John; he had hunted there from a boy, and knew all about that region. His game had been, beaver, otter, black cat (or fisher), sable, moose, etc. Loup cervier (or Canada lynx) were plenty yet in burnt grounds. For food in the woods, he uses partridges, ducks, dried moose-meat, hedge-hog, etc. Loons, too, were good, only "bile 'em good." He told us at some length how he had suffered from starvation when a mere lad, being overtaken by winter when hunting with two grown Indians in the northern part of Maine, and obliged to leave their canoe on account of ice.

Pointing into the bay, he said that it was the way to various lakes which he knew. Only solemn bear-haunted mountains, with their great wooded slopes, were visible; where, as man is not, we suppose some other power to be. My imagination personified the slopes themselves, as if by their very length they would waylay you, and compel you to camp again on them before night. Some invisible glutton would seem to drop from the trees and gnaw at the heart of the solitary hunter who threaded those woods; and yet I was tempted to walk there. The Indian said that he had been along there several times.

I asked him how he guided himself in the woods. "O," said he, "I can tell good many ways." When I pressed him further, he answered, "Sometimes I lookum side hill," and he glanced toward a high hill or mountain on the eastern shore, "great difference between the north and south, see where the sun has shone most. So trees, — the large limbs bend toward south. Sometimes I lookum locks" (rocks). I asked what he saw on the rocks, but he did not describe anything in particular, answering vaguely, in a mysterious or drawling tone, "Bare locks on lake shore, — great difference between north, south, east, west side,—can tell what the sun has shone on." "Suppose," said I, "that I should take you in a dark night, right up here into the middle of the woods a hundred miles, set you down, and turn you round quickly twenty times, could you steer straight to Oldtown?" "O yer," said he, "have done pretty much same thing. I will tell you. Some years ago I met an old white hunter at Millinocket; very good hunter. He said he could go anywhere in the woods. He wanted to hunt with me that day, so we start. We chase a moose all the forenoon, round and round, till middle of afternoon, when we kill him. Then I said to him, 'Now you go straight to camp. Don't go round and round where we've been, but go straight.' He said, 'I can't do that. I don't know where I am.' 'Where you think camp?' I asked. He pointed so. Then I laugh at him. I take the lead and go right off the other way, cross our tracks many times, straight camp." "How do you do that?" asked I. "Oh, I can't tell *you,*" he replied. "Great difference between me and white man."

It appeared as if the sources of information were so various that he did not give a distinct, conscious attention to any one, and so could not readily refer to any when questioned about it, but he found his way very much as an animal does. Perhaps what is commonly called instinct in the animal, in this case is merely a sharpened and educated sense. Often, when an Indian says, "I don't know," in regard to the route he is to take, he does not mean what a white man would by those words, for his Indian instinct may tell him still as much as the most confident white man knows. He does not carry things in his head, nor remember the route exactly, like a white man, but relies on himself at the moment. Not having experienced the need of the other sort of knowledge, all labelled and arranged, he has not acquired it.

The white hunter with whom I talked in the stage knew some of the resources of the Indian. He said that he steered by the wind, or by the limbs of the hemlocks, which were largest on the south side; also sometimes, when he knew that there was a lake near, by firing his gun and listening to hear the direction and distance of the echo from over it.

The course we took over this lake, and others afterward, was rarely direct, but a succession of curves from point to point, digressing considerably into each of the bays; and this was not merely on account of the wind, for the Indian, looking toward the middle of the lake, said it was hard to go there, easier to keep near the shore, because he thus got over it by successive reaches and saw by the shore how he got along.

The following will suffice for a common experience in crossing lakes in a canoe. As the forenoon advanced the wind increased. The last bay which we crossed before reaching the desolate pier at the Northeast Carry, was two or three miles over, and the wind was southwesterly. After going a third of the way, the waves had increased so as occasionally to wash into the canoe, and we saw that it was worse and worse ahead. At first we might have turned about, but were not willing to. It would have been of no use to follow the curve of the shore, for not only the distance would have been much greater, but the waves ran still higher there on account of the greater sweep the wind had. At any rate it would have been dangerous now to alter our course, because the waves would have struck us at an advantage. It will not do to meet them at right angles, for then they will wash in both sides, but you must take them quartering.[65] So the Indian stood up in the canoe, and exerted all his skill and strength for a mile or two, while I paddled right along in order to give him more steerage-way. For more than a mile he did not allow a single wave to strike the canoe as it would, but turned it quickly from this side to that, so that it would always be on or near the crest of a wave when it broke,

[65] Paddling at an angle to the wind or waves to prevent being struck broadside by the wind or waves, and to avoid riding in the valley of a wave.

where all its force was spent, and we merely settled down with it. At length I jumped out on to the end of the pier, against which the waves were dashing violently, in order to lighten the canoe, and catch it at the landing, which was not much sheltered; but just as I jumped we took in two or three gallons of water. I remarked to the Indian, "You managed that well," to which he replied: "Ver few men do that. Great many waves; when I look out for one, another come quick."

While the Indian went to get cedar-bark, etc., to carry his canoe with, we cooked the dinner on the shore, at this end of the carry, in the midst of a sprinkling rain.

He prepared his canoe for carrying in this wise. He took a cedar shingle or splint eighteen inches long and four or five wide, rounded at one end, that the corners might not be in the way, and tied it with cedar-bark by two holes made midway, near the edge on each side, to the middle cross-bar of the canoe. When the canoe was lifted upon his head bottom up, this shingle, with its rounded end uppermost, distributed the weight over his shoulders and head, while a band of cedar-bark, tied to the cross-bar on each side of the shingle, passed round his breast, and another longer one, outside of the last, round his forehead; also a hand on each side rail served to steer the canoe and keep it from rocking. He thus carried it with his shoulders, head, breast, forehead, and both hands, as if the upper part of his body were all one hand to clasp and hold it. If you know of a better way, I should like to hear of it. A cedar-tree furnished all the gear in this case, as it had the woodwork of the canoe. One of the paddles rested on the cross-bars in the bows. I took the canoe upon my head and found that I could carry it with ease, though the straps were not fitted to my shoulders; but I let him carry it, not caring to establish a different precedent, though he said that if I would carry the canoe, he would take all the rest of the baggage, except my companion's. This shingle remained tied to the cross-bar throughout the voyage, was always ready for the carries, and also served to protect the back of one passenger.

We were obliged to go over this carry twice, our load was so great. But the carries were an agreeable variety, and we improved the opportunity to gather the rare plants which we had seen, when we returned empty-handed.

We reached the Penobscot about four o'clock, and found there some St. Francis Indians[66] encamped on the bank, in the same place where I camped with four Indians four years before. They were making a canoe, and, as then, drying moose-meat. The meat looked very suitable to make a *black* broth[67] at least. Our Indian said it was not good. Their camp was covered with spruce-bark. They had got a young moose, taken in the river a fortnight before, confined in a sort of cage of logs piled up cob-fashion,[68] seven or eight feet high. It was quite tame, about four feet high, and covered with moose-flies. There was a large quantity of cornel (*C. stolonifera*), red maple, and also willow and aspen boughs, stuck through between the logs on all sides, but-ends out, and on their leaves it was browsing. It looked at first as if it were in a bower rather than a pen.

Our Indian said that *he* used *black* spruce-roots to sew canoes with, obtaining it from high lands or mountains. The St. Francis Indian thought that *white* spruce-roots might be best. But the former said, "No good, break, can't split 'em"; also that they were hard to get, deep in ground, but the black were near the surface, on higher land, as well as tougher. He said that the white spruce was *sube-koondark,* black, *skusk.* I told him I thought that I could make a canoe, but he expressed great doubt of it; at any rate, he thought that my work would not be "neat" the first time. An Indian at Greenville had told me that the

66 One of whom was Louis Annance (1794–1875), a trapper and guide, who attended Moor's Indian Charity School, part of Dartmouth College.
67 In ancient Sparta, called μέλας ζωμός (*melas zōmos*), pork cooked in blood, seasoned with vinegar and salt.
68 Ends laid crosswise.

69 In his journal Thoreau identified him only as an "Indian who came to talk with Polis, who made canoes, had made those two for Leonard. . . . He said that he used the red cedar of uplands (*i.e.* arbor-vitae) for ribs, etc." [J 9:488]. He was one of the three sons of Newell Bear.

70 Thoreau described the yellow lily several times in his journal, as on 12 July 1854: "four and a half feet high, with a whorl of four flowers, and two more above, somewhat pyramidal" [J 6:392].

71 Although eaten raw, green corn was commonly served boiled or roasted. The young, milky ear of green corn was an anticipated treat. Thoreau celebrated September in his journal as the "month of green corn and melons and plums and the earliest apples" [J 5:403]. On 29 August 1858 Thoreau wrote: "I remember when boiled green corn was sold piping hot on a muster-field in this town, and my father says that he remembers when it used to be carried about the streets of Boston in large baskets on the bare heads of negro women, and gentlemen would stop, buy an ear, and eat it in the street" [J11:131].

72 The name Matahumkeag is found on Coffin's 1835 map.

winter bark, that is, bark taken off before the sap flows in May, was harder and much better than summer bark.[69]

Having reloaded, we paddled down the Penobscot, which, as the Indian remarked, and even I detected, remembering how it looked before, was uncommonly full. We soon after saw a splendid yellow lily (*Lilium Canadense*) by the shore, which I plucked. It was six feet high, and had twelve flowers, in two whorls, forming a pyramid, such as I have seen in Concord.[70] We afterward saw many more thus tall along this stream, and also still more numerous on the East Branch, and, on the latter, one which I thought approached yet nearer to the *Lilium superbum*. The Indian asked what we called it, and said that the "loots" (roots) were good for soup, that is, to cook with meat, to thicken it, taking the place of flour. They get them in the fall. I dug some, and found a mass of bulbs pretty deep in the earth, two inches in diameter, looking, and even tasting, somewhat like raw green corn on the ear.[71]

When we had gone about three miles down the Penobscot, we saw through the tree-tops a thunder-shower coming up in the west, and we looked out a camping-place in good season, about five o'clock, on the west side, not far below the mouth of what Joe Aitteon, in '53, called Lobster Stream, coming from Lobster Pond. Our present Indian, however, did not admit this name, nor even that of *Matahumkeag*, which is on the map,[72] but called the lake *Beskabekuk*.

I will describe, once for all, the routine of camping at this season. We generally told the Indian that we would stop at the first suitable place, so that he might be on the lookout for it. Having observed a clear, hard, and flat beach to land on, free from mud, and from stones which would injure the canoe, one would run up the bank to see if there were open and level space enough for the camp between the trees, or if it could be easily cleared, preferring at the same time a cool place, on account of insects. Sometimes we paddled a mile or more before finding one to our minds, for where the shore was suitable, the bank would often be too steep, or else too low and grassy, and therefore mosquitoey. We then took out the baggage and drew up the canoe, sometimes turning it over on shore for safety. The Indian cut a path to the spot we had selected, which was usually within two or three rods of the water, and we carried up our baggage. One, perhaps, takes canoe-birch bark, always at hand, and dead dry wood or bark, and kindles a fire five or six feet in front of where we intend to lie. It matters not, commonly, on which side this is, because there is little or no wind in so dense a wood at that season; and then he gets a kettle of water from the river, and takes out the pork, bread, coffee, etc., from their several packages.

Another, meanwhile, having the axe, cuts down the nearest dead rock-maple or other dry hard wood, collecting several large logs to last through the night, also a green stake, with a notch or fork to it, which is slanted over the fire, perhaps resting on a rock or forked stake, to hang the kettle on, and two forked stakes and a pole for the tent.

The third man pitches the tent, cuts a dozen or more pins with his knife, usually of moose-wood, the common underwood, to fasten it down with, and then collects an armful or two of fir-twigs,[73] arbor-vitae, spruce, or hemlock, whichever is at hand, and makes the bed, beginning at either end, and laying the twigs wrong-side up, in regular rows, covering the stub-ends of the last row; first, however, filling the hollows, if there are any, with coarser material. Wrangel says that his guides in Siberia first strewed a quantity of dry brushwood on the ground, and then cedar twigs on that.[74]

Commonly, by the time the bed is made, or within fifteen or twenty minutes, the water boils, the pork is

73 Thoreau's note: "These twigs are called in Rasles' Dictionary, *Sediak.*"
74 Ferdinand Petrovich Wrangel (1796–1870) wrote in *Narrative of an Expedition to the Polar Sea in the Years 1820, 1821, 1822, and 1823,* [42]: "Our guides soon strewed the ground about the fire with a quantity of dry brushwood, on which they placed a layer of the green branches of the dwarf cedar. On this fragrant floor we pitched our three little tents."

fried, and supper is ready. We eat this sitting on the ground, or a stump, if there is any, around a large piece of birch-bark for a table, each holding a dipper in one hand and a piece of ship-bread[75] or fried pork in the other, frequently making a pass with his hand, or thrusting his head into the smoke, to avoid the mosquitoes.

Next, pipes are lit by those who smoke, and veils are donned by those who have them, and we hastily examine and dry our plants, anoint our faces and hands, and go to bed,—and—the mosquitoes.

Though you have nothing to do but see the country, there's rarely any time to spare, hardly enough to examine a plant, before the night or drowsiness is upon you.

Such was the ordinary experience, but this evening we had camped earlier on account of the rain, and had more time.

We found that our camp to-night was on an old, and now more than usually indistinct, supply-road, running along the river. What is called a road there shows no ruts or trace of wheels, for they are not used; nor, indeed, of runners, since they are used only in the winter, when the snow is several feet deep. It is only an indistinct vista through the wood, which it takes an experienced eye to detect.

We had no sooner pitched our tent than the thunder-shower burst on us, and we hastily crept under it, drawing our bags after us, curious to see how much of a shelter our thin cotton roof was going to be in this excursion. Though the violence of the rain forced a fine shower through the cloth before it was fairly wetted and shrunk, with which we were well bedewed, we managed to keep pretty dry, only a box of matches having been left out and spoiled, and before we were aware of it the shower was over, and only the dripping trees imprisoned us.

Wishing to see what fishes there were in the river there, we cast our lines over the wet bushes on the shore, but they were repeatedly swept down the swift stream in vain. So, leaving the Indian, we took the canoe just before dark, and dropped down the river a few rods to fish at the mouth of a sluggish brook on the opposite side. We pushed up this a rod or two, where, perhaps, only a canoe had been before. But though there were a few small fishes, mostly *chivin,* there, we were soon driven off by the mosquitoes. While there we heard the Indian fire his gun twice in such rapid succession that we thought it must be double-barrelled, though we observed afterward that it was single. His object was to clean out and dry it after the rain, and he then loaded it with ball, being now on ground where he expected to meet with large game. This sudden, loud, crashing noise in the still aisles of the forest, affected me like an insult to nature, or ill manners at any rate, as if you were to fire a gun in a hall or temple. It was not heard far, however, except along the river, the sound being rapidly hushed up or absorbed by the damp trees and mossy ground.

The Indian made a little smothered fire of damp leaves close to the back of the camp, that the smoke might drive through and keep out the mosquitoes; but just before we fell asleep this suddenly blazed up, and came near setting fire to the tent. We were considerably molested by mosquitoes at this camp.

SUNDAY, *July 26.*
The note of the white-throated sparrow, a very inspiriting but almost wiry sound, was the first heard in the morning, and with this all the woods rang. This was the prevailing bird in the northern part of Maine. The forest generally was all alive with them at this season, and they were proportionally numerous and musical about Bangor. They evidently breed in that State. Though commonly unseen, their simple *ah, te-te-te, te-te-te, te-te-te,* so sharp and piercing, was as distinct to the ear as the

76 The Concord citizen Edward Jarvis (1803–1884) wrote that election days were for the boys in the town "a day of great expectation and exhilaration. They looked forward to it with fondness and yet with anxiety lest the weather should be unfavorable for out-of-door sports. A large part expected to go hunting birds in the woods and fields. . . . and early on Election Day they went forth on their cruel and wanton amusement."

77 One call of the chickadee is similar to that of the phoebe, as Thoreau noted in his journal of 11 March 1854: "Air full of birds,—bluebirds, song sparrows, chickadee (phoebe notes), and black-birds" [J 6:162].

78 John Franceway, sometimes Brassua, who led a group of twelve ministers and students from the Bangor Theological Seminary in June 1857.

79 George Goodwin (d. 1857).

80 John Smith Sewall (1830–1911), one of the party at the time, later related in a talk before the Bangor Rhetorical Society on 12 April 1858: "That afternoon in Lake Pocwocamus we found the body of a poor lumberman, drowned while driving logs on the river. On the bank we made him a grave—and there he rests beneath a tree, which is fixed with a rude carving of his name and age on a fragment of slate."

81 Thoreau wrote in *Cape Cod* that Eastham was "famous of late years for its camp-meetings, held in a grove near by, to which thousands flock from all parts of the Bay. . . . There are sometimes one hundred and fifty ministers, (!) and five thousand hearers, assembled. The ground, which is called Millennium Grove, is owned by a company in Boston, and is the most suitable, or rather unsuitable, for this purpose, of any that I saw on the Cape. It is fenced, and the frames of the tents are, at all times, to be seen interspersed among the oaks. They have an oven and a pump, and keep all their kitchen utensils and tent coverings and furniture in a permanent building on the spot" [W 4:48].

passage of a spark of fire shot into the darkest of the forest would be to the eye. I thought that they commonly uttered it as they flew. I hear this note for a few days only in the spring, as they go through Concord, and in the fall see them again going southward, but then they are mute. We were commonly aroused by their lively strain very early. What a glorious time they must have in that wilderness, far from mankind and election day![76]

I told the Indian that we would go to church to Chesuncook this (Sunday) morning, some fifteen miles. It was settled weather at last. A few swallows flitted over the water, we heard the white throats along the shore, the phebe notes of the chicadee,[77] and, I believe, red-starts, and moose-flies of large size pursued us in mid-stream.

The Indian thought that we should lie by on Sunday. Said he, "We come here lookum things, look all round; but come Sunday, lock up all that, and then Monday look again." He spoke of an Indian of his acquaintance who had been with some ministers to Ktaadn,[78] and had told him how they conducted. This he described in a low and solemn voice. "They make a long prayer every morning and night, and at every meal. Come Sunday," said he, "they stop 'em, no go at all that day,—keep still,—preach all day,—first one then another, just like church. O, ver good men." "One day," said he, "going along a river, they came to the body of a man in the water,[79] drowned good while, all ready fall to pieces. They go right ashore,—stop there, go no further that day,—they have meeting there, preach and pray just like Sunday. Then they get poles and lift up the body, and they go back and carry the body with them. O, they ver good men."[80]

I judged from this account that their every camp was a camp-meeting, and they had mistaken their route,—they should have gone to Eastham;[81] that they wanted an opportunity to preach somewhere more than to see Ktaadn. I read of another similar party that seem to have spent their time there singing the songs of Zion.[82] I was glad that I did not go to that mountain with such slow coaches.

However, the Indian added, plying the paddle all the while, that if we would go along, he must go with us, he our man, and he suppose that if he no takum pay for what he do Sunday, then ther's no harm, but if he takum pay, then wrong. I told him that he was stricter than white men. Nevertheless, I noticed that he did not forget to reckon in the Sundays at last.

He appeared to be a very religious man, and said his prayers in a loud voice, in Indian, kneeling before the camp, morning and evening,—sometimes scrambling up again in haste when he had forgotten this, and saying them with great rapidity. In the course of the day, he remarked, not very originally, "Poor man rememberum God more than rich."

We soon passed the island where I had camped four years before, and I recognized the very spot. The dead water, a mile or two below it, the Indian called, *Beskabe-kukskishtuk*, from the lake *Beskabekuk*, which empties in above. This dead water, he said, was "a great place for moose always." We saw the grass bent where a moose came out the night before, and the Indian said that he could smell one as far as he could see him; but, he added, that if he should see five or six to-day close by canoe, he no shoot 'em. Accordingly, as he was the only one of the party who had a gun, or had come a-hunting, the moose were safe.

Just below this, a cat-owl flew heavily over the stream, and he, asking if I knew what it was, imitated very well the common *hoo, hoo, hoo, hoorer, hoo,* of our woods; making a hard, guttural sound, "Ugh, ugh, ugh,—ugh, ugh." When we passed the Moose-horn, he said that it had no name. What Joe Aitteon had called Ragmuff, he called *Paytaytequick,* and said that it meant Burnt

82 Thoreau read in Marcus R. Keep's account in Springer's *Forest Life and Forest Trees:* "The day—the place—the topics of remarks—the songs of Zion—all encircled by a kind of Providence, and made effective by the presence of God, will ever be worthy of a grateful remembrance." The songs of Zion were lyrical hymns, following the destruction of Solomon's Temple, that express longing to see the hill of Zion and the city of Jerusalem shine again as in their former glory, as in Psalms 137:3: "For there they that carried us away captive required of us a song and they that wasted us required of us mirth, saying, Sing us one of the songs of Zion."

Ground Stream. We stopped there, where I had stopped before, and I bathed in this tributary. It was shallow but cold, apparently too cold for the Indian, who stood looking on. As we were pushing away again, a white-headed eagle sailed over our heads. A reach some miles above Pine Stream, where there were several islands, the Indian said was *Nonglangyis,* dead-water. Pine Stream he called Black River, and said that its Indian name was *Karsaootuk*. He could go to Caribou Lake that way.

We carried a part of the baggage about Pine Stream Falls, while the Indian went down in the canoe. A Bangor merchant[83] had told us that two men in his employ were drowned some time ago while passing these falls in a batteau, and a third clung to a rock all night, and was taken off in the morning. There were magnificent great purple-fringed orchises on this carry and the neighboring shores. I measured the largest canoe-birch which I saw in this journey near the end of the carry. It was 14½ feet in circumference at two feet from the ground, but at five feet divided into three parts. The canoe-birches thereabouts were commonly marked by conspicuous dark spiral ridges, with a groove between, so that I thought at first that they had been struck by lightning, but, as the Indian said, it was evidently caused by the grain of the tree. He cut a small, woody knob, as big as a filbert, from the trunk of a fir, apparently an old balsam vesicle filled with wood, which he said was good medicine.

After we had embarked and gone half a mile, my companion remembered that he had left his knife, and we paddled back to get it, against the strong and swift current. This taught us the difference between going up and down the stream, for while we were working our way back a quarter of a mile, we should have gone down a mile and a half at least. So we landed, and while he and the Indian were gone back for it, I watched the motions of the foam, a kind of white water-fowl near the shore, forty or fifty rods below. It alternately appeared and disappeared behind the rock, being carried round by an eddy. Even this semblance of life was interesting on that lonely river.

Immediately below these falls was the Chesuncook dead-water, caused by the flowing back of the lake. As we paddled slowly over this, the Indian told us a story of his hunting thereabouts, and something more interesting about himself. It appeared that he had represented his tribe at Augusta,[84] and also once at Washington, where he had met some Western chiefs. He had been consulted at Augusta, and gave advice, which he said was followed, respecting the eastern boundary of Maine, as determined by highlands and streams, at the time of the difficulties on that side. He was employed with the surveyors on the line.[85] Also he had called on Daniel Webster in Boston, at the time of his Bunker Hill oration.[86]

I was surprised to hear him say that he liked to go to Boston, New York, Philadelphia, etc., etc.; that he would like to live there. But then, as if relenting a little, when he thought what a poor figure he would make there, he added, "I suppose, I live in New York, I be poorest hunter, I expect." He understood very well both his superiority and his inferiority to the whites. He criticised the people of the United States as compared with other nations, but the only distinct idea with which he labored was, that they were "very strong," but, like some individuals, "too fast." He must have the credit of saying this just before the general breaking down of railroads and banks.[87] He had a great idea of education, and would occasionally break out into such expressions as this, "Kademy—a-cad-e-my—good thing—I suppose they usum Fifth Reader[88] there. . . . You been college?"

From this dead-water the outlines of the mountains about Ktaadn were visible. The top of Ktaadn was concealed by a cloud, but the Souneunk Mountains were

84 Where the Maine state legislature met.

85 From 27 September to 6 November 1838 Polis was part of the surveying party led by John Gilmore Deane (1785–1839).

86 Daniel Webster (1782–1852), famed orator and senator from Massachusetts, gave his "Address on Laying the Corner-Stone of the Bunker Hill Monument" in 1825.

87 Allusion to the panic, sometimes called the revulsion, of 1857, which began on 24 August with the closing of the New York branch of the Ohio Life Insurance and Trust company. Before the end of the year nearly five thousand businesses closed. The Concord Bank suspended business in October.

88 William Holmes McGuffey's (1800–1873) Rhetorical Guide or Fifth Reader of the Eclectic Series: Containing Elegant Extracts in Prose and Poetry, published in 1844.

nearer, and quite visible. We steered across the north-west end of the lake, from which we looked down south-southeast, the whole length to Joe Merry Mountain, seen over its extremity. It is an agreeable change to cross a lake, after you have been shut up in the woods, not only on account of the greater expanse of water, but also of sky. It is one of the surprises which Nature has in store for the traveller in the forest. To look down, in this case, over eighteen miles of water, was liberating and civilizing even. No doubt, the short distance to which you can see in the woods, and the general twilight, would at length react on the inhabitants, and make them *salvages*. The lakes also reveal the mountains, and give ample scope and range to our thought. The very gulls which we saw sitting on the rocks, like white specks, or circling about, reminded me of custom-house officers. Already there were half a dozen log-huts about this end of the lake, though so far from a road. I perceive that in these woods the earliest settlements are, for various reasons, cluster-ing about the lakes, but partly, I think, for the sake of the neighborhood as the oldest clearings. They are for-est schools[89] already established,—great centres of light. Water is a pioneer which the settler follows, taking ad-vantage of its improvements.

Thus far only I had been before.[90] About noon we turned northward, up a broad kind of estuary, and at its northeast corner found the Caucomgomoc River, and after going about a mile from the lake, reached the Um-bazookskus, which comes in on the right at a point where the former river, coming from the west, turns short to the south. Our course was up the Umbazookskus, but as the Indian knew of a good camping-place, that is, a cool place where there were few mosquitoes, about half a mile further up the Caucomgomoc, we went thither. The latter river, judging from the map, is the longer and principal stream, and, therefore, its name must prevail

89 Schools for the training of foresters, such as were found in Germany in the early nineteenth century.
90 During his 1853 excursion to Chesuncook.

below the junction. So quickly we changed the civilizing sky of Chesuncook for the dark wood of the Caucomgomoc. On reaching the Indian's camping-ground, on the south side, where the bank was about a dozen feet high, I read on the trunk of a fir-tree blazed[91] by an axe an inscription in charcoal which had been left by him. It was surmounted by a drawing of a bear paddling a canoe, which he said was the sign which had been used by his family always. The drawing, though rude, could not be mistaken for anything but a bear, and he doubted my ability to copy it. The inscription ran thus, *verbatim et literatim.*[92] I interline the English of his Indian as he gave it to me.

July 26,
1853.

---

niasoseb
We alone Joseph
Polis   *elioi*
Polis   start
sia   *olta*
for   Oldtown
onke   *ni*
right   away.[93]
quanibi

July 15,
1855.
niasoseb

91 Setting a white mark on a tree by paring off part of the bark or cutting a piece out of the side of the tree.

92 Latin: word for word and letter for letter.

93 Thoreau may have misunderstood Polis's translation; the passage more literally translates as: *niasoseb* (me Joseph) *Polis elioi sia* (Polis—or Little Paul—is how I am called) *olta onke niquanibi* (Oldtown I am connected to now). The single word *niquanibi* may have been split in Thoreau's transcription in his journal, or in Polis's inscription, due to lack of space. Thoreau's lack of a translation of *quanibi* indicates his awareness that it was not a separate word. The spelling in Rasles's *Dictionary of the Abnaki Language* is: *nikkȣañbi.*

He added now below: —

1857,
July 26.
Io. Polis.

This was one of his homes. I saw where he had sometimes stretched his moose-hides on the opposite or sunny north side of the river, where there was a narrow meadow.

After we had selected a place for our camp, and kindled our fire, almost exactly on the site of the Indian's last camp here, he, looking up, observed, "That tree danger." It was a dead part, more than a foot in diameter, of a large canoe-birch, which branched at the ground. This branch, rising thirty feet or more, slanted directly over the spot which we had chosen for our bed. I told him to try it with his axe; but he could not shake it perceptibly, and, therefore, seemed inclined to disregard it, and my companion expressed his willingness to run the risk. But it seemed to me that we should be fools to lie under it, for though the lower part was firm, the top, for aught we knew, might be just ready to fall, and we should at any rate be very uneasy if the wind arose in the night. It is a common accident for men camping in the woods to be killed by a falling tree.[94] So the camp was moved to the other side of the fire.

It was, as usual, a damp and shaggy forest, that Caucomgomoc one, and the most you knew about it was, that on this side it stretched toward the settlements, and on that to still more unfrequented regions. You carried so much topography in your mind always, — and sometimes it seemed to make a considerable difference whether you sat or lay nearer the settlements, or further off, than your companions, — were the rear or frontier man of the camp. But there is really the same difference between

94 Springer wrote in his *Forest Life and Forest Trees:* "Life is constantly endangered in felling the Pine-trees. . . . It is never safe to run from a falling tree in a line directly opposite from the course in which it falls . . . Running from a falling tree in the way above alluded to, I knew a man killed in an instant. . . . To retreat safely, one should run in a direction so as to make nearly a right angle with the falling tree. A man by the name of Hale, a master chopper, cut a Pine which, in its passage down, struck in the crutch of another tree and broke the trunk of the falling one, the top of which pitched back and instantly killed him."

our positions wherever we may be camped, and some are nearer the frontiers on feather-beds in the towns than others on fir-twigs in the backwoods.

The Indian said that the Umbazookskus, being a dead stream with broad meadows, was a good place for moose, and he frequently came a-hunting here, being out alone three weeks or more from Oldtown. He sometimes, also, went a-hunting to the Seboois Lakes, taking the stage, with his gun and ammunition, axe and blanket, hard bread and pork, perhaps for a hundred miles of the way, and jumped off at the wildest place on the road, where he was at once at home, and every rod was a tavern-site for him. Then, after a short journey through the woods, he would build a spruce-bark canoe in one day, putting but few ribs into it, that it might be light, and after doing his hunting with it on the lakes, would return with his furs the same way he had come. Thus you have an Indian availing himself cunningly of the advantages of civilization, without losing any of his woodcraft, but proving himself the more successful hunter for it.

This man was very clever and quick to learn anything in his line. Our tent was of a kind new to him; but when he had once seen it pitched it was surprising how quickly he would find and prepare the pole and forked stakes to pitch it with, cutting and placing them right the first time, though I am sure that the majority of white men would have blundered several times.

This river came from Caucomgomoc Lake, about ten miles further up. Though it was sluggish here, there were falls not far above us, and we saw the foam from them go by from time to time. The Indian said that *Caucomgo-moc* meant Big-gull Lake, (i.e. Herring-gull, I suppose,) *gomoc* meaning lake. Hence this was *Caucomgomoc-took,* or the river from that lake. This was the Penobscot *Caucomgomoc-took;* there was another St. John one not far north. He finds the eggs of this gull, sometimes twenty together, as big as hen's eggs, on rocky ledges on the west side of Millinocket River, for instance, and eats them.

Now I thought I would observe how he spent his Sunday. While I and my companion were looking about at the trees and river, he went to sleep. Indeed, he improved every opportunity to get a nap, whatever the day.

Rambling about the woods at this camp, I noticed that they consisted chiefly of firs, black spruce, and some white, red maple, canoe-birch, and, along the river, the hoary alder, *Alnus incana.* I name them in the order of their abundance. The *Viburnum nudum* was a common shrub, and of smaller plants, there were the dwarf-cornel, great round-leaved orchis, abundant and in bloom (a greenish-white flower growing in little communities), *Uvularia grandiflora,* whose stem tasted like a cucumber, *Pyrola secunda,* apparently the commonest Pyrola in those woods, now out of bloom, *Pyrola elliptica,* and *Chiogenes hispidula.* The *Clintonia borealis,* with ripe berries, was very abundant, and perfectly at home there. Its leaves, disposed commonly in triangles about its stem, were just as handsomely formed and green, and its berries as blue and glossy, as if it grew by some botanist's favorite path.

I could trace the outlines of large birches that had fallen long ago, collapsed and rotted and turned to soil, by faint yellowish-green lines of feather-like moss, eighteen inches wide and twenty or thirty feet long, crossed by other similar lines.

I heard a Maryland yellow-throat's midnight strain, wood-thrush, kingfisher, tweezer-bird or parti-colored warbler, and a night-hawk. I also heard and saw red squirrels, and heard a bull-frog. The Indian said that he heard a snake.

Wild as it was, it was hard for me to get rid of the associations of the settlements. Any steady and monotonous sound, to which I did not distinctly attend, passed for a sound of human industry. The waterfalls which I heard were not without their dams and mills to my imagination,—and several times I found that I had been regarding the steady rushing sound of the wind from over the woods beyond the rivers as that of a train of cars,—the cars at Quebec.[95] Our minds anywhere, when left to themselves, are always thus busily drawing conclusions from false premises.

I asked the Indian to make us a sugar-bowl of birch-bark, which he did, using the great knife which dangled in a sheath from his belt; but the bark broke at the corners when he bent it up, and he said it was not good; that there was a great difference in this respect between the bark of one canoe-birch and that of another, i.e. one cracked more easily than another. I used some thin and delicate sheets of this bark which he split and cut, in my flower-book; thinking it would be good to separate the dried specimens from the green.

My companion, wishing to distinguish between the black and white spruce, asked Polis to show him a twig of the latter, which he did at once, together with the black; indeed, he could distinguish them about as far as he could see them; but as the two twigs appeared very much alike, my companion asked the Indian to point out the difference; whereupon the latter, taking the twigs, instantly remarked, as he passed his hand over them successively in a stroking manner, that the white was rough (i.e. the needles stood up nearly perpendicular), but the black smooth (i.e. as if bent or combed down). This was an obvious difference, both to sight and touch. However, if I remember rightly, this would not serve to distinguish the white spruce from the light-colored variety of the black.[96]

I asked him to let me see him get some black spruce root, and make some thread. Whereupon, without look-

95 St. Andrews and Quebec Rail Road Company was incorporated in 1836 and began operation in 1851.

96 Asa Gray wrote in his *Manual of the Botany of the Northern United States:* "A common variety in New England has lighter-colored or glaucous-green leaves, rather more slender and loosely spreading, and is undistinguishable from the next, except by the cones." The lighter-colored species is the red spruce (*Picea rubens*).

97 Loudon wrote: "In both Sweden and Norway . . . planks [are] fastened together with strings or cords made of the roots. . . . The long and slender roots are made use of to form this kind of strings; and they are rendered flexible by splitting them down the middle, and by boiling them for two or three hours in water mixed with alkali and sea salt. After this, they are dried and twisted into cordage, which is used as a substitute for hemp, both for naval and agricultural purposes."

98 Also known as stone-pitch, a hard pitch caused by heating the pitch to remove or reduce the essential oil.

ing up at the trees overhead, he began to grub in the ground, instantly distinguishing the black spruce roots, and cutting off a slender one, three or four feet long, and as big as a pipe-stem, he split the end with his knife, and taking a half between the thumb and forefinger of each hand, rapidly separated its whole length into two equal semi-cylindrical halves; then giving me another root, he said, "You try." But in my hands it immediately ran off one side, and I got only a very short piece. In short, though it looked very easy, I found that there was a great art in splitting these roots. The split is skillfully humored by bending short with this hand or that, and so kept in the middle. He then took off the bark from each half, pressing a short piece of cedar bark against the convex side with both hands, while he drew the root upward with his teeth. An Indian's teeth are strong, and I noticed that he used his often where we should have used a hand. They amounted to a third hand. He thus obtained, in a moment, a very neat, tough, and flexible string, which he could tie into a knot, or make into a fish-line even. It is said that in Norway and Sweden the roots of the Norway spruce (*Abies excelsa*) are used in the same way for the same purpose.[97] He said that you would be obliged to give half a dollar for spruce root enough for a canoe, thus prepared. He had hired the sewing of his own canoe, though he made all the rest. The root in his canoe was of a pale slate color, probably acquired by exposure to the weather, or perhaps from being boiled in water first.

He had discovered the day before that his canoe leaked a little, and said that it was owing to stepping into it violently, which forced the water under the edge of the horizontal seams on the side. I asked him where he would get pitch to mend it with, for they commonly use hard-pitch,[98] obtained of the whites at Oldtown. He said that he could make something very similar, and equally good, not of spruce gum, or the like, but of material which we had with us; and he wished me to guess what. But I could not, and he would not tell me, though he showed me a ball of it when made, as big as a pea, and like black pitch, saying, at last, that there were some things which a man did not tell even his wife. It may have been his own discovery. In Arnold's expedition the pioneers used for their canoe "the turpentine of the pine, and the scrapings of the pork-bag."[99]

Being curious to see what kind of fishes there were in this dark, deep, sluggish river, I cast in my line just before night, and caught several small somewhat yellowish sucker-like fishes, which the Indian at once rejected, saying that they were *Michigan* fish (i.e. *soft* and *stinking* fish)[100] and good for nothing. Also, he would not touch a pout, which I caught, and said that neither Indians nor whites thereabouts ever ate them, which I thought was singular, since they are esteemed in Massachusetts, and he had told me that he ate hedgehogs, loons, etc. But he said that some small silvery fishes, which I called white chivin, which were similar in size and form to the first, were the best fish in the Penobscot waters, and if I would toss them up the bank to him, he would cook them for me. After cleaning them, not very carefully, leaving the heads on, he laid them on the coals and so broiled them.

Returning from a short walk, he brought a vine in his hand, and asked me if I knew what it was, saying that it made the best tea of anything in the woods. It was the Creeping Snowberry (*Chiogenes hispidula*), which was quite common there, its berries just grown. He called it *cowosnebagosar,* which name implies that it grows where old prostrate trunks have collapsed and rotted. So we determined to have some tea made of this to-night. It had a slight checkerberry flavor, and we both agreed that it was really better than the black tea which we had

99 Quoted from "Arnold's Letters on his Expedition to Canada in 1775": "They were delayed several hours in consequence of injuries to one of their canoes by running upon the limb of a tree in the river. Birch bark was procured, and the roots of cedar for twine, and the canoe was covered with pitch made from the turpentine of the pine and scrapings of the pork bag."

100 The Winnebago nation, which came from the Green Bay area of Lake Michigan, were called "les Puans" ("the stinkards") among the Canadian French. According to Charlevoix "they lived on Fish, which the Lake furnished them in great abundance, the name Puans ['foul-smelling'] was given to them; for along the entire length of the Shore, where their Cabins were built, one saw only rotten Fish, with which the air was tainted." In his journal Thoreau simply wrote: "I think *Michigan* meant 'shit'" [MJ 26 July 1857].

101 On 4 February 1858 Thoreau noted in his journal: "The ledum bears a *general* resemblance to the water andromeda, with its dark reddish-purplish, or rather mulberry, leaves, reflexed; but nearer it is distinguished by its coarseness, the perfect tent form of its upper leaves, and the large, conspicuous terminal roundish (strictly oval) red buds, nearly as big as the swamppink's, but rounded. The woolly stem for a couple of inches beneath the bud is frequently bare and conspicuously club-shaped. The rust on the under sides of the leaves seems of a lighter color than that of Maine. . . . As usual with the finding of new plants, I had a presentiment that I should find the ledum in Concord" [J 10:273–274].

brought. We thought it quite a discovery, and that it might well be dried, and sold in the shops. I, for one, however, am not an old tea-drinker, and cannot speak with authority to others. It would have been particularly good to carry along for a cold drink during the day, the water thereabouts being invariably warm. The Indian said that they also used for tea a certain herb which grew in low ground, which he did not find there, and *Ledum*, or Labrador tea, which I have since found and tried in Concord;[101] also hemlock leaves, the last especially in the winter, when the other plants were covered with snow; and various other things; but he did not approve of *arbor vitae*, which I said I had drunk in those woods. We could have had a new kind of tea every night.

Just before night we saw a *musquash,* (he did not say muskrat,) the only one we saw in this voyage, swimming downward on the opposite side of the stream. The Indian, wishing to get one to eat, hushed us, saying, "Stop, me call 'em"; and sitting flat on the bank, he began to make a curious squeaking, wiry sound with his lips, exerting himself considerably. I was greatly surprised,—thought that I had at last got into the wilderness, and that he was a wild man indeed, to be talking to a musquash! I did not know which of the two was the strangest to me. He seemed suddenly to have quite forsaken humanity, and gone over to the musquash side. The musquash, however, as near as I could see, did not turn aside, though he may have hesitated a little, and the Indian said that he saw our fire; but it was evident that he was in the habit of calling the musquash to him, as he said. An acquaintance of mine who was hunting moose in the woods a month after this, tells me that his Indian in this way repeatedly called the musquash within reach of his paddle in the moonlight, and struck at them.

The Indian said a particularly long prayer this Sunday evening, as if to atone for working in the morning.

MONDAY, July 27.

Having rapidly loaded the canoe, which the Indian always carefully attended to, that it might be well trimmed, and each having taken a look, as usual, to see that nothing was left, we set out again, descending the Caucomgomoc, and turning northeasterly up the *Umbazookskus*. This name, the Indian said, meant *Much Meadow River*. We found it a very meadowy stream, and dead water, and now very wide on account of the rains, though, he said, it was sometimes quite narrow. The space between the woods, chiefly bare meadow, was from fifty to two hundred rods in breadth, and is a rare place for moose. It reminded me of the Concord; and what increased the resemblance, was one old musquash house almost afloat.[102]

In the water on the meadows grew sedges, wool-grass, the common blue-flag abundantly, its flower just showing itself above the high water, as if it were a blue water-lily, and higher in the meadows a great many clumps of a peculiar narrow-leaved willow (*Salix petiolaris*), which is common in our river meadows. It was the prevailing one here, and the Indian said that the musquash ate much of it; and here also grew the red osier (*Cornus stolonifera*), its large fruit now whitish.

Though it was still early in the morning, we saw night-hawks circling over the meadow, and as usually heard the pe-pe[103] (*Muscicapa Cooperi*), which is one of the prevailing birds in these woods, and the robin.

It was unusual for the woods to be so distant from the shore, and there was quite an echo from them, but when I was shouting in order to awake it, the Indian reminded me that I should scare the moose, which he was looking out for, and which we all wanted to see. The word for echo was *Pockadunkquaywayle*.

A broad belt of dead larch-trees along the distant edge of the meadow, against the forest on each side, increased

102 Thoreau wrote on 16 November 1852: "Muskrat-houses completed. Interesting objects looking down a river-reach at this season, and our river should not be represented without one or two of these cones. They are quite conspicuous half a mile distant, and are of too much importance to be omitted in the river landscape" [J 4:413].

103 Name given by Nuttall to the Cooper's, or olive-sided, fly-catcher, of which Thoreau wrote: "Regularly, at short intervals, it utters its monotonous note like *till-till-till* or *pe-pe-pe*" [J 9:408].

104 The fruit of which Thoreau called "a pleasant lively acid fruit" [J 4:170].

105 Newell (or Noel) Bear (or Bair), a Maliseet hunter, trapper, and guide, who was born ca. 1794 and died in 1907 at more than one hundred years of age. He was sometimes referred to as "Old Newell."

106 The Maliseet, a Native American people inhabiting the St. John River valley, were considered by some American officials to be part of British North America and therefore not subject to any American treaties.

the usual wildness of the scenery. The Indian called these juniper, and said that they had been killed by the back water caused by the dam at the outlet of Chesuncook Lake, some twenty miles distant. I plucked at the water's edge the *Asclepias incarnata,* with quite handsome flowers, a brighter red than our variety (the *pulchra*). It was the only form of it which I saw there.

Having paddled several miles up the Umbazook-skus, it suddenly contracted to a mere brook, narrow and swift, the larches and other trees approaching the bank and leaving no open meadow, and we landed to get a black-spruce pole for pushing against the stream. This was the first occasion for one. The one selected was quite slender, cut about ten feet long, merely whittled to a point, and the bark shaved off. The stream, though narrow and swift, was still deep, with a muddy bottom, as I proved by diving to it. Beside the plants which I have mentioned, I observed on the bank here the *Salix cordata* and *rostrata, Ranunculus recurvatus,* and *Rubus triflorus* with ripe fruit.[104]

While we were thus employed, two Indians in a canoe hove in sight round the bushes, coming down stream. Our Indian knew one of them, an old man,[105] and fell into conversation with him in Indian. He belonged at the foot of Moosehead. The other was of another tribe. They were returning from hunting. I asked the younger if they had seen any moose, to which he said no; but I, seeing the moose-hides sticking out from a great bundle made with their blankets in the middle of the canoe, added, "Only their hides." As he was a foreigner,[106] he may have wished to deceive me, for it is against the law for white men and foreigners to kill moose in Maine at this season. But, perhaps, he need not have been alarmed, for the moose-wardens are not very particular. I heard quite directly of one, who being asked by a white man going into the woods what he would say if he killed a moose, answered, "If you bring me a quarter of it, I guess you won't be troubled." His duty being, as he said, only to prevent the "indiscriminate" slaughter of them for their hides. I suppose that he would consider it an *indiscriminate* slaughter when a quarter was not reserved for himself. Such are the perquisites of this office.[107]

We continued along through the most extensive larch wood which I had seen,—tall and slender trees with fantastic branches. But though this was the prevailing tree here, I do not remember that we saw any afterward. You do not find straggling trees of this species here and there throughout the wood, but rather a little forest of them. The same is the case with the white and red pines, and some other trees, greatly to the convenience of the lumberer. They are of a social habit, growing in "veins," "clumps," "groups," or "communities," as the explorers[108] call them, distinguishing them far away, from the top of a hill or a tree, the white pines towering above the surrounding forest, or else they form extensive forests by themselves. I would have liked to come across a large community of pines, which had never been invaded by the lumbering army.

We saw some fresh moose tracks along the shore, but the Indian said that the moose were not driven out of the woods by the flies, as usual at this season, on account of the abundance of water everywhere. The stream was only from one and one half to three rods wide, quite winding, with occasional small islands, meadows, and some very swift and shallow places. When we came to an island, the Indian never hesitated which side to take, as if the current told him which was the shortest and deepest. It was lucky for us that the water was so high. We had to walk but once on this stream, carrying a part of the load, at a swift and shallow reach, while he got up with the canoe,

107 According to the 1852 legislation on moose wardens, the legal perquisites of the office entitled each warden and deputy wardens to "retain three-fourths of all forfeitures accruing their hands for their own use."
108 Those who locate stands of pine for the lumber companies.

109 Jackson wrote in his *Second Annual Report* that the "Umbazookskus continues sluggish and shallow, till within a few miles of the lake of the same name, from whence it flows. It is a smaller stream than the [Caucomgomac], exceedingly crooked, only ten miles long, and almost overgrown with tall grass and lily-pads."

110 Thoreau wrote in *A Week on the Concord and Merrimack Rivers:* "You may sometimes see the curious circular nests of the lamprey eel (*Petromyzon Americanus*), the American stone-sucker, as large as a cart-wheel, a foot or two in height, and sometimes rising half a foot above the surface of the water. They collect these stones, of the size of a hen's egg, with their mouths, as their name implies, and are said to fashion them into circles with their tails" [W 1:31].

111 Although the observation is not included in "Chesuncook," Thoreau noted in his journal on 16 September 1853 that Aitteon "said the stone-heaps (though we saw none) were made by chub" [J 5:424].

112 Hodge wrote: "Mud lake, as its name indicates, is low and muddy. Its level has been found to be fourteen feet above that of the Umbazookskus."

not being obliged to take out, though he said it was very strong water. Once or twice we passed the red wreck of a batteau which had been stove some spring.

While making this portage I saw many splendid specimens of the great purple-fringed orchis, three feet high. It is remarkable that such delicate flowers should here adorn these wilderness paths.

Having resumed our seats in the canoe, I felt the Indian wiping my back, which he had accidentally spat upon. He said it was a sign that I was going to be married.

The Umbazookskus River is called ten miles long.[109] Having poled up the narrowest part some three or four miles, the next opening in the sky was over Umbazookskus Lake, which we suddenly entered about eleven o'clock in the forenoon. It stretches northwesterly four or five miles, with what the Indian called the Caucomgomoc Mountain seen far beyond it. It was an agreeable change.

This lake was very shallow a long distance from the shore, and I saw stone heaps on the bottom, like those in the Assabet at home.[110] The canoe ran into one. The Indian thought that they were made by an eel. Joe Aitteon in 1853 thought that they were made by chub.[111] We crossed the southeast end of the lake to the carry into Mud Pond.

Umbazookskus Lake is the head of the Penobscot in this direction, and Mud Pond is the nearest head of the Allegash, one of the chief sources of the St. John. Hodge, who went through this way to the St. Lawrence in the service of the State, calls the portage here a mile and three quarters long, and states that Mud Pond has been found to be fourteen feet higher than Umbazookskus Lake.[112] As the west branch of the Penobscot at the Moosehead carry is considered about twenty-five feet lower than Moosehead Lake, it appears that the Penobscot in the upper part of its course runs in a broad and shallow valley, between the Kennebec and St. John, and lower than either of them, though, judging from the map, you might expect it to be the highest.

Mud Pond is about half-way from Umbazookskus to Chamberlain Lake, into which it empties, and to which we were bound. The Indian said that this was the wettest carry in the State, and as the season was a very wet one, we anticipated an unpleasant walk. As usual he made one large bundle of the pork-keg,[113] cooking utensils, and other loose traps, by tying them up in his blanket. We should be obliged to go over the carry twice, and our method was to carry one half part way, and then go back for the rest.

Our path ran close by the door of a log-hut in a clearing at this end of the carry, which the Indian, who alone entered it, found to be occupied by a Canadian and his family, and that the man had been blind for a year.[114] He seemed peculiarly unfortunate to be taken blind there, where there were so few eyes to see for him. He could not even be led out of that country by a dog, but must be taken down the rapids as passively as a barrel of flour. This was the first house above Chesuncook, and the last on the Penobscot waters, and was built here, no doubt, because it was the route of the lumberers in the winter and spring.

After a slight ascent from the lake through the springy soil of the Canadian's clearing, we entered on a level and very wet and rocky path through the universal dense evergreen forest, a loosely paved gutter merely, where we went leaping from rock to rock and from side to side, in the vain attempt to keep out of the water and mud. We concluded that it was yet Penobscot water, though there was no flow to it. It was on this carry that the white hunter whom I met in the stage, as he told me, had shot two bears a few months before.[115] They stood directly

113 A small barrel, usually between five and ten pounds.

114 Jules Thurlotte, whose wife, a year later, eloped with Joe Goodblood, a Frenchman. Unable to cope on his own, Thurlotte sold out to Ansel Smith.

115 Thoreau noted in his journal that Hiram Leonard said "that a few months ago he shot 2 bears on the Mudford carry—right in the path" [MJ 23 July 1857].

116 Jackson wrote that that the region "around the upper Allagash lakes . . . comprises the best timber land in the State."
117 Quoted from Jackson's *Second Annual Report.*
118 Telos Cut, or Canal, was built in 1841 to accommodate the passage of lumber between Telos and Webster Lakes.

in the path, and did not turn out for him. They might be excused for not turning out there, or only taking the right as the law directs. He said that at this season bears were found on the mountains and hillsides, in search of berries, and were apt to be saucy, — that we might come across them up Trout Stream; and he added, what I hardly credited, that many Indians slept in their canoes, not daring to sleep on land, on account of them.

Here commences what was called, twenty years ago, the best timber land in the State.[116] This very spot was described as "covered with the greatest abundance of pine,"[117] but now this appeared to me, comparatively, an uncommon tree there, — and yet you did not see where any more could have stood, amid the dense growth of cedar, fir, etc. It was then proposed to cut a canal from lake to lake here, but the outlet was finally made further east, at Telos Lake,[118] as we shall see.

The Indian with his canoe soon disappeared before us; but erelong he came back and told us to take a path which turned off westward, it being better walking, and, at my suggestion, he agreed to leave a bough in the regular carry at that place, that we might not pass it by mistake. Thereafter, he said, we were to keep the main path, and he added, "You see 'em my tracks." But I had not much faith that we could distinguish his tracks, since others had passed over the carry within a few days.

We turned off at the right place, but were soon confused by numerous logging-paths, coming into the one we were on, by which lumberers had been to pick out those pines which I have mentioned. However, we kept what we considered the main path, though it was a winding one, and in this, at long intervals, we distinguished a faint trace of a footstep. This, though comparatively unworn, was at first a better, or, at least, a drier road, than the regular carry which we had left. It led through an arbor-vitae wilderness of the grimmest character. The great fallen and rotting trees had been cut through and rolled aside, and their huge trunks abutted on the path on each side, while others still lay across it two or three feet high. It was impossible for us to discern the Indian's trail in the elastic moss, which, like a thick carpet, covered every rock and fallen tree, as well as the earth. Nevertheless, I did occasionally detect the track of a man, and I gave myself some credit for it. I carried my whole load at once, a heavy knapsack, and a large India-rubber bag, containing our bread and a blanket, swung on a paddle; in all, about sixty pounds; but my companion preferred to make two journeys, by short stages, while I waited for him. We could not be sure that we were not depositing our loads each time further off from the true path.

As I sat waiting for my companion, he would seem to be gone a long time, and I had ample opportunity to make observations on the forest. I now first began to be seriously molested by the black-fly, a very small but perfectly formed fly of that color, about one tenth of an inch long, which I first felt, and then saw, in swarms about me, as I sat by a wider and more than usually doubtful fork in this dark forest-path. The hunters tell bloody stories about them,—how they settle in a ring about your neck, before you know it, and are wiped off in great numbers with your blood. But remembering that I had a wash in my knapsack, prepared by a thoughtful hand in Bangor,[119] I made haste to apply it to my face and hands, and was glad to find it effectual, as long as it was fresh, or for twenty minutes, not only against black flies, but all the insects that molested us. They would not alight on the part thus defended. It was composed of sweet-oil[120] and oil of turpentine, with a little oil of spearmint, and camphor. However, I finally concluded that the remedy was worse than the disease. It was so disagreeable and inconvenient to have your face and hands covered with such a mixture.

119 Probably Thoreau's cousin, Rebecca Thatcher.
120 Olive oil.

Three large slate-colored birds of the jay genus (*Garrulus Canadensis*), the Canada-jay, moose-bird, meat-bird, or what not, came flitting silently and by degrees toward me, and hopped down the limbs inquisitively to within seven or eight feet. They were more clumsy and not nearly so handsome as the blue-jay. Fish-hawks, from the lake, uttered their sharp whistling notes low over the top of the forest near me, as if they were anxious about a nest there.

After I had sat there some time, I noticed at this fork in the path a tree which had been blazed, and the letters "Chamb. L." written on it with red chalk. This I knew to mean Chamberlain Lake. So I concluded that on the whole we were on the right course, though as we had come nearly two miles, and saw no signs of Mud Pond, I did harbor the suspicion that we might be on a direct course to Chamberlain Lake, leaving out Mud Pond. This I found by my map would be about five miles northeasterly, and I then took the bearing by my compass.

My companion having returned with his bag, and also defended his face and hands with the insect-wash, we set forward again. The walking rapidly grew worse, and the path more indistinct, and at length, after passing through a patch of *calla palustris,* still abundantly in bloom, we found ourselves in a more open and regular swamp, made less passable than ordinary by the unusual wetness of the season. We sank a foot deep in water and mud at every step, and sometimes up to our knees, and the trail was almost obliterated, being no more than that a musquash leaves in similar places, when he parts the floating sedge. In fact, it probably was a musquash trail in some places. We concluded that if Mud Pond was as muddy as the approach to it was wet, it certainly deserved its name. It would have been amusing to behold the dogged and deliberate pace at which we entered that swamp, without interchanging a word, as if determined to go through it, though it should come up to our necks. Having penetrated a considerable distance into this, and found a tussuck on which we could deposit our loads, though there was no place to sit, my companion went back for the rest of his pack. I had thought to observe on this carry when we crossed the dividing line between the Penobscot and St. John, but as my feet had hardly been out of water the whole distance, and it was all level and stagnant, I began to despair of finding it. I remembered hearing a good deal about the "highlands" dividing the waters of the Penobscot from those of the St. John, as well as the St. Lawrence, at the time of the northeast boundary dispute, and I observed by my map, that the line claimed by Great Britain as the boundary prior to 1842 passed between Umbazookskus Lake and Mud Pond, so that we had either crossed or were then on it. These, then, according to *her* interpretation of the treaty of '83, were the "highlands which divide those rivers that empty themselves into the St. Lawrence from those which fall into the Atlantic Ocean."[121] Truly an interesting spot to stand on,—if that were it,—though you could not sit down there. I thought that if the commissioners themselves, and the king of Holland[122] with them, had spent a few days here, with their packs upon their backs, looking for that "highland," they would have had an interesting time, and perhaps it would have modified their views of the question somewhat. The king of Holland would have been in his element. Such were my meditations while my companion was gone back for his bag.

It was a cedar swamp, through which the peculiar note of the white-throated sparrow rang loud and clear. There grew the side-saddle flower, Labrador tea, *Kalmia glauca,* and, what was new to me, the low birch (*Betula pumila*), a little round-leafed shrub, two or three feet high only. We thought to name this swamp after the latter.

[121] From the "Preliminary Articles of Peace, November 30, 1782" as incorporated into the Treaty of Paris (1783) that formally ended the American Revolutionary War.

[122] In an effort to settle the boundary dispute between the United States and Great Britain, arguments were made to William I of the Netherlands (1772–1843), who attempted to arbitrate the affair.

After a long while my companion came back, and the Indian with him. We had taken the wrong road, and the Indian had lost us. He had very wisely gone back to the Canadian's camp, and asked him which way we had probably gone, since he could better understand the ways of white men, and he told him correctly that we had undoubtedly taken the supply road to Chamberlain Lake (slender supplies they would get over such a road at this season). The Indian was greatly surprised that we should have taken what he called a "tow" (i.e. tote or toting or supply) road, instead of a carry path,—that we had not followed his tracks,—said it was "strange," and evidently thought little of our woodcraft.

Having held a consultation, and eaten a mouthful of bread, we concluded that it would, perhaps, be nearer for us two now to keep on to Chamberlain Lake, omitting Mud Pond, than to go back and start anew for the last place, though the Indian had never been through this way, and knew nothing about it. In the meanwhile he would go back and finish carrying over his canoe and bundle to Mud Pond, cross that, and go down its outlet and up Chamberlain Lake, and trust to meet us there before night. It was now a little after noon. He supposed that the water in which we stood had flowed back from Mud Pond, which could not be far off eastward, but was unapproachable through the dense cedar swamp.

Keeping on, we were erelong agreeably disappointed by reaching firmer ground, and we crossed a ridge where the path was more distinct, but there was never any out-look over the forest. While descending the last, I saw many specimens of the great round-leaved orchis, of large size; one which I measured had leaves, as usual, flat on the ground, nine and a half inches long, and nine wide, and was two feet high. The dark, damp wilderness is favorable to some of these orchidaceous plants, though they are too delicate for cultivation. I also saw the swamp gooseberry (*Ribes lacustre*), with green fruit, and in all the low ground, where it was not too wet, the *Rubus triflorus* in fruit. At one place I heard a very clear and piercing note from a small hawk, like a single note from a white-throated sparrow, only very much louder, as he dashed through the tree-tops over my head. I wondered that he allowed himself to be disturbed by our presence, since it seemed as if he could not easily find his nest again himself in that wilderness. We also saw and heard several times the red squirrel, and often, as before observed, the bluish scales of the fir cones which it had left on a rock or fallen tree. This, according to the Indian, is the only squirrel found in those woods, except a very few striped ones.[123] It must have a solitary time in that dark evergreen forest, where there is so little life, seventy-five miles from a road as we had come. I wondered how he could call any particular tree there his home; and yet he would run up the stem of one out of the myriads, as if it were an old road to him. How can a hawk ever find him there? I fancied that he must be glad to see us, though he did seem to chide us. One of those sombre fir and spruce woods is not complete unless you hear from out its cavernous mossy and twiggy recesses his fine alarum,—his spruce voice, like the working of the sap through some crack in a tree,—the working of the spruce-beer. Such an impertinent fellow would occasionally try to alarm the wood about me. "O," said I, "I am well acquainted with your family, I know your cousins in Concord very well. Guess the mail's irregular in these parts, and you'd like to hear from 'em." But my overtures were vain, for he would withdraw by his aerial turnpikes into a more distant cedar-top, and spring his rattle again.[124]

We then entered another swamp, at a necessarily slow pace, where the walking was worse than ever, not only on account of the water, but the fallen timber, which often obliterated the indistinct trail entirely. The fallen trees

123 Any of several small rodents with striped markings on the back, but Thoreau used the term in its most common usage as referring to the eastern chipmunk. He identified it more specifically in *A Week on the Concord and Merrimack Rivers*: "The chipping or striped squirrel, *Sciurus striatus* (*Tamias Lysteri*, Aud.)" [W 1:205] and in "Succession of Forest Trees": "How commonly in the Fall you see the cheek-pouches of the striped squirrel distended by a quantity of nuts! This species gets its scientific name *Tamias*, or the steward, from its habit of storing up nuts and other seeds" [W 5:198].

124 In *Walden* Thoreau wrote: "All day long the red squirrels came and went, and afforded me much entertainment by their manoeuvres. One would approach at first warily through the shrub-oaks, running over the snow crust by fits and starts like a leaf blown by the wind, now a few paces this way, with wonderful speed and waste of energy, making inconceivable haste with his 'trotters,' as if it were for a wager, and now as many paces that way, but never getting on more than half a rod at a time; and then suddenly pausing with a ludicrous expression and a gratuitous somerset, as if all the eyes in the universe were fixed on him,—for all the motions of a squirrel, even in the most solitary recesses of the forest, imply spectators as much as those of a dancing girl,—wasting more time in delay and circumspection than would have sufficed to walk the whole distance,—I never saw one walk,—and then suddenly, before you could say Jack Robinson, he would be in the top of a young pitch-pine, winding up his clock and chiding all imaginary spectators, soliloquizing and talking to all the universe at the same time,—for no reason that I could ever detect, or he himself was aware of, I suspect" [Wa 264–265].

were so numerous, that for long distances the route was through a succession of small yards, where we climbed over fences as high as our heads, down into water often up to our knees, and then over another fence into a second yard, and so on; and going back for his bag my companion once lost his way and came back without it. In many places the canoe would have run if it had not been for the fallen timber. Again it would be more open, but equally wet, too wet for trees to grow, and no place to sit down. It was a mossy swamp, which it required the long legs of a moose to traverse, and it is very likely that we scared some of them in our transit, though we saw none. It was ready to echo the growl of a bear, the howl of a wolf, or the scream of a panther; but when you get fairly into the middle of one of these grim forests, you are surprised to find that the larger inhabitants are not at home commonly, but have left only a puny red squirrel to bark at you. Generally speaking, a howling wilderness does not howl: it is the imagination of the traveller that does the howling. I did, however, see one dead porcupine; perhaps he had succumbed to the difficulties of the way. These bristly fellows are a very suitable small fruit of such unkempt wildernesses.

Making a logging-road in the Maine woods is called "swamping" it, and they who do the work are called "swampers." I now perceived the fitness of the term. This was the most perfectly swamped of all the roads I ever saw. Nature must have co-operated with art here. However, I suppose they would tell you that this name took its origin from the fact that the chief work of road-makers in those woods is to make the swamps passable. We came to a stream where the bridge, which had been made of logs tied together with cedar bark, had been broken up, and we got over as we could. This probably emptied into Mud Pond, and perhaps the Indian might have come up it and taken us in there if he had known it.

Such as it was, this ruined bridge was the chief evidence that we were on a path of any kind.

We then crossed another low rising ground, and I, who wore shoes, had an opportunity to wring out my stockings, but my companion, who used boots, had found that this was not a safe experiment for him, for he might not be able to get his wet boots on again. He went over the whole ground, or water, three times, for which reason our progress was very slow; beside that the water softened our feet, and to some extent unfitted them for walking. As I sat waiting for him, it would naturally seem an unaccountable time that he was gone. Therefore, as I could see through the woods that the sun was getting low, and it was uncertain how far the lake might be, even if we were on the right course, and in what part of the world we should find ourselves at nightfall, I proposed that I should push through with what speed I could, leaving boughs to mark my path, and find the lake and the Indian, if possible, before night, and send the latter back to carry my companion's bag.

Having gone about a mile, and got into low ground again, I heard a noise like the note of an owl, which I soon discovered to be made by the Indian, and answering him, we soon came together. He had reached the lake, after crossing Mud Pond, and running some rapids below it, and had come up about a mile and a half on our path. If he had not come back to meet us, we probably should not have found him that night, for the path branched once or twice before reaching this particular part of the lake. So he went back for my companion and his bag, while I kept on. Having waded through another stream where the bridge of logs had been broken up and half floated away,—and this was not altogether worse than our ordinary walking, since it was less muddy,—we continued on, through alternate mud and water, to the shore of Apmoojenegamook Lake, which we reached in

125 The first clearing for Chamberlain Farm was made in 1846. Much of the land on and near the lake was owned by David Pingree (1795–1863), who established a storehouse, or base of supplies, in that region. Eben Smith Coe (1814–1899), who helped establish the farm and was co-proprietor, was on the farm at the time of Thoreau's visit. According to the 1861 *Annual Report upon the Natural History and Geology of Maine,* "Between 200 and 300 acres have been cleared and put into grass. A half a dozen men are constantly employed, and an immense amount of hay, grain and root crops is raised here, and used principally for supplies for men and teams in lumbering in the neighborhood. A large stock of cattle, horses and hogs is also kept on the farm."

season for a late supper, instead of dining there, as we had expected, having gone without our dinner. It was at least five miles by the way we had come, and as my companion had gone over most of it three times, he had walked full a dozen miles, bad as it was. In the winter, when the water is frozen, and the snow is four feet deep, it is no doubt a tolerable path to a footman. As it was, I would not have missed that walk for a good deal. If you want an exact recipe for making such a road, take one part Mud Pond, and dilute it with equal parts of Umbazookskus and Apmoojenegamook; then send a family of musquash through to locate it, look after the grades and culverts, and finish it to their minds, and let a hurricane follow to do the fencing.

We had come out on a point extending into Apmoojenegamook, or Chamberlain Lake, west of the outlet of Mud Pond, where there was a broad, gravelly, and rocky shore, encumbered with bleached logs and trees. We were rejoiced to see such dry things in that part of the world. But at first we did not attend to dryness so much as to mud and wetness. We all three walked into the lake up to our middle to wash our clothes.

This was another noble lake, called twelve miles long, east and west; if you add Telos Lake, which, since the dam was built, has been connected with it by dead water, it will be twenty; and it is apparently from a mile and a half to two miles wide. We were about midway its length, on the south side. We could see the only clearing in these parts, called the "Chamberlain Farm,"[125] with two or three log buildings close together, on the opposite shore, some two and a half miles distant. The smoke of our fire on the shore brought over two men in a canoe from the farm, that being a common signal agreed on when one wishes to cross. It took them about half an hour to come over, and they had their labor for their pains this time. Even the English name of the lake had a wild, woodland sound, reminding me of that Chamberlain who killed Paugus at Lovewell's fight.[126]

After putting on such dry clothes as we had, and hanging the others to dry on the pole which the Indian arranged over the fire, we ate our supper, and lay down on the pebbly shore with our feet to the fire, without pitching our tent, making a thin bed of grass to cover the stones.

Here first I was molested by the little midge called the No-see-em (*Simulium nocivum*, the latter word[127] is not the Latin for no-see-em), especially over the sand at the water's edge, for it is a kind of sand-fly. You would not observe them but for their light-colored wings. They are said to get under your clothes, and produce a feverish heat, which I suppose was what I felt that night.

Our insect foes in this excursion, to sum them up, were, first, mosquitoes, the chief ones, but only troublesome at night, or when we sat still on shore by day; second, black flies (*Simulium molestum*), which molested us more or less on the carries by day, as I have before described, and sometimes in narrower parts of the stream. Harris mistakes when he says that they are not seen after June.[128] Third, moose-flies. The big ones, Polis said, were called *Bososquasis*. It is a stout brown fly, much like a horse-fly, about eleven sixteenths of an inch long, commonly rusty-colored beneath, with unspotted wings. They can bite smartly, according to Polis, but are easily avoided or killed. Fourth, the No-see-ems above mentioned. Of all these, the mosquitoes are the only ones that troubled me seriously; but, as I was provided with a wash and a veil, they have not made any deep impression.

The Indian would not use our wash to protect his face and hands, for fear that it would hurt his skin, nor had he any veil; he, therefore, suffered from insects now, and throughout this journey, more than either of us. I think

126 Paugus was the war chief of the Pequawkets killed during Lovewell's Fight in 1725. John Chamberlain (1692–1758) was apocryphally designated Paugus's vanquisher. Thoreau was familiar with "The Ballad of Lovewell's Fight" and also the *History of the Old Township of Dunstable*, which contained the following account: "Paugus . . . was slain by John Chamberlain, who afterwards settled in Merrimac. After the heat of the conflict was over, weary and faint, Paugus and Chamberlain both went down to the pond to quench their thirst, and to wash out their guns which had become foul by continued firing. There they met and at once recognized each other, for Paugus was known personally to many of the company. Seeing the useless condition of each other's guns, they tacitly agreed to a truce while they were cleaning them. During this process, some words were exchanged, and Paugus said to Chamberlain, 'It is you or I.' Cautiously but with haste they proceeded in their work, for it was a case of life or death. Paugus had nearly finished loading, and was priming his piece, when Chamberlain struck the breech of his gun violently upon the ground, thus causing it to prime itself, and shot Paugus through the heart, the bullet of Paugus at the same instant grazing the head of Chamberlain."

127 *Nocivum* (Latin): hurtful, injurious, noxious.

128 Thaddeus William Harris wrote in *A Report on the Insects of Massachusetts, Injurious to Vegetation* (1841), which Thoreau reviewed in "Natural History of Massachusetts," that swarms of *Simulium molestum* "fill the air during the month of June. . . . They begin to appear in May, and continue about six weeks, after which they are no more seen."

129 Ursa Major, a constellation in the region of the north celestial pole containing the seven stars that form the Big Dipper.

130 The Pleiades, an open star cluster in the constellation Taurus, consisting of several hundred stars, of which six are visible to the naked eye.

131 Any star visible in the morning, and most often used, as here, for the planet Venus.

132 Also known as the polestar, or Polaris: the brightest star at the end of the handle of Ursa Minor, the Little Dipper, and star visually nearest the north celestial pole.

133 One of whom was George Thatcher.

that he suffered more than I did, when neither of us was protected. He regularly tied up his face in his handkerchief, and buried it in his blanket, and he now finally lay down on the sand between us and the fire for the sake of the smoke, which he tried to make enter his blanket about his face, and for the same purpose he lit his pipe and breathed the smoke into his blanket.

As we lay thus on the shore, with nothing between us and the stars, I inquired what stars he was acquainted with, or had names for. They were the Great Bear,[129] which he called by this name, the Seven Stars,[130] which he had no English name for, "the morning star,"[131] and "the north star."[132]

In the middle of the night, as indeed each time that we lay on the shore of a lake, we heard the voice of the loon, loud and distinct, from far over the lake. It is a very wild sound, quite in keeping with the place and the circumstances of the traveller, and very unlike the voice of a bird. I could lie awake for hours listening to it, it is so thrilling. When camping in such a wilderness as this, you are prepared to hear sounds from some of its inhabitants which will give voice to its wildness. Some idea of bears, wolves, or panthers runs in your head naturally, and when this note is first heard very far off at midnight, as you lie with your ear to the ground, — the forest being perfectly still about you, you take it for granted that it is the voice of a wolf or some other wild beast, for only the last part is heard when at a distance, — you conclude that it is a pack of wolves baying the moon, or, perchance, cantering after a moose. Strange as it may seem, the "mooing" of a cow on a mountain-side comes nearest to my idea of the voice of a bear; and this bird's note resembled that. It was the unfailing and characteristic sound of those lakes. We were not so lucky as to hear wolves howl, though that is an occasional serenade. Some friends of mine,[133] who two years ago went up the Caucomgomoc River, were serenaded by wolves while moose-hunting by moonlight. It was a sudden burst, as if a hundred demons had broke loose,—a startling sound enough, which, if any, would make your hair stand on end, and all was still again. It lasted but a moment, and you'd have thought there were twenty of them, when probably there were only two or three. They heard it twice only, and they said that it gave expression to the wilderness which it lacked before. I heard of some men who, while skinning a moose lately in those woods, were driven off from the carcass by a pack of wolves, which ate it up.[134]

This of the loon—I do not mean its laugh, but its looning[135]—is a long-drawn call, as it were, sometimes singularly human to my ear,—*hoo-hoo-ooooo,* like the hallooing of a man on a very high key, having thrown his voice into his head. I have heard a sound exactly like it when breathing heavily through my own nostrils, half awake at ten at night, suggesting my affinity to the loon; as if its language were but a dialect of my own, after all. Formerly, when lying awake at midnight in those woods, I had listened to hear some words or syllables of their language, but it chanced that I listened in vain until I heard the cry of the loon. I have heard it occasionally on the ponds of my native town,[136] but there its wildness is not enhanced by the surrounding scenery.

I was awakened at midnight by some heavy, low-flying bird, probably a loon, flapping by close over my head, along the shore. So, turning the other side of my half-clad body to the fire, I sought slumber again.

TUESDAY, July 28.

When we awoke we found a heavy dew on our blankets. I lay awake very early, and listened to the clear, shrill *ah-tette-tette-te,* of the white-throated sparrow, repeated at short intervals, without the least variation, for half an hour, as if it could not enough express its happiness.

134 Thoreau was told of this by Leonard.

135 Apparently a Thoreau-ism. Thoreau is cited as the source in the 1889 *Century Dictionary.* The term does not appear in any dictionary published before the publication of *Walden,* in which Thoreau wrote: "His usual note was this demoniac laughter, yet somewhat like that of a water-fowl; but occasionally, when he had balked me most successfully and come up a long way off, he uttered a long-drawn unearthly howl, probably more like that of a wolf than any bird; as when a beast puts his muzzle to the ground and deliberately howls. This was his looning,—perhaps the wildest sound that is ever heard here, making the woods ring far and wide" [Wa 226].

136 In "A Natural History of Massachusetts" Thoreau wrote that "when the frosts have tinged the leaves, a solitary loon pays a visit to our retired ponds, where he may lurk undisturbed till the season of moulting is passed, making the woods ring with his wild laughter" [W 5:114].

137 Ecclesiastically, the first of seven canonical
hours, but generally, the time of morning worship,
prayer or song.
138 Doubletop Mountain.

Whether my companions heard it or not, I know not, but it was a kind of matins[137] to me, and the event of that forenoon.

It was a pleasant sunrise, and we had a view of the mountains in the southeast. Ktaadn appeared about southeast by south. A double-topped mountain,[138] about southeast by east, and another portion of the same, east-southeast. The last the Indian called *Nerlumskeechti-cook,* and said that it was at the head of the East Branch, and we should pass near it on our return that way.

We did some more washing in the lake this morning, and with our clothes hung about on the dead trees and rocks, the shore looked like washing-day at home. The Indian, taking the hint, borrowed the soap, and walking into the lake, washed his only cotton shirt on his person, then put on his pants and let it dry on him.

I observed that he wore a cotton shirt, originally white, a greenish flannel one over it, but no waistcoat, flannel drawers, and strong linen or duck pants, which also had been white, blue woollen stockings, cowhide boots, and a Kossuth hat. He carried no change of clothing, but putting on a stout, thick jacket, which he laid aside in the canoe, and seizing a full-sized axe, his gun and ammunition, and a blanket, which would do for a sail or knapsack, if wanted, and strapping on his belt, which contained a large sheath-knife, he walked off at once, ready to be gone all summer. This looked very independent; a few simple and effective tools, and no India-rubber clothing. He was always the first ready to start in the morning, and if it had not held some of our property would not have been obliged to roll up his blanket. Instead of carrying a large bundle of his own extra clothing, etc., he brought back the great-coats of moose tied up in his blanket. I found that his outfit was the result of a long experience, and in the main was hardly to be improved on, unless by washing or an extra shirt.

Wanting a button here, he walked off to a place where some Indians had recently encamped, and searched for one, but I believe in vain.

Having softened our stiffened boots and shoes with the pork fat, the usual disposition of what was left at breakfast, we crossed the lake early, steering in a diagonal direction northwesterly about four miles, to the outlet, which was not to be discovered till we were close to it. The Indian name, *Apmoojenegamook,* means lake that is crossed, because the usual course lies across, and not along it. This is the largest of the Allegash lakes, and was the first St. John's water that we floated on. It is shaped in the main like Chesuncook. There are no mountains or high hills very near it. At Bangor we had been told of a township many miles further northwest; it was indicated to us as containing the highest land thereabouts,[139] where, by climbing a particular tree in the forest, we could get a general idea of the country. I have no doubt that the last was good advice, but we did not go there. We did not now intend to go far down the Allegash, but merely to get a view of the great lakes which are its source, and then return this way to the East Branch of the Penobscot. The water now, by good rights, flowed northward, if it could be said to flow at all.

After reaching the middle of the lake, we found the waves as usual pretty high, and the Indian warned my companion, who was nodding, that he must not allow himself to fall asleep in the canoe lest he should upset us; adding, that when Indians want to sleep in a canoe, they lie down straight on the bottom. But in this crowded one that was impossible. However, he said that he would nudge him if he saw him nodding.

A belt of dead trees stood all around the lake, some far out in the water, with others prostrate behind them, and they made the shore, for the most part, almost inaccessible. This is the effect of the dam at the outlet. Thus

139 Probably the Allagash Mountain area in township 7.

140 Flooded, inundated.

the natural sandy or rocky shore, with its green fringe, was concealed and destroyed. We coasted westward along the north side, searching for the outlet, about one quarter of a mile distant from this savage-looking shore, on which the waves were breaking violently, knowing that it might easily be concealed amid this rubbish, or by the over-lapping of the shore. It is remarkable how little these important gates to a lake are blazoned. There is no triumphal arch over the modest inlet or outlet, but at some undistinguished point it trickles in or out through the uninterrupted forest, almost as through a sponge.

We reached the outlet in about an hour, and carried over the dam there, which is quite a solid structure, and about one quarter of a mile further there was a second dam. The reader will perceive that the result of this particular damming about Chamberlain Lake is, that the head-waters of the St. John are made to flow by Bangor. They have thus dammed all the larger lakes, raising their broad surfaces many feet; Moosehead, for instance, some forty miles long, with its steamer on it; thus turning the forces of nature against herself, that they might float their spoils out of the country. They rapidly run out of these immense forests all the finer, and more accessible pine timber, and then leave the bears to watch the decaying dams, not clearing nor cultivating the land, nor making roads, nor building houses, but leaving it a wilderness, as they found it. In many parts, only these dams remain, like deserted beaver-dams. Think how much land they have flowed,[140] without asking Nature's leave! When the State wishes to endow an academy or university, it grants it a tract of forest land: one saw represents an academy; a gang, a university.

The wilderness experiences a sudden rise of all her streams and lakes, she feels ten thousand vermin gnawing at the base of her noblest trees, many combining, drag them off, jarring over the roots of the survivors, and tumble them into the nearest stream, till the fairest having fallen, they scamper off to ransack some new wilderness, and all is still again. It is as when a migrating army of mice girdles a forest of pines. The chopper fells trees from the same motive that the mouse gnaws them, — to get his living. You tell me that he has a more interesting family than the mouse. That is as it happens. He speaks of a "berth" of timber,[141] a good place for him to get into, just as a worm might. When the chopper would praise a pine, he will commonly tell you that the one he cut was so big that a yoke of oxen stood on its stump; as if that were what the pine had grown for, to become the footstool of oxen. In my mind's eye, I can see these unwieldy tame deer, with a yoke binding them together, and brazen-tipped horns betraying their servitude, taking their stand on the stump of each giant pine in succession through-out this whole forest, and chewing their cud there, until it is nothing but an ox-pasture, and run out at that. As if it were good for the oxen, and some terebinthine[142] or other medicinal quality ascended into their nostrils. Or is their elevated position intended merely as a symbol of the fact that the pastoral comes next in order to the sylvan or hunter life?

The character of the logger's admiration is betrayed by his very mode of expressing it. If he told all that was in his mind, he would say — It was so big that I cut it down and then a yoke of oxen could stand on its stump. He admires the log, the carcass or corpse, more than the tree. Why, my dear sir, the tree might have stood on its own stump, and a great deal more comfortably and firmly than a yoke of oxen can, if you had not cut it down. What right have you to celebrate the virtues of the man you murdered?[143]

The Anglo-American can indeed cut down, and grub up all this waving forest, and make a stump speech,[144] and vote for Buchanan[145] on its ruins, but he cannot con-

141 In Canada an allotted area obtained from the government on a timber license granting rights of property whatsoever in all trees, timber, and lumber cut within the limits of the license during the term thereof, but here used as a general term for an area of forest.
142 Or of pertaining to turpentine.
143 Possible allusion to Shakespeare's *Julius Caesar* III.ii.79: "I come to bury Caesar, not to praise him."
144 Popular political oratory from the frequent early use in the United States of a tree-stump as a rostrum in open-air political meetings.
145 James Buchanan (1791–1868), fifteenth president of the United States (1857–1861), who, trying to maintain a balance between proslavery and antislavery factions, angered radicals in both North and South.

146 Edmund Spenser (1552–1599), author of *The Faerie Queene,* and Dante Alighieri (1265–1321), author of *The Divine Comedy.*

147 First coin not issued by the British government in America, first minted in Massachusetts in 1652, and so-called from the encircled pine tree on the obverse side.

148 New England pronunciation of the word *district.* As Walter Channing (1786–1876) noted in his *Physician's Vacation:* "The New Englander adds a school,—the district (often pronounced *deestrict,* you know,) school."

149 Webster's *American Spelling Book* was dedicated to American, not British, spelling.

150 The dog day cicada (*Tibicen pruinosa*), also known as the harvest fly. On 2 September 1856 Thoreau noted in his journal a "dog-day locust" that "lit on the bottom of my boat . . . and z-ed there. When you hear him you have got to the end of the alphabet and may imagine the &. It has a mark somewhat like a small writing w on the top of its thorax" [J 9.53].

151 Also known as Eagle Lake, which name Thoreau used in "Chesuncook."

verse with the spirit of the tree he fells, he cannot read the poetry and mythology which retire as he advances. He ignorantly erases mythological tablets in order to print his handbills and town-meeting warrants on them. Before he has learned his a b c in the beautiful but mystic lore of the wilderness which Spenser and Dante had just begun to read,[146] he cuts it down, coins a *pine-tree* shilling,[147] (as if to signify the pine's value to him,) puts up a *dee*strict[148] school-house, and introduces Webster's spelling-book.[149]

Below the last dam, the river being swift and shallow, though broad enough, we two walked about half a mile to lighten the canoe. I made it a rule to carry my knapsack when I walked, and also to keep it tied to a cross-bar when in the canoe, that it might be found with the canoe if we should upset.

I heard the dog-day locust[150] here, and afterward on the carries, a sound which I had associated only with more open, if not settled countries. The area for locusts must be small in the Maine woods.

We were now fairly on the Allegash River, which name our Indian said meant hemlock bark. These waters flow northward about 100 miles, at first very feebly, then southeasterly 250 more to the Bay of Fundy. After perhaps two miles of river, we entered Heron Lake,[151] called on the map *Pongokwahem,* scaring up forty or fifty young *shecorways,* sheldrakes, at the entrance, which ran over the water with great rapidity, as usual in a long line.

This was the fourth great lake, lying northwest and southeast, like Chesuncook, and most of the long lakes in that neighborhood, and, judging from the map, it is about ten miles long. We had entered it on the southwest side, and saw a dark mountain northeast over the lake, not very far off nor high, which the Indian said was called *Peaked Mountain,* and used by explorers to look for timber from. There was also some other high land more easterly. The shores were in the same ragged and unsightly condition, encumbered with dead timber, both fallen and standing, as in the last lake, owing to the dam on the Allegash below. Some low points or islands were almost drowned.

I saw something white a mile off on the water, which turned out to be a great gull on a rock in the middle, which the Indian would have been glad to kill and eat, but it flew away long before we were near; and also a flock of summer ducks that were about the rock with it. I asking him about herons, since this was Heron Lake, he said that he found the blue heron's nests in the hardwood trees. I thought that I saw a light-colored object move along the opposite or northern shore, four or five miles distant. He did not know what it could be, unless it were a moose, though he had never seen a white one; but he said that he could distinguish a moose "anywhere on shore, clear across the lake."

Rounding a point, we stood across a bay for a mile and a half or two miles, toward a large island,[152] three or four miles down the lake. We met with ephemerae[153] (shad-fly) midway, about a mile from the shore, and they evidently fly over the whole lake. On Moosehead I had seen a large devil's-needle[154] half a mile from the shore, coming from the middle of the lake, where it was three or four miles wide at least. It had probably crossed. But at last, of course, you come to lakes so large that an insect cannot fly across them; and this, perhaps, will serve to distinguish a large lake from a small one.

We landed on the southeast side of the island, which was rather elevated, and densely wooded, with a rocky shore, in season for an early dinner. Somebody had camped there not long before, and left the frame on which they stretched a moose-hide, which our Indian criticised severely, thinking it showed but little woodcraft.[155] Here were plenty of the shells of crayfish, or fresh-water lob-

152 Pillsbury Island.

153 Any of various fragile winged insects of the order Ephemeroptera that develop from aquatic nymphs and live in the adult stage no longer than a few days; also called dayfly, Mayfly, and shadfly.

154 Also called a darning needle or devil's darning needle: common name for the dragonfly.

155 Thoreau wrote in his journal that Polis "said these were Joe Aitteon's. (He was my Indian 4 years ago) How he told I do not know—He was probably hunting bear—& had left them for the day" [MJ 1 August 1857].

156 Settlements on the American side of the St. John by the French who were expelled from Acadia, in Nova Scotia, by the English in the 1760s.

sters, which had been washed ashore, such as have given a name to some ponds and streams. They are commonly four or five inches long. The Indian proceeded at once to cut a canoe-birch, slanted it up against another tree on the shore, tying it with a withe, and lay down to sleep in its shade.

When we were on the Caucomgomoc, he recommended to us a new way home, the very one which we had first thought of, by the St. John. He even said that it was easier, and would take but little more time than the other, by the east branch of the Penobscot, though very much further round; and taking the map, he showed where we should be each night, for he was familiar with the route. According to his calculation, we should reach the French settlements[156] the next night after this, by keeping northward down the Allegash, and when we got into the main St. John the banks would be more or less settled all the way; as if that were a recommendation. There would be but one or two falls, with short carrying-places, and we should go down the stream very fast, even a hundred miles a day, if the wind allowed; and he indicated where we should carry over into Eel River to save a bend below Woodstock in New Brunswick, and so into the Schoodic Lake, and thence to the Mattawamkeag. It would be about three hundred and sixty miles to Bangor this way, though only about one hundred and sixty by the other; but in the former case we should explore the St. John from its source through two thirds of its course, as well as the Schoodic Lake and Mattawamkeag,—and we were again tempted to go that way. I feared, however, that the banks of the St. John were too much settled. When I asked him which course would take us through the wildest country, he said the route by the East Branch. Partly from this consideration, as also from its shortness, we resolved to adhere to the latter route, and perhaps ascend Ktaadn on the way.[157] We made this island the limit of our excursion in this direction.

We had now seen the largest of the Allegash Lakes. The next dam "was about fifteen miles" further north, down the Allegash, and it was dead water so far. We had been told in Bangor of a man who lived alone, a sort of hermit, at that dam, to take care of it, who spent his time tossing a bullet from one hand to the other, for want of employment,[158]—as if we might want to call on him. This sort of tit-for-tat intercourse between his two hands, bandying to and fro a leaden subject, seems to have been his symbol for society.

This island, according to the map, was about a hundred and ten miles in a straight line north-northwest from Bangor, and about ninety-nine miles east-southeast from Quebec. There was another island visible toward the north end of the lake, with an elevated clearing on it; but we learned afterward that it was not inhabited, had only been used as a pasture for cattle which summered in these woods, though our informant said that there was a hut on the mainland near the outlet of the lake. This unnaturally smooth-shaven, squarish spot, in the midst of the otherwise uninterrupted forest, only reminded us how uninhabited the country was. You would sooner expect to meet with a bear than an ox in such a clearing. At any rate, it must have been a surprise to the bears when they came across it. Such, seen far or near, you know at once to be man's work, for Nature never does it. In order to let in the light to the earth as on a lake, he clears off the forest on the hillsides and plains, and sprinkles fine grass-seed, like an enchanter, and so carpets the earth with a firm sward.

Polis had evidently more curiosity respecting the few settlers in those woods than we. If nothing was said, he took it for granted that we wanted to go straight to the

157 Thoreau wrote in his 28 January 1858 letter to Thomas Wentworth Higginson: "The Indian proposed that we should return to Bangor by the St John & Great Schoodic Lake, which we had thought of ourselves; and he showed us on the map where we should be each night. It was then noon, and the next day night, continuing down the Allegash, we should have been at the Madawaska settlements, having made only one or two portages; and thereafter, on the St John there would be but one or two more falls, with short carries; and if there was not too much wind, we could go down that stream one hundred miles a day. It is settled all the way below Madawaska. He knew the route well. He even said that this was easier, and would take but little more time, though much further, than the route we decided on,—*i.e.*, by Webster Stream, the East Branch, and main Penobscot to Oldtown; but he may have wanted a longer job. We preferred the latter, not only because it was shorter, but because, as he said, it was wilder" [W 6:324–325].

158 Daniel Crockett (d. 1864). Thoreau learned about Crockett from Eben Coe and met Crockett at Chamberlain Farm on 28 July: "Landed on a point at the Chamberlain Farm. . . . I saw there the man, the hermit, who tended the Dam on the Allegash some 15 miles below where we had been—& was said to spend his time tossing a bullet from one hand to the other." He had closed the dam "in order to catch trout—& if we wanted more water to get through the canal we might raise it—for he would like to have it raised" [MJ 28 July 1857].

next log-hut. Having observed that we came by the log-huts at Chesuncook, and the blind Canadian's at the Mud Pond carry, without stopping to communicate with the inhabitants, he took occasion now to suggest that the usual way was, when you came near a house, to go to it, and tell the inhabitants what you had seen or heard, and then they tell you what they had seen; but we laughed, and said that we had had enough of houses for the present, and had come here partly to avoid them.

In the meanwhile, the wind, increasing, blew down the Indian's birch and created such a sea that we found ourselves prisoners on the island, the nearest shore, which was the western, being perhaps a mile distant, and we took the canoe out to prevent its drifting away. We did not know but we should be compelled to spend the rest of the day and the night there. At any rate, the Indian went to sleep again in the shade of his birch, my companion busied himself drying his plants, and I rambled along the shore westward, which was quite stony, and obstructed with fallen bleached or drifted trees for four or five rods in width. I found growing on this broad rocky and gravelly shore the *Salix rostrata, discolor,* and *lucida, Ranunculus recurvatus, Potentilla Norvegica, Scutellaria lateriflora, Eupatorium purpureum, Aster Tradescanti, Mentha Canadensis, Epilobium angustifolium,* abundant, *Lycopus sinuatus, Solidago lanceolata, Spiraea salicifolia, Antennaria margaritacea, Prunella, Rumex acetosella,* Raspberries, Wool-grass, *Onoclea,* etc. The nearest trees were *Betula papyracea* and *excelsa,* and *Populus tremuloides.* I give these names because it was my furthest northern point.

Our Indian said that he was a doctor, and could tell me some medicinal use for every plant I could show him. I immediately tried him. He said that the inner bark of the aspen (*Populus tremuloides*) was good for sore eyes; and so with various other plants, proving himself as good as his word. According to his account, he had acquired such knowledge in his youth from a wise old Indian with whom he associated, and he lamented that the present generation of Indians "had lost a great deal."

He said that the caribou was a "very great runner," that there was none about this lake now, though there used to be many, and pointing to the belt of dead trees caused by the dams, he added, "No likum stump,—when he sees that he scared."

Pointing southeasterly over the lake and distant forest, he observed, "Me go Oldtown in three days." I asked how he would get over the swamps and fallen trees. "O," said he, "in winter all covered, go anywhere on snow-shoes, right across lakes." When I asked how he went, he said, "First I go Ktaadn, west side, then I go Millinocket, then Pamadumcook, then Nickatow, then Lincoln, then Oldtown," or else he went a shorter way by the Piscataquis. What a wilderness walk for a man to take alone! None of your half-mile swamps, none of your mile-wide woods merely, as on the skirts of our towns, without hotels, only a dark mountain or a lake for guide-board and station, over ground much of it impassable in summer!

It reminded me of Prometheus Bound. Here was travelling of the old heroic kind over the unaltered face of nature. From the Allegash, or Hemlock River, and Pongoquahem Lake, across great Apmoojenegamook, and leaving the Nerlumskeechticook Mountain on his left, he takes his way under the bear-haunted slopes of Souneunk and Ktaadn Mountains to Pamadumcook and Millinocket's inland seas, (where often gulls'-eggs may increase his store,) and so on to the forks at Nickatow, (*niasoseb* "we alone Joseph" seeing what our folks see,) ever pushing the boughs of the fir and spruce aside, with his load of furs, contending day and night, night and day, with the shaggy demon vegetation, travelling through the mossy graveyard of trees. Or he could go by

159 Translation, probably Thoreau's, of Aeschylus's *Prometheus Bound* (l. 727), which Thoreau had earlier translated as "rough jaw of the sea" [W 5:302] in his translation published in the January 1843 issue of the *Dial*.

160 Kineo is composed primarily of hornstone, which, like flint, being exceedingly hard, is useful in the making of tools and weapons.

161 In 1507 the German cartographer Martin Waldseemüller (ca. 1470–ca. 1521) made a map on which he gave the name America to the newly discovered continent, naming it after Amerigo Vespucci.

162 According to chapter 648, section 1, of the *Acts and Resolves Passed by the Thirty-First Legislature of the State of Maine, A.D. 1852:* "All sleds used for the transportation of provisions, grain, forage, lumber or merchandize of any kind, over any public road in the county of Aroostook, or that part of the county of Penobscot, over which the Aroostook road passes, drawn by two or more horses or other animals, shall be at least four feet, four inches in width, from outside to outside of the runners thereof."

"that rough tooth of the sea,"[159] Kineo, great source of arrows and of spears to the ancients, when weapons of stone were used.[160] Seeing and hearing moose, caribou, bears, porcupines, lynxes, wolves, and panthers. Places where he might live and die and never hear of the United States, which make such a noise in the world,—never hear of America, so called from the name of a European gentleman.[161]

There is a lumberer's road called the Eagle Lake road, from the Seboois to the east side of this lake. It may seem strange that any road through such a wilderness should be passable, even in winter, when the snow is three or four feet deep, but at that season, wherever lumbering operations are actively carried on, teams are continually passing on the single track, and it becomes as smooth almost as a railway. I am told that in the Aroostook country the sleds are required by law to be of one width, (four feet,)[162] and sleighs must be altered to fit the track, so that one runner may go in one rut and the other follow the horse. Yet it is very bad turning out.

We had for some time seen a thunder-shower coming up from the west over the woods of the island, and heard the muttering of the thunder, though we were in doubt whether it would reach us; but now the darkness rapidly increasing, and a fresh breeze rustling the forest, we hastily put up the plants which we had been drying, and with one consent made a rush for the tent material and set about pitching it. A place was selected and stakes and pins cut in the shortest possible time, and we were pinning it down lest it should be blown away, when the storm suddenly burst over us.

As we lay huddled together under the tent, which leaked considerably about the sides, with our baggage at our feet, we listened to some of the grandest thunder which I ever heard,—rapid peals, round and plump, bang, bang, bang, in succession, like artillery from some fortress in the sky; and the lightning was proportionally brilliant. The Indian said, "It must be good powder." All for the benefit of the moose and us, echoing far over the concealed lakes. I thought it must be a place which the thunder loved, where the lightning practised to keep its hand in, and it would do no harm to shatter a few pines. What had become of the ephemerae and devil's-needles then? Were they prudent enough to seek harbor before the storm? Perhaps their motions might guide the voyageur.

Looking out I perceived that the violent shower falling on the lake had almost instantaneously flattened the waves,—the commander of that fortress had smoothed it for us so,—and it clearing off, we resolved to start immediately, before the wind raised them again.

Going outside, I said that I saw clouds still in the southwest, and heard thunder there. The Indian asked if the thunder went "lound" (round), saying that if it did we should have more rain. I thought that it did. We embarked, nevertheless, and paddled rapidly back toward the dams. The white-throated sparrows on the shore were about, singing, *Ah te, e, e, te, e, e, te,* or else *ah te, e, e, te, e, e, te, e, e, te, e, e.*

At the outlet of Chamberlain Lake we were overtaken by another gusty rain-storm, which compelled us to take shelter, the Indian under his canoe on the bank, and we under the edge of the dam. However, we were more scared than wet. From my covert I could see the Indian peeping out from beneath his canoe to see what had become of the rain. When we had taken our respective places thus once or twice, the rain not coming down in earnest, we commenced rambling about the neighborhood, for the wind had by this time raised such waves on the lake that we could not stir, and we feared that we should be obliged to camp there. We got an early supper on the dam and tried for fish there, while waiting for

163 Variant of *piles*.

the tumult to subside. The fishes were not only few, but small and worthless, and the Indian declared that there were no good fishes in the St. John's waters; that we must wait till we got to the Penobscot waters.

At length, just before sunset, we set out again. It was a wild evening when we coasted up the north side of this Apmoojenegamook Lake. One thunder-storm was just over, and the waves which it had raised were still running with violence, and another storm was now seen coming up in the southwest, far over the lake; but it might be worse in the morning, and we wished to get as far as possible on our way up the lake while we might. It blowed hard against the northern shore about an eighth of a mile distant on our left, and there was just as much sea as our shallow canoe would bear, without our taking unusual care. That which we kept off, and toward which the waves were driving, was as dreary and harborless a shore as you can conceive. For half a dozen rods in width it was a perfect maze of submerged trees, all dead and bare and bleaching, some standing half their original height, others prostrate, and criss-across, above or beneath the surface, and mingled with them were loose trees and limbs and stumps, beating about. Imagine the wharves of the largest city in the world, decayed, and the earth and planking washed away, leaving the spiles[163] standing in loose order, but often of twice the ordinary height, and mingled with and beating against them the wreck of ten thousand navies, all their spars and timbers, while there rises from the water's edge the densest and grimmest wilderness, ready to supply more material when the former fails, and you may get a faint idea of that coast. We could not have landed if we would, without the greatest danger of being swamped; so blow as it might, we must depend on coasting by it. It was twilight, too, and that stormy cloud was advancing rapidly in our rear. It was a pleasant excitement, yet we were glad to reach, at length, in the dusk, the cleared shore of the Chamberlain Farm.

We landed on a low and thinly wooded point there, and while my companions were pitching the tent, I ran up to the house to get some sugar,[164] our six pounds being gone;—it was no wonder they were, for Polis had a sweet tooth. He would first fill his dipper nearly a third full of sugar, and then add the coffee to it. Here was a clearing extending back from the lake to a hill-top, with some dark-colored log buildings and a storehouse in it, and half a dozen men standing in front of the principal hut, greedy for news. Among them was the man who tended the dam on the Allegash and tossed the bullet. He having charge of the dams, and learning that we were going to Webster Stream the next day, told me that some of their men, who were haying at Telos Lake, had shut the dam at the canal there in order to catch trout, and if we wanted more water to take us through the canal we might raise the gate, for he would like to have it raised. The Chamberlain Farm is no doubt a cheerful opening in the woods, but such was the lateness of the hour that it has left but a dusky impression on my mind. As I have said, the influx of light merely is civilizing, yet I fancied that they walked about on Sundays in their clearing somewhat as in a prison-yard.

They were unwilling to spare more than four pounds of brown sugar,[165]—unlocking the storehouse to get it,—since they only kept a little for such cases as this, and they charged twenty cents a pound for it,[166] which certainly it was worth to get it up there.

When I returned to the shore it was quite dark, but we had a rousing fire to warm and dry us by, and a snug apartment behind it. The Indian went up to the house to inquire after a brother who had been absent hunting a year or two, and while another shower was beginning, I groped about cutting spruce and arbor-vitae twigs for

[164] Bought as either a small conical sugarloaf or cut from a larger sugarloaf.

[165] Due to crop failures, sugar was in short supply at this time.

[166] According to "Sugar Trade in the United States in 1859," *New York Times*, 13 January 1859: "The value of Sugars not only in our own market but also, in a measure, those of the producing countries, and in Europe, is always more or less affected by the extent of our domestic crop, and its almost total failure in 1855–6, and its partial deficiency in 1856–7, contributed in no considerable degree to the unparalleled expansion in prices which prevailed in those years."

167 Sometimes called a biscuit oven, a simple metal box (reflector oven) that reflects the heat of a campfire to cook food on a shelf inside the oven.

a bed. I preferred the arbor-vitae on account of its fragrance, and spread it particularly thick about the shoulders. It is remarkable with what pure satisfaction the traveller in these woods will reach his camping-ground on the eve of a tempestuous night like this, as if he had got to his inn, and, rolling himself in his blanket, stretch himself on his six feet by two bed of dripping fir-twigs, with a thin sheet of cotton for roof, snug as a meadow-mouse in its nest. Invariably our best nights were those when it rained, for then we were not troubled with mosquitoes.

You soon come to disregard rain on such excursions, at least in the summer, it is so easy to dry yourself, supposing a dry change of clothing is not to be had. You can much sooner dry you by such a fire as you can make in the woods than in anybody's kitchen, the fireplace is so much larger, and wood so much more abundant. A shed-shaped tent will catch and reflect the heat like a Yankee-baker,[167] and you may be drying while you are sleeping.

Some who have leaky roofs in the towns may have been kept awake, but we were soon lulled asleep by a steady, soaking rain, which lasted all night. To-night, the rain not coming at once with violence, the twigs were soon dried by the reflected heat.

WEDNESDAY, *July 29.*

When we awoke it had done raining, though it was still cloudy. The fire was put out, and the Indian's boots, which stood under the eaves of the tent, were half full of water. He was much more improvident in such respects than either of us, and he had to thank us for keeping his powder dry. We decided to cross the lake at once, before breakfast, or while we could; and before starting I took the bearing of the shore which we wished to strike, south-southeast about three miles distant, lest a sudden misty rain should conceal it when we were midway.

Though the bay in which we were was perfectly quiet and smooth, we found the lake already wide awake outside, but not dangerously or unpleasantly so; nevertheless, when you get out on one of those lakes in a canoe like this, you do not forget that you are completely at the mercy of the wind, and a fickle power it is. The playful waves may at any time become too rude for you in their sport, and play right on over you. We saw a few *shecorways* and a *fish-hawk* thus early, and after much steady paddling and dancing over the dark waves of Apmoojenegamook, we found ourselves in the neighborhood of the southern land, heard the waves breaking on it, and turned our thoughts wholly to that side. After coasting eastward along this shore a mile or two, we breakfasted on a rocky point, the first convenient place that offered.

It was well enough that we crossed thus early, for the waves now ran quite high, and we should have been obliged to go round somewhat, but beyond this point we had comparatively smooth water. You can commonly go along one side or the other of a lake, when you cannot cross it.

The Indian was looking at the hard-wood ridges from time to time, and said that he would like to buy a few hundred acres somewhere about this lake, asking our advice. It was to buy as near the crossing place as possible.

My companion and I having a minute's discussion on some point of ancient history, were amused by the attitude which the Indian, who could not tell what we were talking about, assumed. He constituted himself umpire, and, judging by our air and gesture, he very seriously remarked from time to time, "you beat," or "he beat."

Leaving a spacious bay, a northeasterly prolongation of Chamberlain Lake, on our left, we entered through a short strait into a small lake a couple of miles over, called on the map *Telasinis,* but the Indian had no distinct name for it, and thence into *Telos* Lake, which he called

168 As a result of the Telos Cut.
169 According to Eckstorm, this was Allan B. Farrar (d. ca. 1880s), a trapper who afterward moved to Florida.
170 William Harmon Hunt who, in 1835, made a clearing on the East Branch of the Penobscot River near Stacyville.

Paytaywecongomoc, or Burnt-Ground Lake. This curved round toward the northeast, and may have been three or four miles long as we paddled. He had not been here since 1825. He did not know what Telos meant; thought it was not Indian. He used the word "*Spokelogan*" (for an inlet in the shore which led nowhere), and when I asked its meaning said that there was "no Indian in 'em." There was a clearing, with a house and barn, on the southwest shore, temporarily occupied by some men who were getting the hay, as we had been told; also a clearing for a pasture on a hill on the west side of the lake.

We landed on a rocky point on the northeast side, to look at some Red Pines (*Pinus resinosa*), the first we had noticed, and get some cones, for our few which grow in Concord do not bear any.

The outlet from the lake into the East Branch of the Penobscot is an artificial one,[168] and it was not very apparent where it was exactly, but the lake ran curving far up northeasterly into two narrow valleys or ravines, as if it had for a long time been groping its way toward the Penobscot waters, or remembered when it anciently flowed there; by observing where the horizon was lowest, and following the longest of these, we at length reached the dam, having come about a dozen miles from the last camp. Somebody had left a line set for trout, and the jackknife with which the bait had been cut on the dam beside it, an evidence that man was near, and in a deserted log hut close by a loaf of bread baked in a Yankee-baker. These proved the property of a solitary hunter,[169] whom we soon met, and canoe and gun and traps were not far off. He told us that it was twenty miles further on our route to the foot of Grand Lake, where you could catch as many trout as you wanted, and that the first house below the foot of the lake, on the East Branch, was Hunt's,[170] about forty-five miles further; though there was one about a mile and a half up Trout stream, some fifteen miles ahead, but it was rather a blind route to it. It turned out that, though the stream was in our favor, we did not reach the next house till the morning of the third day after this. The nearest permanently inhabited house behind us was now a dozen miles distant, so that the interval between the two nearest houses on our route was about sixty miles.

This hunter, who was a quite small, sunburnt man, having already carried his canoe over, and baked his loaf, had nothing so interesting and pressing to do as to observe our transit. He had been out a month or more alone. How much more wild and adventurous his life than that of the hunter in Concord woods, who gets back to his house and the mill-dam[171] every night! Yet they in the towns who have wild oats to sow commonly sow them on cultivated and comparatively exhausted ground. And as for the rowdy world in the large cities, so little enterprise has it that it never adventures in this direction, but like vermin clubs together in alleys and drinking-saloons, its highest accomplishment, perchance, to run beside a fire-engine and throw brickbats.[172] But the former is comparatively an independent and successful man, getting his living in a way that he likes, without disturbing his human neighbors. How much more respectable also is the life of the solitary pioneer or settler in these, or any woods,—having real difficulties, not of his own creation, drawing his subsistence directly from nature,—than that of the helpless multitudes in the towns who depend on gratifying the extremely artificial wants of society and are thrown out of employment by hard times!

Here for the first time we found the raspberries really plenty,—that is, on passing the height of land between the Allegash and the East Branch of the Penobscot; the same was true of the blueberries.

Telos Lake, the head of the St. John on this side, and Webster Pond, the head of the East Branch of the Penob-

171 Town center. Concord originated as a mill-dam site, a center of converging roads, from which a settlement grew.
172 Pieces of brick.

173 Thoreau's first visit to Maine was made in 1846; the canal was completed in 1841.
174 Quoted from Springer's *Forest-Life*, although Springer was incorrect regarding the reasons for the digging of the canal.

scot, are only about a mile apart, and they are connected by a ravine, in which but little digging was required to make the water of the former, which is the highest, flow into the latter. This canal, which is something less than a mile long and about four rods wide, was made a few years before my first visit to Maine.[173] Since then the lumber of the upper Allegash and its lakes has been run down the Penobscot, that is, up the Allegash, which here consists principally of a chain of large and stagnant lakes, whose thoroughfares, or river-links, have been made nearly equally stagnant by damming, and then down the Penobscot. The rush of the water has produced such changes in the canal that it has now the appearance of a very rapid mountain stream flowing through a ravine, and you would not suspect that any digging had been required to persuade the waters of the St. John to flow into the Penobscot here. It was so winding that one could see but little way down.

It is stated by Springer, in his "Forest Life," that the cause of this canal being dug was this. According to the treaty of 1842 with Great Britain, it was agreed that all the timber run down the St. John, which rises in Maine, "when within the Province of New Brunswick. . . . shall be dealt with as if it were the produce of the said Province," which was thought by our side to mean that it should be free from taxation. Immediately, the Province, wishing to get something out of the Yankees, levied a duty on all the timber that passed down the St. John; but to satisfy its own subjects "made a corresponding discount on the stumpage charged those hauling timber from the crown lands."[174] The result was that the Yankees made the St. John run the other way, or down the Penobscot, so that the Province lost both its duty and its water, while the Yankees, being greatly enriched, had reason to thank it for the suggestion.

It is wonderful how well watered this country is. As

you paddle across a lake, bays will be pointed out to you, by following up which, and perhaps the tributary stream which empties in, you may, after a short portage, or possibly, at some seasons, none at all, get into another river, which empties far away from the one you are on. Generally, you may go in any direction in a canoe, by making frequent but not very long portages. You are only realizing once more what all nature distinctly remembers here, for no doubt the waters flowed thus in a former geological period, and instead of being a lake country, it was an archipelago. It seems as if the more youthful and impressible streams can hardly resist the numerous invitations and temptations to leave their native beds and run down their neighbors' channels. Your carries are often over half-submerged ground, on the dry channels of a former period. In carrying from one river to another, I did not go over such high and rocky ground as in going about the falls of the same river. For in the former case I was once lost in a swamp, as I have related, and, again, found an artificial canal which appeared to be natural.

I remember once dreaming of pushing a canoe up the rivers of Maine, and that, when I had got so high that the channels were dry, I kept on through the ravines and gorges, nearly as well as before, by pushing a little harder, and now it seemed to me that my dream was partially realized.

Wherever there is a channel for water, there is a road for the canoe. The pilot of the steamer which ran from Oldtown up the Penobscot in 1853[175] told me that she drew only fourteen inches, and would run easily in two feet of water, though they did not like to. It is said that some Western steamers can run on a heavy dew,[176] whence we can imagine what a canoe may do. Montresor,[177] who was sent from Quebec by the English about 1760 to explore the route to the Kennebec, over which Arnold afterward passed,[178] supplied the Penobscot near

175 In his journal of 1853 Thoreau described "the small rivers steamers which run to the Five Islands, built propeller-fashion" [J 5:456].

176 Possible reference to George Stillman Hillard's (1808–1879) *Six Months in Italy*, in which he wrote that the gondola "is so light that they seem able to go, — as a western captain said of his steamer, — wherever there is a heavy dew," or to Edward Robert Sullivan's (1826–1899) *Rambles and Scrambles in North and South America*, referring to "all the old jokes about the steamers drawing so little water, that they can cross the country anywhere after a heavy dew."

177 John Montresor (1736–1799), British military engineer, whose journal of his explorations into the region between Quebec and the Kennebec River was published with "Arnold's Letters on his Expedition to Canada in 1775."

178 In 1775 Benedict Arnold, then a colonel in the service of the American Colonies, was commanded to lead a select army corps through the wilds of the Kennebec, cooperate with other forces ordered to enter Upper Canada by the lakes, and capture Quebec. Montresor's manuscript journal, having fallen into Arnold's hand, was used as his guide on this unsuccessful campaign.

179 Montresor wrote in his journal: "The river was so small that my navigation was often interrupted, and I was obliged to drag my canoes, although I had it supplied by opening the Beaver dams. This is often practised and is of great use in small rivers."

180 Montresor wrote in his journal: "3d July. Continued the portage through the woods. After walking about we launched the canoes into a muddy creek in the middle of a marshy savanna. Upon this creek we advanced miles, and opened a vast number of beaver dams, which were of some use to us. It seems the Governor of Canada had been formerly acquainted with this, and all hunters were by his edict forbid to molest the beavers in this part of the country."

its source with water by opening the beaver-dams, and he says, "This is often done." [179] He afterward states that the Governor of Canada had forbidden to molest the beaver about the outlet of the Kennebec from Moosehead Lake, on account of the service which their dams did by raising the water for navigation. [180]

This canal, so called, was a considerable and extremely rapid and rocky river. The Indian decided that there was water enough in it without raising the dam, which would only make it more violent, and that he would run down it alone, while we carried the greater part of the baggage. Our provision being about half consumed, there was the less left in the canoe. We had thrown away the pork-keg, and wrapt its contents in birch bark, which is the unequalled wrapping-paper of the woods.

Following a moist trail through the forest, we reached the head of Webster Pond about the same time with the Indian, notwithstanding the velocity with which he moved, our route being the most direct. The Indian name of Webster Stream, of which this pond is the source, is, according to him, *Madunkehunk,* i.e. Height of Land, and of the pond, *Madunkehunk-gamooc,* or Height of Land Pond. The latter was two or three miles long. We passed near a pine on its shore which had been splintered by lightning, perhaps the day before. This was the first proper East Branch Penobscot water that we came to.

At the outlet of Webster Lake was another dam, at which we stopped and picked raspberries, while the Indian went down the stream a half-mile through the forest, to see what he had got to contend with. There was a deserted log camp here, apparently used the previous winter, with its "hovel" or barn for cattle. In the hut was a large fir-twig bed, raised two feet from the floor, occupying a large part of the single apartment, a long narrow table against the wall, with a stout log bench before it, and above the table a small window, the only one there was, which admitted a feeble light. It was a simple and strong fort erected against the cold, and suggested what valiant trencher work had been done there. I discovered one or two curious wooden traps, which had not been used for a long time, in the woods near by. The principal part consisted of a long and slender pole.

We got our dinner on the shore, on the upper side of the dam. As we were sitting by our fire, concealed by the earth bank of the dam, a long line of sheldrake, half grown, came waddling over it from the water below, passing within about a rod of us, so that we could almost have caught them in our hands. They were very abundant on all the streams and lakes which we visited, and every two or three hours they would rush away in a long string over the water before us, twenty to fifty of them at once, rarely ever flying, but running with great rapidity up or down the stream, even in the midst of the most violent rapids, and apparently as fast up as down, or else crossing diagonally, the old, as it appeared, behind, and driving them, and flying to the front from time to time, as if to direct them. We also saw many small black dippers, which behaved in a similar manner, and, once or twice, a few black ducks.

An Indian at Oldtown had told us that we should be obliged to carry ten miles between Telos Lake on the St. John's and Second Lake on the East Branch of the Penobscot; but the lumberers whom we met assured us that there would not be more than a mile of carry. It turned out that the Indian, who had lately been over this route, was nearest right, as far as we were concerned. However, if one of us could have assisted the Indian in managing the canoe in the rapids, we might have run the greater part of the way; but as he was alone in the management of the canoe in such places, we were obliged to walk the greater part. I did not feel quite ready to try such an experiment on Webster Stream, which has so bad a reputation. According to my observation, a batteau, properly manned, shoots rapids as a matter of course, which a single Indian with a canoe carries round.

My companion and I carried a good part of the baggage on our shoulders, while the Indian took that which would be least injured by wet in the canoe. We did not know when we should see him again, for he had not been this way since the canal was cut, nor for more than thirty years. He agreed to stop when he got to smooth water, come up and find our path if he could, and halloo for us, and after waiting a reasonable time go on and try again,—and we were to look out in like manner for him.

He commenced by running through the sluice-way and over the dam, as usual, standing up in his tossing canoe, and was soon out of sight behind a point in a wild gorge. This Webster Stream is well known to lumbermen as a difficult one. It is exceedingly rapid and rocky, and also shallow, and can hardly be considered navigable, unless that may mean that what is launched in it is sure to be carried swiftly down it, though it may be dashed to pieces by the way. It is somewhat like navigating a thunder-spout. With commonly an irresistible force urging you on, you have got to choose your own course each moment, between the rocks and shallows, and to get into it, moving forward always with the utmost possible moderation, and often holding on, if you can, that you may inspect the rapids before you.

By the Indian's direction we took an old path on the south side, which appeared to keep down the stream, though at a considerable distance from it, cutting off bends, perhaps to Second Lake, having first taken the course from the map with a compass, which was northeasterly, for safety. It was a wild wood-path, with a few tracks of oxen which had been driven over it, probably to some old camp clearing, for pasturage, mingled with the tracks of moose which had lately used it. We kept on steadily for about an hour without putting down our packs, occasionally winding around or climbing over a fallen tree, for the most part far out of sight and hearing of the river; till, after walking about three miles, we were glad to find that the path came to the river again at an old camp ground, where there was a small opening in the forest, at which we paused. Swiftly as the shallow and rocky river ran here, a continuous rapid with dancing waves, I saw, as I sat on the shore, a long string of sheldrakes, which something scared, run up the opposite side of the stream by me, with the same ease that they commonly did down it, just touching the surface of the waves, and getting an impulse from them as they flowed from under them; but they soon came back, driven by the Indian, who had fallen a little behind us, on account of the windings. He shot round a point just above, and came to land by us with considerable water in his canoe. He had found it, as he said, "very strong water," and had been obliged to land once before to empty out what he had taken in. He complained that it strained him to paddle so hard in order to keep his canoe straight in its course, having no one in the bows to aid him, and, shallow as it was, said that it would be no joke to upset there, for the force of the water was such that he had as lief I would strike him over the head with a paddle as have that water strike him. Seeing him come out of that gap was as if you should pour water down an inclined and zigzag trough, then drop a nutshell into it, and taking a short cut to the bottom, get there in time to see it come out, notwithstanding the rush and tumult, right side up, and only partly full of water.

After a moment's breathing space, while I held his canoe, he was soon out of sight again around another bend, and we, shouldering our packs, resumed our course.

181 The Assabet River is approximately twenty miles long, stretching from Westborough to Concord, where it merges with the Sudbury River to form the Concord River.

182 From 1849 to 1860 Thoreau hired himself out as a surveyor, completing more than 150 surveys. A handbill headed "Land Surveying" read: "Of all kinds, according to the best methods known; the necessary data supplied, in order that the boundaries of Farms may be accurately described in Deeds; *Woods* lotted off distinctly and according to a regular plan; *Roads* laid out, &c., &c. Distinct and accurate Plans of Farms furnished, with the buildings thereon, of any size, and with a scale of feet attached, to accompany the Farm Book, so that the land may be laid out in a winter evening. Areas warranted accurate within almost any degree of exactness, and the Variation of the Compass given, so that the lines can be run again. Apply to Henry D. Thoreau."

We did not at once fall into our path again, but made our way with difficulty along the edge of the river, till at length, striking inland through the forest, we recovered it. Before going a mile we heard the Indian calling to us. He had come up through the woods and along the path to find us, having reached sufficiently smooth water to warrant his taking us in. The shore was about one fourth of a mile distant, through a dense, dark forest, and as he led us back to it, winding rapidly about to the right and left, I had the curiosity to look down carefully, and found that he was following his steps backward. I could only occasionally perceive his trail in the moss, and yet he did not appear to look down nor hesitate an instant, but led us out exactly to his canoe. This surprised me, for without a compass, or the sight or noise of the river to guide us, we could not have kept our course many minutes, and could have retraced our steps but a short distance, with a great deal of pains and very slowly, using a laborious circumspection. But it was evident that he could go back through the forest wherever he had been during the day.

After this rough walking in the dark woods it was an agreeable change to glide down the rapid river in the canoe once more. This river, which was about the size of our Assabet (in Concord),[181] though still very swift, was almost perfectly smooth here, and showed a very visible declivity, a regularly inclined plane, for several miles, like a mirror set a little aslant, on which we coasted down. This very obvious regular descent, particularly plain when I regarded the water-line against the shores, made a singular impression on me, which the swiftness of our motion probably enhanced, so that we seemed to be gliding down a much steeper declivity than we were, and that we could not save ourselves from rapids and falls if we should suddenly come to them. My companion did not perceive this slope, but I have a surveyor's eyes,[182] and I satisfied myself that it was no ocular illusion. You could tell at a glance on approaching such a river, which way the water flowed, though you might perceive no motion. I observed the angle at which a level line would strike the surface, and calculated the amount of fall in a rod, which did not need to be remarkably great to produce this effect.

It was very exhilarating, and the perfection of travelling, quite unlike floating on our dead Concord River,[183] the coasting down this inclined mirror, which was now and then gently winding, down a mountain, indeed, between two evergreen forests, edged with lofty dead white pines, sometimes slanted half-way over the stream, and destined soon to bridge it. I saw some monsters there, nearly destitute of branches, and scarcely diminishing in diameter for eighty or ninety feet.

As we thus swept along, our Indian repeated in a deliberate and drawling tone the words "Daniel Webster, great lawyer," apparently reminded of him by the name of the stream, and he described his calling on him once in Boston, at what he supposed was his boarding-house. He had no business with him, but merely went to pay his respects, as we should say. In answer to our questions, he described his person well enough. It was on the day after Webster delivered his Bunker Hill oration, which I believe Polis heard. The first time he called he waited till he was tired without seeing him, and then went away. The next time, he saw him go by the door of the room in which he was waiting several times, in his shirt-sleeves, without noticing him. He thought that if he had come to see Indians, they would not have treated him so. At length, after very long delay, he came in, walked toward him, and asked in a loud voice, gruffly, "What do you want?" and he, thinking at first, by the motion of his hand, that he was going to strike him, said to himself, "You'd better take care, if you try that I shall know what

183 In *A Week on the Concord and Merrimack Rivers* Thoreau described the Concord River as being "remarkable for the gentleness of its current, which is scarcely perceptible" [W 1:7] and called it "a deep, dark, and dead stream" [W 1:43].

184 In 1825 Webster was serving as a congress-man from Massachusetts. Webster had fallen in the esteem of many of his adherents by his support of the Compromise of 1850 reaffirming fugitive slave laws. The bill called for the return of fugitive slaves found in free states. So strong was the sentiment against Webster in Massachusetts that Emerson wrote several diatribes in his journal, including "Pho! Let Mr Webster for decency's sake shut his lips once & forever on this word. The word *liberty* in the mouth of Mr Webster sounds like the word *love* in the mouth of a courtesan," and "Tell him that he who was their pride in the woods & mountains of New England is now their mortification; that they never name him; they have taken his picture from the wall & torn it—dropped the pieces in the gutter[;] they have taken his book of speeches from the shelf & put it in the stove." In "Slavery in Massachusetts" Thoreau likened Webster to a dung beetle or "dirt-bug and its ball" [W 4:395].

185 Hoar, pulled by the Gold Rush, had gone in 1849 to California, where he had practiced law, and returned to Concord to live in 1857.

to do." He did not like him, and declared that all he said "was not worth talk about a musquash." We suggested that probably Mr. Webster was very busy, and had a great many visitors just then.[184]

Coming to falls and rapids, our easy progress was suddenly terminated. The Indian went along shore to inspect the water, while we climbed over the rocks, picking berries. The peculiar growth of blueberries on the tops of large rocks here made the impression of high land, and indeed this was the Height-of-land stream. When the Indian came back, he remarked, "You got to walk; ver strong water." So, taking out his canoe, he launched it again below the falls, and was soon out of sight. At such times, he would step into the canoe, take up his paddle, and, with an air of mystery, start off, looking far down stream, and keeping his own counsel, as if absorbing all the intelligence of forest and stream into himself; but I sometimes detected a little fun in his face, which could yield to my sympathetic smile, for he was thoroughly good-humored. We meanwhile scrambled along the shore with our packs, without any path. This was the last of *our* boating for the day.

The prevailing rock here was a kind of slate, standing on its edges, and my companion, who was recently from California,[185] thought it exactly like that in which the gold is found, and said that if he had had a pan he would have liked to wash a little of the sand here.

The Indian now got along much faster than we, and waited for us from time to time. I found here the only cool spring that I drank at anywhere on this excursion, a little water filling a hollow in the sandy bank. It was a quite memorable event, and due to the elevation of the country, for wherever else we had been the water in the rivers and the streams emptying in was dead and warm, compared with that of a mountainous region. It was very bad walking along the shore over fallen and drifted trees

and bushes, and rocks, from time to time swinging ourselves round over the water, or else taking to a gravel bar
or going inland. At one place, the Indian being ahead, I
was obliged to take off all my clothes in order to ford a
small but deep stream emptying in, while my companion, who was inland, found a rude bridge, high up in the
woods, and I saw no more of him for some time. I saw
there very fresh moose tracks, found a new golden-rod to
me (perhaps *Solidago thyrsoidea*), and I passed one white-
pine log, which had lodged, in the forest near the edge of
the stream, which was quite five feet in diameter at the
but. Probably its size detained it.

Shortly after this, I overtook the Indian at the edge of
some burnt land, which extended three or four miles at
least, beginning about three miles above Second Lake,
which we were expecting to reach that night, and which
is about ten miles from Telos Lake. This burnt region was
still more rocky than before, but, though comparatively
open, we could not yet see the lake. Not having seen my
companion for some time, I climbed, with the Indian,
a singular high rock on the edge of the river, forming a
narrow ridge only a foot or two wide at top, in order to
look for him; and after calling many times, I at length
heard him answer from a considerable distance inland, he
having taken a trail which led off from the river, perhaps
directly to the lake, and was now in search of the river
again. Seeing a much higher rock, of the same character,
about one third of a mile further east, or down stream,
I proceeded toward it, through the burnt land, in order
to look for the lake from its summit, supposing that the
Indian would keep down the stream in his canoe, and
hallooing all the while that my companion might join
me on the way. Before we came together, I noticed where
a moose, which possibly I had scared by my shouting,
had apparently just run along a large rotten trunk of a
pine, which made a bridge, thirty or forty feet long, over

186 Blackened with soot or other matter, such as ash, collected from combustion.

a hollow, as convenient for him as for me. The tracks were as large as those of an ox, but an ox could not have crossed there. This burnt land was an exceedingly wild and desolate region. Judging by the weeds and sprouts, it appeared to have been burnt about two years before. It was covered with charred trunks, either prostrate or standing, which crocked[186] our clothes and hands, and we could not easily have distinguished a bear there by his color. Great shells of trees, sometimes unburnt without, or burnt on one side only, but black within, stood twenty or forty feet high. The fire had run up inside, as in a chimney, leaving the sap-wood. Sometimes we crossed a rocky ravine fifty feet wide, on a fallen trunk; and there were great fields of fire-weed (*Epilobium angustifolium*) on all sides, the most extensive that I ever saw, which presented great masses of pink. Intermixed with these were blueberry and raspberry bushes.

Having crossed a second rocky ridge, like the first, when I was beginning to ascend the third, the Indian, whom I had left on the shore some fifty rods behind, beckoned to me to come to him, but I made sign that I would first ascend the highest rock before me, whence I expected to see the lake. My companion accompanied me to the top. This was formed just like the others. Being struck with the perfect parallelism of these singular rock-hills, however much one might be in advance of another, I took out my compass and found that they lay north-west and southeast, the rock being on its edge, and sharp edges they were. This one, to speak from memory, was perhaps a third of a mile in length, but quite narrow, rising gradually from the northwest to the height of about eighty feet, but steep on the southeast end. The southwest side was as steep as an ordinary roof, or as we could safely climb; the northeast was an abrupt precipice from which you could jump clean to the bottom, near which the river flowed; while the level top of the ridge, on which you walked along, was only from one to three or four feet in width. For a rude illustration, take the half of a pear cut in two lengthwise, lay it on its flat side, the stem to the northwest, and then halve it vertically in the direction of its length, keeping the southwest half. Such was the general form.

There was a remarkable series of these great rock-waves revealed by the burning; breakers, as it were. No wonder that the river that found its way through them was rapid and obstructed by falls. No doubt the absence of soil on these rocks, or its dryness where there was any, caused this to be a very thorough burning. We could see the lake over the woods, two or three miles ahead, and that the river made an abrupt turn southward around the northwest end of the cliff on which we stood, or a little above us, so that we had cut off a bend, and that there was an important fall in it a short distance below us. I could see the canoe a hundred rods behind, but now on the opposite shore, and supposed that the Indian had concluded to take out and carry round some bad rapids on that side, and that that might be what he had beckoned to me for; but after waiting a while I could still see nothing of him, and I observed to my companion that I wondered where he was, though I began to suspect that he had gone inland to look for the lake from some hill-top on that side, as we had done. This proved to be the case; for after I had started to return to the canoe, I heard a faint halloo, and descried him on the top of a distant rocky hill on that side. But as, after a long time had elapsed, I still saw his canoe in the same place, and he had not returned to it, and appeared in no hurry to do so, and, moreover, as I remembered that he had previously beckoned to me, I thought that there might be something more to delay him than I knew, and began to return northwest, along the ridge, toward the angle in the river. My companion, who had just been separated from us, and had even contemplated the necessity of camping alone, wishing to husband his steps, and yet to keep with us, inquired where I was going; to which I answered, that I was going far enough back to communicate with the Indian, and that then I thought we had better go along the shore together, and keep him in sight.

When we reached the shore, the Indian appeared from out the woods on the opposite side, but on account of the roar of the water it was difficult to communicate with him. He kept along the shore westward to his canoe, while we stopped at the angle where the stream turned southward around the precipice. I again said to my companion, that we would keep along the shore and keep the Indian in sight. We started to do so, being close together, the Indian behind us having launched his canoe again, but just then I saw the latter, who had crossed to our side, forty or fifty rods behind, beckoning to me, and I called to my companion, who had just disappeared behind large rocks at the point of the precipice, three or four rods before me, on his way down the stream, that I was going to help the Indian a moment. I did so,— helped get the canoe over a fall, lying with my breast over a rock, and holding one end while he received it below,— and within ten or fifteen minutes at most I was back again at the point where the river turned southward, in order to catch up with my companion, while Polis glided down the river alone, parallel with me. But to my surprise, when I rounded the precipice, though the shore was bare of trees (not of rocks) for a quarter of a mile at least, my companion was not to be seen. It was as if he had sunk into the earth. This was the more unaccountable to me, because I knew that his feet were since our swamp walk very sore, and that he wished to keep with the party; and besides this was very bad walking, climbing over or about the rocks. I hastened along, hallooing and searching for him, thinking he might be concealed behind a rock, yet doubting if he had not taken the other side of the precipice, but the Indian had got along still faster in his canoe, till he was arrested by the falls, about a quarter of a mile below. He then landed, and said that we could go no further that night. The sun was setting, and on account of falls and rapids we should be obliged to leave this river and carry a good way into another further east. The first thing then was to find my companion, for I was now very much alarmed about him, and I sent the Indian along the shore down stream, which began to be covered with unburnt wood again just below the falls, while I searched backward about the precipice which we had passed. The Indian showed some unwillingness to exert himself, complaining that he was very tired, in consequence of his day's work, that it had strained him very much getting down so many rapids alone; but he went off calling somewhat like an owl. I remembered that my companion was near-sighted, and I feared that he had either fallen from the precipice, or fainted and sunk down amid the rocks beneath it. I shouted and searched above and below this precipice in the twilight till I could not see, expecting nothing less than to find his body beneath it. For half an hour I anticipated and believed only the worst. I thought what I should do the next day, if I did not find him, what I *could* do in such a wilderness, and how his relatives would feel, if I should return without him. I felt that if he were really lost away from the river there, it would be a desperate undertaking to find him; and where were they who could help you? What would it be to raise the country, where there were only two or three camps, twenty or thirty miles apart, and no road, and perhaps nobody at home? Yet we must try the harder, the less the prospect of success.

I rushed down from this precipice to the canoe in order to fire the Indian's gun, but found that my companion had the caps. I was still thinking of getting it off

187 According to H. Parker Huber, Thoreau "confused his directions here; he meant the northern side of Webster Brook."

when the Indian returned. He had not found him, but he said that he had seen his tracks once or twice along the shore. This encouraged me very much. He objected to firing the gun, saying that if my companion heard it, which was not likely, on account of the roar of the stream, it would tempt him to come toward us, and he might break his neck in the dark. For the same reason we refrained from lighting a fire on the highest rock. I proposed that we should both keep down the stream to the lake, or that I should go at any rate, but the Indian said, "No use, can't do anything in the dark; come morning, then we find 'em. No harm,—he make 'em camp. No bad animals here, no gristly bears, such as in California, where he's been,—warm night,—he well off as you and I." I considered that if he was well he could do without us. He had just lived eight years in California, and had plenty of experience with wild beasts and wilder men, was peculiarly accustomed to make journeys of great length, but if he were sick or dead, he was near where we were. The darkness in the woods was by this so thick that it alone decided the question. We must camp where we were. I knew that he had his knapsack, with blanket and matches, and, if well, would fare no worse than we, except that he would have no supper nor society.

This side of the river being so encumbered with rocks, we crossed to the eastern or smoother shore,[187] and proceeded to camp there, within two or three rods of the Falls. We pitched no tent, but lay on the sand, putting a few handfuls of grass and twigs under us, there being no evergreen at hand. For fuel we had some of the charred stumps. Our various bags of provisions had got quite wet in the rapids, and I arranged them about the fire to dry. The fall close by was the principal one on this stream, and it shook the earth under us. It was a cool, because dewy, night; the more so, probably, owing to the nearness of the falls. The Indian complained a good deal, and thought afterward that he got a cold there which occasioned a more serious illness. We were not much troubled by mosquitoes at any rate. I lay awake a good deal from anxiety, but, unaccountably to myself, was at length comparatively at ease respecting him. At first I had apprehended the worst, but now I had little doubt but that I should find him in the morning. From time to time I fancied that I heard his voice calling through the roar of the falls from the opposite side of the river; but it is doubtful if we could have heard him across the stream there. Sometimes I doubted whether the Indian had really seen his tracks, since he manifested an unwillingness to make much of a search, and then my anxiety returned.

It was the most wild and desolate region we had camped in, where, if anywhere, one might expect to meet with befitting inhabitants, but I heard only the squeak of a night-hawk flitting over. The moon in her first quarter, in the fore part of the night, setting over the bare rocky hills, garnished with tall, charred, and hollow stumps or shells of trees, served to reveal the desolation.

THURSDAY, *July 30.*

I aroused the Indian early this morning to go in search of our companion, expecting to find him within a mile or two, further down the stream. The Indian wanted his breakfast first, but I reminded him that my companion had had neither breakfast nor supper. We were obliged first to carry our canoe and baggage over into another stream, the main East Branch, about three fourths of a mile distant, for Webster Stream was no further navigable. We went twice over this carry, and the dewy bushes wet us through like water up to the middle; I hallooed in a high key from time to time, though I had little expectation that I could be heard over the roar of the rapids, and moreover we were necessarily on the opposite side of the stream to him. In going over this portage the last time, the Indian, who was before me with the canoe on his head, stumbled and fell heavily once, and lay for a moment silent, as if in pain. I hastily stepped forward to help him, asking if he was much hurt, but after a moment's pause, without replying, he sprang up and went forward. He was all the way subject to taciturn fits, but they were harmless ones.

We had launched our canoe and gone but little way down the East Branch, when I heard an answering shout from my companion, and soon after saw him standing on a point where there was a clearing a quarter of a mile below, and the smoke of his fire was rising near by. Before I saw him I naturally shouted again and again, but the Indian curtly remarked, "He hears you," as if once was enough. It was just below the mouth of Webster Stream. When we arrived, he was smoking his pipe, and said that he had passed a pretty comfortable night, though it was rather cold, on account of the dew.

It appeared that when we stood together the previous evening, and I was shouting to the Indian across the river, he, being near-sighted, had not seen the Indian nor his canoe, and when I went back to the Indian's assistance, did not see which way I went, and supposed that we were below and not above him, and so, making haste to catch up, he ran away from us. Having reached this clearing, a mile or more below our camp, the night overtook him, and he made a fire in a little hollow, and lay down by it in his blanket, still thinking that we were ahead of him. He thought it likely that he had heard the Indian call once the evening before, but mistook it for an owl. He had seen one botanical rarity before it was dark,—pure white *Epilobium angustifolium* amidst the fields of pink ones, in the burnt lands. He had already stuck up the remnant of a lumberer's shirt, found on the point, on a pole by the water-side, for a signal, and attached a note to it, to inform us that he had gone on to the lake, and that if he did not find us there, he would be back in a couple of hours. If he had not found us soon, he had some thoughts of going back in search of the solitary hunter whom we had met at Telos Lake, ten miles behind, and, if successful, hire him to take him to Bangor. But if this hunter had moved as fast as we, he would have been twenty miles off by this time, and who could guess in what direction? It would have been like looking for a needle in a hay-mow,[188] to search for him in these woods. He had been considering how long he could live on berries alone.

We substituted for his note a card containing our names and destination, and the date of our visit, which Polis neatly enclosed in a piece of birch-bark to keep it dry. This has probably been read by some hunter or explorer ere this.

We all had good appetites for the breakfast which we made haste to cook here, and then, having partially dried our clothes, we glided swiftly down the winding stream toward Second Lake.

As the shores became flatter with frequent gravel and sand bars, and the stream more winding in the lower land near the lake, elms and ash trees made their appearance; also the wild yellow lily (*Lilium Canadense*), some of whose bulbs I collected for a soup. On some ridges the burnt land extended as far as the lake. This was a very beautiful lake, two or three miles long, with high mountains on the southwest side, the (as our Indian said) *Nerlumskeechticook,* i.e. Dead-Water Mountain. It appears to be the same called Carbuncle Mountain on the map. According to Polis, it extends in separate elevations all along this and the next lake, which is much larger. The lake, too, I think, is called by the same name, or perhaps with the addition of *gamoc* or *mooc.*[189] The morning was a bright one, and perfectly still and serene,

188 A mow or mass of hay stored in a barn.
189 Meaning lake or pond.

the lake as smooth as glass, we making the only ripples as we paddled into it. The dark mountains about it were seen through a glaucous mist, and the brilliant white stems of canoe-birches were seen mingled with the other woods around it. The wood-thrush sang on the distant shore, and the laugh of some loons, sporting in a concealed western bay, as if inspired by the morning, came distinct over the lake to us, and, what was remarkable, the echo which ran round the lake was much louder than the original note; probably because, the loons being in a regularly curving bay under the mountain, we were exactly in the focus of many echoes, the sound being reflected like light from a concave mirror. The beauty of the scene may have been enhanced to our eyes by the fact that we had just come together again after a night of some anxiety. This reminded me of the Ambejijis Lake on the West Branch, which I crossed in my first coming to Maine. Having paddled down three quarters of the lake, we came to a stand still, while my companion let down for fish. A white (or whitish) gull sat on a rock which rose above the surface in mid-lake not far off, quite in harmony with the scene; and as we rested there in the warm sun, we heard one loud crashing or crackling sound from the forest, forty or fifty rods distant, as of a stick broken by the foot of some large animal. Even this was an interesting incident there. In the midst of our dreams of giant lake-trout, even then supposed to be nibbling, our fisherman drew up a diminutive red perch, and we took up our paddles again in haste.

It was not apparent where the outlet of this lake was, and while the Indian thought it was in one direction, I thought it was in another. He said, "I bet you fourpence it is there," but he still held on in my direction, which proved to be the right one. As we were approaching the outlet, it being still early in the forenoon, he suddenly exclaimed, "Moose! moose!" and told us to be still.

He put a cap on his gun, and standing up in the stern, rapidly pushed the canoe straight toward the shore and the moose. It was a cow-moose, about thirty rods off, standing in the water by the side of the outlet, partly behind some fallen timber and bushes, and at that distance she did not look very large. She was flapping her large ears, and from time to time poking off the flies with her nose from some part of her body. She did not appear much alarmed by our neighborhood, only occasionally turned her head and looked straight at us, and then gave her attention to the flies again. As we approached nearer, she got out of the water, stood higher and regarded us more suspiciously. Polis pushed the canoe steadily forward in the shallow water, and I for a moment forgot the moose in attending to some pretty rose-colored Polygonums[190] just rising above the surface, but the canoe soon grounded in the mud eight or ten rods distant from the moose, and the Indian seized his gun and prepared to fire. After standing still a moment, she turned slowly, as usual, so as to expose her side, and he improved this moment to fire, over our heads. She thereupon moved off eight or ten rods at a moderate pace, across a shallow bay, to an old standing-place of hers, behind some fallen red maples, on the opposite shore, and there she stood still again a dozen or fourteen rods from us, while the Indian hastily loaded and fired twice at her, without her moving. My companion, who passed him his caps and bullets, said that Polis was as excited as a boy of fifteen, that his hand trembled, and he once put his ramrod back upside down. This was remarkable for so experienced a hunter. Perhaps he was anxious to make a good shot before us. The white hunter had told me that the Indians were not good shots, because they were excited, though he said that we had got a good hunter with us.

The Indian now pushed quickly and quietly back, and a long distance round, in order to get into the outlet, —

190 Any of the plants classified under the genus *Polygonum* and characterized by stems with knot-like joints and conspicuous sheathlike stipules that Thoreau described in *A Week on the Concord and Merrimack Rivers:* "The small rose-colored polygonum raised its head proudly above the water on either hand, and flowering at this season and in these localities, in front of dense fields of the white species which skirted the sides of the stream, its little streak of red looked very rare and precious" [W 1:18].

for he had fired over the neck of a peninsula between it and the lake,—till we approached the place where the moose had stood, when he exclaimed, "She is a goner," and was surprised that we did not see her as soon as he did. There, to be sure, she lay perfectly dead, with her tongue hanging out, just where she had stood to receive the last shots, looking unexpectedly large and horse-like, and we saw where the bullets had scored the trees.

Using a tape, I found that the moose measured just six feet from the shoulder to the tip of the hoof, and was eight feet long as she lay. Some portions of the body, for a foot in diameter, were almost covered with flies, apparently the common fly of our woods, with a dark spot on the wing, and not the very large ones which occasionally pursued us in mid-stream, though both are called moose-flies.

Polis, preparing to skin the moose, asked me to help him find a stone on which to sharpen his large knife. It being all a flat alluvial ground where the moose had fallen, covered with red maples, etc., this was no easy matter; we searched far and wide, a long time, till at length I found a flat kind of slate-stone, and soon after he returned with a similar one, on which he soon made his knife very sharp.

While he was skinning the moose, I proceeded to ascertain what kind of fishes were to be found in the sluggish and muddy outlet. The greatest difficulty was to find a pole. It was almost impossible to find a slender, straight pole ten or twelve feet long in those woods. You might search half an hour in vain. They are commonly spruce, arbor-vitae, fir, etc., short, stout, and branchy, and do not make good fish-poles, even after you have patiently cut off all their tough and scraggy branches. The fishes were red perch and chivin.

The Indian having cut off a large piece of sirloin, the upper lip and the tongue, wrapped them in the hide, and placed them in the bottom of the canoe, observing that there was "one man," meaning the weight of one. Our load had previously been reduced some thirty pounds, but a hundred pounds were now added, a serious addition, which made our quarters still more narrow, and considerably increased the danger on the lakes and rapids, as well as the labor of the carries. The skin was ours according to custom, since the Indian was in our employ, but we did not think of claiming it. He being a skilful dresser of moose-hides, would make it worth seven or eight dollars to him, as I was told. He said that he sometimes earned fifty or sixty dollars in a day at them; he had killed ten moose in one day, though the skinning and all took two days. This was the way he had got his property. There were the tracks of a calf thereabouts, which he said would come "by, by," and he could get it if we cared to wait, but I cast cold water on the project.

We continued along the outlet toward Grand Lake, through a swampy region, by a long, winding, and narrow dead water, very much choked up by wood, where we were obliged to land sometimes in order to get the canoe over a log. It was hard to find any channel, and we did not know but we should be lost in the swamp. It abounded in ducks, as usual. At length we reached Grand Lake, which the Indian called *Matungamook.*

At the head of this we saw, coming in from the southwest, with a sweep apparently from a gorge in the mountains, Trout Stream, or *Uncardnerheese,* which name, the Indian said, had something to do with mountains.

We stopped to dine on an interesting high rocky island,[191] soon after entering Matungamook Lake, securing our canoe to the cliffy shore. It is always pleasant to step from a boat on to a large rock or cliff. Here was a good opportunity to dry our dewy blankets on the open sunny rock. Indians had recently camped here, and accidentally burned over the western end of the island, and

191 Louse Island, also known now as Thoreau Island.

192 In Loudon's *Arboretum et Fruticetum Britanicum,* from which the references to Michaux's
North American Sylva and Sir John Richardson's
(1787–1865) *Fauna boreali-americana* are taken.

Polis picked up a gun-case of blue broadcloth, and said
that he knew the Indian it belonged to, and would carry
it to him. His tribe is not so large but he may know all its
effects. We proceeded to make a fire and cook our dinner
amid some pines, where our predecessors had done the
same, while the Indian busied himself about his moose-
hide on the shore, for he said that he thought it a good
plan for one to do all the cooking, i.e. I suppose if that
one were not himself. A peculiar evergreen overhung our
fire, which at first glance looked like a pitch pine (*Pinus
rigida*), with leaves little more than an inch long, spruce-
like, but we found it[192] to be the *Pinus Banksiana,*—
"Banks's, or the Labrador Pine," also called Scrub Pine,
Gray Pine, etc., a new tree to us. These must have been
good specimens, for several were thirty or thirty-five feet
high, which is two or three times the height commonly
assigned them. Michaux says that it grows further north
than any of our pines, but he did not find it any where
more than ten feet high. Richardson found it forty feet
high and upward, and states that the porcupine feeds on
its bark. Here also grew the Red Pine (*Pinus resinosa*).

I saw where the Indians had made canoes in a little
secluded hollow in the woods, on the top of the rock,
where they were out of the wind, and large piles of
whittlings remained. This must have been a favorite resort for their ancestors, and, indeed, we found here the
point of an arrow-head, such as they have not used for
two centuries and now know not how to make. The
Indian, picking up a stone, remarked to me, "That very
strange lock (rock)." It was a piece of horn-stone, which
I told him his tribe had probably brought here centuries
before to make arrow-heads of. He also picked up a yellowish curved bone by the side of our fireplace and asked
me to guess what it was. It was one of the upper incisors
of a beaver, on which some party had feasted within a

year or two. I found also most of the teeth, and the skull, etc. We here dined on fried moose-meat.

One who was my companion in my two previous excursions to these woods,[193] tells me that when hunting up the Caucomgomoc, about two years ago, he found himself dining one day on moose-meat, mud-turtle, trout, and beaver, and he thought that there were few places in the world where these dishes could easily be brought together on one table.

After the almost incessant rapids and falls of the Madunkehunk (Height-of-Land, or Webster Stream), we had just passed through the dead-water of Second Lake, and were now in the much larger dead-water of Grand Lake, and I thought the Indian was entitled to take an extra nap here. Ktaadn, near which we were to pass the next day, is said to mean "Highest Land." So much geography is there in their names. The Indian navigator naturally distinguishes by a name those parts of a stream where he has encountered quick water and falls, and again, the lakes and smooth water where he can rest his weary arms, since those are the most interesting and memorable parts to him. The very sight of the *Nerlumskeechticook,* or Dead-Water Mountains, a day's journey off over the forest, as we first saw them, must awaken in him pleasing memories. And not less interesting is it to the white traveller, when he is crossing a placid lake in these out-of-the-way woods, perhaps thinking that he is in some sense one of the earlier discoverers of it, to be reminded that it was thus well known and suitably named by Indian hunters perhaps a thousand years ago.

Ascending the precipitous rock which formed this long narrow island, I was surprised to find that its summit was a narrow ridge, with a precipice on one side, and that its axis of elevation extended from northwest to southeast, exactly like that of the great rocky ridges

193 George Thatcher.

194 Engraved ideograms and pictographs. In *Walden* Thoreau wrote: "In the Indian gazettes a wigwam was the symbol of a day's march, and a row of them cut or painted on the bark of a tree signified that so many times they had camped" [Wa 27].

at the commencement of the Burnt Ground, ten miles northwesterly. The same arrangement prevailed here, and we could plainly see that the mountain ridges on the west of the lake trended the same way. Splendid large harebells nodded over the edge and in the clefts of the cliff, and the blueberries (*Vaccinium Canadense*) were for the first time really abundant in the thin soil on its top. There was no lack of them henceforward on the East Branch. There was a fine view hence over the sparkling lake, which looked pure and deep, and had two or three, in all, rocky islands in it. Our blankets being dry, we set out again, the Indian as usual having left his gazette[194] on a tree. This time it was we three in a canoe, my companion smoking. We paddled southward down this handsome lake, which appeared to extend nearly as far east as south, keeping near the western shore, just outside a small island, under the dark *Nerlumskeechticook* mountain. For I had observed on my map that this was the course. It was three or four miles across it. It struck me that the outline of this mountain on the southwest of the lake, and of another beyond it, was not only like that of the huge rock waves of Webster Stream, but in the main like Kineo, on Moosehead Lake, having a similar but less abrupt precipice at the southeast end; in short, that all the prominent hills and ridges hereabouts were larger or smaller Kineos, and that possibly there was such a relation between Kineo and the rocks of Webster Stream.

The Indian did not know exactly where the outlet was, whether at the extreme southwest angle or more easterly, and had asked to see my plan at the last stopping-place, but I had forgotten to show it to him. As usual, he went feeling his way by a middle course between two probable points, from which he could diverge either way at last without losing much distance. In approaching the south shore, as the clouds looked gusty, and the waves ran pretty high, we so steered as to get partly under the lee of an island, though at a great distance from it.

I could not distinguish the outlet till we were almost in it, and heard the water falling over the dam there.

Here was a considerable fall, and a very substantial dam, but no sign of a cabin or camp. The hunter whom we met at Telos Lake had told us that there were plenty of trout here, but at this hour they did not rise to the bait, only cousin trout, from the very midst of the rushing waters. There are not so many fishes in these rivers as in the Concord.

While we loitered here, Polis took occasion to cut with his big knife some of the hair from his moose-hide, and so lightened and prepared it for drying. I noticed at several old Indian camps in the woods the pile of hair which they had cut from their hides.

Having carried over the dam, he darted down the rapids, leaving us to walk for a mile or more, where for the most part there was no path, but very thick and difficult travelling near the stream. At length he would call to let us know where he was waiting for us with his canoe, when, on account of the windings of the stream, we did not know where the shore was, but he did not call often enough, forgetting that we were not Indians. He seemed to be very saving of his breath,—yet he would be surprised if we went by, or did not strike the right spot. This was not because he was unaccommodating, but a proof of superior manners. Indians like to get along with the least possible communication and ado. He was really paying us a great compliment all the while, thinking that we preferred a hint to a kick.

At length, climbing over the willows and fallen trees, when this was easier than to go round or under them, we overtook the canoe, and glided down the stream in smooth but swift water for several miles. I here observed again, as at Webster Stream, and on a still larger scale the next day, that the river was a smooth and regularly inclined plane down which we coasted. As we thus glided along we started the first black ducks which we had distinguished.

We decided to camp early to-night, that we might have ample time before dark; so we stopped at the first favorable shore, where there was a narrow gravelly beach on the western side, some five miles below the outlet of the lake. It was an interesting spot, where the river began to make a great bend to the east, and the last of the peculiar moose-faced *Nerlumskeechticook* mountains not far southwest of Grand Lake rose dark in the northwest a short distance behind, displaying its gray precipitous southeast side, but we could not see this without coming out upon the shore.

Two steps from the water on either side, and you come to the abrupt bushy and rooty if not turfy edge of the bank, four or five feet high, where the interminable forest begins, as if the stream had but just cut its way through it.

It is surprising on stepping ashore anywhere into this unbroken wilderness to see so often, at least within a few rods of the river, the marks of the axe, made by lumberers who have either camped here, or driven logs past in previous springs. You will see perchance where, going on the same errand that you do, they have cut large chips from a tall white-pine stump for their fire. While we were pitching the camp and getting supper, the Indian cut the rest of the hair from his moose-hide, and proceeded to extend it vertically on a temporary frame between two small trees, half a dozen feet from the opposite side of the fire, lashing and stretching it with arbor-vitae bark, which was always at hand, and in this case was stripped from one of the trees it was tied to. Asking for a new kind of tea, he made us some, pretty good, of the checkerberry

(*Gaultheria procumbens*), which covered the ground, dropping a little bunch of it tied up with cedar bark into the kettle; but it was not quite equal to the *Chiogenes*. We called this therefore Checkerberry-tea Camp.

I was struck with the abundance of the *Linnaea borealis,* checkerberry, and *Chiogenes hispidula,* almost everywhere in the Maine woods. The wintergreen (*Chimaphila umbellata*) was still in bloom here, and *Clintonia* berries were abundant and ripe. This handsome plant is one of the most common in that forest. We here first noticed the moose-wood in fruit on the banks. The prevailing trees were spruce (commonly black), arbor-vitae, canoe-birch, (black ash and elms beginning to appear,) yellow birch, red maple, and a little hemlock skulking in the forest. The Indian said that the white-maple punk was the best for tinder, that yellow-birch punk was pretty good, but hard. After supper he put on the moose tongue and lips to boil, cutting out the *septum*. He showed me how to write on the under side of birch bark, with a black spruce twig, which is hard and tough and can be brought to a point.

The Indian wandered off into the woods a short distance just before night, and, coming back, said, "Me found great treasure—fifty, sixty dollars worth." "What's that?" we asked. "Steel traps, under a log, thirty or forty, I didn't count 'em. I guess Indian work—worth three dollars apiece." It was a singular coincidence that he should have chanced to walk to and look under that particular log, in that trackless forest.

I saw chivin and chub in the stream when washing my hands, but my companion tried in vain to catch them. I also heard the sound of bull-frogs from a swamp on the opposite side, thinking at first that they were moose; a duck paddled swiftly by; and sitting in that dusky wilderness, under that dark mountain, by the bright river which was full of reflected light, still I heard the wood-

195 In *Walden* Thoreau also described the loon's unearthly sound: "I would suddenly be startled by his unearthly laugh behind me. . . . He uttered a long-drawn unearthly howl" [Wa 226].

thrush sing, as if no higher civilization could be attained. By this time the night was upon us.

You commonly make your camp just at sundown, and are collecting wood, getting your supper, or pitching your tent while the shades of night are gathering around and adding to the already dense gloom of the forest. You have no time to explore or look around you before it is dark. You may penetrate half a dozen rods further into that twilight wilderness, after some dry bark to kindle your fire with, and wonder what mysteries lie hidden still deeper in it, say at the end of a long day's walk; or you may run down to the shore for a dipper of water, and get a clearer view for a short distance up or down the stream, and while you stand there, see a fish leap, or duck alight in the river, or hear a wood-thrush or robin sing in the woods. That is as if you had been to town or civilized parts. But there is no sauntering off to see the country, and ten or fifteen rods seems a great way from your companions, and you come back with the air of a much travelled man, as from a long journey, with adventures to relate, though you may have heard the crackling of the fire all the while,—and at a hundred rods you might be lost past recovery, and have to camp out. It is all mossy and *moosey*. In some of those dense fir and spruce woods there is hardly room for the smoke to go up. The trees are a *standing* night, and every fir and spruce which you fell is a plume plucked from night's raven wing. Then at night the general stillness is more impressive than any sound, but occasionally you hear the note of an owl further or nearer in the woods, and if near a lake, the semi-human cry of the loons at their unearthly revels.[195]

To-night the Indian lay between the fire and his stretched moose-hide, to avoid the mosquitoes. Indeed, he also made a small smoky fire of damp leaves at his head and his feet, and then as usual rolled up his head in his blanket. We with our veils and our wash were tolerably comfortable, but it would be difficult to pursue any sedentary occupation in the woods at this season: you cannot see to read much by the light of a fire through a veil in the evening, nor handle pencil and paper well with gloves or anointed fingers.

FRIDAY, *July 31.*

The Indian said, "You and I kill moose last night, therefore use 'em best wood. Always use hard wood to cook moose-meat." His "best wood" was rock-maple. He cast the moose's lip into the fire, to burn the hair off, and then rolled it up with the meat to carry along. Observing that we were sitting down to breakfast without any pork, he said, with a very grave look, "Me want some fat," so he was told that he might have as much as he would fry.

We had smooth but swift water for a considerable distance, where we glided rapidly along, scaring up ducks and kingfishers. But as usual, our smooth progress erelong came to an end, and we were obliged to carry canoe and all about half a mile down the right bank, around some rapids or falls. It required sharp eyes sometimes to tell which side was the carry, before you went over the falls, but Polis never failed to land us rightly. The raspberries were particularly abundant and large here, and all hands went to eating them, the Indian remarking on their size.

Often on bare rocky carries the trail was so indistinct that I repeatedly lost it, but when I walked behind him I observed that he could keep it almost like a hound, and rarely hesitated, or, if he paused a moment on a bare rock, his eye immediately detected some sign which would have escaped me. Frequently *we* found no path at all at these places, and were to him unaccountably delayed. He would only say it was "ver strange."

We had heard of a Grand Fall on this stream, and thought that each fall we came to must be it, but after christening several in succession with this name, we gave up the search. There were more Grand or Petty Falls than I can remember.

I cannot tell how many times we had to walk on account of falls or rapids. We were expecting all the while that the river would take a final leap and get to smooth water, but there was no improvement this forenoon. However, the carries were an agreeable variety. So surely as we stepped out of the canoe and stretched our legs we found ourselves in a blueberry and raspberry garden, each side of our rocky trail around the falls being lined with one or both. There was not a carry on the main East Branch where we did not find an abundance of both these berries, for these were the rockiest places, and partially cleared, such as these plants prefer, and there had been none to gather the finest before us.

In our three journeys over the carries, for we were obliged to go over the ground three times whenever the canoe was taken out, we did full justice to the berries, and they were just what we wanted to correct the effect of our hard bread and pork diet. Another name for making a portage would have been going a-berrying. We also found a few *Amelanchier,* or *service* berries, though most were abortive, but they held on rather more generally than they do in Concord. The Indian called them *Pemoymenuk,* and said that they bore much fruit in some places. He sometimes also ate the northern wild red cherries, saying that they were good medicine, but they were scarcely edible.

We bathed and dined at the foot of one of these carries. It was the Indian who commonly reminded us that it was dinner-time, sometimes even by turning the prow to the shore. He once made an indirect, but lengthy apology, by saying that we might think it strange, but that one who worked hard all day was very particular to have his dinner in good season. At the most considerable fall on this stream, when I was walking over the carry, close behind the Indian, he observed a track on the rock, which was but slightly covered with soil, and, stooping, muttered "caribou." When we returned, he observed a much larger track near the same place, where some animal's foot had sunk into a small hollow in the rock, partly filled with grass and earth, and he exclaimed with surprise, "What that?" "Well, what is it?" I asked. Stooping and laying his hand in it, he answered with a mysterious air, and in a half whisper, "Devil [that is, Indian Devil,[196] or cougar]—ledges about here—very bad animal—pull 'em *locks* all to pieces." "How long since it was made?" I asked. "To-day or yesterday," said he. But when I asked him afterward if he was sure it was the devil's track, he said he did not know. I had been told that the scream of a cougar was heard about Ktaadn recently, and we were not far from that mountain.

We spent at least half the time in walking to-day, and the walking was as bad as usual, for the Indian being alone, commonly ran down far below the foot of the carries before he waited for us. The carry-paths themselves were more than usually indistinct, often the route being revealed only by the countless small holes in the fallen timber made by the tacks in the drivers' boots, or where there *was* a slight trail we did not find it. It was a tangled and perplexing thicket, through which we stumbled and threaded our way, and when we had finished a mile of it, our starting-point seemed far away. We were glad that we had not got to walk to Bangor along the banks of this river, which would be a journey of more than a hundred miles. Think of the denseness of the forest, the fallen trees and rocks, the windings of the river, the streams emptying in and the frequent swamps to be crossed. It made you shudder. Yet the Indian from time to time pointed out to us where he had thus crept along day after day when he was a boy of ten, and in a starving condition. He had been hunting far north of this with

196 Of this animal Springer wrote: "There is an animal in the deep recesses of our forests, evidently belonging to the feline race, which, on account of its ferocity, is significantly called 'Indian Devil'—in the Indian language, 'the Lunk Soos'; a terror to the Indians, and the only animal in New England of which they stand in dread. You may speak of the moose, the bear, and the wolf even, and the red man is ready for the chase and the encounter. But name the object of his dread, and he will significantly shake his head, while he exclaims, 'He all one debil.'"

two grown Indians. The winter came on unexpectedly early, and the ice compelled them to leave their canoe at Grand Lake, and walk down the bank. They shouldered their furs and started for Oldtown. The snow was not deep enough for snow-shoes, or to cover the inequalities of the ground. Polis was soon too weak to carry any burden; but he managed to catch one otter. This was the most they all had to eat on this journey, and he remembered how good the yellow-lily roots were, made into a soup with the otter oil. He shared this food equally with the other two, but being so small he suffered much more than they. He waded through the Mattawamkeag at its mouth, when it was freezing cold and came up to his chin, and he, being very weak and emaciated, expected to be swept away. The first house which they reached was at Lincoln, and thereabouts they met a white teamster with supplies, who seeing their condition gave them as much of his load as they could eat. For six months after getting home he was very low, and did not expect to live, and was perhaps always the worse for it.

We could not find much more than half of this day's journey on our maps (the "Map of the Public Lands of Maine and Massachusetts," and "Colton's Railroad and Township Map of Maine," which copies the former). By the maps there was not more than fifteen miles between camps, at the outside, and yet we had been busily progressing all day, and much of the time very rapidly.

For seven or eight miles below that succession of "Grand" falls, the aspect of the banks as well as the character of the stream was changed. After passing a tributary from the northeast, perhaps Bowlin Stream,[197] we had good swift smooth water, with a regular slope, such as I have described. Low, grassy banks and muddy shores began. Many elms, as well as maples, and more ash trees overhung the stream, and supplanted the spruce.

My lily-roots having been lost when the canoe was

taken out at a carry, I landed late in the afternoon, at a low and grassy place amid maples, to gather more. It was slow work grubbing them up amid the sand, and the mosquitoes were all the while feasting on me. Mosquitoes, black flies, etc., pursued us in mid-channel, and we were glad sometimes to get into violent rapids, for then we escaped them.

A red-headed woodpecker flew across the river, and the Indian remarked that it was good to eat. As we glided swiftly down the inclined plane of the river, a great cat-owl launched itself away from a stump on the bank, and flew heavily across the stream, and the Indian, as usual, imitated its note. Soon the same bird flew back in front of us, and we afterwards passed it perched on a tree. Soon afterward a white-headed eagle sailed down the stream before us. We drove him several miles, while we were looking for a good place to camp, for we expected to be overtaken by a shower, —and still we could distinguish him by his white tail, sailing away from time to time from some tree by the shore still further down the stream. Some shecorways, being surprised by us, a part of them dived, and we passed directly over them, and could trace their course here and there by a bubble on the surface, but we did not see them come up. Polis detected once or twice what he called a "tow" road, an indistinct path leading into the forest. In the meanwhile we passed the mouth of the Seboois on our left. This did not look so large as our stream, which was indeed the main one. It was some time before we found a camping-place, for the shore was either too grassy and muddy, where mosquitoes abounded, or too steep a hillside. The Indian said that there were but few mosquitoes on a steep hillside. We examined a good place, where somebody had camped a long time; but it seemed pitiful to occupy an old site, where there was so much room to choose, so we continued on. We at length found a place to our

198 English axiom appearing in variant forms in the seventeenth century, as in John Arbuthnot's (1667–1735) fourth *John Bull* pamphlet: "The little I have is free, and I can call it my own; hame's hame, be it never so hamely."

199 Match for lighting candles, lamps, and the like.

200 Crop the snuff, the burning part or wick.

201 William Kirby (1759–1850) and William Spence (1783–1860) wrote in *An Introduction to Entomology* that the gnat "keep us awake by the ceaseless hum of their rapid wings (which, according to the Baron C. de Latour, are vibrated 3000 times per minute)." Baron Charles Cagniard de la Tour (1777–1859) invented an acoustical instrument that measured the number of vibrations corresponding to a particular pitch.

minds, on the west bank, about a mile below the mouth of the Seboois, where, in a very dense spruce wood above a gravelly shore, there seemed to be but few insects. The trees were so thick that we were obliged to clear a space to build our fire and lie down in, and the young spruce trees that were left were like the wall of an apartment rising around us. We were obliged to pull ourselves up a steep bank to get there. But the place which you have selected for your camp, though never so rough and grim, begins at once to have its attractions, and becomes a very centre of civilization to you: "Home is home, be it never so homely."[198]

It turned out that the mosquitoes were more numerous here than we had found them before, and the Indian complained a good deal, though he lay, as the night before, between three fires and his stretched hide. As I sat on a stump by the fire, with a veil and gloves on trying to read, he observed, "I make you candle," and in a minute he took a piece of birch bark about two inches wide and rolled it hard, like an allumette[199] fifteen inches long, lit it, and fixed it by the other end horizontally in a split stick three feet high, stuck it in the ground, turning the blazing end to the wind, and telling me to snuff[200] it from time to time. It answered the purpose of a candle pretty well.

I noticed, as I had done before, that there was a lull among the mosquitoes about midnight, and that they began again in the morning. Nature is thus merciful. But apparently they need rest as well as we. Few if any creatures are equally active all night. As soon as it was light I saw, through my veil, that the inside of the tent about our heads was quite blackened with myriads, each one of their wings when flying, as has been calculated, vibrating some three thousand times in a minute,[201] and their combined hum was almost as bad to endure as their stings. I had an uncomfortable night on this account, though I am not sure that one succeeded in his attempt to sting me.

We did not suffer so much from insects on this excursion as the statements of some who have explored these woods in midsummer led us to anticipate. Yet I have no doubt that at some seasons and in some places they are a much more serious pest. The Jesuit Hierome Lalemant, of Quebec, reporting the death of Father Reni Menard,[202] who was abandoned, lost his way, and died in the woods, among the Ontarios[203] near Lake Superior, in 1661, dwells chiefly on his probable sufferings from the attacks of mosquitoes when too weak to defend himself, adding that there was a frightful number of them in those parts, "and so insupportable," says he, "that the three Frenchmen who have made that voyage, affirm that there was no other means of defending one's self but to run always without stopping, and it was even necessary for two of them to be employed in driving off these creatures while the third wanted to drink, otherwise he could not have done it."[204] I have no doubt that this was said in good faith.

AUGUST I.

I caught two or three large red chivin (*Leuciscus pulchellus*) early this morning, within twenty feet of the camp, which, added to the moose-tongue, that had been left in the kettle boiling over night, and to our other stores, made a sumptuous breakfast. The Indian made us some hemlock tea instead of coffee, and we were not obliged to go as far as China for it; indeed, not quite so far as for the fish. This was tolerable, though he said it was not strong enough. It was interesting to see so simple a dish as a kettle of water with a handful of green hemlock sprigs in it, boiling over the huge fire in the open air, the leaves fast losing their lively green color, and know that it was for our breakfast.

202 René Ménard (1604–1661), who disappeared into the forest in the Wisconsin district in August 1661.
203 Huron.
204 Thoreau's translation of Jérôme Lallemant (1593–1665) in *Relation de ci qui s'est passé en la Nouvelle France en les années 1661 et 1662* (Paris, 1663).

We were glad to embark once more, and leave some of the mosquitoes behind. We had passed the *Wassataquoik* without perceiving it. This, according to the Indian, is the name of the main East Branch itself, and not properly applied to this small tributary alone, as on the maps.

We found that we had camped about a mile above Hunt's, which is on the east bank, and is the last house for those who ascend Ktaadn on this side.

We also had expected to ascend it from this point, but omitted it on account of the chafed feet of one of my companions. The Indian, however, suggested that perhaps he might get a pair of moccasins at this place, and that he could walk very easily in them without hurting his feet, wearing several pairs of stockings, and he said beside that they were so porous that when you had taken in water it all drained out again in a little while. We stopped to get some sugar, but found that the family had moved away, and the house was unoccupied, except temporarily by some men who were getting the hay. They told us that the road to Ktaadn left the river eight miles above; also that perhaps we could get some sugar at Fisk's, fourteen miles below. I do not remember that we saw the mountain at all from the river. I noticed a seine here stretched on the bank, which probably had been used to catch salmon. Just below this, on the west bank, we saw a moose-hide stretched, and with it a bear-skin, which was comparatively very small. I was the more interested in this sight, because it was near here that a townsman of ours, then quite a lad, and alone, killed a large bear some years ago.[205] The Indian said that they belonged to Joe Aitteon, my last guide, but how he told I do not know. He was probably hunting near, and had left them for the day. Finding that we were going directly to Oldtown, he regretted that he had not taken more of the moose-meat to his family, saying that in a short time, by drying it, he could have made it so light as to have brought away the greater part, leaving the bones. We once or twice inquired after the lip, which is a famous tit-bit, but he said, "That go Oldtown for my old woman; don't get it every day."

Maples grew more and more numerous. It was lowering,[206] and rained a little during the forenoon, and, as we expected a wetting, we stopped early and dined on the east side of a small expansion of the river, just above what are probably called Whetstone Falls, about a dozen miles below Hunt's. There were pretty fresh moose-tracks by the water-side. There were singular long ridges hereabouts, called "horsebacks,"[207] covered with ferns. My companion having lost his pipe asked the Indian if he could not make him one. "O yer," said he, and in a minute rolled up one of birch-bark, telling him to wet the bowl from time to time. Here also he left his gazette on a tree.

We carried round the falls just below, on the west side. The rocks were on their edges, and very sharp. The distance was about three fourths of a mile. When we had carried over one load, the Indian returned by the shore, and I by the path; and though I made no particular haste, I was nevertheless surprised to find him at the other end as soon as I. It was remarkable how easily he got along over the worst ground. He said to me, "I take canoe and you take the rest, suppose you can keep along with me?" I thought that he meant, that while he ran down the rapids I should keep along the shore, and be ready to assist him from time to time, as I had done before; but as the walking would be very bad, I answered, "I suppose you will go too fast for me, but I will try." But I was to go by the path, he said. This I thought would not help the matter, I should have so far to go to get to the river-side when he wanted me. But neither was this what he meant. He was proposing a race over the carry, and asked

206 Overcast; darkened by clouds.

207 The *Sixth Annual Report of the Secretary of the Maine Board of Agriculture* described them as a "curious class of alluvial ridges . . . found in great abundance in Maine, and scarcely occur out of the State, which are known by the provincial name of horsebacks. They are found mostly in the unsettled districts, and have never been carefully explored by geologists. We are not ready to theorize upon their origin until more details of their structure and distribution are known. In general they may be described as narrow ridges of coarse gravel and sand from thirty to forty feet high, situated in a level country, with sometimes an undulating summit, and the two ends are of nearly the some elevation above the ocean."

me if I thought I could keep along with him by the same path, adding that I must be pretty smart to do it. As his load, the canoe, would be much the heaviest and bulkiest, though the simplest, I thought that I ought to be able to do it, and said that I would try. So I proceeded to gather up the gun, axe, paddle, kettle, frying-pan, plates, dippers, carpets, etc., etc., and while I was thus engaged he threw me his cow-hide boots. "What, are these in the bargain?" I asked. "O yer," said he; but before I could make a bundle of my load I saw him disappearing over a hill with the canoe on his head; so, hastily scraping the various articles together, I started on the run, and immediately went by him in the bushes, but I had no sooner left him out of sight in a rocky hollow, than the greasy plates, dippers, etc., took to themselves wings, and while I was employed in gathering them up again, he went by me; but hastily pressing the sooty kettle to my side, I started once more, and soon passing him again, I saw him no more on the carry. I do not mention this as anything of a feat, for it was but poor running on my part, and he was obliged to move with great caution for fear of breaking his canoe as well as his neck. When he made his appearance, puffing and panting like myself, in answer to my inquiries where he had been, he said, "Locks (rocks) cut 'em feet," and laughing added, "O, me love to play sometimes." He said that he and his companions when they came to carries several miles long used to try who would get over first; each perhaps with a canoe on his head. I bore the sign of the kettle on my brown linen sack for the rest of the voyage.

We made a second carry on the east side, around some falls about a mile below this. On the mainland were Norway pines, indicating a new geological formation, and it was such a dry and sandy soil as we had not noticed before.

As we approached the mouth of the East Branch, we

passed two or three huts, the first sign of civilization after Hunt's, though we saw no road as yet; we heard a cow-bell, and even saw an infant held up to a small square window to see us pass, but apparently the infant and the mother that held it were the only inhabitants then at home for several miles. This took the wind out of our sails, reminding us that we were travellers surely, while it was a native of the soil, and had the advantage of us. Conversation flagged. I would only hear the Indian, per-haps, ask my companion, "You load my pipe?" He said that he smoked alder bark, for medicine. On entering the West Branch at Nickatow it appeared much larger than the East. Polis remarked that the former was all gone and lost now, that it was all smooth water hence to Oldtown, and he threw away his pole which was cut on the Umbazookskus. Thinking of the rapids, he said once or twice, that you wouldn't catch him to go East Branch again; but he did not by any means mean all that he said.

Things are quite changed since I was here eleven years ago. Where there were but one or two houses, I now found quite a village, with saw-mills and a store (the latter was locked, but its contents were so much the more safely stored), and there was a stage-road to Mattawam-keag, and the rumor of a stage. Indeed, a steamer had as-cended thus far once, when the water was very high. But we were not able to get any sugar, only a better shingle to lean our backs against.

We camped about two miles below Nickatow, on the south side of the West Branch, covering with fresh twigs the withered bed of a former traveller, and feeling that we were now in a settled country, especially when in the evening we heard an ox sneeze in its wild pasture across the river. Wherever you land along the frequented part of the river, you have not far to go to find these sites of temporary inns, the withered bed of flattened twigs,

208 The procedure is described in William Kelly's (1791–1855) *Excursion to California over the Prairies, Rocky Mountains, and Great Sierra Nevada:* "It is made by cutting off a large piece of flesh from a carcase, together with the skin, then paring away a good margin of the meat, so as to afford a selvage of hide that will lap over what remains in the centre . . . and then skewer or tie it up closely, placing it on hot embers or stones made red hot (which we did), when, if carefully tended, before the hide is burned through the meat is thoroughly done, juicy and savoury beyond conception, being stewed in its own peculiar gravy."

209 Traditional story that may have originated in Portugal, with variations spreading throughout Europe and Scandinavia, also known as "stone soup," "nail soup," and "beggar's broth." A poor traveler convinces an old woman that he will make soup if he is given a pot of boiling water in which to put his stone. As the stone broth boils, the traveler asks for some salt, and then for some potatoes or carrots, that the woman gladly gives as she watches the miracle of a bountiful soup being made from a stone.

the charred sticks, and perhaps the tent-poles. And not long since, similar beds were spread along the Connecticut, the Hudson, and the Delaware, and longer still ago, by the Thames and Seine, and they now help to make the soil where private and public gardens, mansions and palaces are. We could not get fir twigs for our bed here, and the spruce was harsh in comparison, having more twig in proportion to its leaf, but we improved it somewhat with hemlock. The Indian remarked as before, "Must have hard wood to cook moose-meat," as if that were a maxim, and proceeded to get it. My companion cooked some in California fashion, winding a long string of the meat round a stick and slowly turning it in his hand before the fire.[208] It was very good. But the Indian not approving of the mode, or because he was not allowed to cook it his own way, would not taste it. After the regular supper we attempted to make a lily soup of the bulbs which I had brought along, for I wished to learn all I could before I got out of the woods. Following the Indian's directions, for he began to be sick, I washed the bulbs carefully, minced some moose-meat and some pork, salted and boiled all together, but we had not patience to try the experiment fairly, for he said it must be boiled till the roots were completely softened so as to thicken the soup like flour; but though we left it on all night, we found it dried to the kettle in the morning, and not yet boiled to a flour. Perhaps the roots were not ripe enough, for they commonly gather them in the fall. As it was, it was palatable enough, but it reminded me of the Irishman's limestone broth.[209] The other ingredients were enough alone. The Indian's name for these bulbs was *Sheepnoc*. I stirred the soup by accident with a striped maple or moose-wood stick, which I had peeled, and he remarked that its bark was an emetic.

He prepared to camp as usual between his moose-hide and the fire, but it beginning to rain suddenly, he took refuge under the tent with us, and gave us a song before falling asleep. It rained hard in the night and spoiled another box of matches for us, which the Indian had left out, for he was very careless; but, as usual, we had so much the better night for the rain, since it kept the mosquitoes down.

SUNDAY, *August 2,*
was a cloudy and unpromising morning. One of us observed to the Indian, "You did not stretch your moose-hide last night, did you, Mr. Polis?" Whereat he replied, in a tone of surprise, though perhaps not of ill humor: "What you ask me that question for? Suppose I stretch 'em, you see 'em. May be your way talking, may be all right, no Indian way." I had observed that he did not wish to answer the same question more than once, and was often silent when it was put again for the sake of certainty, as if he were moody. Not that he was incommunicative, for he frequently commenced a long-winded narrative of his own accord,—repeated at length the tradition of some old battle, or some passage in the recent history of his tribe in which he had acted a prominent part, from time to time drawing a long breath, and resuming the thread of his tale, with the true story-teller's leisureliness, perhaps after shooting a rapid,—prefacing with "we-e-ll, by-by," etc., as he paddled along. Especially after the day's work was over, and he had put himself in posture for the night, he would be unexpectedly sociable, exhibit even the *bonhommie* of a Frenchman, and we would fall asleep before he got through his periods.

Nickatow is called eleven miles from Mattawamkeag by the river. Our camp was, therefore, about nine miles from the latter place.

210 A universal cure-all first manufactured in New York City circa 1835.

211 In his journal Thoreau wrote more generally: "It seemed to me that he made a greater ado about his sickness than a white man would have done" [MJ] 2 August 1857].

The Indian was quite sick this morning with the colic. I thought that he was the worse for the moose-meat he had eaten.

We reached the Mattawamkeag at half past eight in the morning, in the midst of a drizzling rain, and after buying some sugar set out again.

The Indian growing much worse, we stopped in the north part of Lincoln to get some brandy for him, but failing in this, an apothecary recommended Brandreth's pills,[210] which he refused to take, because he was not acquainted with them. He said to me, "Me doctor—first study my case, find out what ail 'em—then I know what to take." We dropped down a little further, and stopped at mid-forenoon on an island and made him a dipper of tea. Here too we dined and did some washing and botanizing, while he lay on the bank. In the afternoon we went on a little further, though the Indian was no better. "*Burntibus,*" as he called it, was a long smooth lake-like reach below the Five Islands. He said that he owned a hundred acres somewhere up this way. As a thunder-shower appeared to be coming up, we stopped opposite a barn on the west bank, in Chester, about a mile above Lincoln. Here at last we were obliged to spend the rest of the day and night, on account of our patient, whose sickness did not abate. He lay groaning under his canoe on the bank, looking very woe-begone, yet it was only a common case of colic. You would not have thought, if you had seen him lying about thus, that he was the proprietor of so many acres in that neighborhood, was worth $6,000, and had been to Washington. It seemed to me that, like the Irish, he made a greater ado about his sickness than a Yankee does,[211] and was more alarmed about himself. We talked somewhat of leaving him with his people in Lincoln,—for that is one of their homes,—and taking the stage the next day, but he objected on account of the expense, saying, "Suppose me well in morning, you and I go Oldtown by noon."

As we were taking our tea at twilight, while he lay groaning still under his canoe, having at length found out "what ail him," he asked me to get him a dipper of water. Taking the dipper in one hand, he seized his powder-horn with the other, and pouring into it a charge or two of powder, stirred it up with his finger, and drank it off. This was all he took to-day after breakfast beside his tea.

To save the trouble of pitching our tent, when we had secured our stores from wandering dogs, we camped in the solitary half-open barn near the bank, with the permission of the owner, lying on new-mown hay four feet deep. The fragrance of the hay, in which many ferns, etc. were mingled, was agreeable, though it was quite alive with grasshoppers which you could hear crawling through it. This served to graduate our approach to houses and feather-beds. In the night some large bird, probably an owl, flitted through over our heads, and very early in the morning we were awakened by the twittering of swallows which had their nests there.

MONDAY, *August 3.*

We started early before breakfast, the Indian being considerably better, and soon glided by Lincoln, and after another long and handsome lake-like reach, we stopped to breakfast on the west shore, two or three miles below this town.

We frequently passed Indian islands with their small houses on them. The Governor, Aitteon, lives on one of them, in Lincoln.

The Penobscot Indians seem to be more social, even, than the whites. Ever and anon in the deepest wilderness of Maine you come to the log-hut of a Yankee or Canada

212 The steamer *Mattanawcook* began service on the Penobscot in 1848.

settler, but a Penobscot never takes up his residence in such a solitude. They are not even scattered about on their islands in the Penobscot, which are all within the settlements, but gathered together on two or three,— though not always on the best soil,—evidently for the sake of society. I saw one or two houses not now used by them, because, as our Indian Polis said, they were too solitary.

The small river emptying in at Lincoln is the Matanawcook, which also, we noticed, was the name of a steamer[212] moored there. So we paddled and floated along, looking into the mouths of rivers. When passing the Mohawk Rips, or, as the Indian called them, "Mohog lips," four or five miles below Lincoln, he told us at length the story of a fight between his tribe and the Mohawks there, anciently,—how the latter were overcome by stratagem, the Penobscots using concealed knives,— but they could not for a long time kill the Mohawk chief, who was a very large and strong man, though he was attacked by several canoes at once, when swimming alone in the river.

From time to time we met Indians in their canoes, going up river. Our man did not commonly approach them, but exchanged a few words with them at a distance in his tongue. These were the first Indians we had met since leaving the *Umbazookskus*.

At Piscataquis Falls, just above the river of that name, we walked over the wooden railroad on the eastern shore, about one and a half miles long, while the Indian glided down the rapids. The steamer from Oldtown stops here, and passengers take a new boat above. Piscataquis, whose mouth we here passed, means "branch." It is obstructed by falls at its mouth, but can be navigated with batteaux or canoes above through a settled country, even to the neighborhood of Moosehead Lake, and we had thought at first of going that way. We were not obliged to get out of the canoe after this on account of falls or rapids, nor, indeed, was it quite necessary here. We took less notice of the scenery to-day, because we were in quite a settled country. The river became broad and sluggish, and we saw a blue heron winging its way slowly down the stream before us.

We passed the Passadumkeag River on our left and saw the blue *Olamon* mountains at a distance in the south-east. Hereabouts our Indian told us at length the story of their contention with the priest respecting schools. He thought a great deal of education and had recommended it to his tribe. His argument in its favor was, that if you had been to college and learnt to calculate, you could "keep 'em property,—no other way." He said that his boy[213] was the best scholar in the school at Oldtown, to which he went with whites. He himself is a Protestant, and goes to church regularly in Oldtown. According to his account, a good many of his tribe are Protestants, and many of the Catholics also are in favor of schools. Some years ago they had a schoolmaster, a Protestant, whom they liked very well. The priest came[214] and said that they must send him away, and finally he had such influence, telling them that they would go to the bad place at last if they retained him, that they sent him away. The school party, though numerous, were about giving up. Bishop Fenwick[215] came from Boston and used his influence against them. But our Indian told his side that they must not give up, must hold on, they were the strongest. If they gave up, then they would have no party. But they answered that it was "no use, priest too strong, we'd better give up." At length he persuaded them to make a stand.

The priest was going for a sign to cut down the liberty-pole. So Polis and his party had a secret meeting about it; he got ready fifteen or twenty stout young men, "stript 'em naked, and painted 'em like old times," and told them

213 Newell Polis, who was listed in the 1858 census of the Penobscot Indians as age fourteen.
214 John Bapst (1815–1879).
215 Benedict Joseph Fenwick (1782–1846), although according to Eugene Vetromile (1819–1891), a Jesuit priest stationed in Oldtown (ca. 1855–1880), it was Fenwick's successor, John Bernard Fitzpatrick (1812–1866), who was the bishop involved.

216 Term often used to denote the soul or spirit.

that when the priest and his party went to cut down the liberty-pole, they were to rush up, take hold of it and prevent them, and he assured them that there would be no war, only a noise, "no war where priest is." He kept his men concealed in a house near by, and when the priest's party were about to cut down the liberty-pole, the fall of which would have been a death-blow to the school party, he gave a signal, and his young men rushed out and seized the pole. There was a great uproar, and they were about coming to blows, but the priest interfered, saying, "No war, no war," and so the pole stands, and the school goes on still.

We thought that it showed a good deal of tact in him, to seize this occasion and take his stand on it; proving how well he understood those with whom he had to deal.

The Olamon River comes in from the east in Greenbush a few miles below the Passadumkeag. When we asked the meaning of this name, the Indian said that there was an island opposite its mouth which was called *Olarmon.* That in old times, when visitors were coming to Oldtown, they used to stop there to dress and fix up or paint themselves. "What is that which ladies used?" he asked. Rouge? Red vermilion? "Yer," he said, "that is *larmon,* a kind of clay or red paint, which they used to get here."

We decided that we too would stop at this island, and fix up our inner man,[216] at least, by dining.

It was a large island with an abundance of hemp-nettle, but I did not notice any kind of red paint there. The Olamon River, at its mouth at least, is a dead stream. There was another large island in that neighborhood, which the Indian called "*Soogle*" (i.e. Sugar) Island.

About a dozen miles before reaching Oldtown he inquired, "How you like 'em your pilot?" But we postponed an answer till we had got quite back again.

The *Sunkhaze,* another short dead stream, comes in from the east two miles above Oldtown. There is said to be some of the best deer ground in Maine on this stream. Asking the meaning of this name, the Indian said, "Suppose you are going down Penobscot, just like me, and you see a canoe come out of bank and go along before you, but you no see 'em stream. That is *Sunkhaze.*"

He had previously complimented me on my paddling, saying that I paddled "just like anybody," giving me an Indian name which meant "great paddler."[217] When off this stream he said to me, who sat in the bows, "Me teach you paddle." So turning toward the shore he got out, came forward and placed my hands as he wished. He placed one of them quite outside the boat, and the other parallel with the first, grasping the paddle near the end, not over the flat extremity, and told me to slide it back and forth on the side of the canoe. This, I found, was a great improvement which I had not thought of, saving me the labor of lifting the paddle each time, and I wondered that he had not suggested it before. It is true, before our baggage was reduced we had been obliged to sit with our legs drawn up, and our knees above the side of the canoe, which would have prevented our paddling thus, or perhaps he was afraid of wearing out his canoe, by constant friction on the side.

I told him that I had been accustomed to sit in the stern, and, lifting my paddle at each stroke, give it a twist in order to steer, the boat only getting a pry on the side each time, and I still paddled partly as if in the stern. He then wanted to see me paddle in the stern. So, changing paddles, for he had the longer and better one, and turning end for end, he sitting flat on the bottom and I on the cross-bar, he began to paddle very hard, trying to turn the canoe, looking over his shoulder and laughing, but finding it in vain he relaxed his efforts, though we still sped along a mile or two very swiftly. He said that he

217 No record of this Indian name is extant in Thoreau's journal.

218 Thoreau wrote in his 28 January 1858 letter to Thomas Wentworth Higginson that in general "the Indian can paddle twice as far in a day as he commonly does" [C 508].

219 Between Orson and Indian Islands.

220 Polis's.

221 Mary Polis (ca. 1818–1890)

222 This was the 48 × 44-inch "Map of Oldtown, Penobscot Co., Maine," published in 1855 by E. M. Woodford in Philadelphia.

223 Either the *Bangor Courier* or the *Bangor Journal*, both of which were published at this time.

224 Thoreau and Hoar remained in Maine several days longer: "*Aug. 4. Tuesday.* A.M.—Rode to Pushaw Lake with Thatcher and Hoar.

"Duck-meat, apparently a new kind, there. T. thinks there's little if any red cedar about Bangor.

"*Aug. 5. Wednesday.* To my surprise found on the dinner-table at Thatcher's the *Vaccinium Oxycoccus.* T. did not know it was anything unusual, but bought it at such a rate per bushel of Mr. Such-a-one, who brought it to market. They call it the 'bog cranberry.' I did not perceive that it differed from the common, unless that it was rather more skinny. . . .

"P.M.—Rode to Old Fort Hill at the bend of the Penobscot some three miles above Bangor, to look for the site of the Indian town,—perhaps the ancient Negas? Found several arrowheads and two little dark and crumbling fragments of Indian earthenware, like black earth.

"*Aug. 6. Thursday.* A.M.—To the high hill and ponds in Bucksport, some ten or more miles out.

"A withdrawn, wooded, and somewhat mountainous country. There was a little trout-pond just over the highest hill, very muddy, surrounded by a broad belt of yellow lily pads. Over this we pushed with great difficulty on a rickety raft of small logs, using poles thirty feet long, which stuck in the mud. The pond was about twenty-five feet deep in the middle, and our poles would stick up there and hold the raft. There was no apparent inlet, but a small outlet. The water was not clear nor particularly cold, and you would have said it was

had no fault to find with my paddling in the stern, but I complained that he did not paddle according to his own directions in the bows.[218]

Opposite the Sunkhaze is the main boom of the Penobscot, where the logs from far up the river are collected and assorted.

As we drew near to Oldtown I asked Polis if he was not glad to get home again; but there was no relenting to his wildness, and he said, "It makes no difference to me where I am." Such is the Indian's pretence always.

We approached the Indian Island through the narrow strait called "Cook."[219] He said, "I 'xpect we take in some water there, river so high,—never see it so high at this season. Very rough water there, but short; swamp steamboat once. Don't you paddle till I tell you, then you paddle right along." It was a very short rapid. When we were in the midst of it he shouted "paddle," and we shot through without taking in a drop.

Soon after the Indian houses came in sight, but I could not at first tell my companion which of two or three large white ones was our guide's. He said it was the one with blinds.

We landed opposite his door at about four in the afternoon, having come some forty miles this day. From the Piscataquis we had come remarkably and unaccountably quick, probably as fast as the stage on the bank, though the last dozen miles was dead water.

Polis wanted to sell us his canoe, said it would last seven or eight years, or with care, perhaps ten; but we were not ready to buy it.

We stopped for an hour at his house, where my companion shaved with his[220] razor, which he pronounced in very good condition. Mrs. P.[221] wore a hat and had a silver brooch on her breast, but she was not introduced to us. The house was roomy and neat. A large new map of Oldtown and the Indian Island hung on the wall,[222] and a clock opposite to it. Wishing to know when the cars left Oldtown, Polis's son brought one of the last Bangor papers,[223] which I saw was directed to "Joseph Polis," from the office.

This was the last that I saw of Joe Polis. We took the last train, and reached Bangor that night.[224]

the very place for pouts, yet T. said that the only fish there caught were brook trout, at any time of day. You fish with a line only, sinking twenty feet from the raft. The water was full of insects, which looked very much like the little brown chips or bits of wood which make coarse sawdust, with legs, running over the submerged part of the raft, etc. I suppose this pond owed its trout to its elevation and being fed by springs. It seems they do not require swift or clear water, sandy bottom, etc. Are caught like pouts without any art. We had many bites and caught one.

"*Aug. 7. Friday.* P.M.—Take cars for Portland, and at evening the boat for Boston. A great deal of cat-tail flag by railroad between Penobscot and Kennebec. Fine large ponds about Belgrade.

"*Aug. 8. Saturday.* Get home at 8.30 A.M."
[J 9:501–503, 10:3].

Appendix

I. Trees.

The prevailing trees (I speak only of what I saw) on the east and west branches of the Penobscot and on the upper part of the Allegash were the fir, spruce (both black and white), and arbor-vitae, or "cedar." The fir has the darkest foliage, and, together with the spruce, makes a very dense "black growth," especially on the upper parts of the rivers. A dealer in lumber with whom I talked called the former a weed, and it is commonly regarded as fit neither for timber nor fuel. But it is more sought after as an ornamental tree than any other evergreen of these woods except the arbor-vitae. The black spruce is much more common than the white. Both are tall and slender trees. The arbor-vitae, which is of a more cheerful hue, with its light-green fans, is also tall and slender, though sometimes two feet in diameter. It often fills the swamps.

Mingled with the former, and also here and there forming extensive and more open woods by themselves, indicating, it is said, a better soil, were canoe and yellow birches (the former was always at hand for kindling a fire,—we saw no small white-birches in that wilderness), and sugar and red maples.

The Aspen (*Populus tremuloides*) was very common on burnt grounds. We saw many straggling white pines, commonly unsound trees, which had therefore been skipped by the choppers; these were the largest trees we saw; and we occasionally passed a small wood in which this was the prevailing tree; but I did not notice nearly so many of these trees as I can see in a single walk in Concord. The speckled or hoary alder (*Alnus incana*) abounds everywhere along the muddy banks of rivers and lakes, and in swamps. Hemlock could commonly be found for tea, but was nowhere abundant. Yet F. A. Michaux states that in Maine, Vermont, and the upper part of New Hampshire, etc., the hemlock forms three fourths of the evergreen woods, the rest being black spruce.[1] It belongs to cold hillsides.

The elm and black ash were very common along the lower and stiller parts of the streams, where the shores were flat and grassy or there were low gravelly islands. They made a pleasing variety in the scenery, and we felt as if nearer home while gliding past them.

The above fourteen trees made the bulk of the woods which we saw.

The larch (Juniper), beech, and Norway pine (*Pinus resinosa,* red pine), were only occasionally seen in particular places. The *Pinus Banksiana* (gray or Northern scrub-pine), and a single small red oak (*Quercus rubra*) only, are on islands in Grand Lake, on the East Branch.

The above are almost all peculiarly Northern trees, and found chiefly, if not solely, on mountains southward.

II. Flowers and Shrubs.

It appears that in a forest like this the great majority of flowers, shrubs, and grasses are confined to the banks of the rivers and lakes, and to the meadows, more open swamps, burnt lands, and mountain-tops; comparatively very few indeed penetrate the woods. There is no such dispersion even of wild-flowers as is commonly supposed, or as exists in a cleared and settled country. Most of our wild-flowers, so called, may be considered as naturalized

1 Michaux wrote in *The North American Sylva:* "The Hemlock Spruce is known only by this name throughout the United States, and by that of *Pérusse* among the French inhabitants of Canada. It is natural to the coldest regions of the New World, and begins to appear about Hudson's Bay, in latitude 51°; near lake St. John and in the neighbourhood of Quebec it fills the forests, and in Nova Scotia, New Brunswick, the District of Maine, the State of Vermont and the upper part of New Hampshire, where I have observed it, it forms three quarters of the evergreen woods, of which the remainder consists of the Black Spruce."

2 The literal French: protected ones.

3 The landlord at Sangerville, unidentified further.

in the localities where they grow. Rivers and lakes are the great protectors of such plants against the aggressions of the forest, by their annual rise and fall keeping open a narrow strip where these more delicate plants have light and space in which to grow. They are the *protégés*[2] of the rivers. These narrow and straggling bands and isolated groups are, in a sense, the pioneers of civilization. Birds, quadrupeds, insects, and man also, in the main, follow the flowers, and the latter in his turn makes more room for them and for berry-bearing shrubs, birds, and small quadrupeds. One settler[3] told me that not only blackberries and raspberries, but mountain-maples came in, in the clearing and burning.

Though plants are often referred to primitive woods as their locality, it cannot be true of very many, unless the woods are supposed to include such localities as I have mentioned. Only those which require but little light, and can bear the drip of the trees, penetrate the woods, and these have commonly more beauty in their leaves than in their pale and almost colorless blossoms.

The prevailing flowers and conspicuous small plants of the *woods,* which I noticed, were: *Clintonia borealis, Linnaea,* checkerberry (*Gaultheria procumbens*), *Aralia nudicaulis* (wild sarsaparilla), great round-leaved orchis, *Dalibarda repens, Chiogenes hispidula* (creeping snowberry), *Oxalis acetosella* (common wood-sorrel), *Aster acuminatus, Pyrola secunda* (one-sided pyrola), *Medeola Virginica* (Indian cucumber-root), small *Circaea* (enchanter's nightshade), and perhaps *Cornus Canadensis* (dwarf cornel).

Of these, the last of July, 1857, only the *Aster acuminatus* and great round-leaved *orchis* were conspicuously in bloom.

The most common flowers of the *river* and *lake shores* were: *Thalictrum cornuti* (meadow-rue), *Hypericum ellipticum, mutilum,* and *Canadense* (St. John's-wort), horsemint, horehound, *Lycopus Virginicus* and *Europaeus,* var. *sinuatus* (bugle-weed), *Scutellaria galericulata* (skull-cap), *Solidago lanceolata* and *squarrosa* East Branch (golden-rod), *Diplopappus umbellatus* (double-bristled aster), *Aster radula, Cicuta maculata* and *bulbifera* (water-hemlock), meadow-sweet, *Lysimachia stricta* and *ciliata* (loose-strife), *Galium trifidum* (small bed-straw), *Lilium Canadense* (wild yellow-lily), *Platanthera peraoena* and *psycodes* (great purple orchis and small purple-fringed orchis), *Mimulus ringens* (monkey-flower), dock (water), blue flag, *Hydrocotyle Americana* (marsh pennywort), *Sanicula Canadensis?* (black snake-root), *Clematis Virginiana?* (common virgin's-bower), *Nasturtium palustre* (marsh cress), *Ranunculus recurvatus* (hooked crowfoot), *Asclepias incarnata* (swamp milkweed), *Aster Tradescanti* (Tradescant's aster), *Aster miser,* also *longifolius, Eupatorium purpureum* especially lake shores (Joe-Pye-weed), *Apocynum Cannabinum* East Branch (Indian hemp), *Polygonum cilinode* (bind-weed), and others. Not to mention among inferior orders wool-grass and the sensitive fern.

In the *water, Nuphar advena* (yellow pond-lily), some *potamogetons* (pond-weed), *Sagittaria variabilis* (arrow-head), *Sium lineare?* (water-parsnip).

Of these, those conspicuously in flower the last of July, 1857, were: rue, *Solidago lanceolata* and *squarrosa, Diplopappus umbellatus, Aster radula, Lilium Canadense,* great and small purple orchis, *Mimulus ringens,* blue flag, virgin's-bower, etc.

The characteristic flowers in *swamps* were: *Rubus triflorus* (dwarf raspberry), *Calla palustris* (water-arum), and *Sarracenia purpurea* (pitcher-plant). On *burnt grounds: Epilobium angustifolium,* in full bloom (great willow-herb), and *Erechthites hieracifolia* (fire-weed). On *cliffs: Campanula rotundifolia* (harebell), *Cornus Canadensis* (dwarf cornel), *Arctostaphylos uva-ursi* (bearberry),

4 On 15 June 1852 Thoreau wrote in his journal: "I see the fringed purple orchis, unexpectedly beautiful, though a pale lilac purple,—a large spike of purple flowers. I find two,—the *grandiflora* of Bigelow and *fimbriata* of Gray. Bigelow thinks it the most beautiful of all the orchises. I am not prepared to say it is the most beautiful wild flower I have found this year. Why does it grow there only, far in a swamp, remote from public view? It is somewhat fragrant, reminding me of the lady's-slipper. Is it not significant that some rare and delicate and beautiful flowers should be found only in unfrequented wild swamps?" [J 4:103–104].

Potentilla tridentata (mountain cinquefoil), *Pteris aquilina* (common brake). At *old camps, carries, and logging-paths: Cirsium arvense* (Canada thistle), *Prunella vulgaris* (common self-heal), clover, herd's-grass, *Achillea millefolium* (common yarrow), *Leucanthemum vulgare* (white-weed), *Aster macrophyllus, Halenia deflexa* East Branch (spurred gentian), *Antennaria margaritacea* (pearly everlasting), *Actaea rubra* and *alba,* wet carries (red and white cohosh), *Desmodium Canadense* (tick-trefoil), sorrel.

The handsomest and most interesting flowers were the great purple orchises, rising ever and anon, with their great purple spikes perfectly erect, amid the shrubs and grasses of the shore. It seemed strange that they should be made to grow there in such profusion, seen of moose and moose-hunters only, while they are so rare in Concord.[4] I have never seen this species flowering nearly so late with us, or with the small one.

The prevailing underwoods were: *Dirca palustris* (moose-wood), *Acer spicatum* (mountain maple), *Viburnum lantanoides* (hobble-bush), and frequently *Taxus baccata,* var. *Canadensis* (American yew).

The prevailing shrubs and small trees along the shore were: *osier rouge* and alders (before mentioned), sallows, or small willows, of two or three kinds, as *Salix humilis, rostrata,* and *discolor?, Sambucus Canadensis* (black elder), rose, *Viburnum opulus* and *nudum* (cranberry-tree and withe-rod), *Pyrus Americana* (American mountain-ash), *Corylus rostrata* (beaked hazel-nut), *Diervilla trifida* (bush honeysuckle), *Prunus Virginiana* (choke-cherry), *Myrica gale* (sweet-gale), *Nemopanthes Canadensis* (mountain holly), *Cephalanthus occidentalis* (button-bush), *Ribes prostratum,* in some places (fetid currant).

More particularly of shrubs and small trees in *swamps:* some willows, *Kalmia glauca* (pale laurel), *Ledum latifolium* and *palustre* (Labrador tea), *Ribes lacustre* (swamp gooseberry), and in one place *Betula pumila* (low birch).

At *camps and carries:* raspberry, *Vaccinium Canadense* (Canada blueberry), *Prunus Pennsylvanica* also along shore (wild red cherry), *Amelanchier Canadensis* (shadbush), *Sambucus pubens* (red-berried elder). Among those peculiar to the *mountains* would be the *Vaccinium vitis-idaea* (cow-berry).

Of plants commonly regarded as *introduced* from Europe, I observed at Ansel Smith's clearing, Chesuncook, abundant in 1857: *Ranunculus acris* (buttercups), *Plantago major* (common plantain)[5], *Chenopodium album* (lamb's-quarters), *Capsella bursa-pastoris,* 1853 (shepherd's-purse), *Spergula arvensis,* also, north shore of Moosehead, in 1853, and elsewhere, 1857 (corn-spurrey), *Taraxacum dens-leonis* — regarded as indigenous by Gray,[6] but evidently introduced there — (common dandelion), *Polygonum Persicaria* and *hydropiper,* by a logging-path in woods at Smith's (lady's-thumb and smart-weed), *Rumex acetosella,* common at carries, (sheep-sorrel), *Trifolium pratense,* 1853 and 1857, and carries frequent (red clover), *Leucanthemum vulgare,* carries (white weed), *Phleum pratense,* carries, 1853 and 1857 (herd's-grass), *Verbena hastata* (blue vervain), *Cirsium arvense,* abundant at camps 1857 (Canada thistle), *Rumex crispus?,* West Branch, 1853? (curled dock), *Verbascum thapsus,* between Bangor and lake, 1853 (common mullein).

It appears that I saw about a dozen plants which had accompanied man as far into the woods as Chesuncook, and had naturalized themselves there, in 1853. Plants begin thus early to spring by the side of a logging-path, — a mere vista through the woods, which can only be used in the winter, on account of the stumps and fallen trees, — which at length are the roadside plants in old settlements. The pioneers of such are planted in part by the first cattle, which cannot be summered in the woods.[7]

5 A broad-leaved perennial sometimes called "the white man's foot" from its association with the coming of the Europeans. Longfellow wrote in The Song of Hiawatha:

> Wheresoe'er they tread, beneath them
> Springs a flower unknown among us,
> Springs the White-man's Foot in blossom.

6 Gray wrote in his *New Manual of Botany:* "Pastures and fields everywhere: probably indigenous in the North."

7 For more on Thoreau's theories on the introduction of plants, cf. "The Succession of Forest Trees," first published in *the New York Weekly Tribune,* 6 October 1860, and collected in the posthumous volume *Excursions.*

8 Also known as *Fraxinus nigra*.

9 There is no indication in Thoreau's journal whether this reference was from the 1853 or the 1857 excursion. The only reference to the yellow ash in Thoreau's journal, indicating that the Indian may have been from his 1846 excursion, was from 21 May 1851: "I should like to see a description of the Yellow Ash which grows in Maine" [PJ 3:228].

10 A variation of black ash.

III. List of Plants.

The following is a list of the plants which I noticed in the Maine woods, in the years 1853 and 1857. (Those marked* not in woods.)

I. THOSE WHICH ATTAINED THE HEIGHT OF TREES.

Alnus incana (speckled or hoary alder), abundant along streams, etc.

Thuja occidentalis (American arbor-vitae), one of the prevailing.

Fraxinus sambucifolia[8] (black ash), very common, especially near dead water. The Indian[9] spoke of "yellow ash"[10] as also found there.

Populus tremuloides (American aspen), very common, especially on burnt lands, almost as white as birches.

Populus grandidentata (large-toothed aspen), perhaps two or three.

Fagus ferruginea (American beech), not uncommon, at least on the West Branch (saw more in 1846).

Betula papyracea (canoe-birch), prevailing everywhere and about Bangor.

Betula excelsa (yellow birch), very common.

Betula lenta (black birch), on the West Branch, in 1853.

*Betula alba** (American white birch), about Bangor only.

Ulmus Americana (American or white elm), West Branch and low down the East Branch, i.e. on the lower and alluvial part of the river, very common.

Larix Americana (American or black larch), very common on the Umbazookskus, some elsewhere.

Abies Canadensis (hemlock-spruce), not abundant, some on the West Branch, and a little everywhere.

Acer saccharinum (sugar maple), very common.

Acer rubrum (red or swamp maple), very common.

Acer dasycarpum (white or silver maple), a little low on East Branch and in Chesuncook woods.

Quercus rubra (red oak), one on an island in Grand Lake, East Branch, and, according to a settler,[11] a few on the east side of Chesuncook Lake; a few also about Bangor in 1853.

Pinus strobus (white pine), scattered along, most abundant at Heron Lake.

Pinus resinosa (red pine), Telos and Grand Lake, a little afterwards here and there.

Abies balsamea (balsam fir), perhaps the most common tree, especially in the upper parts of rivers.

Abies nigra[12] (black or double spruce), next to the last the most common, if not equally common, and on mountains.

Abies alba (white or single spruce), common with the last along the rivers.

Pinus Banksiana (gray or Northern scrub-pine), a few on an island in Grand Lake.

Twenty-three in all (23).

2. SMALL TREES AND SHRUBS.

Prunus depressa (dwarf-cherry), on gravel-bars, East Branch, near Hunt's, with green fruit, obviously distinct from the *pumila* of river and meadows.

Vaccinium corymbosum (common swamp blueberry), Bucksport.

Vaccinium Canadense (Canada blueberry), carries and rocky hills everywhere as far south as Bucksport.

Vaccinium Pennsylvanicum (dwarf-blueberry?), Whetstone Falls.

Betula pumila (low birch), Mud Pond Swamp.

11 Thoreau learned that "there was a little red oak across the lake" [MJ 18 September 1853] when visiting Ansel Smith's clearing. The settler was probably Smith's brother.

12 Now *Picea mariana*. *Abies nigra* may be a conflation of other nineteenth-century scientific names for the black spruce: *Abies mariana*, *Picea nigra*, and *Pinus nigra*.

Prinos verticillatus (black alder), 1857, now placed with *Ilex* by Gray, 2d ed.[13]

Cephalanthus occidentalis (button-bush).

Prunus Pennsylvanica (wild red cherry), very common at camps, carries, etc., along rivers; fruit ripe, August 1, 1857.

Prunus Virginiana (choke-cherry), river-side, common.

Cornus alternifolia (alternate-leaved cornel), West Branch, 1853.

Ribes prostratum (fetid currant), common along streams, as Webster Stream.

Sambucus Canadensis (common elder), common along river-sides.

Sambucus pubens (red-berried elder), not quite so common, roadsides toward Moosehead, and on carries afterward, fruit beautiful.

Ribes lacustre (swamp-gooseberry), swamps, common, Mud Pond Swamp and Webster Stream; not ripe July 29, 1857.

Corylus rostrata (beaked hazel-nut), common.

Taxus baccata, var. *Canadensis* (American yew), a common under-shrub at an island in West Branch and Chesuncook woods.

Viburnum lantanoides (hobble-bush), common, especially in Chesuncook woods; fruit ripe in September, 1853, not in July, 1857.

Viburnum opulus (cranberry-tree), on West Branch; one in flower still, July 25, 1857.

Viburnum nudum (withe-rod), common along rivers.

Kalmia glauca (pale laurel), swamps, common, as at Moosehead carry and Chamberlain swamp.

Kalmia angustifolia (lamb-kill), with *Kalmia glauca*.

Acer spicatum (mountain maple), a prevailing underwood.

Acer striatum (striped maple), in fruit July 30, 1857;

green the first year; green, striped with white, the second; darker, the third, with dark blotches.

Cornus stolonifera (red-osier dogwood), prevailing shrub on shore of West Branch; fruit still white in August, 1857.

Pyrus Americana (American mountain ash), common along shores.

Amelanchier Canadensis (shad-bush), rocky carries, etc.; considerable fruit in 1857.

Rubus strigosus (wild red raspberry), very abundant, burnt grounds, camps, and carries, but not ripe till we got to Chamberlain dam and on East Branch.

Rosa Carolina (swamp-rose), common on the shores of lakes, etc.

*Rhus typhina** (stag-horn sumac).

Myrica gale (sweet-gale), common.

Nemopanthes Canadensis (mountain holly), common in low ground, Moosehead carry, and on Mount Kineo.

Crataegus (*coccinea?* scarlet-fruited thorn), not uncommon; with hard fruit in September, 1853.

Salix (near to *petiolaris,* petioled willow), very common in Umbazookskus meadows.

Salix rostrata (long-beaked willow), common.

Salix humilis (low bush-willow), common.

Salix discolor (glaucous willow?).

Salix lucida (shining willow), at island in Heron Lake.

Dirca palustris (moose-wood), common.

In all, 38.

3. SMALL SHRUBS AND HERBACEOUS PLANTS.

Agrimonia Eupatoria (common agrimony), not uncommon.

Circaea Alpina (enchanter's nightshade), very common in woods.

Nasturtium palustre (marsh cress), var. *hispidum,* common as at A. Smith's.

Aralia hispida (bristly sarsaparilla), on West Branch, both years.

Aralia nudicaulis (wild sarsaparilla), Chesuncook woods.

Sagittaria variabilis (arrow-head), common at Moosehead and afterward.

Arum triphyllum (Indian turnip), now *arisaema,* Moosehead carry in 1853.

Asclepias incarnata (swamp milk-weed), Umbazookskus River and after, redder than ours, and a different variety from our var. *pulchra.*

Aster acuminatus (pointed-leaved aster), the prevailing aster in woods, not long open on East Branch July 31st; two or more feet high.

Aster macrophyllus (large-leaved aster), common, and the whole plant surprisingly fragrant, like a medicinal herb, just out at Telos Dam July 29, 1857, and after to Bangor and Bucksport; bluish flower (in woods on Pine Stream and at Chesuncook in 1853).

Aster radula (rough-leaved aster), common, Moosehead carry and after.

Aster miser (petty aster), in 1853 on West Branch, and common on Chesuncook shore.

Aster longifolius (willow-leaved blue aster), 1853, Moosehead and Chesuncook shores.

Aster cordifolius (heart-leaved aster), 1853, West Branch.

Aster Tradescanti (Tradescant's aster), 1857. A narrow-leaved one Chesuncook shore, 1853.

Aster, *longifolius*-like, with small flowers, West Branch, 1853.

Aster puniceus (rough-stemmed aster), Pine Stream.

Diplopappus umbellatus (large *diplopappus* aster), common along river.

Arctostaphylos uva-ursi (bear-berry), Kineo, etc., 1857.

Polygonum cilinode (fringe-jointed false buckwheat), common.

Bidens cernua (bur-marigold), 1853, West Branch.

Ranunculus acris (buttercups), abundant at Smith's, Chesuncook, 1853.

Rubus triflorus (dwarf-raspberry), low grounds and swamps, common.

*Utricularia vulgaris** (greater bladder-wort), Pushaw.

Iris versicolor (larger blue-flag), common Moosehead, West Branch, Umbazookskus, etc.

Sparganium (bur-reed).

Calla palustris (water-arum), in bloom July 27, 1857, Mud Pond Swamp.

Lobelia cardinalis (cardinal-flower), apparently common, but out of bloom August, 1857.

Cerastium nutans (clammy wild chickweed?).

Gaultheria procumbens (checkerberry), prevailing everywhere in woods along banks of rivers.

*Stellaria media** (common chickweed), Bangor.

Chiogenes hispidula (creeping snowberry), very common in woods.

Cicuta maculata (water-hemlock).

Cicuta bulbifera (bulb-bearing water-hemlock), Penobscot and Chesuncook shore, 1853.

Galium trifidum (small bed-straw), common.

Galium Aparine (cleavers?), Chesuncook, 1853.

Galium, one kind on Pine Stream, 1853.

Trifolium pratense (red-clover), on carries, etc.

Actaea spicata, var. *alba* (white cohosh), Chesuncook woods 1853, and East Branch 1857.

Actaea var. *rubra* (red cohosh), East Branch 1857.

Vaccinium vitis-idaea (cow-berry), Ktaadn, very abundant.

Cornus Canadensis (dwarf-cornel), in woods Chesuncook 1853; just ripe at Kineo July 24, 1857, common; still in bloom, Moosehead carry September 16, 1853.

Medeola Virginica (Indian cucumber-root), West Branch and Chesuncook woods.

Dalibarda repens (Dalibarda), Moosehead carry and after, common. In flower still, August 1, 1857.

Taraxacum dens-leonis (common dandelion), Smith's 1853, only there. Is it not foreign?

Diervilla trifida (bush honeysuckle), very common.

Rumex hydrolapathum? (great water-dock), in 1857; noticed it was large-seeded in 1853, common.

Rumex crispus? (curled-dock), West Branch 1853.

Apocynum cannabinum (Indian hemp), Kineo, *Bradford,* and East Branch 1857, at Whetstone Falls.

Apocynum androsaemifolium (spreading dogbane), Kineo, *Bradford.*

Clintonia borealis (Clintonia), all over woods; fruit just ripening July 25, 1857.

A *lemna* (duckweed),* Pushaw 1857.

Elodea Virginica (marsh St. John's-wort), Moosehead 1853.

Epilobium angustifolium (great willow-herb), great fields on burnt lands; some white at Webster Stream.

Epilobium coloratum (purple-veined willow-herb), once in 1857.

Eupatorium purpureum (Joe-Pye-weed), Heron, Moosehead, and Chesuncook lake-shores, common.

Allium (onion), a new kind to me in bloom, without bulbs above, on rocks near Whetstone Falls? East Branch.

Halenia deflexa (spurred gentian), carries on East Branch, common.

Geranium Robertianum (Herb Robert).

Solidago lanceolata (bushy golden-rod), very common.

Solidago, one of the three-ribbed, in both years.

Solidago thyrsoidea (large mountain golden-rod), one on Webster Stream.

Solidago squarrosa (large-spiked golden-rod), the most common on East Branch.

Solidago altissima (rough hairy golden-rod), not uncommon both years.

Coptis trifolia (three-leaved gold-thread).

Smilax herbacea (carrion-flower), not uncommon both years.

Spiraea tomentosa* (hardhack), Bangor.

Campanula rotundifolia (harebell), cliffs Kineo, Grand Lake, etc.

Hieracium (hawk-weed), not uncommon.

Veratrum viride (American white hellebore).

Lycopus Virginicus (bugle-weed), 1857.

Lycopus Europaeus (water-horehound), var. *sinuatus,* Heron Lake shore.

Chenopodium album (lamb's-quarters), Smith's.

Mentha Canadensis (wild mint), very common.

Galeopsis tetrahit (common hemp-nettle), Olamon Isle, abundant, and below, in prime August 3, 1857.

Houstonia caerulea (bluets), now *Oldenlandia* (Gray, 2d ed.), 1857.

Hydrocotyle Americana (marsh pennywort), common.

Hypericum ellipticum (elliptical-leaved St. John's-wort), common.

Hypericum mutilum (small St. John's-wort), both years, common.

Hypericum Canadense (Canadian St. John's-wort), Moosehead Lake and Chesuncook shores, 1853.

Trientalis Americana (star-flower), Pine Stream, 1853.

Lobelia inflata (Indian tobacco).

Spiranthes cernua (ladies' tresses), Kineo and after.

Nabalus (rattlesnake root), 1857; *altissimus* (tall white lettuce), Chesuncook woods, 1853.

Antennaria margaritacea (pearly everlasting), common, Moosehead, Smith's, etc.

Lilium Canadense (wild yellow lily), very common and large, West and East Branch; one on East Branch, 1857, with strongly revolute petals, and leaves perfectly smooth beneath, but not larger than the last, and apparently only a variety.

Linnaea borealis (Linnaea), almost everywhere in woods.

Lobelia Dortmanna (water-lobelia), pond in Bucksport.

Lysimachia ciliata (hairy-stalked loosestrife), very common, Chesuncook shore and East Branch.

Lysimachia stricta (upright loosestrife), very common.

Microstylis ophioglossoides (adder's-mouth), Kineo.

Spiraea salicifolia (common meadow-sweet), common.

Mimulus ringens (monkey-flower), common, lakeshores, etc.

Scutellaria galericulata (skullcap), very common.

Scutellaria lateriflora (mad-dog skullcap), Heron Lake, 1857, Chesuncook, 1853.

Platanthera psycodes (small purple-fringed orchis), very common, East Branch and Chesuncook, 1853.

Platanthera fimbriata (large purple-fringed orchis), very common, West Branch and Umbazookskus, 1857.

Platanthera orbiculata (large round-leaved orchis), very common in woods, Moosehead and Chamberlain carries, Caucomgomoc, etc.

Amphicarpaea monoica (hog peanut).

Aralia racemosa (spikenard), common, Moosehead carry, Telos Lake, etc., and after; out about August 1, 1857.

Plantago major (common plantain), common in open land at Smith's in 1853.

*Pontederia cordata** (pickerel-weed), only near Old-town, 1857.

Potamogeton (pond-weed), not common.

Potentilla tridentata (mountain cinquefoil), Kineo.

Potentilla Norvegica (cinquefoil), Heron Lake shore and Smith's.

Polygonum amphibium (water-persicaria), var. *aquaticum,* Second Lake.

Polygonum Persicaria (lady's-thumb), log-path Chesuncook, 1853.

Nuphar advena (yellow pond-lily), not abundant.

Nymphaea odorata (sweet water-lily), a few in West Branch, 1853.

Polygonum hydropiper (smart-weed), log-path, Chesuncook.

Pyrola secunda (one-sided pyrola), very common, Caucomgomoc.

Pyrola elliptica (shin-leaf), Caucomgomoc River.

Ranunculus Flammula (spearwort, var. *reptans*).

Ranunculus recurvatus (hooked crowfoot), Umbazookskus landing, etc.

*Typha latifolia** (common cat-tail or reed-mace), extremely abundant between Bangor and Portland.

Sanicula Marylandica (black snake-root), Moosehead carry and after.

Aralia nudicaulis (wild sarsaparilla).

Capsella bursa-pastoris (shepherd's-purse), Smith's, 1853.

Prunella vulgaris (self-heal), very common everywhere.

Erechthites hieracifolia (fireweed), 1857, and Smith's open land, 1853.

Sarracenia purpurea (pitcher-plant), Mud Pond swamp.

Smilacina bifolia (false Solomon's-seal), 1857, and Chesuncook woods, 1853.

Smilacina racemosa (false spikenard?), Umbazookskus carry (July 27, 1853).

Veronica scutellata (marsh speedwell).

Spergula arvensis (corn spurrey), 1857, not uncommon, 1853, Moosehead and Smith's.

Fragaria (strawberry), 1853 Smith's, 1857 Bucksport.

Thalictrum Cornuti (meadow-rue), very common, especially along rivers, tall, and conspicuously in bloom in July, 1857.

Cirsium arvense (Canada thistle), abundant at camps and highway sides in the north of Maine.

Cirsium muticum (swamp-thistle), well in bloom Webster Stream, August 31.

Rumex acetosella (sheep-sorrel), common by river and log-paths, as Chesuncook log-path.

Impatiens fulva (spotted touch-me-not).

Trillium erythrocarpum (painted trillium), common West Branch and Moosehead carry.

Verbena hastata (blue vervain).

Clematis Virginiana (common virgin's-bower), common on river banks, feathered in September, 1853, in bloom July, 1857.

Leucanthemum vulgare (white-weed).

Sium lineare (water-parsnip), 1857, and Chesuncook shore, 1853.

Achillea millefolium (common yarrow), by river and log-paths, and Smith's.

Desmodium Canadense (Canadian tick-trefoil), not uncommon.

Oxalis acetosella (common wood-sorrel), still out July 25, 1853, at Moosehead carry and after.

Oxalis stricta (yellow wood-sorrel), 1853, at Smith's and his wood-path.

Liparis liliifolia (tway-blade), Kineo, *Bradford.*

Uvularia grandiflora (large-flowered bellwort), woods, common.

Uvularia sessilifolia (sessile-leaved bellwort), Chesuncook woods, 1853.

In all, 145.

4. OF LOWER ORDER.

Scirpus Eriophorum (wool-grass), very common, especially on low islands. A coarse grass, four or five feet high, along the river.

Phleum pratense (herd's-grass), on carries, at camps and clearings.

Equisetum sylvaticum (sylvatic horse-tail).

Pteris aquilina (brake), Kineo and after.

Onoclea sensibilis (sensitive-fern), very common along the river sides; some on the gravelly shore of Heron Lake Island.

Polypodium Dryopteris (brittle polypody).

Woodsia Ilvensis (rusty Woodsia), Kineo.

Lycopodium lucidulum (toothed club-moss).

Usnea (a parmeliaceous[14] lichen), common on various trees.

IV. List of Birds which I saw in Maine between July 24 and August 3, 1857.

A very small hawk at Great Falls, on Webster Stream.

Haliaetus leucocephalus (white-headed or bald-eagle), at Ragmuff, and above and below Hunt's, and on pond below Mattawamkeag.

Pandion haliaetus (fish-hawk or osprey), heard, also seen on East Branch.

Bubo Virginianus (cat-owl), near Camp Island, also above mouth of Seboois, from a stump back and forth, also near Hunt's on a tree.

Icterus phoeniceus (red-winged blackbird), Umbazookskus River.

14 Belonging to or having the characters of the genus *Parmelia* or the family *Parmeliaceae,* thus foliose, resembling a leaf in shape.

Corvus Americanus (American crow), a few, as at outlet of Grand Lake; a peculiar cawing.

Fringilla Canadensis (tree-sparrow), think I saw one on Mount Kineo July 24, which behaved as if it had a nest there.

Garrulus cristatus (blue-jay).

Parus atricapillus (chicadee), a few.

Muscicapa tyrannus (king-bird).

Muscicapa Cooperi (olive-sided fly-catcher), everywhere a prevailing bird.

Muscicapa virens (wood pewee), Moosehead, and I think beyond.

Muscicapa ruticilla (American redstart), Moosehead.

Vireo olivaceus (red-eyed vireo), everywhere common.

Turdus migratorius (red-breasted robin), some everywhere.

Turdus melodus (wood-thrush), common in all the woods.

Turdus Wilsonii (Wilson's thrush), Moosehead and beyond.

Turdus aurocapillus (golden-crowned thrush or ovenbird), Moosehead.

Fringilla albicollis (white-throated sparrow), Kineo and after, apparently nesting; the prevailing bird early and late.

Fringilla melodia (song-sparrow), at Moosehead or beyond.

Sylvia pinus (pine warbler), one part of voyage.

Muscicapa acadica (small pewee), common.

Trichas Marylandica (Maryland yellow-throat), everywhere.

Coccyzus Americanus? (yellow-billed cuckoo), common.

Picus erythrocephalus (red-headed woodpecker), heard and saw; and good to eat.

Sitta Carolinensis? (white-breasted American nut-hatch), heard.

Alcedo alcyon (belted kingfisher), very common.

Caprimulgus Americanus (night-hawk).

Tetrao umbellus (partridge), Moosehead carry, etc.

Tetrao cupido? (pinnated grouse), Webster Stream.

Ardea caerulea (blue heron), lower part of Penobscot.

Totanus macularius (spotted sandpiper or peetweet), everywhere.

Larus argentatus? (herring-gull), Heron Lake on rocks, and Chamberlain. Smaller gull on Second Lake.

Anas obscura (dusky or black duck), once in East Branch.

Anas sponsa (summer or wood duck), everywhere.

Fuligula albeola (spirit duck or dipper), common.

Colymbus glacialis (great Northern diver or loon), in all the lakes.

Mergus Merganser (buff-breasted merganser or shel-drake), common on lakes and rivers.

A swallow; the night-warbler (?) once or twice.

V. Quadrupeds.

A bat on West Branch; beaver skull at Grand Lake; Mr. Thatcher ate beaver with moose on the Caucomgo-moc. A muskrat on the last stream; the red squirrel is common in the depths of the woods; a dead porcupine on Chamberlain road; a cow moose and tracks of calf; skin of a bear, just killed.

VI. Outfit for an Excursion.[15]

The following will be a good outfit for one who wishes to make an excursion of *twelve* days into the Maine woods in July, with a companion, and one Indian for the same purposes that I did.

15 Anticipated in Thoreau's 28 January 1858 letter to Higginson: "Perhaps you would like a few more details. We used (three of us) exactly twenty-six pounds of hard bread, fourteen pounds of pork, three pounds of coffee, twelve pounds of sugar (and could have used more), besides a little tea, Indian meal, and rice,—and plenty of berries and moose-meat. This was faring very luxuriously. I had not formerly carried coffee, sugar, or rice. But for solid food, I decide that it is not worth the while to carry anything but hard bread and pork, whatever your tastes and habits may be. These wear best, and you have no time nor dishes in which to cook any thing else. Of course you will take a little Indian meal to fry fish in; and half a dozen lemons also, if you have sugar, will be very refreshing,—for the water is warm.

"To save time, the sugar, coffee, tea, salt, etc., should be in separate water-tight bags, labeled, and tied with a leather string; and all the provisions and blankets should be put into two large india-rubber bags, if you can find them water tight. Ours were not. A four-quart tin pail makes a good kettle for all purposes, and tin plates are portable and convenient. Don't forget an india-rubber knapsack, with a large flap,—plenty of dish-cloths, old newspapers, strings, and twenty-five feet of strong cord. Of india-rubber clothing, the most you can wear, if any, is a very light coat,—and that you cannot work in" [W 6:326–327].

16 The part of one's clothing that covers the breast; especially, the portion of a shirt that covers the bosom, generally made of finer material than the rest.

17 As described in "The Allegash and East Branch," Thoreau's wash was "composed of sweet-oil and oil of turpentine, with a little oil of spearmint, and camphor."

18 Netting placed over the bed to protect the sleeper from mosquitoes.

19 Thoreau carried only hard bread, or hardtack, on his Maine excursions. He may have meant to write "Soft and hard bread" to indicate a small amount of fresh bread, as on his 1860 excursion to Mount Monadnock: "2 lbs. hard-bread . . . ½ loaf home-made bread" [J 14:52].

20 To correct the constipating effect of eating too much pork and bread, as in his eating of berries in "The Allegash and East Branch": "In our three journeys over the carries, for we were obliged to go over the ground three times whenever the canoe was taken out, we did full justice to the berries, and they were just what we wanted to correct the effect of our hard bread and pork diet."

Wear, — a check shirt, stout old shoes, thick socks, a neck ribbon, thick waistcoat, thick pants, old Kossuth hat, a linen sac.

Carry, — in an India-rubber knapsack, with a large flap, two shirts (check), one pair thick socks, one pair drawers, one flannel shirt, two pocket-handkerchiefs, a light India-rubber coat or a thick woollen one, two bosoms[16] and collars to go and come with, one napkin, pins, needles, thread, one blanket, best gray, seven feet long.

Tent, six by seven feet, and four feet high in middle, will do; veil and gloves and insect-wash,[17] or, better, mosquito-bars[18] to cover all at night; best pocket-map, and perhaps description of the route; compass; plant-book and red blotting-paper; paper and stamps, botany, small pocket spy-glass for birds, pocket microscope, tape-measure, insect-boxes.

Axe, full size if possible, jackknife, fish-lines, two only apiece, with a few hooks and corks ready, and with pork for bait in a packet, rigged; matches (some also in a small vial in the waistcoat pocket); soap, two pieces; large knife and iron spoon (for all); three or four old newspapers, much twine, and several rags for dishcloths; twenty feet of strong cord, four-quart tin pail for kettle, two tin dippers, three tin plates, a fry-pan.

Provisions. — Soft hard bread,[19] twenty-eight pounds; pork, sixteen pounds; sugar, twelve pounds; one pound black tea or three pounds coffee, one box or a pint of salt, one quart Indian meal, to fry fish in; six lemons, good to correct the pork[20] and warm water; perhaps two or three pounds of rice, for variety. You will probably get some berries, fish, etc., beside.

A gun is not worth the carriage, unless you go as hunters. The pork should be in an open keg, sawed to fit; the sugar, tea or coffee, meal, salt, etc., should be put in separate water-tight India-rubber bags, tied with a leather string; and all the provisions, and part of the rest of the baggage, put into two large India-rubber bags, which have been proved to be water-tight and durable. Expense of preceding outfit is twenty-four dollars.

An Indian may be hired for about one dollar and fifty cents per day, and perhaps fifty cents a week for his canoe (this depends on the demand). The canoe should be a strong and tight one. This expense will be nineteen dollars.

Such an excursion need not cost more than twenty-five dollars apiece, starting at the foot of Moosehead, if you already possess or can borrow a reasonable part of the outfit. If you take an Indian and canoe at Oldtown, it will cost seven or eight dollars more to transport them to the lake.

VII. A List of Indian Words.

1. *Ktaadn,* said to mean *Highest Land.* Rasles puts for mountain, *Pemadené;* for *Grai, pierre à éguiser,*[21] *Kidadañgan.* (v. Potter.)[22]

Mattawamkeag, place where two rivers meet. (Indian of carry.) (v. Williamson's History of Maine,[23] and Willis.)[24]

Molunkus.

Ebeeme, rock.

Noliseemack; other name, Shad Pond.

Kecunnilessu, chicadee.

Nipsquecohossus, woodcock.

Skuscumonsuk, kingfisher. Has it not the pl. termination *uk* here, or *suk?*

Wassus, bear. *Asess␛s.*[25] Rasles.

Lunxus, Indian-devil.

Upahsis, mountain-ash.

} Joe.

Moose, (is it called, or does it mean, wood-eater?). *M␛s,* Rasles.

21 French: whetstone.

22 Chandler Eastman Potter (1807–1868) wrote in the appendix to "Language of the Abnaquies" in *Collections of the Maine Historical Society,* vol. 4 (1856): "*Ktaadn.* This is doubtless a corruption of *Kees,* (high,) and *Auke,* (a place,) and meaning A high place."

23 According to a note in Williamson's *History of the State of Maine,* "Metawamkeag means a stream running over a *gravelly bed* at its mouth." It is Necotok, defined in the note immediately above Metawamkeag, that means "where two streams come together, forming an *acute angle.*"

24 William Willis's (1794–1870) "Language of the Abnaquies, or Eastern Indians" in *Collections of the Maine Historical Society,* vol. 4 (1856).

25 On the character 8, Rasles wrote: "They have several letters which are sounded wholly from the throat without any motion of the lips; *ou,* for example; is one of the number, and in writing, we denote this by the figure 8, in order to distinguish it from other characters." Pickering wrote that for the figure 8 in the printed edition of Rasles's Dictionary he used the "character 8, borrowed from the Greeks." He further wrote: "The Greek character 8, as above observed, is called by Rasles a guttural; but by this term he only means, that the lips are not used in uttering it; in other words, he calls it guttural merely in contradistinction to labial, and not to denote that strong, rough sound which in popular language is called guttural and is found in the Spanish and Oriental languages. On comparing those words in which it occurs, with the corresponding ones of the kindred dialects, the Massachusetts and the Delaware, there can be no doubt that it represents the same elementary sound which, in the Massachusetts dialect, Eliot denoted by oo and W, and in the Delaware, Mr. Heckewelder denoted by W; and of which, he observes, that 'before a vowel it sounds the same as in English; before a consonant it represents a whistled sound of which I cannot well give you an idea on paper.'"

26 Thoreau's translation of *rouges, mauvais* in Rasles.

27 French: book, letter, painting, handwriting.

28 The exact identification of Nicholai, called the "son-in-law of Neptune" and "the Governor's son-in-law" in "Chesuncook," is unclear. Thoreau may have confused the name, or the relationship with Neptune, or both. Nicholai may have been Neptune's son-in-law Tomer Nicola, who married his daughter, Mary Malt; Neptune's son Piel-Nicola Neptune; or Neptune's illegitimate son Peol Nicola.

29 French: bay, or cove, in the lake.

30 Springer wrote that Penobscot "signifies stony or rocky river."

31 Thoreau's translation of *le lieu-où il y en a [herbes]* in Rasles.

32 Allusion to John Montresor in "Arnold's Letters on His Expedition to Canada in 1775."

Katahdinauguoh, said to mean mountains about Ktaadn.

Ebemena, tree-cranberry. *Ibimin, nar,* red, bad fruit.[26] Rasles. } Joe.

Wighiggin, a bill or writing. *Asiχigan,* "*Livre, lettre, peinture, écriture.*"[27] Rasles. } Indian of carry.

Sebamook, Large-bay Lake. *Pegsasebem;* add *ar* for plural, *lac* or *étang.* Rasles. *sañrinañgamek,* anse dans un lac.[29] Rasles. *Mspame,* large water. Polis.

Sebago and *Sebec,* large open water.

Chesuncook, place where many streams empty in. (v. Willis and Potter.)

Caucomgomoc, Gull Lake. (*Caucomgomoc,* the lake; *Caucomgomoc-took,* the river, Polis.)

Pammadumcook.

Kenduskieg, Little Eel River. (v. Willis.) Nicholai.

Penobscot, Rocky River. *Pnapesks,* stone. (Rasles.) (v. Springer.)[30] } Indian of carry.

Umbazookskus, meadow stream. (Much-meadow river, Polis.)

Millinocket, place of Islands.

Souneunk, that runs between Mountains.

Aboljacarmegus, Smooth-ledge Falls and Dead-water.

Aboljacarmeguscook, the river there.

Musketicook, Dead Stream. (Indian of carry.) *Meski'ks,* or *Meskikäi'ks,* a place where there is grass.[31] (Rasles.) *Muskéeticook,* Dead water. (Polis.)

Mattahumkeag, Sand-creek Pond.
Piscataquis, branch of a river. } Nicholai.

Shecorways, sheldrakes.
Naramekechus, peetweet.
Medawisla, loon. } Polis.

Orignal, Moosehead Lake. (Montresor.)[32]

(Nicholai.[28])

(Tahmunt, etc.)

(Nicholai.)

Chor-chor-que, usnea.
Adelungquamooktum, wood-thrush.
Bematinichtik, high land generally. }
(mountain, *Pemadené,* Rasles.) } Polis.
Maquoxigil, bark of red osier, Indian
tobacco.

Kineo, flint (Williamson); (old Indian hunter,
Hodge.)[33]

Artoosoqu', phosphorescence.
Subekoondark, white spruce.
Skusk, black spruce.
Beskabekuk, the "Lobster Lake" of maps.
Beskabekukshishtook, the dead water
below the island.
Paytaytequick, Burnt-Ground Stream,
what Joe called *Ragmuff.*
Nonglangyis, the name of a dead-water
between the last and Pine Stream.
Karsaootuk, Black River (or Pine
Stream). *Mkazésighen,* black.[34] Rasles.
Michigan, fimus. Polis applied it to a } Polis.
sucker, or a poor, good-for-nothing fish.
Fiante (?), *mitsegan,* Rasles. (Pickering puts
the ? after the first word.)[35]
Cowosnebagosar, Chiogenes hispidula,
means, grows where trees have rotted.
Pockadunkquaywayle, echo.
Pagadaňkŝéśé'rré. Rasles.
Bososquasis, moose-fly.
Nerlumskeechticook (or *quoik?*),
(or *skeetcook*), Dead water, and applied to
the mountains near.
Apmoojenegamook, lake that is crossed.
Allegash, hemlock-bark. (v. Willis.)
Paytaywecongomec, Burnt-Ground Lake,
Telos.

33 Williamson is the authority for the definition, while James Hodge is Thoreau's source for deriving the name Kineo from that of an old Indian hunter: "Mt. Kenio receives its name from that of an old Indian, who formerly lived and hunted in its vicinity."

34 Thoreau's translation of *noir* in Rasles.

35 The dictionary was edited for publication by John Pickering (1777–1846) from Rasles's manuscript. Pickering wrote in his "Supplementary Notes and Observations": "Where a word was not wholly illegible, but the reading doubtful, a note of interrogation is placed immediately after it, in brackets, thus [?]."

36 Thoreau's translation of *noirs* in Rasles.

37 Pickering wrote: "In the ancient Massachusetts language, for example, the plural of the *animate* nouns was formed in *og* or *ok*, and of *inanimate* nouns in *ash*. . . . In the Abnaki also, the plural *animate* ended in *ak*, but the plural *inanimate*, in *ar*."

38 Thoreau's translation of "*blanches, plus grosses que des* penak" in Rasles.

39 Allusion to a footnote in Williamson: "Passadumkeag means, where the water falls into the river *above the falls.—Indian.*"

40 French: above the mountain.

41 Thoreau's translation of *Vermillon, pinture* in Rasles.

42 Thoreau's translation of *j'entre dans la riv. [rivière] . . . l'embouchure* in Rasles.

43 Thoreau's translation of *Hache* in Rasles.

44 French: river that forks.

Madunkehunk, Height-of-land Stream (Webster Stream). ⎫

Madunkehunk-gamooc, Height-of-land Lake.

Matungamooc, Grand Lake.

Uncardnerheese, Trout Stream.

Wassataquoik (or *-cook*), Salmon River, East Branch. (v. Willis.) ⎬ Polis.

Pemoymenuk, Amelanchier berries. "*Pemäaïmin, nak,* a black fruit."[36] Rasles. Has it not here the plural ending?[37]

Sheepnoc, Lilium Canadense bulbs. "*Sipen, nak,* white, larger than *penak*."[38] Rasles.

Paytgumkiss, Petticoat (where a small river comes into the Penobscot below Nickatow).

Burntibus, a lake-like reach in the Penobscot. ⎭

Passadumkeag, "where the water falls into the Penobscot above the falls." (Williamson.)[39] *Pañsidañkisi* is, *au dessus de la montagne.*[40] Rasles.

Olarmon, or *larmon,* (Polis) red paint. "Vermilion, paint,[41] *šrámañ*." Rasles.

Sunkhaze, "See canoe come out; no see 'em stream." (Polis.) The mouth of a river,[42] according to Rasles, is *Sañghedé'tegŝé.* The place where one stream empties into another, thus ♂, is *sañktâiïsi.* (v. Willis.)

Tomhegan Brook (at Moosehead). "Hatchet,[43] *temahígan*." Rasles.

Nickatow, "*Niketaŝtegŝé,* or *Niketstegŝé, rivière qui fourche.*"[44] Rasles.

2. FROM WILLIAM WILLIS, ON THE LANGUAGE OF THE ABNAQUIES. MAINE HIST. COLL., VOL. IV

Abalajako-megus (river near Ktaadn).

Aitteon (name of a pond and sachem).

Apmogenegamook (name of a lake).

Allagash, a bark camp.[45] Sockbasin,[46] a Penobscot, told him, "The Indians gave this name to the lake from the fact of their keeping a hunting-camp there."

Bamonewengamock (head of Allagash), Cross Lake. (Sockbasin.)

Chesuncook, Big Lake. (Sockbasin.)

Caucongamock (a lake).

Ebeeme, mountains that have plums on them. (Sockbasin.)

Ktaadn. Sockbasin pronounced this Ka-tah-din, and said it meant "large mountain or large thing."

Kenduskeag, the place of Eels.

Kineo, flint, mountain on the border of Moosehead Lake.

Metawamkeag, a river with a smooth gravelly bottom. (Sockbasin.)

Metanawcook.

Millinoket, a lake with many islands in it. (Sockbasin.)

Matakeunk (river).

Molunkus (river).

Nickatow, Neccotoh, where two streams meet ("Forks of the Penobscot").

Negas (Indian village on the Kenduskeag).

Orignal (Montresor's name for Moosehead Lake).

Ponguongamook, Allagash, name of a Mohawk Indian killed there. (Sockbasin.)

Penobscot, Penobskeag, French *Pentagoet* or *Pentagovett.*

Pougohwakem (Heron Lake).

Pemadumcook (lake).

45 Camp constructed with thatched strips of bark.

46 Sockbasin (sometimes Sockabasin) Swasson (sometimes Swassian), whose age was listed as thirty-three in the 1858 Penobscot census, was described by Williamson as "an intelligent Indian of the Penobscot tribe."

47 Joseph Howard's definition—"Seboomook, Our rivers."—was included in Willis's "Language of the Abnaquies."

48 Quoted with minor variants from Potter's letter of 10 November 1855 and published as Appendix to "Language of the Abnaquies." Potter was a member of the New Hampshire legislature as well as an author and editor.

49 Reference to Potter's Appendix to "Language of the Abnaquies," 192.

50 Dr. James Andrew Chute (1811–1838), a graduate of Yale College, who settled in Westport, Kansas, and about whom Potter wrote: "You will perceive that Mr Chute and myself are at variance in our definitions, except perhaps as to *katahdn.*"

Passadumkeag, where water goes into the river above falls. (Williamson.)

Ripogenas (river).

Sunkhaze (river), Dead water.

Souneunk.

Seboomook. Sockbasin says this word means "the shape of a Moose's head, and was given to the lake which now bears the English name." *Howard* says differently.[47]

Seboois, a brook, a small river. (Sockbasin.)

Sebec (river).

Sebago, great water.

Telos (lake).

Telasinis (lake).

Umbagog (lake), doubled up; so called from its form. (Sockbasin.)

Umbazookscus (lake).

Wassatiquoik, a mountain river. (Sockbasin.)

Judge C. E. Potter of Manchester, New Hampshire, adds in November, 1855:—

"*Chesuncook.* This is formed from *Chesunk,* or *Sehunk* (a goose), and *Auke* (a place), and means 'The Goose Place.' Chesunk, or Sehunk, is the sound made by the wild geese when flying."[48]

Ktaadn. This is doubtless a corruption of *Kees* (high), and *Auke* (a place).

Penobscot, Penapse (stone, rock-place), and *Auke* (place).

Suncook, Goose-place, *Sehunk-auke.*

The Judge says that *schoot* means to rush, and hence *schoodic* from this and *auke* (a place where water rushes), and that *schoon* means the same; and that the Marble-head people and others have derived the words *scoon* and *scoot* from the Indians, and hence schooner;[49] refers to a Mr. Chute.[50]

The End.

Supplement

Editor's note: The following account from Thoreau's journal of 22 September 1853 on the building of a canoe was not included as part of *The Maine Woods*. The text is taken from *The Writings of Henry D. Thoreau* [J 5:428–431], with corrections made from Thoreau's manuscript journal.

Behind one house, an Indian had nearly finished one canoe and was just beginning another, outdoors. I looked very narrowly at the process and had already carefully examined and measured our birch. We asked this Indian his name. He answered readily and pleasantly, "My name is Old John Pennyweight." Said he got his bark at the head of Passadumkeag, fifty miles off. Took him two days to find one tree that was suitable; had to look very sharp to be sure the bark was not imperfect. But once he made two birches out of one tree. Took the bark off with a shovel made of rock maple, three or four inches wide. It took him a fortnight or three weeks to complete a canoe after he had got the materials ready. They sometimes made them of spruce bark, and also of skins, but they were not so good as birch. Boats of three hides were quicker made. This was the best time to get the birch bark. It would not come off in the winter. (I had heard Joe say of a certain canoe that it was made of summer bark.) They scrape all the inner bark off, and in the canoe the bark is wrong side outward.

He had the ribs of a canoe, all got out of cedar,— the first step in making a canoe, after materials have been brought together,—and each one shaped for the particular place it was to hold in the canoe. As both ends are alike, there will be two ribs alike. These two were placed close together, and the next in succession each way were placed next on each side, and thus tied up in bundles of fourteen to sixteen till all were made. In the bundle I examined, they were two and a half inches wide in the middle narrowing to the ends. He would untie a bundle, take out the inmost, or longest, or several, and place them on their ends in a very large iron kettle of hot water over a fire, turning them from time to time. Then, taking one of the inmost or longest ones, he bent and shaped it with much labor over his knee, giving it with his eyes the shape it was to have in the canoe. It was then tied firmly and held in that shape with the reddish cedar bark. Sometimes he was obliged to tie a straight piece of wood on tangent-wise to the rib, and, with a bark tie, draw out a side of the rib to that. Then each succeeding smaller rib in one half the bundle is forced into this. The first bundles of fourteen or sixteen making two bundles of steamed and bent and tied-up ribs; and thus all are left to dry in that shape.

I was sorry that I could not be there to witness the next step in making a canoe, for I was much struck by the *method* of this work, and the process deserves to be minutely described,—as much, at least, as most of the white man's arts, accounts of which now fill the journals. I do not know how the bark is made to hug so tightly the ribs, unless they are driven into place somewhat like a hoop. One of the next things must be to make the long, thin sheathing of cedar, less than half an inch thick, of pieces half the length of the birch, reaching each way close together beneath the ribs, and quite thin toward the edges of the canoe. However, I examined the canoe that was nearly done with minuteness. The edge or taffrail is composed first of two long strips of cedar, rather stout, one on each side. Four narrow hardwood (rock maple) cross-bars, artfully shaped so that no strength may be wasted, keep these apart, give firmness to the whole, and answer for seats. The ends of the ribs come up behind or outside this taffrail and are nailed to it with a shingle nail. Pennyweight said they formerly used wooden pegs.[1] The edge of the bark is brought up level with this, and a very slender triangular cleat of cedar is nailed on over it and flush with the surface of the taffrail. Then there are ties of split white spruce bark (looking like split bamboo) through the bark, between the ribs, and around these two strips of cedar, and over the two strips one flat and thin strip covering the ties, making smooth work and coming out flush with the under strips. Thus the edge of the canoe is completed. Owing to the form of the canoe, there must be some seams near the edge on the sides about eighteen inches apart, and pieces of bark are put under them. The edges of the bark are carefully sewed together at the ends and, in our canoe, a strip of canvas covered with pitch was laid (doubled) over the edge. They use rosin now, but pitch formerly. Canoe is nearly straight on bottom—straight in principle—and not so rounded the other way as is supposed. *Vide* this section in middle. The sides bulge out an inch or so beyond the rail. There is an additional piece of bark, four or five inches wide, along each side in the middle for four or five feet, for protection, and a similar protecting strip for eighteen inches on each side at the ends. The canoe rises about one foot in the last five or six feet. There is an oval piece of cedar for stiffness inside, within a foot of each end, and near this the ribs are bent short to breaking. Beyond there are no ribs, but sheaths and a small keel-like piece, and the hollow is filled with shavings. Lightness, above all, is studied in the construction. Nails and rosin were all the modern things I noticed. The maker used one of those curved knives, and worked very hard at bending the knees.

1 Thoreau's note: "Polis canoe in '57 had them."

Choice of Copy Text

The text for *The Maine Woods: A Fully Annotated Edition* has been newly established upon the following editorial principles established by this editor.

The first edition of *The Maine Woods*, published in 1864 by Houghton Mifflin, was the second of several posthumous volumes edited by Thoreau's sister, Sophia, and Ellery Channing. Although the first of the two pieces in the volume, "Ktaadn" and "Chesuncook," were previously published in periodical journals, the third piece, "The Allegash and East Branch," and the Appendix were not. To remain as close as possible to an authoritative text, the copy text for *The Maine Woods: A Fully Annotated Edition* is as follows:

- "Ktaadn": the first printing of "Ktaadn, and the Maine Woods" in Sartain's *Union Magazine of Literature and Art*.
- "Chesuncook": the first printing of "Chesuncook" in the *Atlantic Monthly*.
- "The Allegash and East Branch": the 1864 edition of *The Maine Woods*, prepared by Sophia Thoreau and William Ellery Channing.
- "Appendix": the 1864 edition of *The Maine Woods*, prepared by Sophia Thoreau and William Ellery Channing.

In addition, editorial emendations may be based upon the following sources to help determine Thoreau's intent:

- Journal, manuscript, and fair draft versions of portions of the text;

- Thoreau's corrected copy of the first printing of "Ktaadn, and the Maine Woods" in Sartain's *Union Magazine of Literature and Art* held in the Berg Collection of the New York Public Library;
- The following editions of *The Maine Woods:*
  - Boston: Ticknor and Fields, 1864;
  - Boston: Houghton Mifflin, 1894;
  - Boston: Houghton Mifflin, 1906;
- Source texts quoted by Thoreau in *The Maine Woods*.

No attempt to modernize the text has been made. It is my intention that the text should remain as close as possible to the text Thoreau presented. However, a certain consistency within the text is desirable, particularly in the case of this volume, the copy text of which was prepared under several variant editorial policies. Although Thoreau was not consistent in his spelling or punctuation, it is my intention to impose some consistency in regard to spelling and punctuation based upon Thoreau's use as represented in the above sources as well as his other writings, and all such decisions will be carefully noted. All this is further complicated by the lack of a final authoritative text for the work known as *The Maine Woods*.

When a line was omitted from his essay "Chesuncook" during periodical publication, Thoreau wrote, "I hardly need to say that this is a liberty which I will not permit to be taken with my MS. The editor has, in this case, no more right to omit a sentiment than to insert one, or put words into my mouth." This is too often taken as Thoreau's final word on editors and the editorial process. As he wrote: "I do not ask anybody to adopt my opinions, but I do expect that when they ask for them to print, they will print them, or obtain my consent to their alteration or omission. I should not read many books if I thought that they had been thus *expurgated*."

Thoreau is clear that his thought and opinion must not be altered. He has considerably less concern for other corrections, what he called "other cases of comparatively little importance to me." Thoreau's spelling errors, punctuation errors, or slips of the pen, should not stand simply because the author failed, or did not live long enough, to correct them.

That the essays comprising this volume were published under varying editorial policies presents the editor of *The Maine Woods* with a difficult choice to the extent that "Ktaadn" published as an essay and "Ktaadn" published as a chapter in *The Maine Woods* may demand different approaches. Ultimately it is the editor's job to remain faithful to the author's intentions while fulfilling an obligation to the intended reader. I hope that I may have done both.

Textual Notes and Emendations

Ktaadn

1:1	title emended from *Ktaadn, and the Maine Woods* as emended in MW 1864
1:3	*No. I. / THE WILDS OF THE PENOB-SCOT.* deleted as in Thoreau's corrected copy of Sartain's *Union Magazine* (New York Public Library, The Henry W. and Albert A. Berg Collection of English and American Literature) and as emended in MW 1864
1:18	*to* inserted as emended in MW 1864
1:32–33	*mosquitoes, and midges,* inserted as emended in MW 1864
2:4	comma: having examined multiple copies of Sartain's *Union Magazine,* I have determined that what appears as a period after *1836* is caused by an eroded comma and thus does not necessitate emendation
2:26	*other* inserted as in Thoreau's corrected copy of Sartain's *Union Magazine*
3:3	*the* corrected to *this* as in Thoreau's corrected copy of Sartain's *Union Magazine* and as emended in MW 1864
3:12	comma inserted after *perchance* as emended in MW 1864
3:29	*exceedingly light and beautiful*

emended to *light and shapely* as in MW 1864

3:31	*shoulders. They are from eighteen to twenty-five* emended to *shoulders, from twenty to thirty* as in MW 1864
3:35	*rock* emended to *rocks* as in Thoreau's corrected copy of Sartain's *Union Magazine* and as emended in MW 1864
3:36–4:1	*commonly* inserted as emended in MW 1864
4:1	*or other hard-wood* inserted as emended in MW 1864
4:2	*inward are* inserted as emended in MW 1864
4:9	*, or often in a single trip,* inserted as emended in MW 1864
4:28–29	*shabby and forlorn,* corrected to *shabby, forlorn, and* as emended in MW 1864
4:31	*abroadstead* corrected to *abroad-steads* as emended in MW 1864
4:31	*there* emended to *their* as in Thoreau's corrected copy of Sartain's *Union Magazine* and as emended in MW 1864
4:33	*a hunting* emended to *a-hunting* following usage once in "Chesuncook" and three times in "The Allegash and East Branch"
4:34	*Abenaki's* emended to *Abenaki* as emended in MW 1864

4:36   *the ancient Tarrantines* emended to *once a powerful tribe* as emended in MW 1864

5:11   *very shallow* emended to *shallow* as emended in MW 1864

5:15   *Military* deleted after *Houlton* as in Thoreau's corrected copy of Sartain's *Union Magazine* and as emended in MW 1864

5:33   *is* emended to *was* as emended in MW 1864

5:34   *talk* emended to *talked* as emended in MW 1864

5:35   *cannot* emended to *could not* as emended in MW 1864

6:7   *observations* emended to *asseverations* as in Thoreau's corrected copy of Sartain's *Union Magazine* and as emended in MW 1864

6:24   *Spring* emended to *spring* as emended in MW 1864

6:26   *a very* emended to *a* as emended in MW 1864

6:28   *here called the Military road,* inserted as emended in MW 1864

6:36   *regular shanties* emended to *small huts* as emended in MW 1864

7:28   *chieferman* emended to *chiefer man* as in Thoreau's corrected copy of Sartain's *Union Magazine*

7:35–36   parentheses emended to brackets as in Thoreau's corrected copy of Sartain's *Union Magazine* and as emended in MW 1864

8:1   *west branch* emended to *West Branch* as in Thoreau's corrected

copy of Sartain's *Union Magazine* and as emended in MW 1864

8:2   *on* emended to *or* as in Thoreau's corrected copy of Sartain's *Union Magazine* and as emended in MW 1864

8:6   *no* emended to *so* as in Thoreau's corrected copy of Sartain's *Union Magazine* and as emended in MW 1864

8:12   *&c.* expanded to *etc.* as emended in MW 1906

8:25   *larch, cedar,* emended to *larch,* as emended in MW 1864

8:33   *easily* inserted as emended in MW 1864

9:5   *After* emended to *We had* as emended in MW 1864

9:15–16   *demand. The supply is always equal to the demand, and* emended to *demand—the supply is always equal to the demand,—and* as in Thoreau's corrected copy of Sartain's *Union Magazine*

9:36   *swallows* emended to *shallows* as in Thoreau's corrected copy of Sartain's *Union Magazine* and as emended in MW 1864

10:5–6   *carribou* emended to *caribou* as elsewhere in "Ktaadn" and as emended in MW 1906

10:14   *war* emended to *man* as in Thoreau's corrected copy of Sartain's *Union Magazine* and as emended in MW 1864

10:18   *sight; and there* emended to *sight.*

There as in Thoreau's corrected copy of Sartain's *Union Magazine* and as emended in MW 1864

10:21   *boys* emended to *bags* as in Thoreau's corrected copy of Sartain's *Union Magazine* and as emended in MW 1864

10:33   *was* inserted as emended in MW 1864

10:36   *him* emended to *his customer* as emended in MW 1864

11:11   *canalès* emended to *canalés* as in Thoreau's journal [PJ 2:289] and as emended in MW 1906

11:20   *canes* emended to *cones* as in Thoreau's corrected copy of Sartain's *Union Magazine* and as emended in MW 1864

12:3   *immigrant* emended to *emigrant* as emended in MW 1864

12:3–4   *New-York* emended to *New York* following usage in "Chesuncook" and "The Allegash and East Branch" and as emended in MW 1906

12:10   *[END OF PART I.]* deleted as emended in MW 1864

12:11   *No. II. / LIFE IN THE WILDERNESS.* deleted as in Thoreau's corrected copy of Sartain's *Union Magazine* and as emended in MW 1864

12:14   *Why,* emended to *Why* as in Thoreau's corrected copy of Sartain's *Union Magazine* and as emended in MW 1864

13:10   *backwood's* emended to *backwoods* as emended in MW 1864

14:1–2   *Winter and Spring* emended to *winter and spring* as emended in MW 1864

14:2–3   *Summer* emended to *summer* as emended in MW 1864

14:8   *Mattascunk* emended to *Mattaseunk* as emended in MW 1906

14:11   *track* emended to *tract* as in Thoreau's corrected copy of Sartain's *Union Magazine* and as emended in MW 1864

14:21   *New-York* emended to *New York* to conform to usage in "Chesuncook" and "The Allegash and East Branch" and as emended in MW 1906

14:28   *learn* emended to *teach* as in Thoreau's corrected copy of Sartain's *Union Magazine* and as emended in MW 1864

15:17   *name* emended to *names* as in Thoreau's corrected copy of Sartain's *Union Magazine* and as emended in MW 1864

15:26   *The Seboois, or East Branch, a quite* emended to *the East Branch a large and* as emended in MW 1864

16:31   *loggers'* emended to *logger's* following usage later in this same paragraph: *logger's fare.*

17:4   *and lichen* inserted as emended in MW 1864

17:12   *raw pork* emended to *pork, often raw* as emended in MW 1864

17:23   *Spring* emended to *spring* as emended in MW 1864

18:6	*Seboois* emended to *East Branch* as emended in MW 1864
18:22–23	*bounded on all sides but the river, abruptly by* emended to *bounded abruptly on all sides but the river, by* as in Thoreau's corrected copy of Sartain's *Union Magazine* and as emended in MW 1864
19:1	*Springs* emended to *springs* as emended in MW 1864
19:18	*ever-lasting* emended to *everlasting* following form in "Chesuncook" and "Appendix"
19:24–25	*Summer and Winter* emended to *summer and winter* as emended in MW 1864
19:32	*economise* emended to *economize* as emended in MW 1864
19:35	*the upper part of* inserted as emended in MW 1864
20:6–7	*(Vaccinium Vitis-Idaea)* inserted as emended in MW 1864
21:3	*tomatos* emended to *tomatoes* as emended in MW 1864
21:12	*States'* emended to *State's* as in Thoreau's journal—"But to settling on the state's lands there was no such hindrance—" [PJ 2:300] and as emended in MW 1906
21:22	closing quotation mark moved from 21:28 as in Thoreau's corrected copy of Sartain's *Union Magazine* and as emended in MW 1864
21:24	*'yellow hammer'* emended to *"yellow hammer"* as emended in MW 1864
21:28	closing quotation mark moved

	from end of paragraph at 21:22 as in Thoreau's corrected copy of Sartain's *Union Magazine* and as emended in MW 1864
22:10	*some of* inserted as in Thoreau's corrected copy of Sartain's *Union Magazine* and as emended in MW 1864
22:11	*was* emended to *were* as in Thoreau's corrected copy of Sartain's *Union Magazine* and as emended in MW 1864
22:17	*ceilings* emended to *ceiling* as in MW 1906
22:23	*Spring* emended to *spring* as emended in MW 1864
23:27	*Lake* emended to *Lakes* as in Thoreau's corrected copy of Sartain's *Union Magazine* and as emended in MW 1864
24:17	*them* emended to *him* as in Thoreau's corrected copy of Sartain's *Union Magazine* and as emended in MW 1864
24:34	*lamprey-eel* emended to *lamprey-eel's or sucker's* as emended in MW 1864
25:5	*laid* emended to *lain* as in Thoreau's journal [PJ 2:305]
25:23	*in the pickle* emended to *in pickle* as in Thoreau's corrected copy of Sartain's *Union Magazine* and as emended in MW 1864
26:11–12	*backwoods'* emended to *backwoods* as emended in MW 1864
27:12	*buried* emended to *busied* as in Thoreau's corrected copy of Sar-

tain's *Union Magazine* and as
emended in MW 1864

27:19   *the* emended to *this* as in Thoreau's
corrected copy of Sartain's *Union
Magazine* and as emended in MW
1864

28:6   *, whom we did not know,* inserted as
emended in MW 1864

28:12   *at any rate* emended to *for the most
part* as emended in MW 1864

28:23   *torrents'* emended to *torrent's* as in
Thoreau's source, Thomas Camp-
bell's *Poetical Works of Thomas
Campbell,* and as emended in MW
1864

28:29   *Summer* emended to *summer* as
emended in MW 1864

28:33   *Winter* emended to *winter* as
emended in MW 1864

28:35   *train* emended to *team* as emended
in MW 1864

29:9   *Spring* emended to *spring* as
emended in MW 1864

29:11   *moss* emended to *lichens* as emended
in MW 1864

29:26   *Summer* emended to *summer* as
emended in MW 1864

29:33   *logger's* emended to *loggers'* as indicated by the plural in Thoreau's
journal—"we filed into the rude
lumberers' camp" [PJ 2:309]—and
as emended in MW 1894

30:9   *had* emended to *made* as in
Thoreau's corrected copy of Sartain's *Union Magazine* and as
emended in MW 1864

30:10   *liberty* emended to *Liberty* as in
Thoreau's corrected copy of Sar-
tain's *Union Magazine* and as
emended in MW 1864

30:23   *, even here white* emended to *even
here, white* as emended in MW 1864

31:1   *batteau* emended to *batteaux* as
in Thoreau's corrected copy of
Sartain's *Union Magazine* and as
emended in MW 1864

31:4   *[END OF PART II.]* deleted as
emended in MW 1864

31:5   *No. III. / BOATING ON THE LAKES*
deleted as in Thoreau's corrected
copy of Sartain's *Union Magazine*
and as emended in MW 1864

31:34   *white pine* emended to *white-pine*
to be consistent with usage as an
adjective and as emended in MW
1906

32:16   *Allagash* emended to *Allegash* as
emended in MW 1906

32:16   period inserted after *St* as emended
in MW 1864

32:17   *Indian* emended to *Indian's* as
in Thoreau's corrected copy of
Sartain's *Union Magazine* and as
emended in MW 1864

33:25   *timid red deer or* emended to *timid*
as emended in MW 1864

33:29   *fast;* emended to *fast,* as emended in
MW 1864

33:30   *The rapids are near, and the daylight's past,* emended to *The Rapids
are near and the daylight's past!* as
emended in MW 1864

33:33   *description* emended to *experience* as in Thoreau's corrected copy of Sartain's *Union Magazine* and as emended in MW 1864

33:33   *exactly this* emended to *a similar* as emended in MW 1864

33:35   *Utawa's* emended to *Utawas'* as emended in MW 1864

34:2   *curl;* emended to *curl!* as emended in MW 1864

34:3   *But* emended to *But,* as emended in MW 1864

34:4   *Oh, sweetly we'll rest our laboring* emended to *O sweetly we'll rest our weary* as emended in MW 1864

34:6   *Utawa's* emended to *Utawas'* as emended in MW 1864

34:6   *moon* emended to *moon,* as emended in MW 1864

34:15   *isle,* emended to *isle!* as emended in MW 1864

34:15   *prayer* emended to *prayers* as in Thoreau's corrected copy of Sartain's *Union Magazine* and as emended in MW 1864

34:16   *Grant us cool heavens* emended to *O grant us cool days* as emended in MW 1864

34:16   *air* emended to *airs* as in Thoreau's corrected copy of Sartain's *Union Magazine; airs.* emended to *airs!* as emended in MW 1864

34:23   *rills* emended to *rill* as in Thoreau's corrected copy of Sartain's *Union Magazine* and as emended in MW 1864

35:21   *fiendlike* emended to *fiend-like* to follow usage as in *clapboard-like* and *river-like* and as emended in MW 1906

36:2   *north-east* emended to *northeast* as emended in MW 1864

37:20   *that* emended to *the* as in Thoreau's corrected copy of Sartain's *Union Magazine* and as emended in MW 1864

37:35   *&c.* expanded to *etc.* as emended in MW 1906

37:35   *as:* emended to *as* as in Thoreau's corrected copy of Sartain's *Union Magazine* and as emended in MW 1864

37:35–36   *Y—girdle—crow-foot* emended to *Y-girdle-crowfoot* as in Thoreau's journal (PJ 2:283)

38:21–26   *He uses a few . . . on sidewalks.* inserted as emended in MW 1864

38:23   *feruled* emended to *ferruled* as emended in MW 1894

38:34–39:26   *I quote Michaux . . . thirty years."* inserted as emended in MW 1864.

39:22   *drawn* corrected to *sawn* as in all translations of Michaux available to Thoreau, as well as in his probable source, John Claudius Loudon's *Arboretum et fruticetum Britanicum*

40:9   *logger's* emended to *loggers'* as indicated by the plural in a related sentence in the journal: "I could imagine what tales the loggers told here" [PJ 2:320]

40:14   *camping* emended to *tamping* as

40:23   *whole* emended to *rest of the* as in Thoreau's corrected copy of Sartain's *Union Magazine* and as emended in MW 1864

40:36   *Pochwockomus* emended to *Pockwockomus* as in Thoreau's corrected copy of Sartain's *Union Magazine* and as emended in MW 1864

41:11   *lake,* emended to *lake* as in Thoreau's journal [PJ 2:325]

41:17   *outlet* emended to *inlet* following the emendation of Joseph J. Moldenhauer in MW 1972 (46) and his explanation that "'outlet' clearly violates the sense of Thoreau's explanations and examples" [MW 1972:410]

42:10–11   *five to eight* emended to *three to five or six* as emended in MW 1864

42:13–14   *, or else there are two at the bows* inserted as emended in MW 1864

43:8   *our* emended to *one's* as in Thoreau's journal [PJ 2:322]

44:9   *aligators* emended to *alligators* as emended in MW 1864

45:8   *apt* emended to *wont* as in Thoreau's corrected copy of Sartain's *Union Magazine*

46:6   *batteau* emended to *batteaux* as in Thoreau's corrected copy of Sartain's *Union Magazine* and as emended in MW 1864

47:12   *Sowadnechunk* emended to *Sowad-* *nehunk* as in Thoreau's corrected copy of Sartain's *Union Magazine* and as emended in MW 1864

47:20   *[END OF PART III.]* deleted as emended in MW 1864

47:21   *No. IV. / THE ASCENT OF KTAADN.* deleted as in Thoreau's corrected copy of Sartain's *Union Magazine* and as emended in MW 1864

47:29   *leucisci pulchelli* emended to *Leucisci pulchelli* and italicized as emended in MW 1864

48:11   *swam* emended to *swum* following Thoreau's use of the past participle at 150:32

48:27–33   *Lescarbot, writing in . . . less numerous* inserted as emended in MW 1864

48:36   *lopt* emended to *lopped* as in Thoreau's journal [PJ 2:330] and as emended in MW 1906

49:10   *fire* emended to *flame* as emended in MW 1864

49:35   *areas* emended to *arcs* as in Thoreau's corrected copy of Sartain's *Union Magazine* and as emended in MW 1864

50:24   *land, still* emended to *land still,* as in Thoreau's corrected copy of Sartain's *Union Magazine*

51:35   *twelve hundred* emended to *sometimes one thousand* as emended in MW 1864

51:36   *five-feet* emended to *five-foot* as in Thoreau's journal [PJ 2:333] and emended in MW 1894

53:17   *cornet* emended to *cornel* as in Thoreau's corrected copy of Sartain's *Union Magazine* and as emended in MW 1864

53:19   *Blue-berries* emended to *Blueberries* as emended in MW 1864

53:24   *blue-berries* emended to *blueberries* as emended in MW 1864

54:22   *Satan's,* emended to *Satan's* as in Thoreau's corrected copy of Sartain's *Union Magazine* and as emended in MW 1864

54:25   *pinus nigra* emended to *Abies nigra* and italicized as emended in MW 1864

55:6   *nests* emended to *dens* as emended in MW 1864

56:4   *we* emended to *were* as in Thoreau's corrected copy of Sartain's *Union Magazine* and as emended in MW 1864

56:8   *aeriel* emended to *aerial* as in Thoreau's journal [PJ 2:338] and as emended in MW 1864

56:13   *fire-tree* emended to *fir-tree* as emended in MW 1864

56:19   *altogether* emended to *all together* as in Thoreau's corrected copy of Sartain's *Union Magazine* and as emended in MW 1906

56:28   *mist, the* emended to *mist. The* as in Thoreau's corrected copy of Sartain's *Union Magazine* and as emended in MW 1864

57:14   *winds'* emended to *wind's* as emended in MW 1864

59:7   *in* emended to *on* as emended in MW 1864

59:12   *Seboois or East* emended to *east* as emended in MW 1864

59:20   *blue berries* emended to *blueberries* as emended in MW 1864

59:27–28   *that immeasurable* emended to *that,—immeasurable* as emended in MW 1864

60:15   *had rode* emended to *had ridden* following Thoreau's use of the past participle in "Chesuncook," 81:35

62:30   [*END OF PART IV.*] deleted as emended in MW 1864

62:31   *No. V. / THE RETURN JOURNEY.* deleted as in Thoreau's corrected copy of Sartain's *Union Magazine* and as emended in MW 1864

64:17   *recognised* emended to *recognized* as emended in MW 1864

65:18   *three-quarters* emended to *three quarters* as emended in MW 1906

65:30   *before* corrected to *below* as in Thoreau's source, Charles Thomas Jackson's *Second Annual Report on the Geology of the Public Lands*

65:30   *lay* corrected to *lays* as in Thoreau's source, Jackson's *Second Annual Report*

66:34   period: having examined multiple copies of Sartain's *Union Magazine*, I have determined that what appears to be a missing period is caused by an eroded period that appears faintly printed in some

	copies and thus does not necessitate emendation
67:19	*table-rock* emended to *Table Rock* to conform to its use as a place name and as emended in MW 1906
68:6	*tillnight* emended to *till night* as emended in MW 1864
68:9	*almost* inserted as emended in MW 1864
68:24	*lake* emended to *Lake* as emended in MW 1864
69:8	*Saute* emended to *Sault* as emended in MW 1906, although *de St. Marie* has been retained as an acceptable and common variant of Sault Sainte Marie
69:12	*lake* emended to *Lake* as emended in MW 1906
69:28	*cried when* emended to *cried, when* as emended in MW 1864
69:29	*daylight.* emended to *daylight,* as emended in MW 1864
71:15	*scows* emended to *aeons* as in Thoreau's corrected copy of Sartain's *Union Magazine* and as emended in MW 1864
71:22	*race* emended to *face* as emended in MW 1864
72:27	*forests* emended to *forest* as emended in MW 1864
72:33	*mosquitos* emended to *mosquitoes* as emended in MW 1864
73:7–18	*What a place . . . pines among* inserted as emended in MW 1864
73:35	*New-York* emended to the non-hyphenated form to conform to

usage in "Chesuncook" and "The Allegash and East Branch"

74:3	*head-quarters* emended to *head-waters* as in Thoreau's corrected copy of Sartain's *Union Magazine* and as emended in MW 1864

Chesuncook

76:9	*At 5,* emended to *At 5* as in Thoreau's fair-copy manuscript (MS Lowell 9, Houghton Library, Harvard University) and as emended in MW 1906
76:9	*185-* emended to *1853* as indicated by Thoreau's letter of 5 March 1858 to James Russell Lowell—"If there is no objection you can print the whole date as 1853" [C 509]—and as emended in MW 1864
76:32	*get* emended to *yet* as in MW 1864
77:7	*boot-black* emended to *blacker* as in Thoreau's fair-copy manuscript
77:20	*the monster's* has been retained over the fair-copy manuscript use of the pronoun *his* to avoid possible confusion over the noun to which the pronoun refers
77:21	*Manheigan* emended to *Monhegan* as in Thoreau's fair-copy manuscript and as emended in MW 1906
79:4	*Katadn* emended to *Ktaadn* as in Thoreau's manuscript journal (MJ 12 September 1853) and as emended in MW 1864

79:28   *aster acuminatus* emended to *Aster acuminatus* and italicized as in MW 1906

80:5   *farther* emended to *further* as in Thoreau's fair-copy manuscript

81:31   *farther* emended to *further* as in Thoreau's fair-copy manuscript

84:24   *farther* emended to *further* as in Thoreau's fair-copy manuscript

84:25   *north-west* emended to *northwest* as in MW 1864

85:23   *mean while* emended to *meanwhile* as in MW 1864

86:15   *kalmia glauca* emended to *Kalmia glauca* and italicized as emended in MW 1906

86:15–16   *(which was still in fruit, and a second time in bloom,)* emended to *which was still in fruit and a second time in bloom,* as in Thoreau's fair-copy manuscript

86:16–17   *Clintonia and Linnaea borealis* italicized as emended in MW 1906

86:17   as Thoreau's manuscript journal clearly indicated to which plant the word *moxon* referred, the MW 1864 reading of *which last* has been followed over the fair-copy manuscript reading of *which last (?)*

86:19–20   *aster radula, diplopappus umbellatus, solidago lanceolatus* emended to *Aster radula, Diplopappus umbellatus, Solidago lanceolatus* and italicized as emended in MW 1906

87:22   *carryman's* emended to *carry-man's* as in Thoreau's fair-copy manuscript and to follow usage in the preceding paragraph

87:35   *suspected spot* emended to *place* as in Thoreau's fair-copy manuscript

88:1   *set* emended to *placed* as in Thoreau's fair-copy manuscript and as emended in MW 1906

88:35   *dead water* has been retained over the one-word form *deadwater* found in Thoreau's fair-copy manuscript in only this one instance

89:7   *the common and rarely* inserted as in Thoreau's fair-copy manuscript

89:32   *one or* has been retained over the fair-copy manuscript use of *or* as being an inclusive range for the distance represented in Thoreau's journal: "1½ ms distant in a SW direction" (MJ 16 September 1853)

89:36   *chickadees* emended to *chicadees* as Thoreau's preferred spelling and as emended in MW 1864

90:1   *chickadee* emended to *chicadee* as Thoreau's preferred spelling and as emended in MW 1864

90:34   *spot* emended to *place* as in Thoreau's fair-copy manuscript

91:3   *farther* emended to *further* as in Thoreau's fair-copy manuscript

93:27   *They work* emended to *Working* as in Thoreau's fair-copy manuscript

93:28   *let* emended to *letting* as in Thoreau's fair-copy manuscript

93:28   *and live without* emended to *without* as in Thoreau's fair-copy manuscript

94:1   *ugh-ugh-ugh, or oo-oo-oo-oo* emended to *ugh ugh ugh, or oo oo oo oo* as in Thoreau's fair-copy manuscript

94:2   *oo-o-o-o-o-o-o-o* has been retained over the nonhyphenated fair-text manuscript form, following Thoreau's journal (MJ 16 September 1853) as being more indicative of the prolonged sound

94:15–16   *and also that of the caribou and the deer* emended to *and also the caribou and deer* as in Thoreau's fair-copy manuscript

94:22   *is* emended to *was* as in Thoreau's fair-copy manuscript

94:28   *affording* emended to *which afforded* as in Thoreau's fair-copy manuscript

95:12   *inhabitants* emended to *inhabitant* as in Thoreau's fair-copy manuscript

96:16   *thus* emended to *this* as in Thoreau's fair-copy manuscript and in Thoreau's journal (MJ 16 September 1853)

96:20   *had* has been retained over the fair-copy manuscript use of *has* as being parallel to usage in Thoreau's source, *Jesuit Relations*

96:30   *on* emended to *on to* as in Thoreau's fair-copy manuscript

97:5   *chickadee* emended to *chickaree* as in Thoreau's fair-copy manuscript

98:30   *chickadee* emended to *chicadee* as

Thoreau's preferred spelling and as emended in MW 1864.

100:20   *[To be continued.]* deleted as in MW 1864

100:21   *[Continued.]* deleted as in MW 1864

101:15   *Katadn* emended to *Ktaadn* as in Thoreau's journal (MJ 17 September 1853) and as emended in MW 1864

102:6   *farthest* emended to *furthest* as in Thoreau's fair-copy manuscript

102:12   *north-east* emended to *northeast* as in MW 1864

103:17   *Clintonia Borealis* emended to *Clintonia borealis* and italicized as emended in MW 1906 and as found later in this essay and in "Appendix"

104:10   *aster macrophyllus* emended to *Aster macrophyllus* and italicized as emended in MW 1906 and as found in "Appendix"

105:11–14   *[Indeed . . . woods.]* inserted as in MW 1864

105:19   *some* emended to *an* as in Thoreau's fair-copy manuscript

106:1   *Megaceros Hibernicus* italicized as emended in MW 1906

106:4   *upward* emended to *upwards* as in Thoreau's fair-copy manuscript and Thoreau's source, Gideon Algernon Mantell's *Wonders of Geology*

106:22   *an* emended to *one* as in Thoreau's fair-copy manuscript

107:5   *hide* italicized to reflect emphasis in Thoreau's fair-copy manuscript

107:34	*farther* emended to *further* as in Thoreau's fair-copy manuscript
107:36	*aster puniceus* emended to *Aster puniceus* and italicized as emended in MW 1906 and as found in "Appendix"
109:9–10	*This stream was much more unfrequented than the main one* emended to *This was much more unfrequented than the main stream* as in Thoreau's fair-copy manuscript
109:27	*oo-oo-oo-oo-oo-oo* has been retained over the nonhyphenated fair-text manuscript form, following the form at 94:2 and in Thoreau's journal (MJ 17 September 1853) as being more indicative of the prolonged sound
110:2	*near as is possible to come to being a hunter and miss it,* emended to *near to being a hunter and miss it, as possible* as in Thoreau's fair-copy manuscript
112:19	*to have been* emended to *was* as in Thoreau's fair-copy manuscript
112:36–113:2	line restored as in MW 1864. This line was excised without Thoreau's approval. On 22 June 1858 Thoreau wrote to James Russell Lowell, editor of the *Atlantic Monthly*:

Dear Sir,

    When I received the proof of that portion of my story printed in the July number of your magazine, I was surprised to find that the sentence—"It is as immortal as I am, and perchance will go to as high a heaven, there to tower above me still."—(which comes directly after the words "heals my cuts," page 230, tenth line from the top,) had been crossed out, and it occurred to me that, after all, it was of some consequence that I should see the proofs; supposing, of course, that my "Stet" &c in the margin would be respected, as I perceive that it was in other cases of comparatively little importance to me. However, I have just noticed that that sentence was, in a very mean and cowardly manner, omitted. I hardly need to say that this is a liberty which I will not permit to be taken with my MS. The editor has, in this case, no more right to omit a sentiment than to insert one, or put words into my mouth.

    I do not ask anybody to adopt my opinions, but I do expect that when they ask for them to print, they will print them, or obtain my consent to their alteration or omission. I should not read many books if I thought that they had been thus *expurgated*.

    I feel this treatment to be an insult, though not intended as such, for it is to presume that I can be hired to suppress my opinions.

    I do not mean to charge you

with this omission, for I cannot believe that you knew anything about it, but there must be a responsible editor somewhere, and you, to whom I entrusted my MS. are the only party that I know in this matter. I therefore write to ask if you sanction this omission, and if there are any other sentiments to be omitted in the remainder of my article. If you do not sanction it— or whether you do or not—will you do me the justice to print that sentence, as an omitted one, indicating its place, in the August number?

I am not willing to be associated in any way, unnecessarily, with parties who will confess themselves so bigoted & timid as this implies. I could excuse a man who was afraid of an uplifted fist, but if one habitually manifests fear at the utterance of a sincere thought, I must think that his life is a kind of nightmare continued into broad daylight. It is hard to conceive of one so completely *derivative*. Is this the avowed character of the Atlantic Monthly? I should like an early reply.

Yrs truly,
Henry D. Thoreau [C 515-516]

113:30	*Katadn* emended to *Ktaadn* as emended in MW 1864
113:30	*Katahdinauquoh* emended to *Ka-tahdinauguoh* following the spelling in Thoreau's journal (MJ 18 September 1853), "Appendix," and Thoreau's source, Moses Greenleaf's *Survey of the State of Maine*
114:2	*Katadn* emended to *Ktaadn* as in MW 1864
114:16	*Ansell* emended to *Ansel* as in "Appendix" and following the spelling found on Ansel Smith's gravestone
114:17–18	*bateaux* emended to *batteaux* and italics removed as in Thoreau's journal (MJ 18 September 1853) and as emended in MW 1906
117:1	*bateau* emended to *batteau* and italics removed as in Thoreau's journal (MJ 18 September 1853) and as emended in MW 1906
117:8	*Ansell* emended to *Ansel* as in "Appendix" and following the spelling found on Ansel Smith's gravestone
119:6	*Sharpe's* emended from a common contemporary misspelling to *Sharps'* as the correct form of the possessive for the inventor, Christian Sharps, and as emended in MW 1894. MW 1906 incorrectly re-emended to *Sharp's*. Thoreau used the incorrect form *Sharpe's* in both "A Plea for Captain John Brown" in James Redpath's *Echoes of Harper's Ferry* (Boston: Thayer and Eldridge, 1860) and "The Last Days of John Brown" (*Liberator*, 27 July 1860), again incorrectly emended to

	Sharp's in the 1906 edition of those works
119:36	*bed-room* emended to *bedroom* as in Thoreau's journal (MJ 18 September 1853) and as emended in MW 1864
120:8	*there,—* emended to *then* as in Thoreau's journal (MJ 26 October 1853)
120:33	*[To be continued.]* deleted as in MW 1864
120:34	*[Concluded.]* deleted as in MW 1864
124:13	*1588* emended to *1592* as the correct publication date for volume 2 of Theodore De Bry's *Collectiones Peregrinationum in Indiam Orientalem et Indiam Occidentalem*
128:23	*aianbé* emended to *aïanbé* as in Thoreau's Indian notebooks (volume 10) and as in Thoreau's source, Father Sébastian Rasles's *Dictionary of the Abnaki Language*
128:23	*hèrar* emended to *hè ʼrar* as in Thoreau's source, Rasles's *Dictionary of the Abnaki Language.* Thoreau mistranscribed this word in his Indian notebooks, leaving out the mark of aspiration.
130:28	*Cusabesex* emended to *Cusabexsex* as in Thoreau's journal (MJ 19 September 1853) and the *Map of the Public Lands of Maine and Massachusetts*
133:3	the following passage, completing this paragraph, deleted as in MW 1864:

At the carry-man's camp I saw many little birds, brownish and yellowish, with some white tail-feathers, hopping on the wood-pile, in company with the slate-colored snow-bird, (*Fringilla hiemalis,*) but more familiar than they. The lumberers said that they came round their camps, and they gave them a vulgar name. Their simple and lively note, which was heard in all the woods, was very familiar to me, though I had never before chanced to see the bird while uttering it, and it interested me not a little, because I had had many a vain chase in a spring-morning in the direction of that sound, in order to identify the bird. On the 28th of the next month, (October,) I saw in my yard, in a drizzling day, many of the same kinds of birds flitting about amid the weeds, and uttering a faint *chip* merely. There was one full-plumaged Yellow-crowned Warbler (*Sylvia coronata*) among them, and I saw that the others were the young birds of the season. They had followed me from Moosehead and the North. I have since frequently seen the full-plumaged ones while uttering that note in the spring.

133:20	*bateau* emended to *batteau* and italics removed as in Thoreau's jour-

nal (MJ 20 September 1853) and as emended in MW 1906

134:36   *bateau* emended to *batteau* and italics removed as in Thoreau's journal (MJ 22 September 1853) and as emended in MW 1906

137:11   *character* emended to *characters* as in Thoreau's source, John Josselyn's *Account of Two Voyages to New-England*

138:28   *bateau* emended to *batteau* and italics removed as in Thoreau's journal (MJ 22 September 1853) and as emended in MW 1906

139:11–12   *butt-end* emended to *but-end* as in MW 1864 and Thoreau's usage in *Walden* ("The Ponds")

140:1   *Katadn* emended to *Ktaadn* as emended in MW 1864

141:16   *top* emended to *tops* as in Thoreau's source, William Gilpin's *Observations on the Western Parts of England*

145:7   *re-creation* emended to *recreation* as in Thoreau's journal (MJ 13 November 1857) and as emended in MW 1858, although MW 1906 re-emended to *re-creation*. A similar situation appeared in *Walden*—"Having bathed he sat down to recreate his intellectual man" [Wa 213]—in which some editors retained the hyphenated form although none of the draft versions of *Walden* indicated that Thoreau intended to use a hyphenated form in the text.

The Allegash and East Branch

146:19–20   paragraph break inserted as in Huntington Library manuscript HM13199

146:22   *father* emended to *father,* as in Huntington manuscript HM13199

146:22   *the* emended to *a* as in Thoreau's journal (MJ 22 July 1857) and Huntington manuscript HM13199

146:23   *me* emended to *us* as in Huntington manuscript HM13199

147:22–23   paragraph break inserted as in Huntington manuscript HM13199

147:29   *trustworthy* emended to *reliable* as indicated in Thoreau's manuscript journal (MJ 22 July 1857)—"known to be a particularly steady & reliable man"—and as in Huntington manuscript HM13199

147:33   *&c.* expanded to *etc.* as emended in MW 1906

148:6   *the Indian* emended to *Polis* as in Thoreau's journal (MJ 22 July 1857) and Huntington manuscript HM13199

149:27   *two* emended to *nine* following Thoreau's indication in his journal (MJ 23 July 1857) that the fare was three dollars per person

150:5   *farther* emended to *further* following Thoreau's predominant usage

150:7   *Pistigouche* emended to *Ristigouche* as in Thoreau's journal (MJ 23 July 1857) and as emended in MW 1894

150:12   *address* emended to *dress* as indicated by the phrase "gentlemanly dressed man" in Thoreau's journal (MJ 23 July 1857)

150:25   *farther* emended to *further* following Thoreau's predominant usage

152:10   *singing* emended to *ringing* following the probable reading in Thoreau's journal (MJ 23 July 1857) and as emended in MW 1906

152:11   *season* emended to *seasons* as in Thoreau's journal (MJ 23 July 1857)

156:36   *Mt.* expanded to *Mount* as emended in MW 1906

157:8   *realility* emended to *reality* as in Thoreau's journal (MJ 24 July 1857)—"He asked the meaning of reality which one of us used"—and as emended in MW 1906

157:10   *is* emended to *is,* as emended in the 1894 Riverside edition

157:18   *ne* emended to *m* as in Thoreau's Journal of 5 March 1858— "putting an *m* after the word *too*" [J 10:291]—and as emended in MW 1906

157:20   *m ar* emended to *m-ah* as indicated in Thoreau's journal of 5 March 1858—"emphasizing and prolonging that sound, as, 'They carried them home toom-ah,'" [J 10:291]—and as emended in MW 1906

158:28   *she* emended to *and she* as in Thoreau's journal (MJ 23 July 1857) and as emended in MW 1906

160:3   *it.* emended to *it!* as in Thoreau's journal (MJ 30 October 1857) and as emended in MW 1906

160:8   *&c.* expanded to *etc.* as emended in MW 1906

160:14   *succeeding* emended to *succeeded* as emended in MW 1906

161:6   *farther* emended to *further* as in Thoreau's journal (MJ 24 July 1857)

162:6   *&c.* expanded to *etc.* as emended in MW 1906

162:8   *&c.* expanded to *etc.* as emended in MW 1906

164:31–32 *to (the V. Pennsylvanicum) our* emended to *to the V. Pennsylvanicum, our* as emended in MW 1906

168:36   italics added to reflect emphasis in Thoreau's journal (MJ 30 September 1857)

170:13   *farther* emended to *further* following Thoreau's predominant usage

171:6   *&c.* expanded to *etc.* as emended in MW 1906

171:9   *&c.* expanded to *etc.* as emended in MW 1906

171:29   *side-hill* emended to *side hill* as in Thoreau's journal (MJ 25 July 1857)

171:36–172:1 *N. S. E. W.* emended to *north, south, east, west* as emended in MW 1906

172:12   *now* emended to *'Now* as emended in MW 1906

172:13   *straight.* emended to *straight.'* as emended in MW 1906

172:14   *I* emended to *'I* as emended in MW 1906

172:14	*that,* emended to *that.* as in Thoreau's journal (MJ 25 July 1857)
172:14	*am. Where* emended to *am.' 'Where* as implied in Thoreau's journal: "I don't know where I am— Where you think camp—" (MJ 25 July 1957)
172:15	*camp?* emended to *camp?'* as emended in MW 1906
172:18	*O* emended to *Oh* as in the non-capitalized form in journal (MJ 25 July 1857) and as emended in MW 1906
172:31	*exactly* emended to *exactly,* as in Thoreau's journal (MJ 25 July 1857) and as emended in MW 1906
173:17	*northeast carry* emended to *Northeast Carry* following its use as a place name at 170:10
173:23	*course* emended to *curve* as in Thoreau's journal (MJ 25 July 1857)
174:10	*&c.* expanded to *etc.* as emended in MW 1906
174:18	*crossbar* emended to *cross-bar* as emended in MW 1906
174:31	*crossbars* emended to *cross-bars* as emended in MW 1906
175:2	*crossbar* emended to *cross-bar* as emended in MW 1906
175:9	*empty handed* (dropped end-of-line hyphenation) emended to *empty-handed*
176:3	*he* emended to *we* as in Thoreau's journal (MJ 25 July 1857) and as emended in MW 1906

177:16	*&c.* expanded to *etc.* as emended in MW 1906
177:27	*hem lock* without end-of-line hyphenation emended to *hemlock* as emended in MW 1906
177:note 73	*Rasle's* emended to *Rasles'*
179:34	*Wilson did not know where they bred, and says, "Their only note is a kind of chip."* following *that State.* deleted as in MW 1906. The reference is to Alexander Wilson's (1766-1813) *American Ornithology.*
180:28	*farther* emended to *further* following Thoreau's predominant usage
181:21–22	*Beska bekukskishtuk* emended to *Beskabekukskishtuk* as in Thoreau's journal (MJ 26 July 1857) and as emended in MW 1906
181:36	*Pay tay te quick* emended to *Pay-taytequick* as in "Appendix" and as emended in MW 1906
182:4	*beaked* emended to *headed* as in Thoreau's journal (MJ 26 July 1857) and as emended in MW 1906
182:12	*beateau* emended to *batteau* as in Thoreau's journal (MJ 26 July 1857) and as emended in MW 1906
183:19	*&c., &c.* expanded to *etc., etc.* as emended in MW 1906
184:34	*farther* emended to *further* as in Thoreau's journal (MJ 26 July 1857)
185:14–20	*[The figure of a bear in a boat.]* emended to Thoreau's rendition of Polis's gazette as in Thoreau's journal (MJ 26 July 1857)

185:24   *Niasoseb* emended to noncapitalized initial letter and final period deleted as in Thoreau's journal (MJ 26 July 1857) and as emended in MW 1906

185:25   final period deleted as in Thoreau's journal (MJ 26 July 1857) and as emended in MW 1906

185:27   *clioi* emended to *elioli* as in Thoreau's journal (MJ 26 July 1857) and as emended in MW 1906

185:30–32   *ouke ni*
right away.
quambi
emended to
onke ni
right away.
quanibi
ouke emended to *onke* as in Thoreau's journal (MJ 26 July 1857) and as emended in MW 1906; *quambi* emended to the italicized form as emended in MW 1906 and emended to *quanibi* as in Thoreau's journal (MJ 26 July 1857) and following more closely the spelling in Rasles's *Dictionary of the Abnaki Language.* The split *ni quanibi* has been retained following Thoreau's indication that this was a literal transcription of Polis's inscription

185:36   *niasoseb* emended to noncapitalized initial letter and final period deleted as in Thoreau's journal (MJ 26 July 1857) and as emended in MW 1906

186:34   *farther* emended to *further* following Thoreau's predominant usage

187:9   *blankets* emended to *blanket* as in journal—"his gun & ammunition & a blanket" (MJ 28 July 1857)—and as indicated in "Appendix" that "one blanket" is under "Outfit for an Excursion."

187:29   *farther* emended to *further* following Thoreau's predominant usage

187:33–34   *Caucomgomoctook* emended to *Caucomgomoc-took* as in Thoreau's journal (MJ 26 July 1857) and found in the following sentence and in "Appendix"

187:35   *!* emended to *;* as emended in MW 1906

188:31   *kingfisher (tweezer bird),* emended to *kingfisher, tweezer-bird* as emended in MW 1906

191:19   *&c.* expanded to *etc.* as emended in MW 1906

193:20   *Pepe* emended to noncapitalized and nonitalicized form as emended in MW 1906 and to the hyphenated form found in Thoreau's journal (MJ 27 July 1857)

196:3   *beateau* emended to *batteau* as in Thoreau's journal (MJ 30 July 1857 and 5 October 1857) and as emended in MW 1906

196:13   *polled* emended to *poled* as in Thoreau's journal (MJ 27 July 1857) and as emended in MW 1906

196:13   *point* emended to *part* as in Thoreau's journal (MJ 27 July 1857) and as emended in MW 1906

196:28   *bend* emended to *head* as in

	Thoreau's journal (MJ 27 July 1857) and as emended in MW 1906
197:2	*Johns* emended to *John* as emended in MW 1906
198:15	*&c.* expanded to *etc.* as emended in MW 1906
198:16	*farther* emended to *further* as in Thoreau's journal (MJ 27 July 1857)
199:14	*farther* emended to *further* following Thoreau's predominant usage
199:29	*black-flies* emended to *black flies* following Thoreau's predominant usage
201:34	*Low Birch* emended to noncapitalized form as emended in MW 1906 and as found in "Appendix"
204:25	*"swamping it"* emended to *"swamping" it* as emended in MW 1906
206:23	*Tebos* emended to *Telos* as in Thoreau's journal (MJ 27 July 1857) and as emended in MW 1894
207:26	*rusty colored* emended to *rusty-colored* as emended in MW 1906
210:8–9	*Nerlumskeechticook* emended to italicized form as found in "The Allegash and East Branch"
210:33	*&c.* expanded to *etc.* as emended in MW 1906
211:9	*Apmoojenegamook* emended to italicized form as in MW 1906
211:15	*farther* emended to *further* as in Thoreau's journal (MJ 28 July 1857)
212:14	*farther* emended to *further* as in Thoreau's journal (MJ 28 July 1857)
212:29–32	Sophia Thoreau indicated in Houghton Library (Harvard University) MS Am 278.5 that the sentence *When the State . . . university.* was to be inserted at this point. Although the insertion here was possibly an error, interrupting the continuity of the two paragraphs, there is no unequivocal authorial indication that would allow for its removal or placement elsewhere and so has been allowed to stand
213:26	*say, it* emended to *say—It* as in Huntington manuscript HM13199
216:12	*farther* emended to *further* as in Thoreau's journal (MJ 28 July 1857)
217:4	*farther* emended to *further* as in Thoreau's journal (MJ 28 July 1857)
218:10	*mean while* emended to *meanwhile* as in MW 1906
218:25	*abundant.* emended to *abundant*
218:26	*minatus* emended to *sinuatus* as emended in MW 1906
218:27	*margaratacea* emended to *margaritacea* as in Thoreau's journal (MJ 28 July 1857) and as found in "Appendix"
218:28	*&c.* expanded to *etc.* as emended in MW 1906
218:30	*farthest* emended to *furthest* following Thoreau's predominant usage
219:15	*Nickatou* emended to *Nickatow* as in "Ktaadn" and in "Appendix"
219:31	*of the* emended to *at* as in Thoreau's journal (MJ 6 October 1857)
219:31	*Nickatou* emended to *Nickatow* as in "Ktaadn" and in "Appendix"
219:32	*nia soseb* emended to *niasoseb* as at

185:24 and 185:36 and as emended in MW 1906

221:27   *we ran* emended to *we* following the emendation of Moldenhauer in MW 1972 (238) based upon the supposition that *ran* may be the result of an "imperfect or forgotten cancellation" and as indicated by context of the journal—"compelled us to get under the edge of the dam" (MJ 28 July 1857)

222:8   *raised* emended to *raised were* as in Thoreau's journal (MJ 30 October 1857)

224:35   *S.S.E.* expanded to *south-southeast*

225:8   *she-cor-ways* emended to *shecorways* as in Thoreau's journal (MJ 28 July 1857), as emended in MW 1906, and as found in "Appendix"

226:1   *Paytaywecomgomoc* emended to *Paytaywecongomoc* as in Thoreau's journal (MJ 29 July 1857) and as found in "Appendix"

226:27–28   *on a deserted log* emended to *in a deserted log hut* following the emendation of Moldenhauer in MW 1972 (243) based on the context as indicated in manuscript drafts and Thoreau's journal (MJ 7 and 31 October 1857)

226:31   *farther* emended to *further* following Thoreau's predominant usage

226:35   *farther* emended to *further* following Thoreau's predominant usage

229:29   *1854* emended to *1853* as in reference to Thoreau's journal entry of 26 October 1853: "A hand told me that they drew only fourteen inches of water and could run easily in two feet of water, though they did not like to" [J 5:457].

230:21   *Madunkchunk* emended to *Madunkehunk* as in Thoreau's journal (MJ 29 July 1857) and as found in "Appendix"

230:22   *Madunkchunk* emended to *Madunkehunk* as in Thoreau's journal (MJ 29 July 1857) and as found in "Appendix"

231:1   *sim ple* (dropped end-of-line hyphenation) emended to *simple* as emended in MW 1906

232:1   *bateau* emended to *batteau* as emended in MW 1906

234:1   *paths* emended to *path* as in Thoreau's journal (MJ 29 July 1857) and as emended in MW 1906

237:28   *farther* emended to *further* as in Thoreau's journal (MJ 29 July 1857)

240:28   *trees, without rocks,* emended to *trees (not of rocks)* as in Thoreau's journal (MJ 29 July 1857)

241:5   *farther* emended to *further* as in Thoreau's journal (MJ 29 July 1857)

241:7–8   *farther* emended to *further* as in Thoreau's journal (MJ 29 July 1857)

242:22   *blankets* emended to *blanket* as in Thoreau's journal (MJ 29 July 1857) and as indicated in "Appendix" that "one blanket" is listed under "Outfit for an Excursion"

243:26	*farther* emended to *further* as in Thoreau's journal (MJ 30 July 1857)
243:31	*farther* emended to *further* as in Thoreau's journal (MJ 30 July 1857)
246:1	*ripple* emended to *ripples* as in Houghton MS Am 278.5
246:4	*were seen* inserted as in Houghton MS Am 278.5
246:10	*loon* emended to *loons* as in Houghton MS Am 278.5
246:23	*crushing* emended to *crashing* as in Thoreau's journal (MJ 6 October 1857)
247:30	*up-side* emended to *upside* as emended in MW 1906
248:8	*scarred* emended to *scored* as in Houghton MS Am 278.5
248:30	*&c.* emended to *etc.* as in MW 1906
248:31	*&c.* emended to *etc.* as in MW 1906
250:10	*P.* emended to *Pinus* as found in Thoreau's usage for *Pinus resinosa* and *Pinus Banksiana* in this essay
250:14	*&c.* emended to *etc.* as in MW 1906
250:15–19	*thirty-five feet high.* emended to *thirty-five feet high, which is 2 or 3 times the height commonly assigned them. Michaux says that it grows further north than any of our pines, but he did not find it any where more than 10 feet high.* as in Houghton MS Am 278.5 and as indicated in Thoreau's journal (MJ 30 July 1857). The numerals have been emended to the respective words
251:2	*&c.* emended to *etc.* as in MW 1906
251:10–11	*Madunkchunk* emended to *Ma-*
	dunkehunk as in Thoreau's journal (MJ 30 July 1857) and as found in "Appendix"
251:19	*forks* emended to *falls* as in Thoreau's journal (MJ 30 July 1857)
251:22	*more arable* emended to *memorable* as in Thoreau's journal (MJ 30 July 1857)
251:36	*ridge* emended to *ridges* as in Houghton MS Am 278.5
256:8	*farther* emended to *further* following Thoreau's predominant usage
256:29–30	*farther* emended to *further* following Thoreau's predominant usage
257:6	the text following *anointed fingers.* in MW 1864, *On the mainland . . . falling asleep.*, moved to its correct placement at 266:32–269:3 as in the 1899 corrected impression
258:21	*a berrying* emended to *a-berrying* as emended in MW 1906
259:10	*lodges* emended to *ledges* as in Thoreau's journal (MJ 31 July 1857) and as emended in MW 1906
261:5	*&c.* expanded to *etc.* as emended in MW 1906
261:20	*farther* emended to *further* following Thoreau's predominant usage
261:26	*mean while* emended to *meanwhile* as in MW 1906
263:3	paragraph break inserted as in Huntington manuscript HM13199
266:7	*&c., &c.,* expanded to *etc., etc.,* as emended in MW 1906
266:15	*&c.* expanded to *etc.* as emended in MW 1906

266:26   *Rocks (locks)* emended to *Locks (rocks)* to follow Thoreau's representations of Polis's vocalizations at 171:32–33: "Sometimes I lookum locks (rocks)" and at 250:30–31: "That very strange lock (rock)."

266:31   *west* emended to *east* as in Thoreau's journal (MJ 1 August 1857)

266:32–269:3   *On the mainland . . . before falling asleep.* at 257:6 moved to its correct placement here as in the 1899 corrected impression and all subsequent editions

267:12   *Nickertow* emended to *Nickatow* as in "Ktaadn" and in "Appendix"

267:29   *Nickertow* emended to *Nickatow* as in "Ktaadn" and in "Appendix"

269:9–10   SUNDAY, *August 2, —*
Was a cloudy
emended to
      SUNDAY, *August 2,*
was following Thoreau's intention as indicated in Thoreau's journal (MJ 2 August 1857), where *was* was inserted to form a sentence connecting the date and the description

269:27   *"we-e-ll-* emended to *"we-e-ll,* as indicated in Thoreau's journal (MJ 2 August 1857) with the final hyphen emended to a comma as emended in MW 1906

269:27   *&c.* expanded to *etc.* as emended in MW 1906

269:34   *Nickertow* emended to *Nickatow* as in "Ktaadn" and in "Appendix"

270:13   *farther* emended to *further* as in Thoreau's journal (MJ 2 August 1857)

270:17   *farther* emended to *further* as in Thoreau's journal (MJ 2 August 1857)

271:16   *&c.* expanded to *etc.* as emended in MW 1906

271:31   *Islands* emended to *islands* as in Thoreau's journal (MJ 3 August 1857) and as in Thoreau's usage in "Ktaadn"

271:32   *in* emended to *on* as in Thoreau's journal (MJ 3 August 1857), the preposition referring to the islands, not the houses

272:10–11   *Matanancook* emended to *Matanawcook* as in Thoreau's journal (MJ 3 August 1857)

272:33   *beateaux* emended to *batteaux* as emended in MW 1906

274:31   *Olarmon* emended to *Olamon* as in Thoreau's journal (MJ 3 August 1857) and as emended in MW 1894

275:5   *we* emended to *me* in Thoreau's journal (MJ 3 August 1857)

275:27–28   *and lifting my paddle at each stroke,* emended to *and, lifting my paddle at each stroke, give it a twist in order to steer, the boat only* as in Thoreau's journal (MJ 3 August 1857) and as emended in MW 1906, although the punctuation as implied by dashes in the journal—"twist in order to steer—the boat only"—has been retained in this emendation

275:33	*crossbar* emended to *cross-bar* as emended in MW 1906
276:2	*accord ing* (dropped end-of-line hyphenation) emended to *according*
276:26	*or the boat* emended to *on the bank* as in Houghton MS Am 278.5

Appendix

279:19	*&c.* emended to *etc.* as in MW 1906
280:31	*1858* emended to *1857* as the only year in which Thoreau was in Maine in July
281:17	*apparently, lake* emended to *especially lake* following Thoreau's journal: "Eupat. purpuream esp. Lake Shores" (MJ 4 October 1857)
281:29	*&c.* expanded to *etc.* as emended in MW 1906
282:4	*herds* emended to *herd's* as emended in MW 1906
282:23	; emended to , following Thoreau's punctuation throughout these lists
282:28–29	*bush-honeysuckle* emended to *bush honeysuckle* following form later in "Appendix" and as emended in MW 1906
283:19	*1853* emended to *1853 and 1857* as indicated in Thoreau's journal (MJ 8 October 1857)
283:21	*1853-7* emended to *1853 and 1857* as emended in MW 1906
284:10	*&c.* expanded to *etc.* as emended in MW 1906
284:28	asterisk added indicating plants "not in woods" following another

	plant from the same location: "*Spiraea tomentosa** (hardhack), Bangor"
286:1	*verticillata* emended to *verticillatus* as emended in MW 1906
286:1	*alder, '57)* emended to *alder), 1857* as emended in MW 1906
286:5	*&c.* expanded to *etc.* as emended in MW 1906
286:12	*on* emended to *as* as in Thoreau's journal (MJ 7 October 1857)
287:9	*&c.* expanded to *etc.* as emended in MW 1906
287:12	*Cham berlain* (dropped end-of-line hyphenation) emended to *Chamberlain* as emended in MW 1906
287:14	*&c.* expanded to *etc.* as emended in MW 1906
287:27	*lake* emended to *Lake* as emended in MW 1906
288:17	*South* emended to *East* to correctly identify Thoreau's location on 31 July 1857
288:34	*longifolius like* emended to *longifolius-like* as emended in MW 1906
289:3	*&c.* expanded to *etc.* as emended in MW 1906
289:7	*Smith's dam* emended to *Smith's,* as in Thoreau's journal (MJ 7 October 1857)
289:13	*&c.* expanded to *etc.* as emended in MW 1906
289:31	*&c.* expanded to *etc.* as emended in MW 1906

290:12   *large seeded* emended to *large-seeded* as in MW 1906

290:20   asterisk added indicating plants "not in woods" following another plant from the same location: "*Utricularia vulgaris** (greater bladderwort), Pushaw"

291:13   *&c.* expanded to *etc.* as emended in MW 1906

291:34   *cernuus* emended to *cernua* as in Thoreau's journal (MJ 7 October 1857) and as emended in MW 1906

292:2   *&c.* expanded to *etc.* as emended in MW 1906

292:20   *&c.* expanded to *etc.* as emended in MW 1906

292:30   *&c.* expanded to *etc.* as emended in MW 1906

292:31   *monocea* emended to *monoica* as in Thoreau's journal (MJ 7 October 1857) and as emended in MW 1906

292:33   *&c.* expanded to *etc.* as emended in MW 1906

293:21   *&c.* expanded to *etc.* as in MW 1906

295:33   *Schoonis* emended to *Seboois* from the indication in "The Allegash and East Branch" that Thoreau saw "a great cat-owl launched itself away from a stump on the bank" before they "passed the mouth of the Seboois"

296:9   *Cooperii* emended to *Cooperi* following Thoreau's spelling in "The Allegash and East Branch" and as

found in Wilson's *American Ornithology*

297:5   *&c.* expanded to *etc.* as emended in MW 1906

297:15   *albicola* emended to *albeola* as emended in MW 1906 and as found in Wilson's *American Ornithology*

297:17–20   *all the lakes. A swallow; the night-warbler? once or twice.*

Mergus Merganser (buff-breasted merganser or sheldrake), common on lakes and rivers.

emended to

all the lakes.

Mergus Merganser (buff-breasted merganser or sheldrake), common on lakes and rivers.

A swallow; the night-warbler (?) once or twice.

as emended in MW 1906

298:11   *Tent, —six* emended to *Tent, six* following the emendation of Joseph J. Moldenhauer in MW 1972 (319) and his explanation that "'*Tent, — six*' implies a parallelism with the categorical paragraph beginnings, '*Wear, —*' and '*Carry, —*'" (MW 1972:476)

298:26   *hardbread* emended to *hard bread* as found in "Ktaadn," "Chesuncook," and "The Allegash and East Branch"

298:32   *&c.* expanded to *etc.* as emended in MW 1906

298:35   *&c.* expanded to *etc.* as emended in MW 1906

299:19   *Katadn* emended to *Ktaadn* as emended in MW 1906

299:19   *Land,* emended to *Land.*

299:19   *Rale* emended to *Rasles* as Thoreau's usual spelling and as emended in MW 1906

299:20   *Mt.* expanded and emended to nonitalicized form *mountain* following Thoreau's source, Rasles's *Dictionary of the Abnaki Language:* "MONTAGNE, *pemadené*"

299:20   *Pemadene* emended to *Pemadené* as in Thoreau's source, Rasles's *Dictionary of the Abnaki Language*

299:20–21   *aiguiser, Kitadaügen* emended to *éguiser, Kidadañgan* as in Thoreau's source, Rasles's *Dictionary of the Abnaki Language*

299:32   *bear,* emended to *bear.*

299:32   *aouessous* emended to *Asess8s* as in Thoreau's source, Rasles's *Dictionary of the Abnaki Language;* capitalized as initial word

299:32   *Rale* emended to *Rasles* as Thoreau's usual spelling and as emended in MW 1906

299:35   *eater?)* emended to *eater?).*

299:36   *mous* emended to *M8s* as in Thoreau's source, Rasles's *Dictionary of the Abnaki Language;* capitalized as initial word

299:36   *Rale* emended to *Rasles* as Thoreau's usual spelling and as emended in MW 1906

300:3   *Ibibimin* emended to *Ibimin* as in Thoreau's source Rasles's *Dictionary of the Abnaki Language*

300:4   *Rale* emended to *Rasles* as Thoreau's usual spelling and as emended in MW 1906

300:5   *writing,* emended to *writing.*

300:5   *aouixigan* emended to *Asiχigan* as in Thoreau's source, Rasles's *Dictionary of the Abnaki Language;* capitalized as initial word

300:5   *Ind'n* expanded to full form, *Indian*

300:6   *ceinture* emended to *écriture* as in Thoreau's source, Rasles's *Dictionary of the Abnaki Language*

300:6   *Rale* emended to *Rasles* as Thoreau's usual spelling and as emended in MW 1906

300:7   *Lake,* emended to *Lake.*

300:7   *Peqouasebem* emended to *Peg8asebem* as in Thoreau's source, Rasles's *Dictionary of the Abnaki Language*

300:8   *Rale* emended to *Rasles* as Thoreau's usual spelling and as emended in MW 1906

300:9   *Ouaürinaügamek* emended to *8añrinañgamek* as in Thoreau's source, Rasles's *Dictionary of the Abnaki Language*

300:9   *Rale* emended to *Rasles* as Thoreau's usual spelling and as emended in MW 1906

300:12   *&c.* expanded to *etc.* as emended in MW 1906

300:15   *caucomgomoc-took* emended to capitalized form *Caucomgomoc-took* as a place name

300:18   *Puapeskou* emended to *Pnapesk8* as in Thoreau's source, Rasles's *Dictionary of the Abnaki Language*

300:18   *Ind'n* expanded to full form, *Indian*

300:19   *(Rale v.* emended to *Rasles.) (v.* following the form of similar entries in this list; *Rale* emended to *Rasles* as Thoreau's usual spelling and as emended in MW 1906

300:27   *Muskiticook* emended to *Musketicook* as in "The Allegash and East Branch"

300:28   *Meskikou, or Meskikouikou* emended to *Meski'k8, or Meskik8i'k8* as in Thoreau's source, Rasles's *Dictionary of the Abnaki Language*

300:29   *Rale* emended to *Rasles* as Thoreau's usual spelling and as emended in MW 1906

301:3   *Bematruichtik* emended to *Bematinichtik* as in Thoreau's journal (MJ 24 July 1857)

301:4   *Mt.* expanded and emended to nonitalicized form *mountain* following Thoreau's source, Rasles's *Dictionary of the Abnaki Language:* "MONTAGNE, *pemadené*"

301:4   *Rale* emended to *Rasles* as Thoreau's usual spelling and as emended in MW 1906

301:7–8   *(Williamson; old Indian hunter).(Hodge.)* emended to *(Williamson); (old Indian hunter, Hodge.)* to properly reflect Thoreau's sources

301:13   *Beskabekuk shishtook* emended to *Beskabekukshishtook* following the one-word form as in "The Allegash and East Branch"

301:17   *Nonlangyis* emended to *Nonglangyis* as in "The Allegash and East Branch"

301:20   *Mkazéouighen* emended to *Mkazésighen* as in Thoreau's source, Rasles's *Dictionary of the Abnaki Language*

301:20   *Rale* emended to *Rasles* as Thoreau's usual spelling and as emended in MW 1906

301:23   *(?)* emended to *(?),* as in Thoreau's source, Rasles's *Dictionary of the Abnaki Language*

301:23   *Rale* emended to *Rasles* as Thoreau's usual spelling and as emended in MW 1906

301:28   *Pagadanumlkoueouérré* emended to *Pagadañk8ésé'rré* as in Thoreau's source, Rasles's *Dictionary of the Abnaki Language*

301:28   *Rale* emended to *Rasles* as Thoreau's usual spelling and as emended in MW 1906

301:29   *Bororquasis* emended to *Bososquasis* as in "The Allegash and East Branch"

301:30   *Nerlumskeechtcook* emended to *Nerlumskeechticook* as in "The Allegash and East Branch"

301:33   *Apmoojeuegamook* emended to *Apmoojenegamook* as in "The Allegash and East Branch"

302:9   *berries,* emended to *berries.* following the form of similar entries in this list

302:10   *Pemouaimin* emended to *Pemŝaïmin* as in Thoreau's source, Rasles's *Dictionary of the Abnaki Language*

302:11   *fruit. Rale."* emended to *fruit."* *Rasles. Rale* emended to *Rasles* as Thoreau's usual spelling and as emended in MW 1906

302:14   *Rale* emended to *Rasles* as Thoreau's usual spelling and as emended in MW 1906

302:20   *Paüsidaükioui* emended to *Pañsidañkisi* as in Thoreau's source, Rasles's *Dictionary of the Abnaki Language*

302:21   *Rale* emended to *Rasles* as Thoreau's usual spelling and as emended in MW 1906

302:23   *Ourámaü* emended to *ŝrámañ* as in Thoreau's source, Rasles's *Dictionary of the Abnaki Language*

302:23   *Rale* emended to *Rasles* as Thoreau's usual spelling and as emended in MW 1906

302:24   *ho, see* emended to *no see* as in MW 1906

302:24   *Rale* emended to *Rasles* as Thoreau's usual spelling and as emended in MW 1906

302:25   *Saüghedétegoué* emended to *Sañghedé'tegŝé* as in Thoreau's source, Rasles's *Dictionary of the Abnaki Language*

302:26   *saüktaüoui* emended to *sañktâiïsi* as in Thoreau's source, Rasles's *Dictionary of the Abnaki Language*

302:27   *Br.* expanded to *Brook*

302:27–28   *Hatchet* emended to nonitalicized form following the form of similar entries in this list, and *temahigan* emended to *temahígan* as in Thoreau's source, Rasles's *Dictionary of the Abnaki Language*

302:28   *Rale* emended to *Rasles* as Thoreau's usual spelling and as emended in MW 1906

302:29   *Nicketaoutegué, or Niketoutegoue* emended to *Niketaŝtegŝé, or Niketstegŝé* as in Thoreau's source, Rasles's *Dictionary of the Abnaki Language*

302:30   *Rale* emended to *Rasles* as Thoreau's usual spelling and as emended in MW 1906

303:7   *Allagash (a bark camp)* emended to *Allagash, a bark camp* as in Thoreau's source, William Willis's "Language of the Abnaquies, or Eastern Indians"

303:10   *, head of Allegash,* emended to *(head of Allegash),* as in Thoreau's source, Willis's "Language of the Abnaquies"

303:16   *pronounces* emended to *pronounced* as in Thoreau's source, Willis's "Language of the Abnaquies"

303:18   *(the place of Eels)* emended to *, the place of Eels* as in Thoreau's source,

Willis's "Language of the Abnaquies"

303:19   *(flint)* emended to *, flint* as in Thoreau's source, Willis's "Language of the Abnaquies"

303:19–20   *border, &c,* expanded to *border of Moosehead Lake.* as in Thoreau's source, Willis's "Language of the Abnaquies"

303:28   *Nicketow* emended to *Nickatow* as in "Ktaadn" and as found in "Appendix"

303:28   *Neccotoh* emended to italicized form as in Thoreau's source, Willis's "Language of the Abnaquies"

303:34   *Pentagoet, &c.* expanded to *Pentagoet or Pentagovett.* as in Thoreau's source, Willis's "Language of the Abnaquies"

303:35   *Pougohwaken* emended to *Pougohwakem* as in Thoreau's source, Willis's "Language of the Abnaquies"

304:3   *Ripogenus* emended to *Ripogenas* as in Thoreau's source, Willis's "Language of the Abnaquies"

304:7–8   *lake," &c.* expanded to *lake which now bears the English name."* as in Thoreau's source, Willis's "Language of the Abnaquies"

304:11   *Sebago (great water).* emended to *Sebago, great water.* as in Thoreau's source, Willis's "Language of the Abnaquies"

304:13   *Telasiuis* emended to *Telasinis* as

in Thoreau's source, Willis's "Language of the Abnaquies"

304:16   *Umbazookskus* emended to *Umbazookscus* as in Thoreau's source, Willis's "Language of the Abnaquies"

304:20   *Schunk* emended to *Sehunk* as in Thoreau's source, Willis's "Language of the Abnaquies"

304:22   *Schunk* emended to *Sehunk* as in Thoreau's source, Willis's "Language of the Abnaquies"

304:27   *Schunk-auke* emended to *Sehunk-auke* as in Thoreau's source, Willis's "Language of the Abnaquies"

Supplement

305:30–31   *have been* inserted

306:11   *single* emended to *shingle* as in Thoreau's journal (MJ 22 September 1853)

End-of-Line Hyphenation

The two lists below record end-of-line hyphenations. The following list shows the form adopted in the current text for compound or possible compound words that were hyphenated at the end of a line in the respective copy texts.

KTAADN

3:20–21   becalmed
5:2   pow-wows
6:31   wigwams

7:3	island-side	65:18	three quarters
8:2	to-morrow	68:19	reshingling
8:26	fir-balsam	69:20	playthings
9:33	arrow-heads	72:27	woodpecker
10:30	hay-scales		
14:28	picture-books		
17:24	yellow-birch		
18:5	overlook		CHESUNCOOK
19:6	backwoods		
20:24	long-handled	76:27	village-like
22:2	everywhere	76:35	sea-sickness
23:20	buck-beans	80:33	outdoor
27:25	boatmen	81:20	lowlands
28:33	highway	83:14	lumberman
29:1	sled-track	83:24	well-appointed
29:2	evergreen	83:25	life-seats
30:26	puffballs	85:17	however
33:16	unearthly	86:18	large-flowered
33:20	big-throated	86:24	trumpet-weed
36:24	thoroughfare	86:24	arbor-vitae
37:3–4	thoroughfare	89:8	large-toothed
39:9	canoe-birch	89:20	lily-stems
41:7	dead-water	90:7	*nipsquecohossus*
44:12	overshoot	90:7	*skuscumonsuck*
45:31	poke-logs-in	90:9–10	Moose-tracks
46:20	notwithstanding	90:12	crowfoot
49:12	arbor-vitae	90:32	wool-grass
51:14	full-grown	91:25	fir-twigs
53:35	daylight	94:2	*oo-o-o-o-o-o-o-o*
54:5	spruce-trees	95:16–17	horned-owl
54:25	spruce-trees	95:31	something
55:20	side-hill	97:10	under-shrub
56:31	rocking-stones	97:31	hobble-bush
57:19	cloud-works	99:17	without
59:23	cranberries	100:1–2	arbor-vitaes
61:15	green-jacketed	100:25	pine-boards
		100:32	somewhat
		101:30	whereupon

101:36	half-inquisitive		164:29	harebells
103:3	*moose*-men		165:5	twayblade
103:3	footsteps		169:36	myself
103:25	blood-stain		171:11	overtaken
104:10	*macrophyllus*		173:18	southwesterly
105:21	cross-stake		175:16	spruce-bark
109:1	thereabouts		176:23	camping-place
109:1	standstill		178:3	birch-bark
111:19–20	afternoon		178:25–26	thunder-shower
112:11	everything		181:16	rememberum
112:24	township		182:17	canoe-birch
115:27	white-lead		182:36	water-fowl
117:23	black-ash		184:1–2	northwest
121:17	frying-pan		184:2–3	south-southwest
121:31	pigeon-woodpecker		189:10–11	birch-bark
121:32	white-pine		193:17–18	water-lily
121:36	fish-hawk		193:25	night-hawks
124:7	headboard		199:29	black flies
128:33	last-mentioned		200:19	northeasterly
130:3	Large-Bay		201:11	"highlands"
136:1	therefore		209:29–30	outlook
137:7	forefoot		203:32	cedar-top
140:32	white-pines		204:30–31	road-makers
142:23	meeting-house		210:8	east-southeast
143:2	pear-trees		211:15	northwest
144:16	woodman's		214:10	spelling-book
			214:32–33	southwest
			216:19–20	carrying-places
THE ALLEGASH AND EAST BRANCH			219:12–13	snow-shoes
			219:20	guide-board
151:14	anything		224:8–9	meadow-mouse
154:21	southwest		224:17–18	shed-shaped
156:34–35	bluebirds		224:18–19	Yankee-baker
158:5	somebody		226:28–29	Yankee-baker
160:23	Whereupon		232:17	lumbermen
162:2	headway		232:33–34	northeasterly
163:3	overcast			

237:8	golden-rod
239:7–8	rock-waves
241:18	near-sighted
244:28	overtook
246:32	fourpence
247:15	rose-colored
249:26–27	southwest
251:6	himself
257:10	rock-maple
257:13	breakfast
257:18	erelong
258:6	forenoon
265:11–12	moose-tracks
268:1	tent-poles
269:11–12	moose-hide
269:20	long-winded
269:25	story-teller's
269:30–31	Frenchman
270:20–21	thunder-shower
273:8–9	southeast
274:17–18	Greenbush

APPENDIX

278:14	arbor-vitae
280:12	mountain-maples
280:23	checkerberry
281:6	meadow-sweet
281:9	purple-fringed
282:5–6	white-weed
282:20	hobble-bush
283:17	lady's-thumb
283:18	sheep-sorrel
286:16	river-sides
286:16	roadsides
294:11	highway

294:33	wood-path
297:17	muskrat
298:17	tape-measure
298:21	waistcoat
298:36	India-rubber

The following list shows words hyphenated at the end of a line in this edition that should be considered intentionally hyphenated compounds. All other words that are hyphenated at the end of a line in this edition but do not appear on this list should be considered as a single word.

1:33–34	no-see-ems
4:2–3	white-pine
4:16–17	washerwoman-looking
8:25–26	arbor-vitae
8:28–29	grass-plots
16:22–23	arbor-vitae
19:17–18	life-everlasting
19:23–24	tea-kettle
20:24–25	axe-helves
23:6–7	tea-kettle
26:32–33	thunder-shower
30:32–33	twenty-nine
38:8–9	boom-head
44:33–34	hand-bill
48:34–35	cedar-twigs
49:12–13	arbor-vitae
53:29–30	camping-ground
67:27–28	back-water
71:18–19	moose-meat
72:23–24	moss-grown
74:15–16	No-man's
83:21–22	life-boat
84:12–13	twenty-one

84:36–85:1	round-topped	176:21–22	thunder-shower
87:23–24	fir-twigs	178:25–26	thunder-shower
90:9–10	Moose-tracks	184:2–3	south-southeast
91:17–18	moose-hunting	187:33–34	*Caucomgomoc-took*
94:31–32	arbor-vitae	189:10–11	birch-bark
95:16–17	horned-owl	190:34–35	hard-pitch
95:26–27	fungus-like	193:18–19	water-lily
96:29–30	half-extinguished	200:2–3	meat-bird
97:26–27	berry-bearing	204:30–31	road-makers
98:31–32	wood-lots	209:26–27	low-flying
100:1–2	arbor-vitaes	209:33–34	*ah-tette-tette-te*
100:26–27	arrow-points	213:14–15	brazen-tipped
101:2–3	spear-head	215:12–13	hard-wood
101:36–102:1	half-frightened	216:19–20	carrying-places
105:1–2	two-foot	218:1–2	log-huts
111:10–11	camping-ground	219:12–13	snow-shoes
113:12–13	Pine-Stream	224:8–9	meadow-mouse
115:7–8	weather-boards	224:17–18	shed-shaped
123:35–36	patched-up	224:18–19	Yankee-baker
124:34–35	moose-hide	226:28–29	Yankee-baker
124:36–125:1	twenty-two	227:20–21	fire-engine
132:2–3	moose-hides	230:13–14	pork-keg
133:19–20	manly-looking	237:9–10	white-pine
135:29–30	grave-yard	238:25–26	rock-hills
137:23–24	son-in-law	239:7–8	rock-waves
138:19–20	Four-pence-ha'penny	248:15–16	moose-flies
139:10–11	hard-wood	250:6–7	moose-hide
139:11–12	but-end	250:11–12	spruce-like
142:3–4	pine-forest	255:36–256:1	wood-thrush
154:27–28	wrong-side-up	256:30–31	semi-human
157:34–35	Dead-water	261:10–11	cat-owl
162:19–20	clearing-up	261:29–30	camping-place
163:36–164:1	arrow-heads	265:11–12	moose-tracks
167:19–20	sap-wood	265:34–35	river-side
168:4–5	long-continued	267:2–3	cow-bell
171:8–9	moose-meat	268:36–269:1	moose-hide

269:11–12	moose-hide	283:3–4	shad-bush
270:20–21	thunder-shower	283:29–30	logging-path
273:33–34	liberty-pole	288:32–33	narrow-leaved
274:29–30	hemp-nettle	291:26–27	John's-wort
281:3–4	golden-rod	292:19–20	lake-shores
281:5–6	water-hemlock	296:22–23	oven-bird
281:23–24	arrow-head	298:14–15	plant-book
282:2–3	logging-paths	299:10–11	twenty-five
282:5–6	white-weed		

Bibliography

for I love to quote so good authority . . .— Thoreau, A Week on the Concord and Merrimack Rivers

Aesop. *Aesop's Fables: A New Version, Chiefly from Original Sources and Others,* with design on wood by Thomas Bewick by Thomas Tames. London: John Murray, 1848.

American Society for Promoting the Civilization and General Improvement of the Indian Tribes Within the United States. *First Annual Report.* New Haven: Printed for the Society, 1824.

American State Papers, Indian Affairs. Washington, D.C., 1834.

Andersson, Charles John (Karl Johann). *Lake Ngami; or, Explorations and Discoveries During Four Years Wandering in the Wilds of Southwestern Africa.* New York: Harper and Brothers, 1856.

Angelo, Ray. *Botanical Index to the Journal of Henry David Thoreau.* Salt Lake City: Peregrine Smith, 1984.

Annual Report of the Secretary of the Maine Board of Agriculture. Augusta: Stevens and Sayward, 1861.

Arnold, Benedict. "Arnold's Letters on His Expedition to Canada in 1775." *Collections of the Maine Historical Society,* 1st series, 1 (1831).

Audubon, John James. *The Birds of North America, from Drawings Made in the United States and Their Territories.* New York: J. J. Audubon; Philadelphia: J. B. Chevalier, 1840–1844.

Audubon, John James, and John Bachman. *The Viviparous Quadrupeds of North America.* New York: J. J. Audubon, 1845–1848.

Bailey, Jacob Whitman. "Account of an Excursion to Mount Katahdin in Maine." *American Journal of Science and Art,* July 1837.

Bailey, Nathan. *A New Universal Etymological English Dictionary.* London: T. Osborne and J. Snipton, 1755.

Barber, John Warner. *Historical Collections, Being a General Collection of Interesting Facts, Traditions, Biographical Sketches, Anecdotes, &c., Relating to the History and Antiquities of Every Town in Massachusetts, with Geographical Descriptions.* Worcester: Dorr, Howland, 1841.

Barber, John Warner, and Henry Howe. *Our Whole Country; or, The Past and Present of the United States, Historical and Descriptive.* Cincinnati: Henry Howe, 1861.

Bennett, Dean B. *The Wilderness from Chamberlain Farm: A Story of Hope for the American Wild.* Washington, D.C.: Island/Shearwater, 2001.

Bigelow, Jacob. *American Medical Botany.* Boston: Cummings and Hilliard, 1817–1820.

Blount, Thomas. *Glossographia Anglicana Nova; or, Dictionary Interpreting Such Hard Words of Whatever Language as are at Present Used in the English Tongue.* London: Dan. Brown, 1707.

Borst, Raymond. *The Thoreau Log: A Documentary Life of Henry David Thoreau, 1817–1862.* New York: G. K. Hall, 1992.

Botkin, Benjamin Albert, ed. *A Treasury of American Folklore: Stories, Ballads, and Traditions of the People.* New York: Crown, 1944.

Bourque, Bruce J. *Twelve Thousand Years: American Indians in Maine.* Lincoln: University of Nebraska Press, 2004.

Buffon, Georges Louis Leclerc, comte de. *Natural History, General and Particular.* Translated into English, illustrated with above 300 copper-plates, and occasional notes and observations by William Smellie. London: W. Strahan and T. Cadell, 1785.

Cameron, Kenneth Walter. *The Massachusetts Lyceum Dur-*

ing the American Renaissance. Hartford, Conn.: Transcendental Books, 1969.

Campbell, Thomas. *Poetical Works of Thomas Campbell, Including Theodoric, and Many Other Pieces Not Contained in Any Former Edition*. Philadelphia: J. Crissy and J. Grigg, 1826.

Canby, Henry Seidel. *Thoreau*. Boston: Houghton Mifflin, 1939.

Carlyle, Thomas. *Sartor Resartus*. London: J. Fraser, 1834.

Catlan, George. *Letters and Notes on the Manners, Customs, and Conditions of the North American Indians*. Philadelphia: William P. Hazard, 1857.

The Century Dictionary: An Encyclopedic Dictionary of the English Language. New York: Century, 1889–1910.

Channing, Walter. *A Physician's Vacation; or, A Summer in Europe*. Boston: Ticknor and Fields, 1856.

Channing, William Ellery. *Thoreau, the Poet-Naturalist; with Memorial Verses*. New edition, enlarged and edited by F. B. Sanborn. Boston: C. E. Goodspeed, 1902.

Charlevoix, Pierre-François-Xavier de. *Histoire et description générale de la Nouvelle France Collections of the Massachusetts Historical Society for the Year 1794*. Boston: The Society, 1794.

Chevalier, Michel. *Society, Manners, and Politics in the United States, Being a Series of Letters on North America*. Boston: Weeks, Jordan, 1839.

Coffin, George W. "A Plan of the Public Lands in the State of Maine Surveyed Under Instructions from the Commissioners and Agents of the States of Massachusetts and Maine. . . . Copied from the Original Surveys . . . and Corrected by Geo. W. Coffin, Land Agent of the Commonwealth of Massachusetts . . ." Drawn on stone by J. Eddy. Boston: Pendleton's Lithography, 1835.

Collections of the Maine Historical Society. Portland: The Society, 1831.

Collections of the Massachusetts Historical Society. Boston: The Society, 1819.

Collections of the New York Historical Society. New York: The Society, 1857.

Colton, Calvin. *Tour of the American Lakes, and Among the Indians of the North-West Territory in 1830*. London: F. Westley and A. H. Davis, 1833.

Committee on Indian Affairs of the House of Representatives. *American State Papers, Indian Affairs*. Washington, D.C.: 1832–1834.

Concord, Massachusetts: Births, Marriages, and Deaths, 1635–1850. Concord: The Town, 1895.

Cooper, James Fenimore. *The Pioneers*. New York: G. Putnam, 1853.

Cosbey, Robert C. "Thoreau on Katahdin." *Appalachia*, June 1961.

Culbertson, Thaddeus A. "A Journal of an Expedition to the Mauvaises Terres and the Upper Missouri in 1850." *5th Annual Report of the Board of Regents [Smithsonian Institution]*. Washington, D.C.: Smithsonian Institution, 1851.

Dana, Richard Henry, Jr. *Two Years Before the Mast: A Personal Narrative*. Boston: Houghton Mifflin, 1887.

Deane, John G. *John Deane's Journal of the Exploration of the Northeast Boundary*. Maine Historical Society, coll. S-6365, misc. box 192/2.

De Bry, Theodore. *Collectiones Peregrinationum in Indiam Orientalem et Indiam Occidentalem, XXV partibus comprehensae, a Theodoro, Joan: Theodoro de Bry, et a Matheo Merian pulicatae*. Frankfurt: Wecheli, 1590–1634.

De Laski, John Kimball. "Dr. Young's Botanical Expedition," *Bangor Daily Whig and Courier*, 9 September 1847.

Dickens, Charles. "The Noble Savage." *Household Words*, 11 June 1853.

Dietz, Lew. *The Allagash*. New York: Holt, Rinehart and Winston, [1968].

Eastman, Mary. *Dahcotah; or, Life and Legends of the Sioux Around Fort Snelling*. New York: Wiley, 1849.

Eckstorm, Fanny. Unpublished correspondence with Walter Harding, October 1840, Walter Harding Collection, Thoreau Society Collections, Thoreau Institute at Walden Woods.

———. *Old John Neptune and Other Maine Indian Shamans.* Portland, Maine: Southworth-Anthoensen, 1945.

Emerson, Edward. *Early Years of the Saturday Club, 1855–1870.* Boston: Houghton Mifflin, 1918.

Emerson, Ralph Waldo. *The Collected Works of Ralph Waldo Emerson.* Cambridge: Harvard University Press, 1971–.

———. *The Complete Works of Ralph Waldo Emerson.* Centenary edition. Boston: Houghton Mifflin, 1903.

———. *The Journals and Miscellaneous Notebooks of Ralph Waldo Emerson.* Edited by William H. Gilman et al. Cambridge: Harvard University Press, 1960–1982.

———. *The Letters of Ralph Waldo Emerson.* Edited by Ralph L. Rusk and Eleanor Tilton. New York: Columbia University Press, 1939–1995.

———. *The Topical Notebooks of Ralph Waldo Emerson.* Edited by Susan Sutton Smith. Columbia: University of Missouri Press, 1990–1994.

Finley, Anthony. *A New General Atlas, Comprising a Complete Set of Maps, Representing the Grand Division of the Globe, Together with Several Empires, Kingdoms, and States in the World; Compiled from the Best Authorities, and Corrected by the Most Recent Discoveries.* Philadelphia: Anthony Finley, 1824.

First Annual Report of the American Society for Promoting the Civilization and General Improvement of the Indian Tribes Within the United States. New Haven: S. Converse, 1824.

Fleck, Richard. *Henry Thoreau and John Muir Among the Indians.* Hamden, Conn.: Archon, 1985.

Gardner, Daniel Pereira. *The Farmer's Dictionary: A Vocabulary of the Technical Terms Recently Introduced into Agriculture and Horticulture from Various Sciences.* New York: Harper and Brothers, 1854.

Gilpin, William. *Observations on the Western Parts of England, Relative Chiefly to Picturesque Beauty.* London: T. Cadell and W. Davies, 1808.

Goethe, Johann Wolfgang van. *Conversations with Goethe in the Last Years of his Life.* Translated by S. M. Fuller. Boston: Hilliard, Gray, 1839.

———. *Gespräche mit Goethe in den Letzten Jahren seines Lebens. 1823–1832.* Compiled by Johann Peter Eckermann. Leipzig: F. A. Brockhaus, 1837–1848.

——— *Werke: Vollstandige Ausgabe Letzer Hand.* Stuttgart and Tübingen: J. G. Cotta, 1828–1833.

Gray, Asa. *A Manual of the Botany of the Northern United States.* Boston: J. Munroe, 1856.

Greenleaf, Moses. *A Survey of the State of Maine.* Portland, Maine: Shirley and Hyde, 1829.

Harding, Walter. *The Days of Henry Thoreau.* Enlarged and corrected edition. New York: Dover, 1982.

Hariot, Thomas. *A Brief and True Report of the New Found Land of Virginia.* London, 1590.

Harris, Thaddeus William. *A Report on the Insects of Massachusetts, Injurious to Vegetation.* Cambridge: Folson, Wells and Thurston, 1841.

Hawkins, Alfred. *Hawkins's Picture of Quebec with Historical Recollections.* Quebec, 1834.

Hawthorne, Nathaniel. *The American Notebooks.* Edited by Claude M. Simpson. Columbus: Ohio State University Press, 1972.

Hayward, John. *The New England Gazetteer.* Concord, N.H.: L. S. Boyd and W. White, 1839.

Henry, Alexander. *Travels and Adventures in Canada and the Indian Territories Between the Years 1760 and 1776.* New York: I. Riley, 1809.

History of the Old Township of Dunstable: Nashua, Nashville, Hollis, Hudson, Litchfield, and Merrimac, N.H., Dunstable and Tyngsborough, Mass. Nashua, N.H.: C. T. Gill, 1846.

Hitchcock, Edward. *Report on the Geology, Mineralogy, Botany, and Zoology of Massachusetts: Made and Published by Order of the Government of That State.* Amherst: Press of J. S. and C. Adams, 1833.

Homer. *The Iliad of Homer.* Translated by Alexander Pope. Baltimore: Philip H. Nicklin, Fielding Lucas, Jun. and Samuel Jeffries, 1812.

Hoole, Samuel. *Modern manners; or, The Country Cousins in*

a Series of Poetical Epistles. London: Printed for J. Dodsley, 1782.

Howarth, William L. The Book of Concord: Thoreau's Life as a Writer. New York: Viking, 1982.

———. The Literary Manuscripts of Henry David Thoreau. Columbus: Ohio State University Press, 1974.

———. Thoreau in the Mountains: Writings by Henry David Thoreau. Commentary by William Howarth. New York: Farrar, Straus, Giroux, 1982.

Hubbard, Lucius Lee. Woods and Lakes of Maine: A Trip from Moosehead Lake to New Brunswick in a Birch-Bark Canoe to Which Are Added Some Indian Place-Names and Their Meanings Now First Published. Boston: James Osgood, 1884.

Huber, J. Parker. The Wildest Country: Exploring Thoreau's Maine. Boston: Appalachian Mountain Club, 2008.

Humboldt, Alexander von. Views of Nature; or, Contemplations on the Sublime Phenomena of Creation. London, 1850.

Jackson, Charles T. Report on the Geology of the State of Maine: 1st–3rd. Maine Geological Survey, 1836–1839.

Jalbert, Russell, and Ned Jalbert. Mocotaugan: The Story and Art of the Crooked Knife, the Woodlands Indian's Indispensable Survival Tool. Nantucket, Mass.: Metacom, 2003.

Jesuit Relations: Relations de ce qui s'est Passé en la Nouvelle France, et l'Années 1633–1672. Paris: [imprint varies], 1633–1672.

Josselyn, John. An Account of Two Voyages to New-England. London: G. Widdows, 1675.

Keep, Marcus R. "Katahdin." Bangor Democrat, 7 December 1847.

———. "Mount Katahdin, Again." Bangor Democrat, 9 October 1849.

Kelly, William. An Excursion to California over the Prairies, Rocky Mountains, and Great Sierra Nevada. London: Chapman and Hall, 1861.

Kirby, William, and William Spence. An Introduction to Entomology; or, Elements of the Natural History of Insects. Philadelphia: Lea and Blanchard, 1846.

Krutch, Joseph Wood. Henry David Thoreau. New York: W. Sloane, 1948.

Larrabee, William Clark. "Excursion to Mount Ktaadn." Lincoln Telegraph, 23 January 1840.

Lemprière, John. Bibliotheca classica; or, A Dictionary of All the Principal Names and Terms Relating to the Geography, Topography, History, Literature, and Mythology of Antiquity and of the Ancients, with a Chronological Table. Revised and corrected, and divided, under separate head into three parts . . . by Lorenzo L. Da Ponte and John D. Ogilby. New York: W. E. Dean, 1837.

Lewis, Alonzo. The History of Lynn, Including Nahant. Boston: Samuel N. Dickinson, 1844.

Loudon, John Claudius. Arboretum et fruticetum Britanicum; or, The Trees and Shrubs of Britain, Native and Foreign, Hardy and Half-hardy, Pictorially and Botanically Delineated, and Scientifically and Popularly Described. London: John Claudius Loudon, 1844.

Lowell, James Russell. "A Moosehead Journal." Putnam's Magazine, November 1853.

Mactaggart, John. Three Years in Canada: An Account of the Actual State of the Country in 1826–7–8. London: H. Colburn, 1829.

Mantell, Gideon Algernon. The Wonders of Geology. Boston: Bradbury, Soden, 1845.

"Map of Oldtown, Penobscot Co., Maine." Philadelphia: E. M. Woodford, 1855.

Meltzer, Milton, and Walter Harding. A Thoreau Profile. New York: Crowell, 1962.

A Memorial of Daniel Webster, from the City of Boston. Boston: Little, Brown, 1853.

Meyers, J. C. Sketches on a Tour Through the Northern and Eastern States, the Canadas, and Nova Scotia. Harrisonburg, Va.: J. H. Wartmann and Bros., 1849.

Michaux, François André. The North American Sylva; or, A Description of the Forest Trees of the United States, Canada and Nova Scotia. Paris: C. d'Hautel, 1818–1819.

Montresor, John. "Montresor's Journal." In "Arnold's Letters on His Expedition to Canada in 1775," Collections of the Maine Historical Society.

Neff, John W. *Katahdin, an Historic Journey: Legends, Explorations, and Preservation of Maine's Highest Peak.* Boston: Appalachian Mountain Club Books, 2006.

Parish, Elijah. *A Compendious System of Universal Geography, Designed for Schools.* Newburyport, Mass.: Thomas and Whipple, 1807.

———. *A New System of Modern Geography; or, A General Description of All the Considerable Countries in the World.* Newburyport, Mass.: E. Little, 1812.

Paul, Sherman. *The Shores of America: Thoreau's Inward Exploration.* Urbana: University of Illinois Press, 1958.

Pauthier, Jean-Pierre-Guillaume. *Confucius et Mencius: Les quatre livres de philosophie moral et politique de la Chine.* Paris: Bibliothèque-Charpentier, 1841.

Pawling, Micah A. *Wabanaki Homeland and the New State of Maine: The 1820 Journal and Plans of Survey of Joseph Treat.* Edited by Micah A. Pawling. Amherst: University of Massachusetts Press, in conjunction with the Penobscot Indian Nation, Indian Island, Maine, 2008.

Percy, Thomas. *Reliques of Ancient English Poetry; or, A Collection of Old Ballads.* Philadelphia: Published by James E. Moore, 1823.

Poirier, Richard. *A World Elsewhere: The Place of Style in American Literature.* New York: Oxford University Press, 1966.

Potter, Chandler Eastman. Appendix to "Language of the Abnaquies." *Collections of the Maine Historical Society,* vol. 4 (1856).

Public Laws of the State of Maine. Hallowell, Maine: Glazier, Masters, Smith, 1852.

Rasles, Father Sébastian. *Dictionary of the Abnaki Language in North America,* published from the original manuscript of the author with an introductory memoir and notes by John Pickering. *Memoirs of the American Academy of Arts and Sciences,* 1833.

Regnaut, Cristophe. *A Veritable Account of the Martyrdom and Blessed death of Father Jean de Brebœuf and of Father Gabriel L'Alemant, in New France, in the country of the Hurons, by the Iroquois, enemies of the Faith. In Jesuit Relations.*

Ridlon, Gideon T., Sr. "Recollections of Governor John Neptune of the Penobscots." In *White Pine and Blue Water: A State of Maine Reader,* edited by Henry Beston. New York: Farrar, Straus, 1950.

Robertson, William. *The History of America.* London: J. Richardson, 1822.

Robinson, Rowland Evans. *Silver Fields, and Other Sketches of a Farmer-Sportsman.* Boston: Houghton Mifflin, 1921.

Sanborn, Franklin Benjamin. *The Life of Henry David Thoreau: Including Many Essays Hitherto Unpublished, and Some Account of His Family and Friends.* Boston: Houghton Mifflin, 1917.

———. *Recollections of Seventy Years.* Boston: Gorham, 1909.

Sattelmeyer, Robert. *Thoreau's Reading: A Study in Intellectual History with Bibliographical Catalogue.* Princeton: Princeton University Press, 1988.

Sayre, Robert. *Thoreau and the American Indian.* Princeton: Princeton University Press, 1977.

Sewall, John Smith. "Trip to Katahdin." *Bangor Theological Seminary Library Bulletin,* Spring 1999.

Shea, John G. "The Jogues Papers." *Collections of the New-York Historical Society,* 1857.

Smith, John. *A Description of New England.* In Lewis, *History of Lynn.*

The Spirituality of the American Transcendentalists: Selected Writings of Ralph Waldo Emerson, Amos Bronson Alcott, Theodore Parker, and Henry David Thoreau. Edited by Catherine L. Albanese. Macon, Ga.: Mercer University Press, 1988.

Springer, John S. *Forest Life and Forest Trees: Comprising Winter Camp-Life Among the Loggers, and Wild-Wood Adventure; with Descriptions of Lumbering Operations on the Various Rivers of Maine and New Brunswick.* New York: Harper and Brothers, 1851.

Stowell, Robert F. *A Thoreau Gazetteer.* Edited by William L. Howarth. Princeton: Princeton University Press, 1970.

Studies in the American Renaissance. Edited by Joel Myerson. Charlottesville: University Press of Virginia, 1977–1996.

Thoreau, Henry D. "Chesuncook." *Atlantic Monthly,* June–August 1858.

———. *The Correspondence of Henry David Thoreau.* Edited by Walter Harding and Carl Bode. New York: New York University Press, 1958.

———. *The Essays of Henry D. Thoreau.* Edited by Lewis Hyde. New York: North Point, 2002.

———. *I to Myself: An Annotated Selection from the Journal of Henry David Thoreau.* Edited by Jeffrey S. Cramer. New Haven: Yale University Press, 2007.

———. *Journal.* Edited by John C. Broderick et al. Princeton: Princeton University Press, 1981–.

———. *The Journal of Henry Thoreau.* Edited by Bradford Torrey and Francis H. Allen. Boston: Houghton Mifflin, 1906.

———. "Ktaadn, and the Maine Woods." *Sartain's Union Magazine,* July–November 1848.

———. *The Maine Woods.* Boston: Ticknor and Fields, 1864.

———. *The Maine Woods.* Boston: Houghton Mifflin, 1894.

———. *The Maine Woods.* Edited by Joseph J. Moldenhauer. Princeton: Princeton University Press, 1972.

———. *The Maine Woods.* Edited by Richard F. Fleck and Koh Kasegawa. Tokyo: Hokuseido, 1983.

———. *The Maine Woods. Les Forêts du Maine.* Translated and edited by François Specq. Paris: Edition Rue d'Ulm, 2004.

———. *Thoreau on Birds.* Edited by Helen Cruickshank. New York: McGraw-Hill, 1964.

———. *Thoreau's Fact Book in the Harry Elkins Widener Collection.* Hartford: Transcendental Books, 1966.

———. *Thoreau's Literary Notebook in the Library of Congress.* Edited by K. W. Cameron. Hartford: Transcendental Books, 1964.

———. *Walden: A Fully Annotated Edition.* Edited by Jeffrey S. Cramer. New Haven: Yale University Press, 2004.

———. *The Writings of Henry D. Thoreau.* Walden edition. Boston: Houghton Mifflin, 1906.

Thoreau Society Bulletin. Geneseo, N.Y.: Thoreau Society, 1941–.

Torrey, John, and Asa Gray. *A Flora of North America.* New York: Wiley and Putnam, 1838–1843.

Treat, Joseph. *Wabanaki Homeland and the New State of Maine: The 1820 Journal and Plans of Survey of Joseph Treat.* Edited by Micah A. Pawling. Amherst: University of Massachusetts Press, 2007.

Trench, Richard Chenevix. *The Study of Words.* New York: Redfield, 1852.

Turner, Charles Turner, Jr. "A Description of Natardin or Catardin Mountain: Being an Extract from a Letter Written by Charles Turner, Jun. Esq. in the Summer of 1804 . . ." *Collections of the Massachusetts Historical Society.*

Van Doren, Mark. *Henry David Thoreau: A Study.* Boston: Houghton Mifflin, 1916.

Vetromile, Eugene. *The Abnakis and Their History; or, Historical Notices on the Aborigines of Acadia.* New York: James B. Kirker, 1866.

Walker, John. *A Critical Pronouncing Dictionary, and Expositor of the English Language.* New York: Collins and Hannay, 1823.

Warburton, George. *The Conquest of Canada.* New York: Harper and Brothers, 1850.

Webster, Noah. *American Dictionary of the English Language.* Springfield: G. and C. Merriam, 1848.

Williamson, Joseph. *History of the City of Belfast in the State of Maine.* Portland: Loring, Short and Harmon, 1877–1913.

Williamson, William D. *The History of the State of Maine.* Hallowell: Glazier, Masters, 1832.

Willis, Nathaniel Parker. *Famous Persons and Places*. Auburn, N.Y.: Alden and Beardsley, 1855.

Willis, William. "The Language of the Abnaquies, or Eastern Indians." *Collections of the Maine Historical Society*, vol. 4 (1856)

Wood, William. *New England's Prospect, Being a True, Lively, and Experimental Description of that Part of America Commonly Called New-England*. Boston: Thomas and John Fleet, 1764.

Young, Aaron, Jr. *A Flora of Maine, Illustrated with Specimens from Nature, Arranged According to the Natural System, and Containing Descriptions of All the Known Indigenous Plants Growing in the State . . .* Bangor: S.S. Smith, 1848.

———. "Report: Botanical Exploration of Mt. Katahdn. Notes on the Journey—1847." *Maine Farmer*, March 16, April 13, 20, 27, May 4, 11, 18, 25, 1848.

Index